LESSER-KNOWN
W O M E N

LESSER-KNOWN
W·O·M·E·N

A BIOGRAPHICAL DICTIONARY

BEVERLY E. GOLEMBA

LYNNE RIENNER PUBLISHERS ■ BOULDER & LONDON

R
4
920
W872.Go

Published in the United States of America in 1992 by
Lynne Rienner Publishers, Inc.
1800 30th Street, Boulder, Colorado 80301

and in the United Kingdom by
Lynne Rienner Publishers, Inc.
3 Henrietta Street, Covent Garden, London WC2E 8LU

Library of Congress Cataloging-in-Publication Data
Golemba, Beverly E., 1935-
    Lesser-known women: a biographical dictionary/Beverly E. Golemba.
      p.   cm.
    Includes bibliographical references and index.
    ISBN 1-55587-301-4
    1. Women—Biography—Dictionaries.   I. Title.
CT3203.G57 1992
920.72—dc20   91-41182
                                                         CIP

British Cataloguing in Publication Data
A Cataloguing in Publication record for this book
is available from the British Library.

Printed and bound in the United States of America

The paper used in this publication meets the requirements
of the American National Standard for Permanence of
Paper for Printed Library Materials Z39.48-1984.

*This book is dedicated to the memories of
my grandmother, Ruth Bennett Shorrock,
and of my friend, Bette W. Leicach*

If one struggling sister in the great human family, while listening to the history of my life, gain courage to meet and brave severest trials; if she learn to look upon them as blessings in disguise; if she be strengthened in the performance of "daily duties," however "hardly paid"; if she be inspired with faith in the power imparted to a strong will, whose end is good—then I am amply rewarded for my labor.
—Anna Cora Mowatt, *Autobiography of an Actress*

Contents

Acknowledgments

When I was granted sabbatical leave to devote my full time to this book, I worked a fourteen-hour day, seven days a week, but I now look back upon that time as one of the most joyous of my life. I have been astounded by the lives of the women I researched, I have developed an admiration and affection for them, and I was reluctant to omit the names of any of them even when it was necessary to do so.

The willingness to help and the encouragement I received from individuals and library personnel has been an added benefit of doing this work, and I would like to acknowledge my appreciation to them.

Bernard S. Parker, vice-president of Saint Leo College, and Shirley J. Geoffroy, associate dean of the Military Education Program of the college, were instrumental in arranging sabbatical leave for me.

Christie Vernon, the Saint Leo College Military Education Program librarian at Langley Air Force Base in Virginia, worked with me for twenty-eight months researching material. When I felt I had exhausted every possible avenue for information, she would draw on her knowledge to find the right rock to look under. The personnel at the Langley Air Force Base library, especially Sheryl Crosby, the interlibrary-loan officer, always responded professionally and cheerfully to my numerous requests for material.

The following universities and colleges provided me with invaluable help: the Mugar Memorial Library of Boston University; Bryant College in Rhode Island; the Cornell Law Association; Dartmouth College; Dull Knife Memorial College in

Lame Deer, Montana; Hampton University and Felix Malval of
the Hampton University Archives; the University of Hawaii at
Manoa; Howard University; Universidad de Puerto Rico; Rhode
Island College; Vassar College; the William Paterson College of
New Jersey; the College of William and Mary. Also, Brown
University Library granted me reading privileges at two critical
stages in my work.

The following public and private libraries and librarians
were also of great assistance: Alaska State Library; Boston Public
Library; the Brenthurst Library of Johannesburg, South Africa;
Chicago Public Library; Craven-Pamlica-Carteret Regional
Library of New Bern, North Carolina; Sadye E. Whitt of the
Enoch Pratt Free Library, Baltimore, Maryland; Hampton Public
Library in Virginia; Shirley Kiefer of the Hartford Public
Library, Connecticut; Josephus Nelson of the Library of Congress;
Pawtucket Public Library, Rhode Island; and the Tonawanda
Indian Community Library of Akron, New York.

The state and federal agencies that provided information
were the Division of Historical and Cultural Affairs for the
State of Delaware; the Office of the President, Iceland; Mary-
land State Archives; Mississippi Department of Archives and
History; N. Puksta, director of the Navy Nurse Corps; the U.S.
Department of the Interior; and the Veterans Administration,
New Bern, North Carolina.

The following historical societies and private collections
were responsive to my requests: Essex Institute, Salem, Massa-
chusetts; Massachusetts Historical Society; Seeing Eye, Inc.,
Morristown, New Jersey; Old Colony Historical Society; Temple
Beth El library, Providence, Rhode Island; The Historical
Society of the Tonawandas, Inc., New York; El Paso County
Historical Society, Texas; Maureen Taylor of the Rhode Island
Historical Society; and the Virginia Historical Society.

There are individuals to whom I owe a debt of gratitude for
help, encouragement, and support: Paul Brill, who provided me
with information on the LaFlesche family and a warm account of
his long association with the Omaha tribe; Lynn Roy-Macaulay,
who shared her research on Flemmie Kittrell with me; Madelyn
Brady of Virginia Wesleyan College; Melody Kingsley, Saint Leo
College, who faithfully coded, recorded, and filed thousands of
sheets of information; Lelia McDonald, who provided me with
books on several interesting women; and a special thanks to

David Vance, Saint Leo College, for his professional work on the computer. I am also indebted to my publisher, Lynne Rienner Publishers, especially Martha Peacock, for patience and guidance. My family has also been very supportive throughout this long project: my sister Patricia Beezer made trips to Boston to get information for me; my niece Keggie Sugrue willingly spent many days at the library with me and also did research on her own; and my daughters, Carol Gautreaux and Wendy Havunen, gave me the help, support, and encouragement I needed. Friends and colleagues too numerous to name gave their support.

I am indebted to my husband, Michael, who despite his busy practice not only helped edit my work but often helped me at the library and gave both solicited and unsolicited criticism. He was also chief cook and housekeeper during much of the time that I worked on this book and hardly complained when all I made for dinner were reservations.

I acknowledge my debt of appreciation to all the individuals and institutions that made it possible for me to write this book, and I wish to share the credit for it with them.

Beverly E. Golemba
Associate Professor of Sociology
St. Leo College, Langley Air Force Base, Virginia

Introduction

The philosopher Plato thought the soul had no gender, that intrinsic qualities should be the only critera for judging people. A century later, about 350 B.C., Aristotle stated that since women were less rational than men, it was natural for men to rule women—it would, in fact, be beneficial to them. This Platonic-Aristotelian contradiction has been argued ever since.

Taking a clear stand on the issue, I have compiled this book to help reevaluate history by bringing to light accomplishments of women that have largely gone unrecognized for centuries. A secondary purpose is to give women a sense of continuity and historical roots, to change common perceptions of women, and to contribute to the effort to change women's status.

A review of history shows that a gender-based division of work and privilege was one of the earliest complexities to develop after humans formed social groups. The validation of this division came from the perception that it was universal, a characteristic of all societies. It is true that research has shown clearly that not every society divided labor by gender, and not every job was universally viewed as being either "women's work" or "men's work." However, since most known civilizations, and particularly the most influential ones, did divide the labor force by gender and did assign a lower value to work done by women than by men, we came to think of men as superior. Male efforts were more valued; hence, there was more reason to record them. Another outcome of the gender-superiority value system was that society in general and families in particular encouraged and financed the education and accomplishment of men, but not of women.

1

The mundane—but necessary for survival—work of rearing children, caring for the home, and tending to the sick and aged was given to women and assigned a lesser significance. Men were considered rightly free of these obligations.

Although not all men were successful in acquiring wealth and prestige, most did acquire power over their wives and children, freely using them for their own economic gain. Since a critical component of social organization is belief in and adherence to social norms, not only were women considered by men to be second-class citizens, they themselves accepted this as right and proper.

These three developmental components—male superiority, female subjugation, and collusion between the sexes—created the social reality that has dominated the world for centuries. It is only in very recent times that this view of reality has been challenged. While history only recorded the accomplishments of men, more recent history is now recording the challenge to this social structure.

One of the strategies long used to support the status quo has been to dismiss female accomplishments by relegating them to the phenomenon of "exception." By evaluating "exceptional" women as different—unusual, unladylike, unfeminine, sometimes even deviant and dangerous—society has been able to acknowledge outstanding female performance without altering inferior female status.

The chronological presentation of women's achievements in this book is intended to highlight the fact that women have consistently made outstanding contributions over the centuries; a 400-year period, beginning in 1600, was selected as representative of what women have accomplished in the past and are accomplishing now.

A difficulty in using a chronological order for the book is that there are some years for which I could find no representative woman, while for other years there were more women than could be included. This is attributable in part to social circumstances. For example, there were far fewer women physicians to select from in the seventeenth century than in the twentieth, and more poets in the eighteenth century than could be included. There were periods when a woman seeking equal rights was one of many, while at other times one woman's was the lone voice .

The countries I selected for inclusion in this dictionary are meant to represent the widest possible cultural divergence and to reflect the full range of legal and social customs that affect women. Likewise, while not every field of endeavor is included, those selected are representative of the ones in which women have made contributions. I chose women who were not only accomplished and little recognized but also most representative of their country, their field of endeavor, and their social circumstances.

The process of gathering data for this book provided a wealth of interesting information about women. Most of the data came from published sources; however, it was not uncommon to have to search for material in out-of-print books or in archival copies of documents. Historical societies and government agencies were frequently the only sources of information. And more than occasionally just one individual was the only person to possess the particular information sought (once, it was the great-granddaughter of a Native American chief who provided me with the information I needed and directed me to the tribe's historian, Paul Brill).

The difficulties I encountered while doing the research reflect the unevenness of the recording of women's accomplishments. Often a woman was acknowledged only as the wife, mother, or daughter of a man, or her work was credited to her husband, father, or brother. Women's names were often translated from another language into English with several different spellings. The work of women was often deprecated: a commonly used phrase was "her work did not outlive her," and voluminous work was evaluated as trite simply because the woman in question had been so productive. While there is today a focus on the progress of women in the field of business, the work of many contemporary women in a variety of fields is not yet appreciated, and these women are not yet being written about. It was, therefore, difficult to determine which present-day women are making unrecognized but valuable contributions. Perhaps not enough years have passed to accurately assess current endeavors.

The women I researched seem to fall into one of two categories: those who were assertive and self-assured enough to persevere, and those too modest or timid to fully explore their potential. There were women who defied custom and sometimes even family in order to realize their ambition, and others who bent to tradition after an initial success. Some in this second category were so modest that they published anonymously or allowed their work to be exploited or plagiarized by fathers or husbands. In both categories, some women were tragic victims of their gender or situations. As would be expected, in all cases the circumstances of women's lives were reflected in their behavior and statements, whether militant or fatalistic or something in between.

By recording the contributions of women over several centuries, while at the same time being aware of the male contributions that were recognized during the same period, we can correct the misconceptions that women for the most part accomplished nothing, and that the history of women is less significant than that of men. We can identify with these little-known women in our own personal ways, and they can become for us a beacon—or a warning. They act as a beacon to guide and encourage us toward our goals, but they serve too as a warning of the circumstances and attitudes that can limit us.

Not every woman whose accomplishments are noteworthy could be discovered in researching this book. I hope that others will take up the challenge of finding them.

Dictionary

1600 Francesca Caccini (1587–1640) Italy

Except for the opera she wrote in 1625, the first by a woman, most of Caccini's work has been lost. A gifted young woman who composed and played several instruments, she made her singing debut in 1600 when she sang at the wedding of Henry IV and Marie de Medicis. She later became a singer at court and was one of its highest-paid musicians. She was the daughter of the famous composer Giulio Caccini; her sister was also a singer at the courts of Florence. (*Sources*: 116, 327, 595, 731)

1608 Louyse Bourgeois (1563–1636) France

Bourgeois studied midwifery under the tutelage of her husband and another physician. Working among the poor for five years while waiting to join the guild, she noted the effects that poor maternal nutrition had on both babies and mothers. She went on to become the midwife to important women, among them Queen Marie de Medicis, for whom she delivered seven children. It is interesting to note that she was paid more for the birth of a male than a female. As was true for other women in the medical field (see DOROTHEA ERXLEBEN), the death of one of Bourgeois's patients gave male physicians the opportunity to criticize women practitioners in general. Her greatest contribution was the book that she wrote in 1608 on midwifery, in which she described the female reproductive system, the importance of good prenatal care, signs of fetal death, and the need for induction of labor when there was evidence of distress. (*Sources*: 9, 17, 146, 348, 512)

1608 Clara Peeters (1594–1657?) Belgium

Little is known about Peeters as an individual or as an artist. Her first work, a still life, is dated 1608, when she was only fourteen. There is no evidence that she studied under the known artists of the time, but her work is too professional to be simply that of a young girl. Since so many of her paintings have survived, it is likely her artistry was recognized in her own lifetime. Because Peeters's works predate other known Flemish still-life paintings, she probably studied outside Belgium. Twenty-four of her paintings, all still lifes (although she was known to include a self-portrait as a reflection in an object), are noted for their rich color and bold asymmetry. A number of her paintings are in the Prado Museum. (*Sources*: 359, 374, 395, 407, 598, 607, 717, 726)

1609　Rebecca Tiktiner　(?–1650) Czechoslovakia

Tiktiner was the first woman to be published in Yiddish. Her book on religion and religious duties appeared in Prague in 1609 and in Krakow in 1618 during a period of relatively little discrimination against Jews. (*Sources*: 123, 410, 635)

1610　Jeanne-Françoise Chantal　(1572–1641) France

A wealthy widow with four children by the time she was twenty-eight, Chantal devoted her life to the teaching and care of others. In 1610 she and Saint Francis de Sales founded the Order of the Visitation, a series of schools where young women could learn to teach and care for sick, poor, and elderly women. By the time of Chantal's death in 1641, eighty-eight such schools had been started, the majority of which Chantal had established after the death of Saint Francis. MADAME DE SÉVIGNÉ, a literary figure in the same century, was Chantal's granddaughter. (*Sources*: 17, 126)

1617　Anne Clifford　(1590–1676) England

Clifford was much admired in her lifetime for her writing, wit, and intelligence, but she is perhaps best known for winning a legal battle over her father's estate, a battle that lasted from his death in 1605 to 1617. Lady Anne was educated by the poet Samuel Daniel; she later erected a monument to him. She was also responsible for the building of two hospitals and the restoration of several churches and castles. (*Sources*: 12, 60, 556)

1622　Marie Le Jars de Gournay　(1566–1645) France

A self-proclaimed feminist, Le Jars de Gournay published her first treatise in the defense of women in 1622 and another shortly thereafter. Her advocacy of education for women and her eccentric life-style and clothing engendered hostility among the literati, although she enjoyed friendships with many of the leading writers and thinkers of her day. Her books were very popular, and she was able to support herself with her writing. She was also known for her translations of several classics. (*Sources*: 60, 558, 651, 728, 731)

1624　Mbande Nzinga, *aka* Jinga　(1582–1663) Angola

As early as 1483, the Portuguese had attempted to set up a base in West Africa in order to carry on slave trading. Although they always had superior weapons, their losses from war and disease kept them from establishing a foothold in Angola until the end of the 1500s. Having grown up under the pall of war and seen so many Mbundu killed, Nzinga was ready to become queen and warrior when she succeeded her brother in 1624. At first the Mbundu were defeated by the Portuguese and forced into the mountains (an exodus that took five years and many lives); Nzinga later made deals with the Dutch, who also were in the area, and used guerrilla tactics to force the Portuguese to a draw after thirty-nine years of fighting. She was eighty-one years old when the war ended. (*Sources*: 60, 558, 647, 658, 708, 731)

1626 Judith Leyster (1609–1660) Netherlands
A noted genre painter, Leyster was fortunate enough to have the support of her family and the opportunity to study with the famous artist Frans Hals. Although Hals greatly influenced her work, Leyster developed her own style, becoming known for the vitality of her paintings. Merriment and joy emanate from her figures. Leyster conveyed this dynamism with bold strokes rather than detail. Another major theme in her paintings was morality. She would often use ordinary life experiences and temptations to preach on canvas about moral behavior. Recognized for her talent, she was made a member of the painters' guild in 1633, opened her own student studio, and was financially successful. (*Sources*: 374, 395, 407, 598, 607, 717, 726)

1630 Sophia Brahe (1556–1643) Denmark
Although Brahe was an educated woman, which was unusual for her time, her capabilities can best be shown through her service to her family. In the late 1500s she ably assisted her brother Tycho, a noted astronomer, in his computation of a lunar eclipse. It was their work that later enabled Johannes Kepler to determine elliptical orbits. Both brother and sister were also interested in astrology. Following the death of her husband, Brahe managed their estate and continued to pursue her interest in chemistry and medicine. She was influential in appeasing her family when her brother wished to marry a commoner and later supported him in a lengthy suit against a man whom he felt had both humiliated and cheated him. She enjoyed some small reputation for her work in alchemy, searching for a way to

artificially produce gold, and formulating compounds praised for their effectiveness. It was this interest that eventually depleted all of her money. (*Sources*: 354, 412, 587)

1635 Elizabeth Pole (1589–1654) United States (England)

The citizens of Taunton, Massachusetts, are still debating whether Pole founded their city. Much of the controversy stems from the paucity, inaccuracy, and differing interpretation of records. What is uncontested is that Pole arrived in the colonies in 1635, owned two farms called Littleworth and Shute, was one of the two founders of the still existing First Parish Church, and also helped set up the ironworks. The women of Taunton had her body reinterred in a new cemetery in 1836 with a monument that had been erected in 1771 proclaiming her the city's founder. Part of the city seal reads "Dux femina facti" (A woman is the leader of the enterprise). (*Sources*: 440, 455, 532, 756, 767)

1636 Anna Van Schurman (1607–1678) Netherlands

Talented and brilliant, Van Schurman is reported to have been able to read by the age of three and later learned to read and write in sixteen languages and to play several musical instruments. She knew and corresponded with many of the best minds of the time. Beginning in 1636 she devoted herself exclusively to scholarship and helped to establish the University of Utrecht. She became a student of the theologian Gisbert Voet (because women were not allowed to attend the university, it was arranged for her to "eavesdrop" on his lectures). During this time she also wrote and published a feminist manifesto urging that reason rather than custom determine female education. When she was about forty-seven, she and her brother, under the influence of the French religious reformer Jean de Labadie, became ascetics. In 1677 she wrote her autobiography, which reflected her belief in mysticism. (*Sources*: 9, 60, 70, 518, 521, 530, 651, 731)

1640 Anna Visscher (1583–1651) Netherlands

Visscher had the good fortune to be born into a talented and cultured family: both her father and her younger sister were noted poets. A diligent worker, she spent twelve years translating the poems of a French woman. Her own poems, written in a style similar to that of her father, were often about famous people of the time. She is best known for the much-improved version of her father's work "Emblems" that she completed in 1640. She was also noted for her embroidery and glass engraving. (*Sources*: 60, 80, 314)

1641 Madeleine de Scudéry (1607–1701) France

De Scudéry's brother, seven years her senior, exploited her literary talent and presented her work as their combined effort (though she occasionally published her work anonymously). Nevertheless, her talent was recognized and appreciated; she was one of the few women given membership in Italian academies —although she was ignored by the French academies, which failed to honor women for another three hundred years. She was much admired by heads of state, as well as by the literati. Her first novel, *Ibrahim*, was written in 1641. She wrote in the romantic and lengthy style of the time; both of her last two novels, which appeared in 1653 and 1660, took four years to write and filled ten volumes. She stopped writing after her brother's death in 1667, but she continued her famous salon. (*Sources*: 521, 651)

1644 Jeanne Mance (1606–1673) France

It was primarily through the efforts of Mance that the third hospital on the North American continent was opened in Montreal in 1644 (the first was established in Mexico City in 1524 and the second in Quebec in 1639). With financial help from Madame Deguillon, the Catholic church, and others, Mance established a Catholic hospital for the care of the native Indians; the church also approved a seminary as part of this endeavor. Constructed of hand-hewn logs, the hospital was staffed by the Sisters of Saint Joseph, now recognized as the oldest nursing group in North America. It was named Hôtel-Dieu after the two hospitals that had been established in Lyons in 542 and in Paris in 660. Each time the hospital burned down it was replaced and enlarged, until it covered seven acres, eventually moving to another site. A deeply religious and caring woman, Mance helped raise nine younger siblings after her parents died. (*Sources*: 17, 244, 492, 437, 551)

1644 Barbara Strozzi (1619–1664) Italy

Strozzi was the adopted daughter of the poet Giulio Strozzi. She was a student of Francesco Cavalli, who, like

Strozzi, had assumed the name of his patron. The influence of Cavalli's early recitative aria technique is apparent in her work; her recitatives are more impassioned works. Her reputation was based on both the notoriety of her life-style and recognition of her talent. Her ability and knowledge as a singer as well as a composer enabled her to develop early pieces for instrument and voice. This was evident in her work published in 1644 in which she combined her adoptive father's poetry with her music. (*Sources*: 15, 431, 714)

1646   Bathsua Makin   (1608–1675) England
Much more is known about Makin's two brothers than about Makin herself: even the dates of her birth and death are uncertain, though her works have survived. Her first known publication, a pamphlet written in 1646, was a plea to Parliament to revise the laws on imprisonment for debt; a later petition for payments in arrears for tutoring the king's daughter was equally unsuccessful. She wrote her most famous work, an *Essay to Revive the Ancient Education of Gentlewomen, in Religion, Manners, Arts and Tongues*, in 1673. In all her writings she cleverly balances her advocacy of education for women against social fears and rejection of educated women. This is most evident in the preface to her essay, in which she presents two arguments written by men, one for and one against educating women. She then asks if female education is really new, if it would not improve them, what its benefits are, and, finally, how to avoid the dangers of coeducation. This last was probably an attempt to gain acceptance for the school she planned to open for young women, the first of its kind in England. She employed an analytical approach, using the rules of English grammar to teach other languages rather than the accepted method of teaching Latin and Greek first. She was a noted poet as well as an educator. (*Sources*: 9, 70, 348, 375, 695)

1647   Margaret Brent   (1601–1671?) United States (England)
Brent arrived in Maryland in 1638. Because in England she had known Lord Baltimore, the governor of the Maryland colony and its proprietor in absentia, she was able to purchase more than 70 acres of land, which she worked to a profit. After having learned of Brent's successes, the governor named her executor of his estate, in 1647. She sold much of his holdings to pay back

wages to soldiers in service to Lord Baltimore. She petitioned the Assembly for two votes in her own right, one as a property owner and the other as the governor's executor, but she was denied both. In 1651 she moved to Virginia. She established the first English-speaking Catholic colony in the state and continued to be financially successful. (*Sources*: 79, 447, 532, 616, 627, 676, 718, 731, 772)

1647   Dorothy Osborne   (1627–1695) England

Osborne was born into an aristocratic family and married the career diplomat Sir William Osborne in 1655. Because of both families' opposition to the marriage and his posts overseas, theirs was a long courtship. Osborne is noted for the letters she wrote to her fiancé, starting in 1647 and lasting throughout their separation. Rather than using the formal style preferred at the time, she wrote in a conversational style that displayed charm and imagination. These letters gave vivid descriptions of the aristocratic life of that period. Sir William was also noted for his writing, and when he retired from service in order to write, he hired the then unknown Jonathan Swift as his secretary. (*Sources*: 36, 53, 80, 275, 420)

1647   Alse Young[s]   (?–1647) United States

There are false assumptions that all women accused of being witches in New England were burned and that all this took place in Salem, Massachusetts. Such misconceptions are probably due in part to Nathaniel Hawthorne's classic *House of the Seven Gables*. The truth is that the first women accused of witchcraft in the United States were hanged in Connecticut about forty years before the Salem witch trials. Not until 1904, with the discovery of the diary of Mathew Grant and its simple entry for May 26, 1647—"Alse Young was hanged"—was the story of Young's hanging in the town of Windsor verified. This is the only recorded information about her. In 1648 Mary Johnson, who gave birth while awaiting execution, became the second victim. In all, between 1647 and 1768 thirty-seven people in Connecticut were hanged for witchcraft. (*Sources*: 97, 711, 719)

1650   Anne Bradstreet   (1612–1672) United States (England)

Bradstreet was born into a genteel family with an ample supply of books, which she was allowed to read. She was married at the age of sixteen and settled in Massachusetts with her husband and parents, when they immigrated to the New World in 1630. She bore eight children and appears to have had a happy but sickly life. It was her brother-in-law who, without Bradstreet's knowledge, had the poems she had written over the years published in England in 1650. In 1678 the volume was reprinted with revisions and new poems that better reflected her talent. One of her descendants was the poet, writer, physician, and jurist Oliver Wendell Holmes. (*Sources*: 375, 457, 522, 532, 558, 562, 627, 731)

1650   Marie Cunitz   (1610–1664) Germany
Considering the period in which she lived, Cunitz was fortunate to have a father (and later a husband) who appreciated her brilliance and encouraged her intellectual pursuits. She is noted as an astronomer because she devoted twenty years to revising Johannes Kepler's *Rudolphine Tables* used to calculate planetary positions. Written while she was in hiding because of the Thirty Years' War, the book was published in 1650. Although she wrote her major work in Latin, she was equally proficient in Hebrew, Greek, and several other languages, and although most of her work was in mathematics, she was also a noted writer, poet, and artist. (*Sources*: 9, 518, 587, 651, 731)

1653   Marie de Sévigné   (1626–1696) France
Orphaned at the age of twelve when her mother died (her father had been killed in a duel six years earlier), de Sévigné was raised by an uncle, an abbé who provided her with an excellent education. She was married in 1644 to a man noted for his infidelities; he died in a duel in 1651. Never remarrying, she established a famous salon in 1653 and surrounded herself with the most literate people of the time. A prolific correspondent, she later became famous for her letters to her daughter. She was not as generous with her time, money, and words to her son, whom she considered to be profligate (though she was known for her own self-indulgence). Her Paris house has been made into a museum of Parisian history. (*Sources*: 70, 107, 558, 651, 731, 769)

1654   (Queen) Christina   (1626–1689) Sweden
Five years old when she became queen, Christina did not rule until she turned eighteen. She hired the French philosopher

René Descartes, a longtime friend, as a tutor and later became noted for her knowledge of Cartesian philosophy. In 1654, at the age of twenty-eight, she abdicated in order to convert to Catholicism and to pursue a less confining and more literary life. She settled in Rome, where she became a member of the sorority the Bluestockings (the *femmes savantes* of the sixteenth century), was a patron to the learned, and established a great library. She made two unsuccessful attempts to return to power, first to establish herself as a monarch in Naples and later to regain the throne of Sweden. (*Sources*: 9, 42, 60, 518, 587, 651)

1658   Madeleine Béjart   (1618–1672) France
    Béjart, an actor, began a professional and personal relationship with the playwright Jean-Baptiste Molière in 1643. A poor actor, Molière soon turned to managing their theatrical group and writing plays. Their performance of Molière's *Amorous Doctor* in 1658 so delighted King Louis XIV that he had Molière write and Béjart perform for his court for more than a decade. In Molière's comedies satirizing the behavior of the aristocracy, Béjart developed classic roles. In 1662 Molière scandalized the court by marrying a young woman who was possibly Béjart's sister or daughter yet continuing his professional and personal relationship with Béjart. This relationship lasted until their deaths, a year apart. (*Sources*: 363, 731)

1659   Sor Juana Inés de la Cruz   (1651–1695) Mexico
    An intellectually precocious child, Sor Juana was reading her grandfather's books by the age of three. In 1659, only eight years old, she wrote her first poem and mastered Latin in twenty lessons. After a few sensational years during which she wrote poetry for the courts and astounded scholars with her knowledge, she entered a religious order that enabled her to continue her intellectual pursuits. She wrote in the Baroque style of the day and, like KATHERINE PHILIPS, she often favored the people she liked by giving them fictitious names in her poems. Flattered by this attention, one countess arranged to have her poetry published in Spain in 1689. De la Cruz later became embroiled in a religious-political controversy and withdrew to a life of devotion and service. (*Sources*: 31, 64, 70, 196, 360, 490, 682, 717, 731)

1661   Wetamoo   (dates unknown) United States (Native American)

Wetamoo became the *squaw sachem* of the Pocasset tribe (which was part of the Wamponoag tribe) upon the death of her husband, Wamsutta, in 1661. Unlike her relative AWASHONKS, Wetamoo preferred to wage war with the colonists. In an account of her capture by the Saggamore tribe written in 1682, Mary Rowlandson describes Wetamoo as a vain woman who spent much time adorning herself with elaborate clothing. Wetamoo led 300 warriors to fight with King Philip, chief of the Wamponoags, against the white settlers. Only twenty-six survived and were captured, but Wetamoo escaped. Her body was recovered after she drowned, her head then displayed on the village green in what is now Taunton, Massachusetts. (*Sources*: 342, 417, 574, 609, 627, 647, 747)

1662   Margaret Lucas [Cavendish]   (1623–1673) England

A vocal antifeminist all her life, Lucas strived to be recognized for her work. Her views are reflected in an essay written in 1662, in which she stated that it was "supposedly women writers" who wrote of their aspiration to be as free and famous as men. She was a complex woman who was a writer, poet, and biographer; she became known by the derogatory name of Mad Madge because of her outrageous clothing. She categorized the writing of history into three types: general, national, and what she called particular, that is, written by those who participated in the historical events they record. It was this third style she chose for her biography of her husband, Mr. Cavendish, known for his loyalty to the king. (*Sources*: 60, 490, 627, 651)

1663   Katherine Philips   (1632–1664) England

Philips was born into a wealthy mercantile family and was educated in a private girls' school. When she was sixteen, she was wed to a man who was fifty-four years old. Only one of the two children of this marriage survived. Her husband's career, fortune, and health seem to have been mercurial most of their married life; both were involved in court and private intrigues. Philips first began writing poetry in 1651 but was not published until 1663. In much of her work, she used fictitious names for the women who had influenced her. She died of smallpox at the apogee of her fame. Her poetry was published posthumously until 1710. (*Sources*: 375, 457, 562, 731, 758)

1669 Marianna Alcoforado (1640–1723) Portugal

It is still debated whether Alcoforado was the author of five celebrated passionate letters allegedly written in 1669 to her lover, Noel Bouton, later the Comte de Chamilly. What is known is that Alcoforado was a young woman who had been placed in a Franciscan convent at that time. The original letters have never been found, though the Vicomte de Guilleragues claimed to have discovered them and translated them into French. The letters were published in France in 1669 under the title *Lettres Portugaises* (Portuguese letters). The controversy about the author of the letters stems from a later discovery of the original royal patent for the book, which named Guilleragues as the author. There is no mention of de Chamilly's confirming or denying the liaison. A revision of the title of this book was used in 1972 by three Portuguese women writers (see BARRENO). (*Sources*: 80, 556)

1670 Aphra Behn (1640–1689) England

An enterprising woman, Behn traveled to Dutch Guiana (Suriname) at an early age, was married in 1663, was widowed in 1665, was a spy in Antwerp in 1666, and spent time in a debtors' prison. By 1670 she was able to support herself by writing. She wrote some five novels and twenty plays that were both scandalous and very popular. Her best-known work is the novel *Oroonoko*, written in 1688, a year before her death, and based on her years in Dutch Guiana. She was the first nonaristocratic woman to be buried in Westminster Abbey. (*Sources*: 348, 351, 370, 375, 457, 521, 558, 562, 651, 695, 731)

1671 Awashonks (dates unknown) United States (Native American)

Little is recorded about Awashonks other than that she was the wife of Tolony, chief of the Sogonates (one of the thirty tribes that were part of the Wamponoag tribe in what is now Rhode Island) and became *squaw sachem* upon the death of her husband. The Plymouth Court in Massachusetts was the powerful governing body in the seventeenth century. It had the right to make treaties with the Indians as well as establish new colonies.

Recognizing the power Awashonks held within the tribes and wanting to establish new colonies, the court signed articles of agreement with her and other tribes in 1671. Awashonks was a cousin to King Philip, chief of the Wamponoags, who went to war with the colonists in 1675. Although she initially supported the war, after seeing the devastation, she decided again to make peace. It is worth noting that history recorded it as King Philip's War and not Awashonk's Peace. (*Sources*: 25, 342, 417, 574, 591, 647, 747, 765)

1671 Jane Sharp (dates unknown) England

Because women were barred from university training, Sharp saw the need for a comprehensive book for midwives. In 1671 she wrote what became the most-used book on midwifery. A detailed discussion of female anatomy, pregnancy and sterility, the stages of labor, and female diseases, the book went through several editions into the next century. (*Sources*: 9, 12, 17, 348, 587, 768)

1675 Maria Merian (1647–1717) Germany

Linnaeus is credited with the first classification of botanical species in 1735; Merian, however, was the first to attempt to classify any species. An entomologist, she preferred to study live insects rather than dead ones. She even raised larvae in order to understand insects in all stages of their development and maturity. She published her first book, a three-volume study of flowers, in 1675. She next went to Dutch Guiana (Suriname), where she studied the insects of the region and the types of fruit they ate. She also acquired a knowledge of the local medicinal cures, publishing a book on the topic in 1705. Her last book, on caterpillars, was published in 1717. Her descriptions were accompanied by beautifully drawn illustrations. (*Sources*: 9, 60, 518, 587, 621, 651, 654)

1676 Cockacoeske (?–1686) United States (Native American)

There are several parallels between Cockacoeske and AWASHONKS, queen of the Sogonates. Very little is known about either prior to their becoming *squaw sachems* upon the deaths of their husbands. Each was a powerful leader and ruled for many years, and each is remembered for treaties with the colonists.

Cockacoeske became *squaw sachem* of the Pamunkey tribe in what is now Tidewater, Virginia, after the death of her husband, Totopotomoi. Having formed a romantic liaison with an Englishman, John West, by whom she had a son, she understood the English language and ways. Ambitious and intelligent, she signed articles of peace with the governing colonial body in 1676 in order to enlarge her area of control over other tribes. This treaty was violated by Nathaniel Bacon; in what is known as Bacon's Rebellion, he attacked the Indians, including the Pamunkeys. Another agreement, the Treaty of Middle Plantation, was reached in 1677, and because of Cockacoeske's stated admiration for the king of England and her desire for peaceful coexistence, the colonists presented her with richly ornamented clothing and a silver medallion. There was peace for the remaining nine years of her rule. (*Sources*: 342, 420, 455, 521, 542, 596, 747)

1677   Elisabeth-Claude de la Guerre   (1666–1729) France
     From a musical family, de la Guerre was considered a brilliant child. As early as 1677 she played the harpsichord, clavichord, and organ and composed sonatas and cantatas. She was greatly favored by King Louis XIV, who ordered FRANÇOISE DE MAINTENON to be one of her academic tutors. In 1694 she wrote an opera, the first composed by a woman to be performed at the Royal Academy of Music. A commemorative medal was struck in her honor posthumously. (*Sources*: 99, 116, 670, 698, 731)

1678   Marie Madeleine de LaFayette   (1634–1693) France
     A lady-in-waiting to the queen, a friend of MADELEINE DE SCUDÉRY, and (separated from her husband after a few years of marriage) a longtime lover of François de La Rochefoucauld, LaFayette was a notable *femme savante*. Although popular in literary circles, where her work was appreciated, she published her books anonymously. Her first novel, published in 1662, was an immediate success, as was her second novel, published in 1670. Her best-known work, *La Princesse de Clèves* (1678), is considered a classic because of its historical value. The three books published after her death, one as late as 1724, were also a tribute to her literary skill. (*Sources*: 41, 233, 490, 562, 731)

1681   Mademoiselle Lafontaine, *aka* La Fontaine   (1655–1738) France

In 1681, at age twenty-six, Lafontaine was the first woman to dance ballet at the Paris Opera. She appeared as the premiere dancer in Jean-Baptiste Lully's ballet *The Triumph of Love*. She went on to create leading roles for herself in nine more of his ballets, dancing until 1693. Prior to her first performance, all roles were danced by males. She received much acclaim for her grace and style, and retired to a convent at about the age of forty. (*Sources*: 15, 478)

1682   Sofya Alekseyevna   (1657–1704) Russia

The eldest daughter of Czar Alexis, Alekseyevna was given an excellent education. Opposed to her half-brother Peter becoming czar, she incited a successful riot. Her brother Ivan V became a coruler with Peter, and she took over the regency in 1682. In order to prevent the palace troops from turning on her, she had their leaders executed or removed. Ignoring dissidents and advice to the contrary, she made a peace pact with Poland to go to war against the Turks in exchange for Kiev and lands east. She also signed a pact with China to further enlarge the Russian territory. Her two attacks on the Crimean Tatars, who were friendly with the Turks, were disasters. Fearing Peter would overthrow her, she again tried to incite a riot. This one was unsuccessful, and she was banished to a convent for the remainder of her life. (*Sources*: 80, 157, 689)

1682   Rachel Ruysch   (1664–1750) Netherlands

Ruysch's artistic talent was recognized at an early age, and at fifteen she was accepted by Willem van Aelst as a student. She did not follow the prescribed style of setting the flowers and fruit for her still-life paintings indoors. Instead, she chose to place them against natural backdrops, such as woodlands. While reflecting the beauty of her subjects, her paintings also reflected the natural environment: birds, insects, and reptiles were often an integral part of her pictures. In one painting a lizard is raiding a nest for its eggs while a bird idly watches. Her earliest works are dated 1682, and she is credited with close to 100 signed and unsigned paintings. In 1693 she married a portrait painter and by the age of forty had given birth to ten children. Ruysch and her husband joined the Dutch painters' guild in 1701, and from 1708 to

printed was *The Rhode Island Almanack for the Year 1737*. She was very successful and also did the printing for the Rhode Island General Assembly; the first piece, more than 300 pages long, sold 500 copies. She turned the business over to her son in 1748. (*Sources*: 93, 447, 455, 756, 763)

1739   Eliza Lucas Pinckney   (1722–1793) United States (England)

Lucas was born in Antigua, where her father was a colonel, and was educated in England, where she learned foreign languages as well as music. In 1738 the family moved to South Carolina. The outbreak of war in 1739 found her father back at his post in Antigua while Lucas and her mother and younger sister remained in South Carolina. Because of her mother's ill health, Lucas was put in charge of running the family's three plantations when she was eighteen. As well as growing cotton, ginger, and other crops, she successfully grew indigo from seeds her father sent from Antigua. She also developed indigo dye, which proved to be highly profitable. In 1744 she married Charles Pinckney and bore four children. During these years she started a silkworm farm. When her husband died in 1758, she continued to run their vast holdings. Later, two of her sons, who were signers of the Declaration of Independence, were granted federal appointments by George Washington. (*Sources*: 60, 490, 627, 651)

1740   Gabrielle-Emilie du Chatelet   (1706–1749) France

Not until she was twenty-two did du Chatelet begin serious study. Prior to that time, she had married, had a family, and, as an aristocrat, led a frivolous life. It was primarily through her (initially amorous) relationship with Voltaire and friendship with other intellectuals that she began her study of mathematics and physics. Her timidity, which lasted throughout her life, caused her great pain and nearly cost her credit for her work. Because of her secretiveness—she submitted or published her work anonymously—she eventually alienated Voltaire and her tutors, the mathematician Pierre Maupertuis and Samuel König. Convinced that the dichotomous arguments between physics and metaphysics could be resolved, she finally published her work under her own name in 1740. She also wrote articles and books on grammar, feminism, and religion. The only true recognition she received during her lifetime was in being made a member of the Italian Academy of Science. (*Sources*: 9, 15, 189, 651)

1744 Elizabeth Murray (1726–1785) United States (Scotland)

Murray was born in Scotland and at the age of thirteen went to North Carolina to manage her unmarried brother's home. After a return visit to Scotland, in 1744 she opened a shop in Boston with the goods she had brought with her. Within ten years she was a successful entrepreneur who taught other women the principles of business and even helped some of them start their own businesses. When she married, she was no longer legally able to maintain her independent business, lacking the necessary stipulation in a prenuptial agreement, but she returned to her business upon her husband's death. Marrying for a second time, she carefully wrote a prenuptial agreement that allowed her to keep both her own business and her assets. Since she had no children of her own, she helped to raise and educate her three nieces, who soon opened their own shop in England (it eventually failed). Although she had lived in Boston many years, she was more sympathetic to the Crown than to the colonies. In 1771 she married for a third time, again with a carefully worded prenuptial agreement, and during the revolutionary war discovered what a coward and spendthrift her third husband was. Not until several years after her death was her husband finally made to meet the conditions set forth in her will. (*Sources*: 44, 262)

1745 Hannah Snell (1723–1792) England

Snell fought as a marine at the battle of Pondicherry in southern India in 1745. She was wounded twelve times, and extracted a bullet from her own groin in order to avoid detection as a woman. Although she revealed her identity at the end of the war, she was nevertheless given a pension. (*Sources*: 136, 420, 558, 614, 647)

1748 Marie Agnesi (1718–1799) Italy

Agnesi's discourse on education for women, written in Latin, was published when she was only nine years old. She published her first book on mathematics by the time she was twenty; by twenty-one she was an honorary professor at the University of

Bologna and enjoyed an international reputation as a scholar. In her second book, on calculus, in 1748, she explained her versed (*versiera*) sine curve. The Latin *versiera* was wrongly translated into *witch*, and this work was mockingly called the "Witch of Agnesi." Agnesi raised twelve siblings after the death of her mother (there were twenty-one children in the family) and, being deeply religious, devoted most of her later life to the care of the sick and helpless. (*Sources*: 46, 80, 152, 427, 521, 621, 676)

1754   Dorothea Erxleben   (1715–1762) Germany
    Because her father, a physician, allowed Erxleben to study along with her brother, she acquired a thirst for knowledge at an early age. She credited both her father and brother with fostering her education. When she petitioned the king to exempt her brother from military service and to allow him to enter the university to study medicine, she also requested that she be admitted. The king granted both her requests. Her acceptance into the university was challenged in a petition. With her father's encouragement, she published a book examining the causes that prevented women from gaining an education. Because war broke out and her brother had to serve, Erxleben did not go to medical school. Instead, she continued her studies with her father, then married a widower with four children and had children of her own. Upon her father's death, she took over his practice; when one of her patients died, she was again challenged by male physicians. This time she responded with a sixteen-page letter and sat for her examination at the university. In 1754 she became the first woman in Germany to receive a medical degree. (*Sources*: 9, 518, 583, 587, 621, 651)

1756   Fanny Abington   (1737–1815) England
    A clever woman, Abington moved from a flower girl on the street to one of the most admired performers in the British theater. After making her debut in 1755 and acquiring a knowledge of haute couture, she joined the famous Drury Lane Players in 1756. Abington soon became one of their most popular performers. (It is interesting to note that in 1773 the Drury Lane Theatre employed twice as many men as women and paid them twice what they paid female performers.) She appeared in both drama and comedy and created many famous roles, performing with this company for eighteen years. She also acted at Covent Garden.

Her sense of style led the public to adopt what came to be known as the Abington cap. (*Sources:* 26, 71, 150, 556)

1757   Jane Colden   (1724–1766) United States

Colden was educated at home by her father, a physician, politician, and (by avocation) botanist. She began to assist her father in botany at a very early age, and as she grew older and corresponded with the famous botanist Linnaeus, she became expert at identifying and classifying plants. Colden was the first to both identify and classify the gardenia. Much like MARIA MERIAN, Colden studied and sketched living plants. By 1757 she had catalogued over 300 classifications of plants, but she did no further work in botany and died nine years later. (*Sources:* 2, 105, 455, 483, 493, 532, 556, 587, 634, 725, 763)

1760   Marie Biheron   (1719–1786) France

Biheron, like ANNA MANZOLINI, made lifelike wax anatomical molds, beginning in 1760. Biheron's work, too, was greatly admired, even by heads of state; the king of Sweden invited her to lecture. Yet Biheron, unlike Manzolini, did not receive a university appointment or any money. She supported herself by giving lessons and by allowing people to view her work in her home for a small fee. (*Sources:* 587, 651)

1760   Anna Manzolini   (1716–1774) Italy

Manzolini's early life followed a traditional pattern: she married at age twenty and gave birth to six children. She took an interest in her husband's work as an anatomist at the University of Bologna and, by helping with dissections, learned the human anatomy. She also became very skilled at molding anatomical parts out of wax. One of her wax molds showed the stages of the fetus and how it was nourished. She frequently gave lectures at the university when her husband became ill, and was given a professorship in 1760, when he died. It was through her acute skill at dissecting that she discovered several anatomical parts previously unknown. Manzolini was offered the chair of anatomy at the University of Milan and was honored by heads of state. She was given membership in the Italian, Russian, and British Royal Societies. Her collection is housed at the University of Bologna. (*Sources:* 60, 518, 587, 651, 731)

1761 Hester Bateman (1709–1794) England

Bateman was the mother of five children when her husband, a silversmith, died in 1760. In order to support her family, she took over the shop in 1761 with the aid of her sons and an apprentice. Her first business came from other silversmiths who needed orders filled, but she soon established a reputation for her own work and registered her mark, H.B., with the Goldsmiths' Hall. She was especially noted for her elegant tea services and other household items in silver. Many of her pieces are now in museums. (*Sources*: 17, 164, 365, 731)

1762 Hannah More (1745–1833) England

More was a poet, playwright, and writer. She received an early education in Latin, French, Italian, and Spanish as well as in mathematics. After a broken love affair, she moved to London and wrote several plays, producing the first in 1762. This was quickly followed by three more equally successful plays. She became a member of the Bluestockings literary sorority and enjoyed the company of both fashionable and learned people. She next turned to writing, her first books appearing in 1773, 1777, and 1779 (the last of the three printed by Horace Walpole, a great admirer of More). In the following decade she wrote poetry. Her best-known poem, "Bas Bleu," was written in honor of her Bluestocking friends; it was published in 1786. Her interest in the conditions of the poor led her to write two tracts. The second, *The Shepherd of Salisbury Plain*, sold more than 2 million copies. A prolific writer, she wrote her last book in 1809 at age sixty-four. (*Sources*: 12, 60, 258, 420, 453, 562, 587, 676, 696, 743)

1763 Catharine Macaulay (1731–1791) England

Although Thomas Macaulay is the better-known historian, almost a hundred years earlier (1763), Catharine Macaulay (no relation) wrote an eight-volume history of England. Unable to attend university, she was educated by her father in Greek and Latin. It was the study of these classical republics that fostered her interest in history. Macaulay's work received international acclaim by such notables as the clergyman-chemist Joseph Priestley and man of letters Horace Walpole. She wrote adversarial treatises on the aristocrats of the day and freedom of the press and wrote passionately about women's education and suffrage. Public opinion of Macaulay was divided.

When, following the death of her first husband, she married a man little more than half her age, the public became indignant and her career ended. Because of her interest in history, she traveled to the United States shortly after the American Revolution and made the acquaintance of George Washington, with whom she continued to correspond upon her return to England. (*Sources*: 490, 500, 695, 758)

1764   Selina Huntington   (1707–1791) United States (England)
Huntington converted to Methodism after she married and became a leader of this new movement after her husband died. She built several chapels, completing the last one in 1764, though these were banned by the courts in 1779. She established her own school of theology for six Oxford students who had been expelled for their belief in Methodism. Related to George Washington, she was interested in the developments in the United States. This interest led her to assist an orphanage in Georgia and to offer financial help as a founder of two now prestigious colleges, Dartmouth and Princeton. (*Sources*: 223, 362, 576, 731)

1765   Mary Katherine Goddard   (1738–1816) United States
Goddard moved from Connecticut to Providence, Rhode Island, to help her brother in his printing business. When her brother moved to open another printing shop in 1765, she took over the printing of the *Providence Gazette*. She took over her brother's new shop in Philadelphia in 1768 and still another in Baltimore in 1775. Not until she ran this last shop did the colophon list her as publisher. In 1777, after all the signers' names had been added, her press printed the first copy of the Declaration of Independence. In 1775 she became the first woman postmaster of Baltimore, holding the position until 1789. For the remaining few years of her life, Goddard operated a bookstore. (*Sources*: 79, 349, 447, 455, 583, 626, 756)

1765   Angelica Kauffman   (1741–1807) Switzerland
Joseph Kauffman, a minor national artist, taught his daughter painting at an early age, and by fifteen Kauffman was commissioned to do several portraits. Although for most of her life she painted portraits because of their popularity, she much preferred and is best known for her historical paintings. She be-

gan to travel abroad to study and, being proficient in several languages, soon established an international clientele and made friendships with important young artists of the time. In 1765 she was given a membership in one of the most prestigious artists' guilds in Rome. In 1766 Kauffman went to England, where she remained for the next fifteen years. She became a founding member of the Royal Academy, for which she created four ceiling panels that are still part of the academy's buildings. In 1781 she married a minor artist who primarily managed her business affairs. In 1782 she moved to Rome, remaining there until her death. She is known as one of the most brilliant neoclassicist artists of her time, and major exhibitions of her work have been presented in recent years. (*Sources*: 374, 390, 395, 407, 573, 598, 607, 717, 726)

1769   Elizabeth Montagu   (1720–1800) England

Known as Queen of the Blues, a reference to her position in the Bluestockings (the aristocratic female intellectuals of that time), Montagu had one of the most fashionable and popular salons. She surrounded herself with the best minds of the time and often helped establish bright but poor writers. She is said to have written several of George Lyttelton's *Dialogues of the Dead* (1760), but it was not until 1769 that she published her *Essay on the Writings and Genius of Shakespear* [sic] under her own name. Her correspondence, published posthumously, is as famous as is her book. (*Sources*: 12, 253)

1770   Mother Ann Lee   (1736–1784) United States (England)

An uneducated factory worker, Lee married in 1758, the same year she joined a new religious sect known as the Shakers (because of their practice of shouting and shaking during worship). Following the deaths of her four children, she became devoutly religious and was named leader of the Shakers. In 1770 she was arrested and confined to the London insane asylum of Bedlam for proselytizing. After her release, Lee left England and moved the Shakers to Albany, New York. A charismatic woman, she established eleven new groups before her death. (*Sources*: 60, 339, 424, 447, 469, 532, 616, 627)

1771   Sophie von Laroche   (1731–1807) Germany

Laroche is credited with writing the first original novel by a woman, *The Story of Fraulein von Sternheim* (1771).

Patterning her works after letters, she introduced the eroticism of women into fiction. Her later writings reflected her interest in the problems of the German people and the need for education for women. A recognized intellectual, she held popular salons frequented by such notables as the poet and philosopher Johann Wolfgang von Goethe. (*Sources*: 288, 518, 521)

1774 Ann Bailey (1742–1825) United States (England)

Bailey arrived in the Virginia area in 1761. She married a pioneer noted for his courage in battles with the Indians; when he was killed in 1774, Bailey assumed the role of male scout and fighter. Known for her marksmanship and riding skill, she soon acquired a reputation as a brave fighter and was given the name White Squaw of the Kanwha by the Indians in the area. She continued her activities after she remarried and is best remembered as the scout who made a 200-mile round-trip to get the ammunition that saved Fort Lee (now Charleston, West Virginia), under Indian attack, in 1791. After being widowed a second time, Bailey retired to Ohio, where she lived to the age of eighty-three. (*Sources*: 105, 439, 449, 531, 548, 616, 667)

1774 Adelaide Labille-Guyard (1749–1803) France

Labille-Guyard was an ambitious painter who was constantly thwarted in her attempts to achieve a high level of recognition. She initially studied under François-Elie Vincent, whom she later married. Her first exhibition was in 1774, and by the time she applied for membership in the Royal Academy in 1783, she had had several major exhibitions as well as numerous commissions. Labille-Guyard and ELISABETH VIGÉE-LEBRUN applied for membership in the Royal Academy at the same time. Because of their reputations, the academy could not refuse them, but the academy did pass a ruling that membership to women would be limited to four. Like other artists of the time, Labille-Guyard painted portraits for the aristocracy to earn money and was also commissioned to paint portraits of the royal family. The assignment was difficult for Labille-Guyard, who favored the revolution and the dissolution of the monarchy. It is ironic that the theme of a large historical canvas she did to further her career was judged too royalist and was destroyed after the revolution. In a further attempt to gain fame, she painted a canvas of herself teaching (1785), as having pupils was important recognition for an artist. She last exhibited her work shortly before her death. (*Sources*: 598, 607, 717)

1776 Nancy Ward (1738?–1824?) United States (Native American)

Ward was born a Cherokee near present-day Knoxville, Tennessee. Because of her bravery at the side of her husband in a battle in which he was killed, Ward earned the name of Beloved Woman and was entitled to rule over the women's council and to condemn or release captives. Ward used her privileges toward promoting peace both among tribes and between the Native Americans and the colonists. In 1776 she warned settlers about an impending attack by another tribe, and she was always quick to pardon white captives and return them to their camps. She was able to arrange for her village to be spared when a large militia invaded the area. Ward also participated in the treaty between the Indians and the whites in South Carolina in 1785. She later married a white settler named Ward, gave birth to a child, and, after her husband abandoned her, opened an inn near the Georgia line. It was here that her Indian name of Nanye-hi was anglicized to Nancy. Theodore Roosevelt gives an account of Nancy Ward in his book *Winning of the West* (1905). (*Sources*: 89, 105, 342, 548, 574, 647, 763)

1776 Mercy Otis Warren (1728–1814) United States

A spirited woman like her close friend Abigail Adams, Warren wrote poems and plays with patriotic themes. Her first success was a play called *The Group* (1776). This was followed by poems and two more plays. In 1805 Warren wrote a three-volume history of the American Revolution. An advocate for women's legal rights and educational opportunities, Warren used her work to create an ideal model for women to emulate. Perhaps because it was always so thoroughly imbued in patriotism, her literary work has not been reprinted. (*Sources*: 70, 339, 361, 490, 627, 758, 763)

1777 Lydia Darragh (1729–1789) United States (Ireland)

Darragh immigrated to the United States in 1753 and settled in Philadelphia to practice nursing and midwifery. Her home having been commandeered by the British during the revolutionary war, Darragh overheard the plans for an attack on

George Washington's army. Because she succeeded in passing these plans on to scouts, the American troops were ready and repelled the attack. (*Sources*: 347, 419, 420, 756, 759)

1778　Fanny [Frances] Burney　(1752–1840) England

As a shy, unobtrusive child, Burney was a keen observer of the activities in the home of her father, Charles Burney, noted composer. His friend, the author Samuel Crisp, befriended her, and she regaled him with the witty and imaginative letters that became her hallmark. Her first book, *Evelina*, published in 1778, launched her reputation as a writer and her acceptance into the literary world. Dr. Samuel Johnson became her friend and traveling companion. Her next book, written in 1782, was also successful, but Burney was devastated when Crisp, Johnson, and a third close friend, Henry Thale, all died at about this time. Burney spent five very unhappy years as a keeper of the robes to the royal family. She married in 1793 at the age of forty-one and gave birth to her only child, a son. In 1796 she wrote the highly acclaimed and lucrative book *Camilla; or, A Picture of Youth*; income from the work enabled her to build a fashionable house. Her only later publication was the memoirs of her father, which she edited. (*Sources*: 4, 46, 80, 181, 521)

1779　Elisabeth Vigée-Lebrun　(1755–1842) France

Vigée-Lebrun's father was a portraitist. Although he died when she was still a young woman, he had both given her lessons himself and provided her with the tutelage of a well-known artist. In order to support herself and her younger brother, Vigée-Lebrun began to paint shortly after her father's death. In 1779 her reputation was established when she was commissioned to paint portraits of the royal family, especially Marie Antoinette, who was the same age as Vigée-Lebrun. This association led to further commissions for paintings of aristocrats. It was only through the queen's intercession that Vigée-Lebrun was accepted into the Royal Academy, which wanted to deny women entrance. She was later made a member of all the major art guilds of Europe. It was during this period that she did a portrait of the famous soprano, ANGELICA CATALINI. Two major incidents marred her life: one was her marriage to an inveterate gambler, and the other was the French Revolution, during which she was forced to flee to Italy. Her reputation preceded her, and she was welcome at court in

Italy, painting many of the Italian aristocrats and members of royal households. She later went to Russia, where she was equally well received and remained for a number of years. Still unable to return to France because of her royalist ties, she moved to England. There she did a portrait of the prince who was later to become King George IV. Eventually, Vigée-Lebrun returned to Paris. Following the deaths of her husband, daughter, and brother, she stopped painting; during her career she completed more than 1,000 works, mostly portraits in oil. (*Sources*: 407, 573, 598, 607, 723)

1781 Mary Willing Byrd (1740–1814) United States

Byrd came from a privileged family in Philadelphia. When she married William Byrd III and moved to Virginia, she expected to continue her comfortable life; within a few years, however, her husband, unable to meet his debts, committed suicide. Left with nine children, Byrd sold property, valuables, and slaves to pay off these debts. When the revolutionary war began, much of Byrd's property was confiscated by the British, who were billeted in her home. Because she was related to the hero-turned-traitor Benedict Arnold, Byrd's letter of appeal to the British for the return of her property was construed as a traitorous act, and Byrd was tried in 1781 as a conspirator. Although not convicted, Byrd's protest that as a woman she had no means of protecting her property, that she had paid all debts and taxes, yet had no right to legal redress, failed to impress the men who had fought the war to gain freedom from oppression. (*Sources*: 21, 439, 760)

1781 Gabrielle Capet (1761–1817) France

Capet, a student of ADELAIDE LABILLE-GUYARD, never reached the heights of her mentor but was a recognized artist in her own right. Capet remained with Labille-Guyard long after she had established her own career, caring for her former teacher until her death. Capet first displayed her works in 1781, in an exhibit that ran for four years. Also in 1781 she was commissioned to paint the royal princesses. When she was later told that she would most likely be admitted into the Royal Academy if she had a sponsor, Capet refused, stating her work had to stand for her. Her painting of the sculptor Augustin Panjou earned her admission into the academy. In all, Capet created over 150 works, but because the majority were miniatures, an underappreciated art form, she has received little recognition since her death. (*Sources*: 374, 395, 607)

1782 Silvia Dubois (1768?–1888) United States (African American)

Dubois's father, Cuffee Bard, was a fifer during the American Revolution. Unable to buy her freedom, her mother, Dorcas Compton, had four different masters during her lifetime; Dubois was left with the third master, Minical Dubois, who ran a farm and tavern in Great Bend, Pennsylvania. Her master had treated her mother well and was kind to Dubois, but whenever he was away, his wife beat Dubois, often unmercifully. In 1782, while hosting a large party at the tavern, Dubois's mistress, anxious to impress her guests, worked Dubois hard and was displeased with everything she did. When her mistress hit her in full sight of the gathering, Dubois returned the blows; since Dubois was a large woman, no one attempted to rescue her mistress. When her master returned, he gave Dubois and her baby their written freedom. After working for a number of different people for years, she retired to property left to her by her paternal grandfather. Dubois's biography was written by C. W. Larison, who conducted long interviews with her. (*Sources*: 495, 507)

1782 Deborah Sampson (1760–1827) United States

Sampson grew up in poverty, although she was a descendant of Governor William Bradford on her maternal side and her grandfathers were Miles Standish and John Alden. In 1782 Sampson disguised herself as a man and enlisted in the Continental army using the name Robert Shurtleff. Factual information about her military career is unclear because Herman Mann, in bringing her to public attention, romanticized her military activities in a book he wrote in 1797. It is known that Sampson served for two years undetected, and it was only when she became ill that her gender was discovered and she was discharged. After her discharge she married and had three children. Ten years later the state of Massachusetts finally granted her a modest pension; only after Paul Revere petitioned Congress was she given a federal pension. In 1838 her husband became the first man to receive a military widow's pension. (*Sources*: 51, 347, 447, 626, 647, 718, 724, 731, 763)

1782   Elizabeth Wolff-Bekker   (1738–1804) Netherlands
Agatha Deken   (1741–1804) Netherlands

It is not possible to write about Wolff-Bekker and Deken without writing about them together. Except for a few pieces, they collaborated on everything they wrote and, after the death of Wolff-Bekker's husband in 1776, shared a life together. They collaborated on two books before writing what is considered their best work, *Sara Burgerhart*, written in 1782. They are credited with writing the first Dutch novel. Wolff-Bekker has been judged the better writer of the two and the stronger personality. Deken died a few weeks after Wolff-Bekker. (*Sources*: 80, 201, 318, 521)

1783   Ekaterina Dashkova   (1743–1810) Russia

In favor of overthrowing the czar and replacing him with Catherine II, Dashkova warned her of a plot against her and even disguised herself as a soldier so as to fight in the subsequent battle. Catherine did not reward Dashkova; in fact, knowing of Dashkova's more liberal political views, Catherine showed her disfavor. Dashkova moved to England, where she remained for twenty years, not returning to Russia until 1782. A year later Catherine made Dashkova the first president of the new Russian Academy. During her tenure she compiled a Russian dictionary and edited a journal. She also wrote several plays. Her memoirs were published posthumously in England in 1840 but did not appear in Russia until 1859. (*Sources*: 200, 347, 518, 621, 731)

1783   Caroline Herschel   (1750–1848) Germany

Herschel was one of the youngest of six children. Over her mother's protest, her father instructed Herschel in music (he was an oboist) and astronomy along with her brothers. After her father's death, she followed her favorite brother, William, to England, where they both tried to establish careers in music. Her brother, however, was more interested in astronomy and began to devote his time to it rather than to music. Herschel became his assistant, William instructing her in algebra, geometry, and trigonometry. Her brother became famous in 1781 with his discovery of the planet Uranus. With a small stipend from the king, he was able to concentrate on astronomy and made further demands on his sister for help. She later stated that her contribution to astronomy was merely helping her brother, but she also admitted that meeting his needs prevented her from doing her own work. In spite of this, she managed to discover three new nebulae in 1783 and eight comets in the next decade. She, too, was then granted a modest stipend. To help her brother, Herschel revised the existing official catalogue of known celestial bodies, adding almost 600 new entries to it in 1798. After the death of her brother, Herschel returned to Germany. William's son, John, also became an astronomer, and she compiled a newer catalogue for him. Although this work was never published, it won her an honorary membership in the Royal Astronomical Society and a gold medal. She was also awarded a medal by the king of Prussia and became a member of the Royal Irish Academy of Science. (*Sources*: 2, 9, 60, 107, 408, 530, 565, 587, 731)

1784   Hannah Adams   (1755–1831) United States

A shy and retiring person, Adams is generally considered to be the first American woman to attempt to support herself by writing. Frail and poorly educated as a child, she learned Latin and Greek from the boarders her family took in when they had a reversal of fortune. She then began compiling notes on religious denominations, publishing the result in 1784. Acclaimed for its copious sources and the impartiality with which it was written, the book was reprinted several times in both the United States and England. Only with the second edition, however, did Adams realize any profit from her work. The first woman allowed to do research at the Boston Athenaeum, Adams next wrote a history of New England. The appearance of an abridged edition for use in schools embroiled her in a bitter controversy with Jedidiah Morse, who published a similar text at about the same time. Her cause championed by influential friends, Adams won an apology (but no monetary compensation) from Morse. She continued to publish primarily religious history books until 1824. Her memoirs were published posthumously in 1832. (*Sources*: 12, 105, 123, 447, 455, 522)

1784   Charlotte Smith   (1749–1806) England

Smith's first book, *Elegiac Sonnets and Other Essays*, published in 1784, was very successful; it went through eleven printings and was translated into Italian and French. Shortly after the book's appearance, Smith left her ne'er-do-well husband and supported her twelve children by her writing. Often considered politically and socially shocking, her books covered such topics as class equality and even the love of a man for a married woman. They were nevertheless praised by such notables as Sir Walter Scott. She wrote more than twenty books, finishing her last work, *Conversations Introducing Poetry for the Use of Children*, in 1804, shortly before her death. (*Sources*: 12, 67, 298, 457, 556, 763)

1786 Susanna Rowson (1762?–1824) United States (England)

Rowson divided much of her time between her native England and her adopted country, producing most of her work in the United States. A portion of her early childhood was spent in the United States, where she and her father were interned as loyalists during the revolutionary war. Upon their return to England, Rowson's literary skill won her a position as governess for the children of a duchess. She wrote her first novel in 1786; her best-known story, *Charlotte, a Tale of Truth*, followed in 1791. With her new husband, Rowson established a theatrical career in the United States. She wrote a total of three successful light comedies, retiring from the theater after a few years to open a girls' school in Boston and to devote more time to her writing. Rowson is credited with eleven novels. (*Sources*: 50, 548)

1790 Joanna Baillie (1762–1851) Scotland

Baillie did not attend school until she was ten years old. Her first book of poetry, published anonymously in 1790, was praised by the Scottish poet Robert Burns, but Baillie did not receive wide acclaim until she published her three-volume, blank verse *Plays on the Passions* between 1798 and 1812. One of these poems was made into a play and presented at the Drury Lane Theatre. Baillie enjoyed her role within many literary circles and became a close friend of Sir Walter Scott. Her second three-volume series of poetry appeared in 1836. (*Sources*: 53, 500, 556, 562, 695, 717, 731)

1790 Judith Murray (1751–1820) United States

Murray was what was known as a "magazine writer," most of her work published in the prestigious magazines of the time.

She was one of only two women whose writing appeared in the earliest known U.S. anthology, published in 1794. Married to a minister who did not object to her writing, Murray is best recognized for her treatise in favor of education for women, which appeared in 1790. (She published earlier articles on equal education under a pseudonym.) Murray was also an advocate of the right of women to be self-supporting. (*Sources*: 627, 699, 728, 756, 758)

1791   Olympe de Gouges   (1748–1793) France

A patriot, a rebel, a playwright, and an early feminist, de Gouges paid with her life for her passionate views. Following the French Revolution, she strongly advocated a return to normalcy that did not allow for the repercussions that were taking place. She pleaded publicly and in court for sparing the life of the king and stopping the bloodshed among her compatriots. She was also vocal in her criticism of Marat and Robespierre, heroes of the revolution. At her own expense, she had pamphlets posted throughout Paris and soon became the object of popular ridicule and, later, anger. She was equally disliked for her manifesto on *The Rights of Women*, published in 1791. Two of her writings eventually led to her being sentenced to death. One was a play in which the hero was Dumouriez, modeled after a general of the same name who suffered a crushing defeat shortly after the play appeared and went into hiding. The second was a well-publicized manifesto entitled *Les Trois Urnes* in which de Gouges advocated the citizens' right to choose one of three forms of government—even another monarchy. She was charged with treason and followed Marie Antoinette and Charlotte Corday (Marat's assassin) to the guillotine. (*Sources*: 125, 361, 466, 651, 728)

1791   Ann Radcliffe   (1764–1823) England

Radcliffe wrote her first novel in 1789 and her second in 1790, but it was her third novel, *A Romance in the Forest* (1791), that launched her career as a gothic writer. She was known for her skillful weaving of romance, terror, and suspense. Except for making brief visits to the Continent after she ended her career, Radcliffe remained a recluse. Although her books often lacked accurate information because she relied on paintings of castles and landscapes to inspire her gothic settings, her works nevertheless stimulated later romantic writers. (*Sources*: 12, 282, 521, 562)

1792   Mary Anne Talbot   (1778–1808) England

Orphaned in 1792, Talbot was turned over to a Captain Bowen, who took her aboard his ship as a cabin boy and gave her the name John Taylor. Bowen was killed at the battle of Flanders, Talbot wounded. For four years, her gender undetected, Talbot served aboard three ships. Her leg was seriously injured in one battle; this and her previous wounds plagued her all her life. When she was captured in 1796, she revealed her gender and was discharged, though afterward she frequently dressed as a man in order to find work. After a brief career on the stage of the Drury Lane Theatre, she became a maid. A combination of poor health and an accident caused her death in 1808. (*Sources*: 621, 647)

1793   Pauline Auzou   (1775–1835) France

A little-known artist, Auzou is especially noted for her historical paintings, an unusual forte for a woman artist of her time. After studying under the historical painter Jean Baptiste Regnault, she had her first exhibit in 1793 at the age of eighteen. She developed her artistic skills to include genre paintings and portraiture, changing her style as she learned more. Influenced by both her teacher and the classicist Jean Ingres, she experimented with some of their style in her own work but also struck out on her own—for example, using artificial lighting effects in several of her paintings (a technique she later abandoned). In several of her works she depicted women in ordinary domestic situations. One of her best-known genre paintings uses children to illustrate the loss of innocence. Auzou won a medal for her achievements in 1808. Although she gave up her own work by 1817, she continued her art school for young women for many years. (*Sources*: 374, 395, 607)

1794   Henriette Campan   (1753–1822) France

Favored by Napoleon, Campan was allowed in 1794 to open one of the first secular schools in France for the education of young women. It was an exclusive school for the daughters of French and foreign aristocrats and diplomats; James Monroe's daughter numbered among its first twenty students, and later Napoleon's sister entered. As enrollment grew Campan moved and enlarged the school. She added a formal dress code of uniforms and colored sashes designating grade levels, still in effect today. In 1805 Campan established a school to provide for young girls from families of modest means, a revolutionary idea at the time. Unfortunately, these families saw no reason to educate their daughters, even though schooling was offered free of charge, and the school eventually educated only royalty. Campan's schools became so popular she founded a third. (*Sources*: 15, 518, 556)

1794 Louise Reichardt (1779–1826) Germany

Reichardt was the daughter of the famous composer Johann Reichardt. She made her singing debut in 1794 and became both a noteworthy singer and composer, occasionally collaborating with her father. In 1813 she opened a singing school in Hamburg and organized concerts to showcase the talents of her students and selected conductors. She is especially known for her translation and arrangement of George Frideric Handel's work. Reichardt composed almost 100 pieces characterized by their melancholy and tenderness. (*Sources*: 116, 714)

1795 Angelica Catalani (1780–1849) Italy

Catalani received her operatic training at the convent of Santa Lucia in Rome and made her debut in Venice in 1795. She next sang in Florence and made her first appearance at La Scala in 1801. She had very successful tours in Paris and London. Her London tour lasted for six years, and she was the first to sing the role of Susanna there in Mozart's *Le Nozze di Figaro*, in 1812. Catalani was admired for her dramatic performance, voice range, and mastery of the bravura style. Her singing career lasted until 1828. (*Sources*: 29, 116, 325, 595, 717, 731)

1795 Rebecca Cole (?–1824) United States

Founded in 1793 in Pawtucket, Rhode Island, the first factory in the United States was the Slater Mill, which employed women and children at meager wages. Few of the women managed to escape their dismal living conditions. Cole was an exception: within two years she held a man's job, and her daughter became the only female mule spinner. Although they often waited months before receiving their pay, Cole and her four children earned enough to support themselves and to purchase a house from Slater for $1,300. (*Sources*: 483, 493, 725, 763)

1795   Maria Edgeworth   (1767–1849) England (Ireland)

Edgeworth grew up in a bustling household of nineteen siblings, a succession of three stepmothers, and a father who greatly influenced her works. Educated in England, she traveled to France and Belgium with her family and was much admired by leading scientists and writers. JANE MARCET and MARY SOMERVILLE were two of her closest friends. Her first book, *Letters for Literary Ladies* (1795), was an appeal for education for women. Her next and perhaps best-known book, *Castle Rackrent*, depicted Irish country life. Her later years were marked by her friendship with Sir Walter Scott. Edgeworth wrote for over thirty years, publishing her last book in 1834. (*Sources:* 9, 60, 469, 562, 731)

1796   Nicole-Barbe Clicquot   (1777–1866) France

Clicquot was born in Reims near a wine-producing region. She married at the age of seventeen and was left a widow with a child at nineteen. Amidst protests and predictions of failure because of a heavy business tax, she took over her husband's winery, which appeared to be a dying business. At the time, winegrowers were only experimenting with the production of champagne, which tended to develop a sediment that seemed impossible to remove. Clicquot found that by storing the bottles upside down and turning and shaking them daily, the sediment would eventually collect against the cork. At an exact moment, the bottles could be opened, the sediment expelled, and the bottles quickly recorked. She also discovered that she could make pink champagne by pressing the grapes as soon as they were picked. Her vineyard became one of the most successful in France and is still the country's third largest champagne producer. (*Sources:* 518, 627)

1799   Theodosia Burr   (1783–1813) United States

Her mother having died, Burr became mistress of the house when she was an adolescent. Her father, Aaron Burr, supervised her education, and she became proficient in mathematics and languages as well as in literature and poetry. When she was sixteen, her father asked that she entertain notables in his absence; she soon gained a reputation as one of the most gracious hostesses of New York. She later married, moved to South Carolina, and had a child but remained devoted to her father—increasingly so as his reputation was attacked. She also stayed with him in Richmond during his trial for treason. When her father was acquitted and left the country, she tried to raise money for his needs and pleaded for his return. Aaron Burr eventually came back to New York, and in spite of the recent death of her only child and her own poor health, Theodosia set out to meet him. Her boat sank in a storm on the way. (*Sources*: 105, 439, 449, 616, 756, 770)

1799   Marie delle Donne   (1776–1842) Italy

Donne graduated from the medical school at the University of Bologna in 1799 with highest honors but, despite the patronage of Napoleon, failed to be named to the chair for physics. Instead, she served as director of the school for midwifery in Bologna. In 1807, with Napoleon's help, Donne was admitted to the French Academy of Science. (*Sources*: 512, 529)

1801   Sidney Morgan   (1783–1859) Ireland

Morgan first attempted to write in 1801 at the age of eighteen; the result, a book of poems, was considered overly sentimental. Three years later she gained more favorable notice with her first novel, *St. Clair*. Her literary reputation was established in 1806 with *The Wild Irish Girl*. Morgan married a physician and author of philosophical tracts and continued to write on a wide range of topics and to create poetry. Her last book was published in 1823. (*Sources*: 485, 521, 556)

1801   Amelia Opie   (1769–1853) England

Born an only child in a wealthy family, Opie did not begin writing until she was thirty-two, shortly after her marriage to a painter. Her first novel, *Father and Daughter* (1801), extolled virtue. During the next twelve years she wrote several books on the same theme, a popular ideal at the time. Opie later became a Quaker and gave much of her time and effort to helping the poor. Her benevolent work was highly praised during her lifetime. (*Sources*: 12, 53, 78, 272, 521, 562)

1802   Sarah Siddons   (1755–1831) England

Siddons was first a sculptor and later an actor. At the beginning of the nineteenth century she quickly rose to stardom, appearing most often in the famous Drury Lane Theatre. One of the noted intellectuals of the time, Madame de Staël, was so impressed by Siddons that she featured the actor in her famous book *Corinne*. Although actors were still considered quite low class, a few, especially tragediennes, were greatly admired. Siddons was known for her stately and dignified stage presence, especially in the role of Cassandra. Having done sculptures of several prominent people, Siddons herself became one of the most popular subjects of other sculptors. The first known exhibit of a bust done by Siddons was at the Royal Academy in 1802, and she sat for such notable sculptors of the day as Campbell, Flaxman, Henning, and the one well-known woman sculptor, Anne Damer. (*Sources*: 96, 348, 381, 607, 717)

1806   Lucy Hutchinson   (1620–1675?) England
The fourth child and first daughter, Hutchinson was encouraged in her learning by her father; after his death, when she was ten, she continued to study on her own. A serious woman, she wrote verse and translated poetry from Greek and Latin. She actively participated in her children's learning, and most of what she wrote was intended only for them. Her husband died in prison after his capture during the British Civil War; using her diary and her husband's letters, Hutchinson wrote about his military career as a legacy for her children. Despite its obvious bias, the book has proved to be valuable, as it is a firsthand account written while the war was in progress. It was not published until 1806, when Hutchinson's heirs recognized its worth. (*Sources*: 53, 375)

1806   Jane Marcet   (1769–1858) England
Marcet's writing career developed as a result of her frustration at not being able to understand the scientific discussions of her husband and his colleagues nor the lectures she attended. It was only after reading and repeating experiments that she was able to comprehend them. This led her to write books on science, primarily for women, using a three-person, conversational style. Her first book appeared in 1806 and went through more than fifteen printings; her two additional books enjoyed equal success. Michael Faraday, who discovered electromagnetism, credits Marcet's first book with introducing him to the field of electrochemistry. (*Sources*: 587, 634, 695)

1807   Felicia Hemans   (1793–1835) England
A brilliant child with a photographic memory, Hemans

published her first book in 1807 at the age of fifteen and had written two more by the age of nineteen, the year she married. She later bore five sons and wrote an additional two books. Her husband deserted her in 1818, and Hemans had to support her family by writing. A prodigious writer, she produced five books (three of them poetry) and two plays before her health failed at age thirty-five. (*Sources*: 12, 16, 457, 562, 731, 758)

1807   Mary Lamb   (1764–1847) England

A tragic figure, Lamb is perhaps best known as the sister of the writer Charles Lamb, who was ten years her junior. Because her brother was frequently away and her father elderly, Lamb became her crippled mother's constant companion. In 1796 Lamb killed her mother, was declared insane, and was placed in the care of her brother. Although she experienced periods of depression, her brother's solicitous care and encouragement brought out her literary talent; she collaborated with him on four children's books and is credited with writing fourteen of the twenty *Tales from Shakespeare*, which appeared in 1807. She outlived her brother by thirteen years. (*Sources*: 12, 47, 235, 500)

1807   Emma Willard   (1787–1870) United States

Willard spent her life working in and for education for women. In 1807 she moved from Connecticut to Vermont to become the principal of a girls' academy and in 1814 opened her own school for young girls. In 1819 she made an appeal to the New York legislature for aid to establish equal educational facilities for women. Turned down by the legislature but urged on by the famous governor, De Witt Clinton, Willard moved her academy to New York and established the Troy Female Seminary. After almost fifty years in education, she represented the United States at the World's Education Convention in 1854. (*Sources*: 12, 34, 60, 74, 97, 317, 447, 469, 486, 527, 587, 699)

1809   Mary Kies   (1752?–?) United States

In 1809 Kies became the first woman to obtain a patent, for her process of straw weaving with silk or thread. Her business was in South Killingly, Connecticut. Very little else is known of her life. (*Sources*: 383, 440, 455)

1811 James Barry (1795?–1865) England

Miranda Stuart chose to live her life disguised as a man, using the name James Barry. Unlike her counterpart, DEBORAH SAMPSON, Stuart kept her gender secret all her life. She studied medicine at Edinburgh, joined the army in 1811, and was sent to South Africa as a surgeon. Having soon established a reputation as a troublemaker because of her concerns for conditions in the local prisons and leper colonies, she was transferred to outposts in Mauritius, Jamaica, and St. Helena. While in St. Helena she fought to have women treated in a separate facility, especially since so many of them had venereal diseases. In 1845 she was transferred to Trinidad, where she contracted yellow fever. The two doctors who treated her kept her secret. Stuart's last post was in Canada as inspector general of hospitals. She retired from the military in 1859. Upon her death in 1865 it was discovered not only that she was a woman but also that she had at some time given birth to a child. (*Sources*: 9, 384, 447, 518, 529, 583, 614, 621)

1811 Mary Reibey (1777–1855) Australia (England)

Reibey was thirteen years old when she was convicted of stealing a horse. As was a common practice in England at the time, she was transported as a debtor to Australia. In 1794 she married a ship's officer, and they decided to start their own business. Her husband imported goods, and Reibey opened a shop to sell them. Reibey, who had seven children at the time of her husband's death in 1811, took over their successful company. She ran the shipping and import business, bought and sold property, and even managed a hotel. She became the most successful businesswoman of her time in Australia. (*Sources*: 558, 621)

1815 Hannah Crocker (1752–1829) United States

Described as a polemicist, Crocker, a wife and mother of ten children, had only limited education, and responded to issues on the grounds of rightness or morality. In 1815, disturbed by criticism of the Masons, she anonymously published a fictitious account of their meetings in defense of the prestigious fraternal organization. Two years later she published an admonition to seamen for their immoral and decadent life-style, hoping that they would be receptive to a woman's well-chosen words. Crocker was not an advocate of full equality for women, but in 1818, influenced by women writers such as HANNAH MORE, she wrote a tract on the God-given intelligence of women and their ability to act with good judgment. She also felt that women should be educated in the event they had to support themselves and their children. (*Sources:* 53, 339, 447, 699)

1815   Sophie Germain   (1776–1831) France

At the age of thirteen, Germain decided she wanted to study mathematics; in order to read the works of the great mathematicians, she first had to teach herself Latin and Greek. When a new college with an eminent mathematics faculty opened nearby, Germain, unable to attend because of her sex, obtained class notes and submitted a paper under a male name. The geometer Joseph Lagrange, one of the professors, learned her identity and offered to tutor her. She also corresponded with other mathematicians. In spite of this help, Germain still suffered gaps in her knowledge, and she was unable to go beyond a certain point in her work. She was awarded the grand prize in 1815 only after submitting her study on elasticity and vibration for the third time. Her explanation of the Fermat theorem remains a seminal work in the field. (*Sources:* 9, 103, 215, 408, 556, 587, 651)

1816   Joanna Bethune   (1770–1860) United States

An educator and humanitarian, Bethune joined her mother in starting a number of schools for the poor. Most of the classes were held in private homes or makeshift quarters on Sundays— hence the term *Sunday schools*. In 1816 Bethune was instrumental in starting the first formal Sunday school, called the Female Union for the Promotion of Sabbath Schools. Opened to black and white female adults and children, the first class of 136 grew to 3,000 students within seven months. In 1817 Bethune and her mother and husband founded the American Sunday School Union. Ten years later Bethune helped to establish the first nursery school for the children of poor working parents and became the school's founding director. Bethune taught school until she was in her late eighties. (*Sources:* 392, 447, 455)

1816   Elizabeth Fry   (1780–1845) England

Fry is considered to be the earliest and most influential person in women's prison reform. As a member of the Society of

Friends, she visited Newgate prison in 1816 and was appalled at the conditions under which women—often along with their children—were jailed. Fry and a group of women obtained permission to institute reforms in the prison, and they began a vigorous program that involved conducting workshops, improving living conditions, installing female supervisors, and offering religious instruction for the women inmates. This group also provided the inmates with additional help upon their release from prison. In 1827 Fry wrote a treatise that later became the prototype for prison reform in the United States. She was also responsible for bettering the conditions of inmates in Italy, Russia, Denmark, Belgium, the Netherlands, and France. For reasons that are still unclear, British authorities in 1835 rescinded the reforms Fry had implemented. In 1840 Fry founded a nondenominational nursing hospital in London. She also worked for the reform of insane asylums. (*Sources*: 126, 351, 500, 507, 512, 706)

1818   Sarah Hall   (1761–1830) United States

Although her father was a learned man and her brothers educated, Hall received no formal schooling. In 1782 she married and moved to Philadelphia, and thirty-four years later began writing for a literary magazine. When she was older than fifty, she learned Hebrew in order to be able to do research for her book *Conversations on the Bible*, which appeared in 1818. It was considered a classic at the time and went into four editions. (*Sources*: 105, 388, 486)

1822   Sara Coleridge   (1802–1852) England

Coleridge was the daughter of Samuel Taylor Coleridge, whose influence on her was evident throughout her life. Aided by the loan of books from the poet Robert Southey, she taught herself Latin, Greek, and several modern languages. Her first known work was a translation from Latin, in 1822; she followed this with a translation of a medieval French work. Coleridge took an active interest in her children's education and in order to promote their learning composed a series of verses that she published in 1834 as *Pretty Lessons in Verse for Good Children*. In 1837 she wrote *Phantasmion*, considered to be her best literary piece. She devoted the rest of her life to editing and annotating her father's works. (*Sources*: 485, 717)

1823   Gertrudis de Avellaneda   (1814–1873) Cuba

As a child Avellaneda became enthralled with the work of Victor Hugo, Lord Byron, and other great writers. One of Cuba's greatest poets served as her tutor during her formative years; she published her first poem in 1823, at the age of nine, and her first play at the age of fifteen. Her family moved to Spain when she was twenty-two, and she met a man she both loved and hated for fifteen years. He eventually married another woman, and his widow published the letters Avellaneda had written during the course of their relationship. Accepted into the literary circles in Spain, Avellaneda dedicated numerous poems to her friends. She wrote novels; and two of her plays, *Leoncia* and *Munio Alfonso*, were immediate successes. She wrote her best play, *Balshazzar*, in 1856. In 1852 her request for the poet Gallego's vacant chair at the Royal Spanish Academy was denied. She was married briefly in 1846 and remarried in 1854. She and her husband moved back to Cuba, but at his death she returned to Spain, where she continued to write until she died in 1873. (*Sources*: 80, 540, 619, 682, 717)

1823   Sarah Hale   (1788–1879) United States

Hale ran a small school starting in 1806 and wrote for newspapers at about the same time. She married in 1813, had five children, and was widowed in her ninth year of marriage. Although she opened a millinery shop in order to support her children, she also managed to publish a book of poetry, *The Genius of Oblivion*, in 1823 and a novel in 1827. The next year she became editor of what became a prestigious women's magazine. In 1855 she published a book with 1,000 entries on women of ancient times. (*Sources*: 14, 447, 450, 455, 469, 486, 522, 567, 718, 758)

1824   Lydia Marie Child   (1802–1880) United States

Child's first two novels on New England life were *Habanok* (1824) and *The Rebels* (1825). She married in 1828, and she and her new husband became interested in the abolition of slavery. In 1833 and 1836 she published works on abolition and edited an antislavery journal; she wrote four books and published a magazine between 1829 and 1855. In 1860 Child published *Correspondence Between Lydia Marie Child and Governor Wise and Mrs. Mason of Virginia*, which sold more than a quarter of a million copies. (*Sources*: 14, 190, 420, 447, 455, 470, 486, 696, 731, 747)

1825   Nancy Hart   (1735?–1830) United States

Like DEBORAH SAMPSON, Hart became a legendary figure for her acts of bravery during the American Revolution. Many of the exploits attributed to her are unverified, but there was a newspaper account published in 1825 about one: when five Tories arrived at her cabin and demanded a meal, she plied them with whiskey, grabbed one of their rifles, killed one of the soldiers and held the rest hostage until help arrived. There is also agreement that she was 6 feet tall—an unusual height for a woman in the 1800s—and was very outspoken. Georgia has honored Hart by erecting a replica of her cabin and naming a county after her. She was also mentioned in the book on Georgia that Joel Chandler Harris (of Uncle Remus fame) wrote in 1896. (*Sources*: 38, 419, 447, 548, 718, 750)

1825   Frances Wright   (1795–1852) United States (Scotland)

After her first trip to the United States, Wright fell in love with the country's democratic principles and promise of opportunity. Her reputation as a writer was established with a book on the United States published in 1821 and printed in four languages. One aspect of American life troubled her deeply; she was determined to help abolish slavery. To that end, in 1825 she purchased 320 acres of what turned out to be swampland near Memphis, Tennessee. Twenty-two slaves were "given" to her or drifted in, and she purchased another eight—far short of the fifty she had planned on to start Nashoba, a utopian farm to prepare slaves for their freedom. Influenced by Thomas Jefferson's idea that emancipation would have to be a slow process, Wright intended for each slave to work for five years developing the farm, learning a trade, and earning back the slave-purchase price, at which time each would be free to leave to become self-sufficient. In spite of Wright's altruistic and lofty goals and even with the later purchase of more land, Nashoba failed. (*Sources*: 584, 627, 676, 696, 756, 772)

1826   Mary Somerville   (1780–1872) Scotland

There was nothing in Somerville's early life to indicate the mathematical brilliance she would begin to display in 1826 when she wrote *On the Magnetizing Power of the More Refrangible Solar Rays*. She had spent her childhood with an aunt who saw no reason to teach her even to read and write; she had a father who, when he later took an interest in her, did not want her to learn more than the basics; her first husband discouraged any further studies. Not literate until she was thirteen, Somerville taught herself French, Greek, and Latin and soon began studying mathematics. After Somerville became a widow and then remarried in 1812, she pursued her interest in mathematics, being tutored by a professor at Edinburgh. By 1831 she had published an English equivalent of Pierre-Simon de Laplace's book on astronomy that became the most used college text for the next century. Somerville also published books on physics, mathematics, and chemistry. In 1835 she and CAROLINE HERSCHEL became the first women members of the Royal Astronomical Society. (*Sources*: 9, 60, 587, 621, 695)

1827 Catharine Beecher (1800–1878) United States

An educator and home economist, Beecher ran the successful Hartford Female Seminary in Connecticut starting in 1827. She taught young women how to run homes efficiently and hygienically and believed household management deserved scientific study. She wrote two widely used books on home economics in 1841 and 1869. (*Sources*: 97, 351, 518, 567, 720, 756)

1827 Louisa Drew (1820–1897) United States (England)

On the London stage since early childhood, Drew immigrated to the United States in 1827 and became a successful performer. When she married her third husband, John Drew, they opened a theater in Philadelphia that came to be called Mrs. John Drew's Arch Street Theatre Company and was one of the most famous in the country. In most of the plays presented, she acted both male and female parts. When her husband died she took over the theater and managed it for thirty-one years. Her son John later teamed with his brother-in-law Maurice Barrymore and thus started the Drew-Barrymore theatrical dynasty. (*Sources*: 205, 447, 556, 616, 756)

1827 Fanny Hensel (1805–1847) Germany

Hensel is a tragic example of a woman denied the right to publish or claim her work. Her parents forbade her to publish her compositions yet encouraged her younger brother, Felix Mendelssohn. Fortunately, Felix recognized his sister's brilliance, and they formed an extraordinarily close personal and professional relationship. Always fearful of offending her parents, Hensel published most of her compositions under her brother's name; the first of the few works published under her own name appeared in 1827. It is reported that when Queen Victoria wanted to compliment Mendelssohn, she sang one of his songs, only to have him tell her that his sister had written it. Hensel is believed to have composed well over 400 works in her secret career. Her death in 1847 devastated her brother, who died only a few months later. (*Sources*: 95, 99, 569, 670)

1827   Judith Montefiore   (1784–1862) England
Montefiore was raised in a devout Jewish family and was devoted to helping her fellow Jews, especially in Palestine. Married to a wealthy and well-known businessman and philanthropist (the first Jew in England to be knighted), Montefiore nevertheless managed to create a reputation in her own right. Well-educated and childless, she accompanied her husband on his trips abroad and kept diaries of the countries they visited. Her interest in Palestine developed after a trip there in 1827, and she spent the remainder of her life raising money to help the Palestinian Jews build hospitals and schools. Her husband established the Judith Lady Montefiore College in her honor following her death in 1862. (*Sources*: 123, 410, 525, 637)

1827   Susannah [Strickland] Moodie   (1803–1885) Canada
Moodie's first articles on country life in Canada appeared in 1827. After developing an interest in abolition, in 1831 she wrote the history of a slave by the name of Mary Prince. In 1840 she returned to Canadian themes, publishing *Forest Life* in 1852 and another book in 1853. She also coedited the *Victoria Magazine* with her husband beginning in 1847. (*Sources*: 12, 255, 473, 717, 731)

1829   Mary Carpenter   (1807–1877) England
Carpenter's compassion for poor children led her to establish a school for girls in 1829. With the experience she gained there, she developed new teaching methods. In 1846 she opened another school where she promoted play as a means to

learn, developed trust between teacher and child, and did not allow the use of corporal punishment. She taught her students both academic and trade skills, often taking them on visits to museums and other places of interest. Finding that some girls did not respond even to this unusual care, Carpenter established cottage-house reform schools in 1854 and 1857 in rural areas. In 1876 she was able to convince the government to provide school meals for poor children. She also traveled to the United States, Canada, France, and India to study the prison systems and living conditions of the poor. (*Sources*: 185, 363, 518)

1829 Annette von Droste-Hülshoff (1797–1848) Germany

Droste-Hülshoff is best known for her exquisite poetic descriptions of her hometown in Westphalia. She also wrote devotional verses. Influenced by the Brothers Grimm and the philosopher Arthur Schopenhauer, she was reclusive and melancholy. In 1842 she published a book on the murder of a Jew in a small village; she explained how the social environment was at the root of the crime. Droste-Hülshoff's work was not particularly appreciated during her lifetime. (*Sources*: 80, 206, 521)

1829 Rebecca Gratz (1781–1869) United States (Jewish American)

Widely recognized as the model for Sir Walter Scott's character Rebecca in *Ivanhoe* (1819), Gratz accomplished much in her own right. She wrote *Letters of Rebecca Gratz* in 1829 and established the first Hebrew Sunday school in Philadelphia in 1838. She was also a noted philanthropist. (*Sources*: 84, 123, 410, 455, 525)

1831 Fredrika Bremer (1801–1865) Sweden (Finland)

Bremer was born in Finland and moved to Sweden with her family when she was three years old. She began to write at an early age, though her first success, with a book entitled *Familjen H.* (Family of H.), did not come until 1831. Many of her succeeding books were also about family life. She received a Swedish gold medal in 1844 for books written in 1837 and 1843. She worked diligently for women's rights and other reforms. In 1852, along with many of the other great women writers of her day, she organized the International Association of Women for Peace. Her books on family life were very popular, but her novel *Hertha*

(1856) and another written in 1858, both advocating more freedom for women, were met with national protest. As well as advocating abolition, she founded an orphanage and a school for girls. (*Sources*: 60, 80, 175, 521, 562, 696, 731)

1831   Prudence Crandall   (1803–1890) United States

In 1831 Crandall opened a school for the wealthy young girls of Canterbury, Connecticut. The school was very successful until she allowed the child of a black farmer to enroll; the townspeople demanded that the child be expelled. An advocate of abolition, Crandall countered by soliciting other black children for her school and then announcing she would close the existing school and reopen it as boarding school for black girls. A battle ensued, the town passing a law prohibiting schools for black children. Crandall was arrested for noncompliance; one jury was divided and a second convicted her, but a judge reversed the decision. The townspeople began to terrorize Crandall and her students and finally set fire to the school. Crandall, who had recently married, moved to Illinois and set up a school in her home. After the death of her husband in 1874, she moved to Kansas and devoted her efforts to women's rights. In 1886 Connecticut granted her a small pension. (*Sources*: 97, 603, 616, 627, 696, 699, 702, 747)

1832   Lydia Sigourney   (1791–1865) United States

Born in Norwich, Connecticut, Sigourney moved to Hartford in 1814 to open a school for girls. Following her marriage to a wealthy businessman, she spent her time writing, publishing her work anonymously. When Sigourney's husband experienced a financial reversal, she began to write for a living. The first book that appeared under her own name was *Biography of Pious Persons*, published in 1832. Critics considered Sigourney's works light and sentimental, but the books were very popular. The city of Hartford named a street in her honor following her death. (*Sources*: 97, 339, 603, 677, 758)

1832   Marie Taglioni   (1804–1884) Italy

Taglioni became a ballet dancer at an early age and quickly rose to stardom. She was not only famous in Italy but went on to become an international star, traveling to perform as far away as Australia, which was unusual for that time. She was one of the first dancers to use shoes with blocked toes. Taglioni choreographed many of the roles in which she danced. She is best known for helping her father, Filippo Taglioni, choreograph *La Sylphide* in 1832, revolutionizing ballet. Taglioni is also credited with introducing the midcalf-length ballet skirt. (*Sources*: 440, 498, 709, 717)

1833   Anne Boivin   (1773–1847) France

Boivin learned midwifery from the famous Marie LaChapelle, later succeeding LaChapelle as director of the Hôtel Dieu as well as serving as director of several other hospitals. Her major contribution to midwifery was the book she wrote in 1833 about uterine diseases; it later became a standard text. An earlier book about midwifery (1812) was translated into several languages. Boivin is credited as the first to listen for a fetal heartbeat with a stethoscope, and she invented the vaginal speculum, still in use today. She was awarded several honorary degrees but never achieved recognition at the University of Paris, where she did most of her work. (*Sources*: 9, 512, 529)

1834   Marie Durocher   (1809–1893) Brazil

Durocher was the first individual to earn a degree at the medical school of Rio de Janeiro, in 1834, and was among the first women physicians in Brazil. She entered medical school after being widowed and left with children to support. Influenced by the midwife ANNE BOIVIN, Durocher concentrated on obstetrics. She remained in active practice for almost sixty years. (*Sources*: 439, 512, 731)

1834?   Maria Anna Fisher   (1819–1911) United States (African American)

Starting around 1834, Fisher sold her homemade biscuits door to door in Philadelphia and eventually earned enough to provide herself with a fourteen-room house and to buy fourteen other houses from which she earned rent. She never raised her initial price of 12.5 cents per biscuit. She left an estate of $70,000 to Hampton Institute, Tuskeegee Institute, and various charities. (*Source*: 391)

1834   Harriet Martineau   (1802–1876) England

Martineau's father provided her and her brother with an equal education. Her first book, *Illustrations of Political*

Economy, in twenty-five volumes, was published in 1834 and was so successful that cabinet ministers invited her to address Parliament. During this same period, she wrote both a ten-volume and five-volume book. In 1837, after visiting the United States, she wrote *Society in America*, followed in 1839 by her first novel, *Deerbook*. Toward the end of her career, Martineau wrote another novel, her autobiography, and a book about the Lake District, where she had retired. (*Sources*: 370, 514, 579, 584, 758)

1835   Bettina von Arnim   (1785–1859) Germany

Arnim was born into a wealthy and artistic family during the romantic period, when women's writing was recognized and appreciated. She was devoted to the poet Johann Wolfgang von Goethe and his mother, both of whom she had known since childhood; her first book, *Correspondence Between Goethe and a Young Girl*, written in 1835, was a reminiscence of time spent with them, as was her second book. In 1844 she wrote a biography of her brother, the poet Clemens Brentano. Two other books (1843 and 1852), describing the plight of the underclass, were intended to draw the attention of King Frederick William III. (*Sources*: 80, 521, 731)

1836   Mary Lyon   (1797–1849) United States

In order to open a women's seminary, Lyon traveled throughout Massachusetts soliciting small donations. With additional financial aid, she incorporated Mount Holyoke Female Seminary, later renamed Mount Holyoke College, in 1836. Originally offering a two-year program, the school extended the curriculum from two to three years. The school also expanded its science courses because of Lyon's emphasis on the need for women to learn science. Although Lyon served as principal, she continued to teach chemistry, her favorite subject. More than 80 percent of the seminary's graduates became teachers. A bust of Lyon was commissioned from Laura Fardin Fraser and presented to the seminary in 1927. (*Sources*: 242, 447, 627, 634, 680, 696, 699)

1837   Charlotte Barnes   (1818–1863) United States

The daughter of parents who worked in theater, Barnes started acting at a young age and appeared on stage in both Boston and New York. She did not become famous until 1837, when she wrote *Octavia Bragaldi, or, The Confession,* a play based on the factual story of a Kentucky officer who killed another colonel for seducing his fiancée. The play was highly successful and was presented in several adaptations for years in many countries. In 1846 Barnes married the manager of Philadelphia's Arch Street Theatre, where she later appeared in numerous plays. (*Sources:* 105, 486)

1837   Laura Bridgman   (1829–1889) United States

Bridgman was a normal child until the age of two, when she contracted scarlet fever that caused her to lose her sight, hearing, and speech, isolating her from the rest of the world. Samuel Howe worked with her at the Perkins Institution for the Blind in Boston. He devised a system of raised letters used in conjunction with the object the letters represented in order to teach Bridgman how to read and write, making her the first blind deaf-mute able to do so. After her pioneering efforts, Bridgman chose to spend the remainder of her life at Perkins, continuing to participate in studies that would help others overcome their sensory impairments. (*Sources:* 105, 447, 556, 616, 722)

1837   Charlotte Cushman   (1816–1876) United States

Cushman was the first U.S.-born woman to become a star in theater in the United States. Although she had had a brief career in opera, she made her acting debut at the Park Company in New York and in 1837 went to Philadelphia, where she appeared in *Guy Mannering* and *Oliver Twist*; she performed in *Macbeth* on alternate nights in Philadelphia and New York. After a triumphant tour in London that lasted several years, Cushman returned to the United States in 1849 and received widespread acclaim for both male and female Shakespearean roles. In 1874 she came out of a twenty-two-year retirement for her greatest performances at the Booth Theater. She was also known for her willingness to help aspiring young performers. (*Sources:* 197, 447, 731)

1837   Mary Ann Lee   (1824?–1899) United States

Lee first danced ballet in 1837 with another child, Augusta Maywood, beginning a public rivalry that led to fame for both dancers. Two years later Lee danced in New York in *La Bayadère,* which became her favorite ballet role. Following a

U.S. tour she studied in Paris. She returned to the United States in 1846 to become the first American ballet dancer to perform in *Giselle*. It was this role that made her known throughout the country. (*Sources*: 447, 512, 709)

1837   Madmoiselle Rachel   (1820–1858) France

Mademoiselle Rachel was the stage name of Eliza Rachel Felix. In 1837 she made her acting debut in Corneille's tragedy *Horace* at the Comédie Française. She was an immediate success and soon became known for her fiery looks and regal bearing. At first she appeared only in classical works, but she soon added the romantic plays of Victor Hugo and Alexandre Dumas, eventually touring throughout the world. Weakened by tuberculosis, she died soon after her return to France. (*Sources*: 42, 281, 521)

1838   Grace Darling   (1815–1842) England

Born into a large family, Darling helped her father, who had followed his father as keeper of the lighthouse on Farne Islands in Northumberland. In 1838 the ship *Forfashire* was wrecked offshore, and Darling rowed out in heavy seas to rescue four men and a woman. With the aid of two of the men, her father rowed out to rescue the remaining four survivors. She and her father both received gold medals from the Humane Society and a large sum of money collected for them; Darling was even asked to appear in a circus. She chose to return to the solitude of the lighthouse, where she died when she was in her late twenties. (*Sources*: 36, 199, 518, 731)

1838   Frances Green   (1805–1878) United States

Green was born in the small town of Smithfield, Rhode Island. She showed literary promise at an early age. Interested in social issues, she used her writing skills to promote reform for women, slaves, and the working class. Her first published book, *Elleanor Eldridge* (1838), was the true story of the legal injustice experienced by a black woman. A sequel entitled *Elleanor's Second Book* appeared the following year. In 1840 and 1858 Green wrote two novels attacking the practice of slavery. Her interest in working conditions was reflected in her books *The Mechanic* (1841) and *Might and Right: By a Rhode Islander* (1844). Green also wrote poetry and was a contributor and editor for several newspapers. With a knowledge and interest in botany, she coauthored *Analytical Class-Book of Botany* with Joseph Congdon in 1855. Shortly after this last book was published, Green divorced her husband and moved to California, where she remarried and continued to write. She wrote her last book, *Beyond the Veil*, the year of her death. (*Sources*: 486, 508)

1839 Sarah Margaret Fuller (1810–1850) United States

Fuller's father was obsessed with his daughter's education: she could read Latin by the age of three and was proficient in foreign languages by her early teens. He died in 1835; Fuller devoted the rest of her life to the education of others. In 1839 she moved to Boston, where she instituted one of the first women's study groups. At this time she also became friendly with Ralph Waldo Emerson and Horace Greeley, learned about transcendentalism, and became editor of the magazine *Dial*. She later moved to New York and became a literary critic for Greeley's *Tribune*. In 1846 Fuller went to Europe, met and married a marquis, and had a child. All three drowned on a trip to the United States. (*Sources*: 14, 24, 60, 64, 79, 212, 358, 447, 455, 486, 522, 561, 680)

1839 Caroline Norton (1808–1877) England

Norton was an early champion of women's legal rights even though she never advocated equality for women in any other sphere. In 1830 she left her husband, who accused her of adultery, a charge dismissed by the court. Her husband then confiscated her inheritance and earnings from her early books of poetry, denying her access to their children. Norton's plea to the queen, her public pamphlets, and her court battle led to the 1839 Custody of Infants Act in which a mother, unless convicted of adultery, had custody of any of her children under the age of seven and access to any other of her children. Norton was also influential in the passage of the Marriage and Divorce Act of 1857, which addressed the legal inequity women faced. The act granted them the legal status of *femme sole* (the right of a woman to own property in her own name) in property rights. Norton's poetry and novels established her as a literary figure as well. (*Sources*: 12, 60, 271, 558, 599, 695)

1839 Elizabeth Peabody (1804–1894) United States

Although Peabody devoted much of her earlier life to education, she is perhaps best known for the bookstore she opened in Boston in 1839. Her store was the only one that carried books by Nathaniel Hawthorne and SARAH MARGARET FULLER, and it became a cultural center for scholars and for followers of transcendentalism. Peabody closed the shop in 1845 to return to teaching and writing. She is generally credited with introducing the concept of the kindergarten into the United States. (*Sources*: 34, 139, 380, 455, 486, 514, 548, 616, 731)

1840   Agnes Strickland   (1796–1874) England
As were her sisters SUSANNAH MOODIE and Catherine Traill, Strickland was a well-known writer. In 1840, in collaboration with another sister, Elizabeth, she wrote a twelve-volume book on the *Lives of the Queens of England*. She wrote a lengthy book on the queens of Scotland and the princesses of England in 1859. Strickland is also noted for her poetry and children's books. (*Sources*: 12, 304, 473, 521)

1841   Caroline Chisholm   (1808–1877) Australia (England)
Chisholm was born in England but moved first to India and then to Australia with her husband. Alone when her husband was away on business, she soon became active in aiding young single women who had immigrated to Australia. In 1841 she opened the Female Immigrants' Home. She also helped those newly arrived to find jobs. In 1849 she was instrumental in the passage of the Colonization Loan Society, which enabled her to assist convict families and others in relocating to Australia. Despite all of her work and renown, she died impoverished, in England. (*Sources*: 558, 621, 731)

1842   Grace Aguilar   (1816–1847) England
Aguilar had already written a book of poetry by the time she was nineteen. Her most significant works were on Judaism; in *The Spirit of Judaism* (1842) and *The Jewish Faith* (1845) she fostered an understanding of her faith yet advocated the return to biblical principles. Her first popular book was *Home Influence* (1847), the only widely read book she published during her short lifetime. Aguilar's two other popular books, about women and the role of women in Judaism, were published posthumously by her mother, in 1850 and 1851. (*Sources*: 123, 154, 556, 731)

1842   Ada Lovelace   (1815–1852) England
Lovelace might have made some far-reaching contributions to mathematics had she not led such a frenetic and frustrated life. The only daughter of Lord Byron, she was denied seeing him. Although she was provided with tutors, the education she needed was not available to women, and she became primarily self-taught. It was only through her correspondance with the noted mathematician and inventor Charles Babbage that she was able to demonstrate her great mathematical ability. She fully understood the prin ciples of the analytical engine that Babbage had designed and in 1842 pointed out to him some of his errors. In her view, this engine could not think but could be used in programming data. Although credited to Lovelace, this theory was published only as an annotation in another scholar's work. Her addictions to opium and alcohol led to the dissipation of the remainder of her life. A recent federally sponsored computer program is named Ada in her honor. (*Sources*: 9, 22, 36, 621, 731)

1842   Charlotte Yonge   (1823–1901) England
Yonge was a deeply religious woman who dedicated her literary talent to the writing of religious books. Starting in 1842 she wrote for the young people's *Monthly Packet*; she donated her earnings to charity. She promoted the Church of England's Oxford movement through her multiple books and tracts. Her most notable books—both on the theme of virtue—are *The Daisy Chain* in 1856 and *A Chronicle of Mistakes* in 1861. (*Sources*: 12, 322, 500, 562, 731)

1843   Louise Farrenc   (1804–1875) France
An accomplished composer, Farrenc was not intimidated by her famous husband, flutist Aristide Farrenc; her work was once judged to be "good enough to be written by a man." She wrote symphonies in 1843, 1846, and 1849, with the last of these pieces receiving high praise in the prestigious *Gazette Musicale*. The first woman to hold a teaching post at the Paris Conservatory, Farrenc composed thirty études for piano, sonatas for violin and cello, and music for wind and string instruments. She also edited her husband's work after his death in 1865. (*Sources*: 33, 525, 654)

1843   Lola Montez   (1818–1861) Ireland

As a naive woman of twenty, Montez attempted to launch a career as a Spanish dancer but was recognized at her debut in London in 1843 as the wife of the army officer from whom she had separated after a year of marriage. Undaunted, she left England for the Continent, where she did establish a career as a dancer and gained a reputation for her numerous romantic liaisons. Her most famous liaison was with the king of Bavaria, who allowed her influence to dictate political policy, which eventually led to the collapse of his monarchy. Montez returned to London and was briefly remarried (despite never having divorced her first husband). After winning audiences on Broadway, she made a successful tour of the United States. The highlight of her career was a performance of the Spider Dance in San Francisco. Montez eventually settled in New York, where she lectured and wrote books on fashion and beauty. She is reported to have experienced a religious conversion in her later years. (*Sources*: 500, 548, 756)

1844   Sarah Bagley   (dates unknown) United States

Bagley worked for labor reform, organizing the Lowell Female Labor Reform Association in 1844 and helping to establish the New England Working Men's Association in 1845. She also helped to found the Industrial Reform Lyceum, which provided a forum for those who wished to speak out for labor reform. In addition, she served as editor of the *Voice of Industry*, a newspaper that women purchased from the men's association. Because of political and business pressure, Massachusetts failed to pass the ten-hour workday that Bagley and others pushed to have legislated. Discouraged and in ill health, she left the labor movement and became the first woman to be hired as a telegrapher. (*Sources*: 447, 455, 532, 681)

1845   Rosa Bonheur   (1822–1899) France

Bonheur's persona was as colorful and famous as her paintings: she remained single throughout her life, was ambitious and independent, smoked cigarettes, preferred the comfort of male attire, and kept her hair short. She and her three siblings aspired to become artists like their father, but Rosa was the only successful one of the four. Bonheur's father was a struggling artist who moved his family to Paris to further his career. This move enabled Bonheur to visit the Louvre, where she copied the masterpieces to teach herself to paint. Her reproductions were so good that she soon found a lucrative market for them as well as for the sculptures she did of animals. Most of her paintings—such as her best-known one, *The Horse Fair*—were of both domestic and wild animals. Bonheur won her first prize in 1845, and at this time her work became popular and expensive. In 1849 she succeeded her father as director of a government-supported art school for girls, a position he had held the year before his death. In the same year she received a gold medal for her painting *Plowing in Nivernais*, which was purchased by the government and hung in the Louvre. In 1853 Bonheur completed her most ambitious project, the huge *Horse Fair*. Following a stay in England, where her work sold well, she purchased an estate in the countryside in France for herself and her childhood friend, Nathalie Micas. Bonheur's success continued and she was awarded numerous prizes; her greatest honor was in being named the first woman officer in the Legion of Honor in 1894. (*Sources*: 353, 374, 390, 395, 407, 440, 598, 607, 639, 726)

1845   Frances Caulkins   (1795–1869) United States

Caulkins attended the school in Norwich, Connecticut, in which LYDIA SIGOURNEY was later principal. Caulkins ran girls' schools in Norwichtown and New London from 1820 to 1834. She began writing in 1842 for the American Tract Society, her works selling millions of copies. Caulkins is best known for *A History of Norwich* (1845) and *History of New London* (1852). These two books stand as classics of local history that rise above parochialism. In 1849 she became the first woman elected to the Massachusetts Historical Society and the only woman member until the next century. (*Sources*: 12, 447, 473, 718)

1845   Ann Mowatt   (1819–1870) United States

Mowatt lived a glamorous, exciting, and varied life. At the age of fifteen she eloped with an older man and immediately began a successful writing career. After her husband declared bankruptcy, she became a literary public reader and later wrote popular books and articles. Her greatest achievement came in 1845 when she wrote and starred in her first play, *Fashion*. Enjoying her new career, she continued in the theater, performing in her second play, *Armand*. Following the death of her husband in 1851, she married a southerner but left him because of their different allegiances during the Civil War. She returned to writing and worked until her death. (*Sources*: 14, 80, 343, 486, 548, 562, 570)

1846 Marie d'Agoult (1805–1876) France

D'Agoult scandalized Paris when, though already married, she ran off to Switzerland with the composer Franz Liszt. This romantic liaison lasted for nine years and produced three children; their son became a count, one daughter married a future prime minister, and the other daughter married the composer Richard Wagner. After separating from Liszt, d'Agoult returned to Paris and began to write under the pen name of Daniel Stern, which she used as her literary pseudonym throughout her career. She published her first novel, *Nelida*, in 1846; she also published essays and articles on politics and philosophy. Her last publication was *Souvenirs*, a book about French aristocratic society. (*Sources*: 153, 490, 731)

1846 Frances Whitcher (1813–1852) United States

Beginning in 1846, Whitcher wrote insightful and lyrical satire about small-town life and its hypocrisy for the *Saturday Gazette* and *Godey's Lady's Book*. She published her stories anonymously, as she was married to the minister of a church in a small town in New York State. Using malapropian vernacular and colloquial language, she wove a pattern of greed, ambition, false gentility, and meanness, all acted out under the guise of propriety. Her wit, humor, and knowledge of underlying motives make her works memorable. When her identity as the author of these stories was revealed, her husband had to resign from his pastorate. Whitcher died six years after she began writing; her last story, "The Widow Spriggins," was published posthumously in 1867. (*Sources*: 447, 455, 522, 548)

1847 Harriet Bishop (1817–1883) United States

Bishop was an educator and a feminist. When teachers were solicited in 1847 to teach on the frontier in the West, she accepted a teaching position in Minnesota, where she established the first public school. The Sunday schools she started became the first Protestant churches in the area. Active in the feminist movement, she became an officer in the American Equal Rights

Association in 1869. Minnesota named an island in Bishop's honor. (*Sources*: 473, 718)

1847   Maria Mitchell   (1818–1889) United States
Encouraged by her father, an amateur astronomer, Mitchell learned about astronomy at an early age. By 1842 she was librarian of the Nantucket Atheneum, Massachusetts. In 1847 she discovered a new comet. One of the first members on the faculty at Vassar College, which opened in 1865, Mitchell was also the first woman elected to the American Academy of Arts and Sciences and in 1870 served as president of the American Association for the Advancement of Women. (*Sources*: 12, 105, 383, 408, 447, 587, 627, 634, 718, 731)

1848   Lucretia Mott   (1793–1880) United States
Mott devoted her life to aiding the oppressed. Raised a Quaker, she became a minister in 1821, and she and her husband became active in the abolition movement; their home was used often as a shelter for runaway slaves. Mott later worked for social reform for freed slaves. In part because of her experience as a teacher who was paid less than her male colleagues and in part because of her association and friendship with the suffragette Elizabeth Cady Stanton, Mott became a strong advocate for women's rights. In 1848 Mott and Stanton organized the convention in Seneca Falls, New York, that was the impetus to the fight for the enfranchisement of women. An active participant all her life, she wrote, traveled, and lectured widely for the women's cause. (*Sources*: 261, 470, 699, 763)

1849   Elizabeth Blackwell   (1821–1910) United States (England)
When Blackwell was eleven, her family immigrated to the United States, where she and her siblings were educated. Following the death of her father, she and her sisters opened a boarding school for girls. Unwilling to marry, Blackwell decided that becoming a physician would shield her from matrimony. After a long struggle, she was admitted to the Geneva College Medical School, which originally believed an application from a woman could only be a prank. Blackwell completed her degree in 1849, then traveled to England and France to further her training. While in Paris, she contracted a disease that left her blind in one

eye. In 1851 she returned to the United States, adopted a child, and opened a hospital in New York that became the New York Infirmary for Women and Children in 1857. She made a second trip to England, in 1859 becoming the first woman physician listed in the Medical Register of the United Kingdom. She returned to the United States and during the Civil War established the first sanitary commission. She also upgraded the requirements at the hospital she had founded, establishing both entrance and exit examinations. In 1875 she retired to England. (*Sources*: 9, 12, 34, 60, 447, 473, 532, 587, 583, 680)

1849   Alice Cary, *aka* Carey   (1820–1871) United States
Cary and her sister Phoebe published their first book of poetry in 1849. Cary published three more books of poetry in 1852, 1855, and 1866. In addition, she wrote for prestigious magazines in New York and published eight books of prose between 1852 and 1868. In 1868 she and her sister were among the founders of Sorosis, a women's literary group similar to the Bluestockings in Europe. (*Sources*: 12, 455, 527, 758)

1849   Ellen Craft   (1827–?) United States (African American)
In 1849 Ellen Craft and her husband, William, owned by separate slaveholders in Georgia, succeeded in one of the most daring and dangerous escapes from slavery. Craft, the daughter of her owner, was so light-skinned she was able to pass for white, whereas the man she considered her husband (slaves were not allowed to marry) was much darker-skinned. Disguised as a well-dressed gentleman with his servant, Craft and her husband stayed at the best hotels on their four-day journey to Philadelphia, using money William had earned from odd jobs. Unable to read or write, she avoided detection by binding her hand so that she needed assistance to sign the hotel registers. Craft became a popular speaker at abolitionist meetings in both the United States and Britain. Allowed to marry when they reached Boston, she and her husband purchased a large farm, which they leased to poor people. The couple died in poverty, still in debt for the land. (*Sources*: 94, 112, 439, 763)

1849   Margaret Oliphant   (1828–1897) Scotland
Oliphant published her first book, *Mrs Maitland of Sunnyside,* in 1849 and wrote three more books before her

marriage in 1852. When her husband died, leaving her with three children to support, she began to write for a living; within a few years she was also supporting her brother's children. The needs of this enlarged family contributed to her tremendous output. Along with successful novels, Oliphant wrote histories and biographies that were considered among her best work. She was also an editor for *Blackwood's Magazine* and wrote three volumes of Blackwood's *Foreign Classics for English Readers*. (*Sources*: 12, 78, 521, 562, 571, 599, 731)

1849   Luise Otto-Peter   (1819–1895) Germany

Though not able to accomplish her feminist goals in Germany during her lifetime, Otto-Peter nevertheless did much toward the eventual change in the legal status of women there. In 1849 she founded a newspaper urging women to participate in government and to demand equality. When her newspaper was suppressed three years later, she formed the Association for Women's Education and started branches in several cities. This organization merged with the National Association of German Women in 1877 and had more than 11,000 members. For several years the association lobbied for more jobs and better opportunities for women but was unsuccessful. Within ten years, however, women in Germany won the right to vote. (*Sources*: 24, 459, 518, 587, 621)

1849   Mary Ellen Pleasant   (1814–1904) United States
(African American)

Pleasant seemed to create as much excitement when she arrived in California in 1849 as the gold rush that started at the same time. Already known as a great cook, she opened a boardinghouse and was soon linked to various scandals. She operated bordellos, coerced a woman in debt to her to claim she was married to a well-known man in order to secure the money she was owed, financed John Brown's raid on Harper's Ferry, and bullied the wealthy banker for whom she was housekeeper into allowing her free rein to spend and do as she pleased. All of this notoriety detracted from the documented evidence of her work on behalf of blacks in California: she engaged in civil rights activities, rescued illegally held slaves, and gained legal and civic rights for blacks. (*Sources*: 94, 120, 447, 508, 627, 718, 757)

1850 Susan Fenimore Cooper (1813–1894) United States

Cooper was the eldest child of the author James Fenimore Cooper. She not only copied manuscripts for her famous father but also authored her own works. In 1850 she wrote *Rural Hours*, later published under the title *Journal of a Naturalist in the United States*. She also wrote the introduction to her father's best-known work, *The Last of the Mohicans*. Although her father forbade any biography after his death, Cooper wrote about him in the preface to a book of his life, first published in 1876. Aside from her literary accomplishments, she was concerned with altruistic projects; she opened an orphanage in 1873. (*Sources*: 105, 109, 110, 486, 548)

1851 Mary Ann Cary (1823–1893) United States (African American)

The oldest of the thirteen children born to Abraham and Harriet Shadd, Cary, like her younger brothers and sisters, carried on her father's civil rights work. She moved to Canada in 1851 to aid blacks who had fled the United States after the Fugitive Slave Act of 1850. She opened a school for them in Windsor and in 1853 founded the *Provincial Freeman*, a newspaper to advance their cause. She recruited blacks in the United States for service in the Civil War and in 1869 moved to Washington, D.C., where she taught school for many years. In 1883, at the age of sixty, Cary was one among a class of four women to graduate from Howard University Law School. (*Sources*: 17, 60, 447, 486, 502, 599, 627, 696, 718)

1851 Eliza Greenfield (1809–1876) United States (African American)

Greenfield was discovered when Elizabeth Greenfield heard her singing and took the young slave home to Philadelphia with her. Mrs. Greenfield arranged for the girl to have private voice lessons and provided for her in her will. Taking the name of her mistress, Greenfield gave her first concert in 1851 in Philadelphia. She was dubbed the Black Swan for her magnificent voice, which had a range that allowed her to sing from contralto to soprano. She left for Europe to continue her studies but shortly after arriving in England discovered that her manager had not given her the funds she needed. Befriended by Harriet Beecher Stowe, who was in England at the time and arranged a concert for her, Greenfield sang before the British aristocracy. Her concerts were so successful that Queen Victoria requested a command performance in 1854. Again left destitute by her manager, Greenfield returned to the United States, where she gave private voice lessons and only occasionally appeared in concerts. (*Sources*: 148, 372, 764)

1851   Myrtilla Miner   (1815–1864) United States
Despite a spinal disorder, Miner was an indefatigable teacher all her life. She began her career in Providence, Rhode Island, but after teaching in Mississippi in 1847, she determined to start a school for blacks. In 1851 in Washington, D.C., Miner opened the Colored Girls School, which met with more success than had PRUDENCE CRANDALL's school in Connecticut twenty years earlier. Harriet Beecher Stowe, one of the many well-known people who funded the project, gave the school part of her royalties from *Uncle Tom's Cabin*. The school closed briefly during the Civil War but reopened and was eventually expanded to become the District of Columbia Teachers' College. (*Sources*: 339, 340, 447, 696, 718)

1852   Delia Bacon   (1811–1859) United States
Bacon devoted her life to trying to prove that Francis Bacon (no relation to her) and others had written plays under the name of William Shakespeare in order to advance a liberal philosophy. By 1852, she was generally known as the first "Baconian." The poet Ralph Waldo Emerson financed her trip to London to meet the historian Thomas Carlyle, who recognized Bacon's frail state of mind. Nathaniel Hawthorne found a publisher for her *Philosophy of the Plays of Shakespeare Unfolded* in 1857. The book met with derision and ridicule she was unable to comprehend, her mental illness having reached an advanced stage by then. She died shortly after returning to the United States. (*Sources*: 105, 486, 556, 616)

1852   Nancy Talbot Clarke   (1825–1901) United States
Clarke, a widowed schoolteacher, enrolled at the Cleveland Medical College (part of Western Reserve College in Ohio) in order to meet a Massachusetts law requiring that a class in physiology be added to the public school curriculum. She was admitted in 1850 under a new ruling allowing women into the

medical school; although the ruling was reversed a year later, Clarke was permitted to remain. In 1852 she became the first woman to graduate from what was then termed a "regular" medical college. Clarke returned to Boston to practice. In 1853, having met the same requirements as male physicians, she applied for membership in the Massachusetts Medical Society but was rejected. (*Sources*: 512, 529, 703)

1852   Matilda Gage   (1826–1898) United States

One of the first feminists, Gage was as closely associated with and known within the women's movement as were Elizabeth Cady Stanton and Susan B. Anthony. Gage's thinking, however, was more revolutionary, as became obvious in an address to a women's convention in 1852. She stated that seeking the vote was not sufficient but that the movement's focus should instead be on changing societal views of women. She said that society had originally been matriarchal in structure and had been overthrown by men, who, with the help of both church and state, established a patriarchal system. Gage believed it was important to research and publicize the centuries of accomplishments by women to support her thesis. Editor and publisher of the official National Woman Suffrage Association newsletter, she wrote a major portion of a history of the women's movement but never received equal credit with Stanton and Anthony as a coauthor. In *Woman, Church and State* (1893), Gage blamed men for usurping the powers of women and vilified the Christian religion for conspiring with men toward this end. The major split with the women's movement came in 1890, when Gage refused to support an alliance between the women's suffrage group and the temperance movement. She demanded wider legal and social reform, including better treatment of Native Americans. Gage broke with the suffragists to form the Woman's National Liberal Union, thereby ceding Stanton and Anthony her place in history. (*Sources*: 4, 440, 699, 728)

1852   Elizabeth Siddal   (1834–1862) England

Siddal was introduced to art through her work as a model for artists. Considered very beautiful, she soon became the exclusive model for the famous painter Dante Gabriel Rossetti and later became his mistress, student, and wife as well. Despite his obvious influence on her work, Siddal's paintings were once valued in their own right. Although she had only two exhibitions, she received an annual payment for her work from the art critic John Ruskin. Siddal died of a drug overdose at the age of twenty-eight. Today she is better known for her place in Rossetti's paintings than for her own small collection. (*Sources:* 395, 607)

1853 Florence Baker (1836–1916) Hungary

Baker led a sometimes frightening but glamorous life. In 1853, at the age of seventeen, she was almost sold as a slave to a Turk (the circumstances leading up to this event are unknown) but was instead bought by the explorer Samuel Baker, who married her. (Baker herself later played the rescuer in a similar situation, adopting a young girl who was also to be sold into slavery.) She accompanied her husband on exotic and often dangerous expeditions for the rest of her life. She became seriously ill on one desert safari but was forced to keep up with the group because there was only enough water for the journey. Later adventures involved a runaway camel, a hyena attack, an all-night search for her husband in the jungle, and battles with the indigenous peoples. The Bakers eventually found Lake Albert, a source of the Nile River. (*Sources:* 27, 28, 518)

1853 Antoinette Blackwell (1825–1921) United States

Blackwell graduated from Oberlin College in 1847 and completed her theological studies there in 1850. She became an ordained minister in 1853, first serving at a Congregational church in New York State. She married ELIZABETH BLACKWELL's brother in 1856. Active in the women's movement, she continued to preach and also wrote four books, including *Studies in General Science* (1869) and *The Physical Basis of Immortality* (1876). (*Sources:* 392, 419, 455, 532)

1853 Frances Gage (1808–1880) United States

Gage was influenced by her parents, who were active reformers. In 1853, married and with eight children, she began to lecture throughout the country against slavery and for women's issues and temperance. Gage was often threatened, and her early articles were refused for publication. In 1867 she published her first novel, *Elsie Magoon*, which depicted women as the victims of intemperate men. In her next novel, *Gertie's*

Sacrifice (1869), she addressed women's intemperance and in her third novel (1870) described a woman forced to marry to escape her drunken father. On the lighter side, using "Aunt Fannie" as a nom de plume, Gage wrote children's stories and witty accounts about women's positions in society. (*Sources*: 53, 328, 584, 627, 763)

1853   Laura Keene   (1826–1873) United States (England)

Keene took up acting after her husband was banished to Australia for debts and she was left with a mother and two daughters to support. She made her acting debut in London in *The Lady of Lyons* in 1851 and appeared at the Royal Lyceum Theatre in 1852. The U.S. producer James W. Wallack saw her perform and arranged for her to move to New York with her family. She was an immediate success in the United States and soon left Wallack for another producer, John Lutz, whom she eventually married. She became a theatrical manager in Baltimore in 1853, one of the first two women (Catherine Sinclair of San Francisco was the other) to hold such a position. Following a tour to San Francisco and Australia, in 1856 she opened the highly successful Laura Keene Theatre in New York. Her greatest part at this time was in *Our American Cousin*, the role she was playing at Ford's Theater the night Abraham Lincoln was assassinated by the actor John Wilkes Booth. It was Keene who was able to identify Booth, and she held the president in her lap until he was moved out of the theater. Ill and in debt after an illustrious career, she retired ten years later. (*Sources*: 105, 447, 518, 548, 556)

1854   Barbara Bodichon   (1827–1891) England

An eclectic person, Bodichon was interested in education, art, and the women's reform movement. She founded Portland Hall, a coeducational school, and helped EMILY DAVIES found Girton College. She studied art under the painter Jean-Baptiste Camille Corot and sold more than 200 of her works. In 1854 Bodichon wrote *A Brief Summary in Plain Language of the Most Important Laws Concerning Women*, which became the basis for the Married Women's Property Bill passed by Parliament in 1857. She married a French physician and divided her time between her work in England and Algiers, where her husband practiced. (*Sources*: 500, 529, 567, 706, 728)

1855 Louise Ackermann (1813–1890) France

Ackermann spent her life in Nice. Like her husband, Paul, she was a noted poet. Her first book of poetry, *Contes*, published in 1855, dealt with what became a central theme of Ackermann's works, the despair of mankind. She wrote four more volumes of poetry; the last, *Oeuvres* (1885), was an autobiographical account. The journals she kept from 1848 to 1869 were published posthumously in 1927 by Marc Citoleaux. (*Sources*: 15, 455, 556)

1855 Ada Clare (1836?–1874) United States

Jane McElhenney was known as Ada Clare throughout her professional career. She moved from her home in South Carolina to New York in 1854 and began writing for the then well-known publication the *Atlas* a year later. Interested in the theater, she also launched a modest career as an actor at about this same time. She moved to Paris in 1857, after the birth of a child fathered by the composer Louis Gottschalk. Returning to New York in 1859, she continued to appear on stage and wrote columns for several newspapers. Clare acquired the additional nickname of Queen of Bohemia as a result of her close association with such literary and bohemian figures as Walt Whitman and Bayard Taylor. In 1866 she wrote a romantic novel called *Only a Woman's Heart*. Clare spent a year in San Francisco writing for two newspapers but went back to New York to resume her acting career. She was appearing in a play at the time of her death. (*Sources*: 64, 548)

1855 Camilla Collett (1813–1895) Norway

Collett grew up in the shadow of her well-known father, a vicar, and her brother, the famous Norwegian poet Henrik Wergeland, and she eventually married a governor. Collett nevertheless carved a place for herself in history as a writer and champion of women's rights. Her first novel, *The Governor's Daughters*, published anonymously in 1855, was the first of several books in which she endorsed both legal and social equality for women. In *Stories* (1861), *Long Nights* (1863), and *Closing Pages* (1873), she portrayed women as the victims of legal, social, and marital laws and customs. Her work influenced the Norwegian writers Henrik Ibsen, Alexander Kielland, and others, yet was never translated into English for publication. (*Sources*: 80, 193, 488, 521)

1855   Cordelia Greene   **(1831–1905) United States**

Greene, who had helped her physician father in his practice, earned her own medical degree from Western Reserve University in 1855. She practiced medicine with her father until his death and then renamed their center the Castile Sanitarium, in Castile, New York. Greene treated women according to the holistic approach, using a combination of medicine, water treatments, diet, and prayer. She became active in the women's movement and counted Susan B. Anthony among her close friends. She never married, but she adopted and raised six children. She funded the library named in her honor in 1897, and her hospital is now a home for the elderly. (*Sources*: 2, 718)

1856   Margarethe Schurz   **(1833–1876) United States (Germany)**

Schurz was born in Hamburg, Germany. In 1852, while visiting her sister in England, she met and married Carl Schurz; the couple settled in Wisconsin. Impressed with the lectures of Friedrich Froebel, founder of the kindergarten system in Germany, she used his principles to teach her first child, Agathe, and other children in her home. She is sometimes credited with starting the first kindergarten in the United States; her husband's military, state, and diplomatic careers, however, kept the family moving and prevented Schurz from establishing a formal school. Always homesick for Germany, she was buried in Hamburg in 1876. In 1929 the women of Wisconsin erected a tablet in honor of her work. (*Sources*: 447, 718)

1856   Marie Zakrzewska   **(1829–1902) United States (Germany)**

Zakrzewska left Germany in 1851 because of the hostility toward female professors at the medical school from which she had recently graduated. Shortly after arriving in the United States, she was befriended by ELIZABETH BLACKWELL, who helped her gain entrance to medical school. They shared a practice after Zakrzewska completed her U.S. medical training in 1856. In 1859 Zakrzewska took a teaching position at the New England Female Medical College of Boston; three years later, after a dispute with the college, she left to found the New England Hospital for Women and Children, which later became the renowned New England Hospital. (*Sources*: 339, 512, 529, 618, 722, 756)

1857   Lakshmi Bai   (1835–1857) India
    Orphaned at an early age and raised by her brothers, Bai
became an excellent rider, archer, and swordswoman. She married
the raja of Jhansi, a city in north-central India. Upon the death of
their only child, the raja named his nephew heir to the throne;
when the raja died, the British challenged the legality of the
succession, and the people of Jhansi joined the mutiny against
British rule. Bai rode in battle for thirteen consecutive days,
escaping only shortly before Jhansi surrendered. She died during
the Tatya Tope group's uprising against the British. She is
reported to have ridden into battle wielding a sword with
both hands, holding her horse's reins in her mouth. (*Sources*: 621,
647)

1857   Carlotta Ferrari   (1837–1907) Italy
    Ferrari studied piano, voice, and composition at the Milan
Conservatory of Music from 1844 to 1850. She wrote her first
opera, *Ugo*, in 1857 at the age of twenty and had to finance
herself the opening performance because she was a woman
composer. The opera was a success, and her work became popular.
Ferrari was commissioned to write a cantata for an official event
in Turin and also to write a requiem mass to mark the anniversary
of the death of King Albert. In addition to writing two other
operas, Ferrari wrote books of verse and an autobiography.
(*Sources*: 99, 431)

1857   Mary Jane Seacole   (1805–1881) Jamaica
    Seacole was born to a Jamaican woman and a Scottish
soldier. Taking over her mother's boardinghouse at the time of
her mother's death, she gained a reputation for her care for
victims of cholera and yellow fever. When the Crimean War
broke out, Seacole volunteered her services but, as an untrained
nurse, was rejected. She remained in Jamaica, cooking and caring
for the wounded, and served as a nurse also in Cuba and Panama.
Although she was given a special celebration in London, where
she moved following the Crimean War, Seacole was left
destitute; she wrote the *Wonderful Adventures of Mrs Seacole in
Many Lands* (1857) to support herself. The book was highly
successful, and Seacole was not only once again popular with the
crowds but also received much attention from Queen Victoria.
(*Sources*: 53, 648)

1858   Dorothea Beale   (1831–1906) England

Beale devoted her life to the education of women. Her first teaching position was at Queen's College, Oxford, where she had been one of the first students. She also taught briefly at Cowan Bridge School, which numbered the Brontë sisters among its students. In 1858 Beale became principal at Cheltenham Ladies' College, building it into a famous school with both a nursery and teacher training school. She also founded St. Hilda's Hall at Oxford, which eventually was incorporated as a college. As part of her efforts to gain acceptance for the education of women, she wrote an exposé in 1869 entitled *A Report on the Education of Girls*. Beale was also a coauthor of *Work and Play in Girls' Schools* in 1898. (*Sources*: 168, 556, 558, 731)

1858   Ida Lewis   (1842–1911) United States

Lewis grew up helping her father, a lighthouse keeper in Newport, Rhode Island. In 1858 she rescued four men from a capsized boat. She continued her brave sea rescues even after her father suffered a stroke. She was given a gold medal, an award from the American Cross of Honor Society, and a small pension from the Carnegie Hero Fund. Her most prized award was the boat she named *Rescue*, given to her by the city of Newport. She continued at the lighthouse after her father's death but was not officially appointed lighthouse keeper until 1879; she remained at her station for twenty-four more years. (*Sources*: 66, 518, 548, 616, 718)

1859   Isabella Beeton   (1836–1865) England

Beeton's cookbook first appeared in serial form in 1859. Later republished as a book, it contained 3,000 recipes and advice on such topics as housekeeping and child care, all compiled from other sources. Beeton also contributed articles to her husband's newspaper, creating the forerunner of the advice column still popular today. She died giving birth to her fourth child. (*Sources*: 40, 473, 621, 731)

1859   Mary Booth   (1831–1889) United States

In order to pursue a career in journalism, Booth left the school where she had taught for several years and moved to New York. She took whatever jobs she could find during the day to support herself and did her writing at night. The *New York Times* eventually hired her, without pay, to write women's and educational columns. She finally achieved success in 1859 with the *History of the City of New York*. She also did many translations; her most successful was of a French book that boosted morale with its sympathetic view of the North in the Civil War. In 1867 Booth became the first editor of the new magazine *Harper's Bazaar*, a position she held for twenty-two years. (*Sources*: 447, 455, 522, 548, 756)

1859 Abigail Duniway (1834–1915) United States

Duniway based her book *Captain Gray's Company* (1859) on the journal she had kept on her family's trip over the Oregon Trail eight years earlier, during which both her mother and brother died. In Portland, starting in 1871, she edited a weekly newspaper, the *New Northwest*, that was controversial because of its open support of women's rights. She also wrote books on the theme of disadvantaged women who overcome their difficulties. Duniway toured the country, lecturing on women's issues. In 1912 she became the first woman in Oregon to cast a vote. (*Sources*: 14, 34, 447, 486, 522, 627, 718)

1859 Adeline Patti (1843–1919) United States (Spain)

Patti was born in Spain to Italian parents who emigrated to the United States in 1844. She began to sing at an early age and in 1859 made her operatic debut in New York, in Donizetti's *Lucia di Lammermoor*. Two years later she performed in Covent Garden in London and followed this with the first performance of *Aida* in Britain. Although she considered the United States her home, Patti made tours throughout the world, amassing a fortune and a devoted following. She was always asked to sing "Home Sweet Home" at the finale of each of her concerts. She made her final appearance on stage in 1914 in England, with the king and queen in attendance. Patti retired to England in 1918 with her third husband. (*Sources*: 15, 36, 279, 447, 468, 500, 548, 731)

1859 Harriet Wilson (dates unknown) United States (African American)

The only record of Harriet Wilson's existence is the book *Our Nig; or, Sketches from the Life of a Free Black*, which she wrote in 1859. Widely believed to be her auto-biography, her novel tells of a child abandoned by her parents and left to live with a family that, with little exception, treated her cruelly. Wilson tells of being beaten often by her mistress and her mistress's daughter, receiving some kindness only from her master and one of his sons. It was these two men who insisted she be allowed to attend school until the age of eleven. After her master and his son died, her life became even more unbearable until she was finally released at her mistress's death. She married and had a son. After her husband left her, she wrote her book in order to earn money to care for her sick child; the child died six months later. Wilson's novel was prologued by letters of endorsement from friends who attested to both the accuracy of her story and her desperate need. (Sources: 495, 769)

1860 Ellen Demorest (1824–1898) United States

Demorest was already a successful milliner for fashion-able New York women when, in 1860, after marrying an amateur inventor, she designed inexpensive and standardized tissue-paper dress patterns. To promote this new product, she and her husband started a women's magazine that evolved into a controversial women's-issues monthly. They had a policy of nondiscriminatory hiring that offended many people. In 1863 the Buttericks challenged the Demorests in court to the patent rights to the tissue-paper patterns and won their claim. The Demorests nevertheless continued their profitable retail and mail-order company and by the 1880s owned a multimillion-dollar business. (*Sources*: 447, 518, 627)

1860 Charlie [Charlotte] Parkhurst (1812–1879) United States

Parkhurst dressed as a man and gave her name as Charlie in order to get a job as a stagecoach driver in California in 1860. After losing an eye in an accident, she was called One-Eyed Charlie. She managed to go undetected for the nineteen years she drove a stagecoach; it was only after her death that her true sex was discovered. She had also managed to quietly vote in the 1868 election under her own name of Charlotte. (*Sources*: 60, 537, 718, 739, 751)

1860   Loreta Velazquez   (1838–?) United States (Cuba)

Velazquez, granddaughter of the famous painter Diego Velázquez, married a young U.S. army officer in 1856. They settled in New Orleans, and by 1860 their three children had all died. At the start of the Civil War, Velazquez urged her husband to rejoin the military on the side of the Confederates. Although her husband refused to have her accompany him into the war—as many women did, to care for their husbands—she waited until he left and then followed him. A wealthy woman, she went to great expense to have a uniform designed for her that would hide her female figure; she also wore a realistic moustache. She joined her husband only shortly before he was killed when his gun misfired. In 1860, with no family left to her, Velazquez took her husband's place, calling herself Lieutenant Harry Buford. She was assigned to a reserve unit but, after engaging in several battles, including the Battle of Bull Run, applied for assignment to a regular unit and a promotion. These were denied. Recognizing the need for information about the enemy's plans, she offered her services as a spy. It is ironic that Velazquez donned female attire as a disguise for her spying activities, and that at one point after returning to New Orleans for a rest, she was temporarily detained as a Union spy. Her second husband also having been killed in the war, she married for a third time, had a child, and traveled throughout the sparsely settled Southwest. During this time she wrote a narrative of her war experiences. (*Sources*: 136, 647, 739, 763)

1861   Mary Ann Bickerdyke   (1817–1901) United States

Bickerdyke had no formal training as a nurse but managed to learn physio-botanic medical nursing at an early age. After her marriage she moved to Cincinnati, where she used her home to help fugitive slaves escape to Canada. In 1861 she went to Cairo, Illinois, to nurse injured Civil War troops; from there she traveled to Savannah, Georgia, at the time of the Battle at Shiloh. Here she gained a reputation for being fearless: she would go out by lantern at night to ensure that there were no injured men left on the battlefield. By 1863 she was assigned to General William Tecumseh Sherman's Fifteenth Corps at his request and won the right to have medical supplies transported by rail to the field hospitals; Sherman is said to have remarked that Bickerdyke "outranked" him. Following the war, she devoted her life to caring for the needy and trying to obtain pensions for veterans. Near the end of her life, she established the Mother Bickerdyke Home for elderly nurses. (*Sources*: 81, 170, 447, 462, 680)

1861 Mary Braddon (1837–1915) England

A prolific writer, Braddon averaged two novels a year, starting in 1861, for the first ten years of her writing career. Her frantic pace was at least partly spurred by the dependence of her lover (later her husband), his five children, and their six children—all of whom Braddon had to support. Along with her witty novels, mostly satires about the supposed asexuality and passivity of women, she wrote nine plays and edited several magazines for many years. Braddon's *Lady Audley's Secret* (1862) and her historical novel *The Infidel* (1900) are considered to be her best works. (*Sources*: 173, 473, 500, 731)

1861 Elizabeth Keckley (1818–1907) United States (African American)

Keckley borrowed $1,200 to secure the release of herself and her son from slavery. She repaid these debts, learned to read and write, and established herself as a popular dressmaker for the fashionable women of Washington, D.C. In 1861 she became dressmaker and confidante to Mary Todd Lincoln, wife of the president. In *Behind the Scenes; or, Thirty Years a Slave, and Four Years in the White House* (1868), Keckley gave very personal and touching accounts of the death of Willie Lincoln at the age of eleven and the death of President Lincoln. With great sympathy, she describes Mrs. Lincoln's agony and later humiliation at having to sell her clothes and jewels to support herself, since the government had not provided for her. The book was not well received at the time because Keckley quoted criticism of members of the government and showed Mrs. Lincoln, who was not popular, in a favorable light. Keckley was one of the founders of the Home for Destitute Women and Children, where she herself had to reside in later years. (*Sources*: 447, 507, 508, 657, 696)

1861 Mary Peake (1823–1862) United States (African American)

In 1861 Peake became the first black teacher at Hampton Institute (now Hampton University). Her first pupils were what were called "contrabands," the free blacks housed at Fort Monroe. Popular myth has it that she taught under a large oak tree called the Emancipation Oak (though she is buried under the tree, she never held classes there). Peake taught for only a year before she died. Most of the information on her life was collected in interviews with Peake and her mother by Reverend Lewis Lockwood and published as *Mary Peake, the Colored Teacher at Fortress Monroe* in 1862. (*Sources*: 391, 455, 508)

1861   Susie King Taylor   (1848–1912) United States (African American)

Taylor was born a slave in Georgia. When the Civil War started, she volunteered her services to a South Carolina unit. She first washed clothes but soon aided in the care of the wounded. Clara Barton, initially reluctant to consider Taylor a nurse, changed her mind when she saw the skill Taylor displayed in her duties. Taylor worked with Barton for the remainder of the war without official recognition; she received neither a salary nor a pension. (*Sources*: 558, 648, 763)

1861   Tz'u Hsi   (1835–1908) China

A concubine of the emperor, Tz'u Hsi was elevated to empress when she bore the emperor a son, his only heir. When the emperor died in 1861, she effectively took over as a coregent with the emperor's brother. The two succeeded in unifying China by crushing three rebellions. They then established schools and modernized the country. Refusing to give up power, she denied her son the regency throughout his life. After his death, she installed her nephew as ruler and removed her coregent. She stepped down in 1889 but reclaimed power when her nephew attempted to establish reforms after China's defeat by Japan in 1895. Attempting to rid China of foreign influence, Tz'u Hsi encouraged the Boxer Rebellion against Britain (1898–1900). (*Sources*: 420, 731)

1862   Belle Boyd   (1844–1900) United States

From a genteel family and educated at Mount Washington College, Boyd was an unlikely candidate for a spy. But when Confederates attacked Front Royal, in Virginia, in 1862 while she was visiting there she took on this role. It was later documented in two reliable sources that Boyd had in fact raced across an open battlefield to warn the advancing forces that the Union army planned to destroy the fort's munitions. On another occasion, she rode 15 miles during the night to deliver secret plans to the Confederates. She was caught spying in July of that same year, sent to prison for one month, and then released with orders to return to the South. She was arrested twice again for spying. In 1864 Boyd requested that Confederate President Jefferson Davis send her to England as a courier; en route she was captured by the Union navy. After arriving in England, she married one of her captors, Samuel Hardinge. Her husband was recalled to the United States and served time in prison. In order to support herself, Boyd wrote her autobiography, *Belle Boyd in Camp and Prison* (1865). Her husband returned to England later that year but died shortly after the birth of their daughter. Boyd next pursued a career on the stage. She remarried, bore three children, and suffered a breakdown before divorcing in 1884. With children to support, she made her spying exploits into a show that toured for several years. She was poverty-stricken and married to a man twenty years her junior when she died in 1900. Boyd's courage and independence are summed up in words from her book: "Though my heart was throbbing, my eyes were dry; not a muscle of my face quivered; no outward sign betrayed the conflicting emotions that raged within." (*Sources*: 62, 105, 419, 627, 650, 693, 718, 756)

1862   Elizabeth Comstock   (1815–1891) United States (England)

Comstock married at thirty-three, was a widow at thirty-six, migrated to Canda at thirty-seven, and remarried at thirty-eight. Having moved to the United States, she became a minister and actively participated in the Underground Railway to assist escaping slaves. She was considered a charismatic speaker and in 1862 was asked to address the Michigan legislature, the first woman to do this. Comstock spent the Civil War in hospitals and prisons, aiding the sick and wounded. She also held a prayer meeting with President Abraham Lincoln. In 1879 Comstock was secretary to the Kansas Freedmen's Relief Association. Noted for her work in the women's movement, she spoke in women's behalf throughout the country and is credited with changing the Quaker philosophy on the rights of women. Comstock continued to lecture until shortly before her death. (*Sources*: 363, 548)

1862 Carrie Cutter (1842–1862) United States

Cutter was eighteen when the Civil War started, and she volunteered to go with her physician father and the New Hampshire regiment to care for the troops. She died at age twenty of a fever contracted while nursing the sick and wounded in North Carolina; she is said to be the first woman to serve and to die in the war. She was buried at the national cemetery in New Bern, North Carolina, next to her fiancé, who had been killed in battle. Her name is on the roll of honor at the Library of Congress. (*Sources*: 129, 662, 718)

1862 Mary Livermore (1820–1905) United States

Livermore spent the early part of her adulthood teaching school in both the North and South. She married a minister who approved of her activities for social reform. A devout Calvinist, she deplored slavery and was anxious to help when the Civil War broke out. In 1862 Livermore was put in charge of the western branch of the U.S. Sanitary Commission, which transported medical supplies to the battlefront. To raise money to purchase supplies, she sold so-called original copies of Lincoln's Emancipation Proclamation. Following the war, Livermore wrote for her husband's church paper, published a very popular memoir of the war, and devoted much energy to the cause of women's suffrage. (*Sources*: 81, 339, 351, 387, 506, 512, 616, 627, 680)

1862 Harriet Phillips (1819–1901) United States

Although it is not certain that Phillips had formal training, she enlisted in the army in 1862 and served as a nurse at the army hospital in St. Louis for two years. Enrolled in the newly opened Female Medical College at the Women's Hospital in Philadelphia, she received only a year of training but returned to the army hospital in 1869 as a head nurse. In 1872 Phillips left the hospital to provide medical care for the American Indians in Wisconsin and later Chinese immigrants in San Francisco. In 1878 she reentered the women's hospital for postgraduate training. She continued her nursing career until 1883. (*Sources*: 81, 355, 455, 462)

1862 Lucy Taylor (1833–1910) United States

Taylor has the distinction of being the first woman to earn a degree in dentistry. Having applied to and been rejected by both medical and dental schools, she served an apprenticeship with a dentist, and since no degree was yet required, she started her dental practice in 1862. Three years later, Taylor was given membership in the Iowa State Dental Society. She was then admitted to dental college and was granted her degree in 1866 after four months of classes. Taylor married, taught her husband dentistry, and in 1867 moved to Kansas, where she and her husband established one of the largest practices in the state. Taylor practiced until 1886. (*Sources*: 447, 455, 548, 718)

1863   Olympia Brown   (1835–1926) United States
Refused admission to the University of Michigan because of her gender, Brown graduated from Antioch College in 1860. She earned a degree in theology from St. Lawrence University in 1863 and became the first ordained woman minister in the United States. She served as minister for two New England churches between 1864 and 1876, during which time she became interested in women's suffrage. She founded the New England Woman Suffrage Association in 1868. From 1884 to 1912 Brown was president of the Wisconsin Woman Suffrage Association and in 1884 became vice-president of the National Woman Suffrage Association. She was unsuccessful in her effort to get Kansas and Wisconsin to pass a bill giving women the right to vote. In 1902 she founded the Federal Suffrage Association, serving first as its vice-president and later as president. Following the death of her husband in 1893, Brown took over his newspaper, the *Racine Times*, and in 1911 published a book entitled *Acquaintances, Old and New, Among Reformers*. (*Sources*: 339, 548, 584, 616, 756)

1863   Julia Cameron   (1815–1879) England
Raised by her family in Calcutta, Cameron went to England in 1860 and led a conventional life as wife and mother of six children. Her career as a portrait photographer did not start until 1863 when, at age forty-eight, she received a camera as a gift. She was soon taking photographs of some of the noted men of the time, such as Sir John Herschel, Robert Browning, Charles Darwin, and the wealthy women Mrs. Herbert Duckworth and ELLEN TERRY. Her works were unique studies of faces focused so as to highlight facial features and obscure clothing and background objects. Despite winning awards in several countries for her

photography, she died in poverty after returning to Calcutta with her husband. (*Sources*: 183, 426, 538, 731)

1863 Rosalía de Castro (1837–1885) Spain

Castro is noted for her use of the Galician language and folklore to express the universal in her poetry and novels. Her best-known poems were published in 1863 and 1880; they give an intimate image of the pain and sorrow of poverty while depicting the joy of life itself. Castro was able to capture the essence of the Galician belief in the unseen but known. She also wrote a book of poetry in Castilian that was published in 1884. (*Sources*: 31, 187, 484, 717)

1863 Rebecca Clarke (1833–1906) United States

Clarke was born and educated in the small village of Norridgewock, Maine. Her career in teaching cut short by the onset of deafness, she began writing, first publishing under a pseudonym. In 1863 Clarke turned her observations of children in her hometown into a series of books that became very popular. Using such title characters as Prudy Parlin, Dotty Dimple, and Flaxie Frizzle, she described antics children were able to identify with. Clarke's two attempts at writing adult books were unsuccessful. (*Sources*: 29, 439, 645)

1863 Emily Davies (1830–1921) England

Unlike her feminist counterparts DOROTHEA BEALE and ELIZABETH GARRETT ANDERSON, Davies used a subtle approach in gaining acceptance for education for women. After Garrett's fight to be licensed to practice medicine, Davies noted, women could not become physicians because they were barred from the universities. In 1863, working through the necessary channels, Davies convinced Cambridge University to allow women to take the Local Cambridge Examination on an experimental basis; by 1865 Cambridge had opened the entrance exam to women. In 1869 Davies founded Girton College for Women, which was later incorporated into the Cambridge University schools. She was also the author of two books on women's education and served on several boards of education. (*Sources*: 473, 518, 558, 587, 621, 695, 731)

1863 Annie Fields (1834–1915) United States

Fields had the good fortune to live in Boston, the cultural hub of the country at that time, and to have such literary giants as Oliver Wendell Holmes, Thomas Bailey Aldrich, Charles Dickens, Nathaniel Hawthorne, and John Greenleaf Whittier for neighbors and friends. Because she was married to a publisher, her home was a gathering place for the literati. In 1863 she began to keep a journal of these intellectual gatherings, providing the basis for many of her books. Her first literary endeavor was a volume of poetry in 1880; in 1881 she wrote a biography of her husband, who had recently died. These works were followed by nine more books of poetry and prose. In 1882 she and SARAH ORNE JEWETT, a successful writer, became close friends and, following a trip to Europe, the two remained companions for the rest of their lives. (*Sources*: 105, 426, 486)

1863 Cornelia Hancock (1840–1927) United States

Hancock's introduction to the Civil War came in 1863 at the Battle of Gettysburg; she had accompanied her physician brother-in-law to offer her services to the injured. She was untrained and at first unappreciated, but she proved her worth and was given charge of the eight tents that were used for amputees. She later tended to the injured of two other battles in Virginia. In 1866 she went to Charleston and started a school for freed blacks that quickly outgrew its quarters and was moved to a large house with funds provided by the Quakers and the Freedmen's Bureau. Hancock remained at the school for ten more years before moving to Philadelphia, where she established schools for poor children and rebuilt slum areas. During these years Hancock was placed in charge of the relief efforts after the Johnstown flood of 1889. She continued her work until her retirement in 1914. (*Sources*: 447, 629, 718, 763, 780)

1863 Mary Walker (1832–1919) United States

Walker's eccentricities superseded her work as a physician; she managed to alienate her medical colleagues, the federal government, women's rights groups, and townspeople. An independent thinker, Walker obtained her medical degree in 1855 and worked as a volunteer in the early part of the Civil War until she was given a post as an army surgeon in 1863. She chose to wear the same uniform as did her fellow male officers, operating in slacks and a tunic. She was known to quarrel with her colleagues and her superiors. Because of her bravery in field hospitals and in crossing enemy lines to treat civilians, Walker was awarded the Congressional Medal of Honor; this honor was withdrawn by a federal review board in 1917 for reasons that are not clear, and all written documentation of the award removed from the records. Following the war, Walker worked for the women's suffrage groups, later abandoning the cause because she believed the Constitution already guaranteed women the right to vote; the women's groups in turn rejected her. She also took to wearing the formal tuxedo that appears in almost all photographs of Walker. She wrote two books (1871 and 1878) that drew little notice. Retiring to the family farm in 1890, she was rebuffed by the townspeople and died poverty-stricken and alone. She would have had little agreement with the medical thesis written in 1850 by fellow physician Charles Gresham in which he stated that at the onset of menses, young women become timid, modest, affectionate, and reserved; Walker, who might have been more admired at a later time, displayed none of these qualities. (*Sources*: 376, 383, 447, 473, 614, 621, 731, 748)

1864   Ednah Cheney   (1824–1904) United States
Cheney graduated from the Joseph Hale Abbott Girls' School in Boston and lectured in philosophy before she began to write. Her first published work was entitled *Handbook for American Citizens* (1864). Cheney wrote four novels between 1870 and 1890 and published her lectures on philosophy and translations of poetry. Her best work is considered to be *Life, Letters and Journals of Louisa May Alcott*, written in 1889. Cheney was one of the founders of the New England Hospital for Women and Children and was active in both the abolition and women's suffrage causes. (*Sources*: 53, 522, 616)

1864   Octavia Hill   (1838–1912) England
In 1864, armed with her grandfather's notable work in public sanitation and trained in finance by her father, Hill undertook the revitalization of a slum neighborhood. She had been given money and three homes by John Ruskin, whom she had interested in her project. By carefully investing this money and never allowing overdue rent, she rebuilt these and other houses into livable homes. She was a strong proponent of open spaces and parks within city neighborhoods. Hill founded an organization that later became a national historical society. Her city planning

ideas were incorporated into an act of Parliament passed in 1909. (*Sources*: 473, 500, 621, 731)

1864   Rebecca Lee   (1840–1881) United States (African American)

Lee was the first black woman to become a university-trained physician. She was granted what was called a "doctoress of medicine" from the New England Female Medical College of Boston in 1864. She practiced in Richmond, Virginia. It was three years before another black woman, REBECCA COLE, was granted a medical degree. (*Sources*: 383, 512, 627, 648, 696, 763)

1865   Hetty Green   (1835–1916) United States

Much envied for her financial wizardry but not well-liked, Green was a remarkable financier and investor. Strongly attached to her father, who had made a fortune in whaling, she parlayed her inheritance of $10 million into $100 million by the end of her life. She not only survived the market crash of 1907 but loaned out millions of dollars to others at 6 percent interest and earned the name, "the Witch of Wall Street." She married in 1867 on the condition that her husband's and her assets remain legally separate, other than the money he used to support her. Apparently traumatized by the death of her father a few years earlier, she developed various eccentricities and became almost wholly obsessed with the acquisition of money. It is reported that she even denied her children medical care other than that offered free of charge. A recluse at the end of her life, she was the richest woman in the country at the time. (*Sources*: 218, 505, 616, 633, 683, 731)

1865   Mary Thompson   (1829–1895) United States

When her father experienced financial problems, Thompson had to take teaching jobs to complete her college education. To be able to teach science courses, she attended the New England Female Medical College in Boston and soon enrolled as a medical student, earning her degree in 1863. She moved to Chicago, where she recognized the need for a hospital for women and children. In 1865, with the help of William Ryder, Thompson founded the Chicago Hospital for Women and Children and became the first woman in Chicago to practice surgery. The hospital burned down in the infamous Chicago fire and was rebuilt in 1871 with the stipulation that twenty-five patients a year be treated without charge. Thompson was also responsible for the founding of the Woman's Medical College of Chicago, which was also destroyed in the fire. It, too, was rebuilt and later became affiliated with Northwestern University; the women's medical college closed in 1902 when women were allowed to enroll in the formerly all-male medical colleges. (*Sources*: 447, 455, 718)

1866   Emily Briggs   (1830–1910) United States
Briggs was hired by a daily newspaper, the *Washington Chronicle*, in 1866 to write a column. More of a social than a political commentator, she wrote under the pseudonym Olivia for sixteen years. An intimate of many Washington notables, including Mary Todd Lincoln, she was the first woman reporter accredited to the White House. In 1892 she became the first president of the Woman's National Press Association. (*Sources*: 455, 522, 718)

1866   Augusta Wilson Evans   (1835–1909) United States
Born and raised in the South, Evans was very proud of her heritage. The first two novels she wrote (1855 and 1859) reflected southern life and were very popular. Encouraged by General Pierre Beauregard, she wrote a novel entitled *Macaria; or, Altars of Sacrifice* in 1863. A patriotic book praising the Confederacy, it was highly successful in the South because of its propaganda value and banned in the North for the same reason. Evans's biggest success came in 1866, when she wrote *St. Elmo*, the title taken from the name of a town; other towns and hotels were renamed St. Elmo because of the book's success. Because her heroes were women who craved independence but succumbed to traditional values in the end, Evans has been called an antifeminist. (*Sources*: 53, 105, 343, 453, 473, 718, 780)

1866   Eliza Orzeszkowa   (1841–1910) Poland
In 1866 Orzeszkowa participated in a reform political movement and was arrested for publishing an underground newspaper. These events were the primary theme in almost all her books. Her literary career spanned forty years, her first work written in 1870 and her eleventh and final book, *Glory to the Defeated*, published in 1910. Five of her books were on women's

rights, with *A Few Words About Women* the first in which she criticized the Polish custom of socializing women to be dependent and docile; she falsely assumed that women in the United States had been emancipated. As a liberal, Orzeszkowa also wrote two books about the prejudice against Jews and strongly advocated for social and legal changes in their status. All of Orzeszkowa's work reflects her concern for and pride in her country. (*Sources*: 80, 274, 731)

1866　Ellen White　(1827–1915) United States

White became a dynamic speaker for the Seventh-Day Adventist religion in the 1840s, raising membership to over 100,000 by the time of her death. Working with her husband, she founded the Western Health Reform Institute in 1866 and the College of Medical Evangelists in California in 1909. She also assisted in the opening of five other Adventist medical centers throughout the country. (*Sources*: 583, 718, 756)

1867　Anne Clough　(1820–1892) England

Clough opened her own school for young women in Liverpool in 1852. She organized a branch of the School-mistresses' Association founded by EMILY DAVIES in 1866 and in 1867 organized a council for the promotion of higher education for women. She was the first headmistress for a women's school, which was incorporated as Newnham College in 1880; she served in this position for twenty-one years. (*Sources*: 191, 473, 500, 587, 731)

1867　Rebecca Cole　(1846–1922) United States (African American)

Cole was only the second black woman, after REBECCA LEE, to earn a medical degree. She graduated in 1867 from the Woman's Medical College of Pennsylvania, then worked with Emily and ELIZABETH BLACKWELL in the slums of New York City, helping to provide medical care for women and children. She later moved to Philadelphia, where she operated both a medical and legal center for women and children. Her last position was as superintendent for the government house for women and children in Washington, D.C. (*Sources*: 483, 493, 725, 763)

1867 Sarah Doremus (1802–1877) United States

An indefatigable worker for social good, Doremus in 1867 became both president of the school she had helped to establish for poor women and children, and the president of the board of directors of the women's hospital she had helped to found twelve years earlier. She had also been president of the Woman's Union Missionary Society organized for the care of women in the Orient. In the final months of her life, Doremus helped to organize the Gould Memorial Home in Italy. The mother of nine children, five of whom she outlived, Doremus gave almost fifty years of her life to charitable causes. She was particularly noted for her organizational skills and practices. (*Sources*: 105, 126, 351, 392, 447, 455, 616)

1867 Katherine [Kate] Field (1838–1896) United States

Field started out in the theater, like her father, an actor, but entered journalism following the publication of her first book, *Adelaide Ristori* (1867). While a journalist in St. Louis, she wrote two additional books in 1873 and 1875. She then went to Washington, D.C., where she wrote her journal, *Kate Field's Washington*, starting in 1891. She was a friend of such notables as Anthony Trollope and George Eliot. (*Sources*: 105, 455, 556)

1867 Edmonia Lewis (1845–1911?) United States (African American)

More is known of Lewis's work than of her life. Daughter of a Native American mother and a black father, she described her early life as being unstable and unsettled. Although she was too wild to stay in school, she attended Oberlin College from 1859 to 1862 and was accused, but not convicted, of poisoning a fellow student. Her career as a sculptor was uncertain until she went to Europe to study in 1865. Lewis's most important work is considered to be her sculpture *Forever Free* (1867), which depicts emancipation. She is especially known for her ability to portray death. Lewis also favored busts of well-known figures such as Henry Wadsworth Longfellow and Abraham Lincoln. One of her personal favorites was a bust of Colonel Robert Gould Shaw, commander of the first black regiment in the Civil War. It is reported that Lewis had caught no more than a glimpse of him as he marched the Fifty-Fourth Regiment through Boston. (*Sources*: 60, 120, 507, 508, 541, 696, 717, 718, 731, 756)

1867 Ellen Scripps (1836–1932) United States (England)

Scripps was born in London and immigrated to the United States with her family at the age of eight. Having the benefit of two years of college, she first began to teach but in 1867 was lured to Michigan by her brother to help him with his newspaper, the *Detroit Evening News*. She thus launched a career in journalism. Scripps also contributed both money and articles to her younger brother's newspaper in Cincinnati. She continued her financial and business interest in both newspapers and eventually owned large shares in several newspapers as well as those run by her family. In later years she moved to California and donated large sums of money to civic projects such as the Scripps Institute of largest grant went toward the founding of the Scripps College for Women in 1927. She was equally generous with the estate she left upon her death in 1932. (*Sources*: 105, 447, 556, 718)

1868 Annie Cary (1842–1921) United States

Cary studied voice in the United States and Italy and made her operatic debut in Germany in 1868. She went on to sing leading roles in Sweden, Britain, Denmark, and Belgium before returning to the United States. In 1877 she became a member of the Academy of Music and the first American woman to sing one of Richard Wagner's works. A popular operatic star, her career was cut short because of illness, and she left the stage in 1881. (*Sources*: 325, 431)

1869 [Frances] Fanny Coppin (1837–1913) United States (African American)

Born into slavery, Coppin had her freedom purchased by an aunt for $125 and moved to Philadelphia. Coppin first attended Rhode Island Normal School and in 1865 went on to become the second African American woman to graduate from Oberlin College. Proficient in Greek, French, and mathematics, she dedicated her life to teaching black children. After teaching briefly at Oberlin, Coppin accepted a position at the newly founded Institute for Colored Youth in Philadelphia; in 1869 she became codirector of the school. Coppin was the president of the Home Missionary Society of the African Methodist Church in 1888 and married a minister, accompanying him on his frequent trips to Africa. In 1913

Coppin authored two books on teaching. (*Sources*: 507, 627, 688)

1869   Ehyophsta   (?–1915) United States (Native American)

Ehyophsta (meaning yellow-haired woman) was a member of the Cheyenne tribe. Little is known of her life until 1869, when her tribe was attacked by the Shoshoni. Ehyophsta joined the men in the fierce battle that took place near the Big Horn Mountains in Montana, killing two of the enemy. When some of the escaping Shoshoni were captured, Ehyophsta killed and scalped one of them, an act other warriors interpreted as great bravery. She was made a member of the prestigious and secret women's council limited to women who had fought courageously in war. (*Sources*: 140, 574, 647)

1869   Margaret Knight   (1838–1914) United States

Although Knight lacked the formal education needed to understand the mechanical principles involved in her inventions, she had the uncanny ability to visualize and construct what was needed to solve a problem. Reported to have invented a safety device for a machine when she was only twelve, her first awareness of the need to patent her work occurred in 1869, when someone attempted to steal one of her designs. This invention was a machine that made the square-bottomed paper bags still in use today. Although she had twenty-seven patents to her credit, she died poor. (It is noteworthy that between 1800 and 1900 more than 8,000 patents were granted to women for their inventions.) (*Sources*: 518, 531, 587, 731)

1869   Arabella Mansfield   (1846–1911) United States

Mansfield graduated from Iowa Wesleyan College in 1866 and, after marrying in 1868, studied law with her husband. In 1869 she became the first woman admitted to the Iowa bar; she earned her L.L.B. in 1872. Despite this honor, Mansfield never practiced law, preferring to teach instead. She taught at Iowa Wesleyan and later at DePauw University, where she became dean of the schools of art and music. Mansfield was also one of the founders of the Iowa Woman Suffrage Society in 1872. (*Sources*: 447, 455, 671, 718)

1870 Emma Albani, *aka* Lajeunesse (1847–1930) Canada

Albani showed early promise as an operatic soprano and in 1868 was sent to France and later to Italy to study voice. She made her debut in 1870 in Italy, adopting the stage name Emma Albani. Her first performance in England was in 1872 at Covent Garden; she remained in Britain for twenty-four years, also giving command performances for Queen Victoria. Albani first performed in the United States in 1874 and returned again in 1883. In 1890 she sang for the first time at the Metropolitan Opera and remained with the company for two years. Except for a brief return to the stage, Albani retired in 1906. She was made a dame of the British Empire in 1925. (*Sources*: 325, 431)

1870 Elizabeth Garrett Anderson (1836–1917) England

After hearing a lecture by the first woman physician in the United States, ELIZABETH BLACKWELL, Anderson was determined to become the first woman physician in England. This proved to be as difficult as she had expected: denied admission to medical school, she studied privately and became a midwife. In 1865, having been granted an apothecary license, she opened a dispensary for women. Anderson took her medical examinations in Paris in 1870 after completing her medical courses in English, meeting her goal to become Britain's first woman physician. Two years later she opened a hospital (now named in her honor) and staffed it with women. Anderson was the author of several books on studying medicine and on child care. In 1908 she accomplished another first for women in England when she was elected mayor of Aldeburgh. (*Sources*: 9, 432, 473, 558, 587, 621, 731)

1870 Millicent Fawcett (1847–1929) England

Fawcett's father and older sister, ELIZABETH GARRETT ANDERSON, set a family precedent for tenacity and belief in women's rights, fighting for years to have Elizabeth granted the right to be the first female physician to practice in England. Carrying on this tradition and encouraged by her husband, a blind professor, Fawcett devoted fifty years of her life to the struggle for women's equality. She gained national attention with the publication of her book *Political Economy for Beginners*, written in 1870 and reprinted nine times. In 1897, as president of the National Union of Women's Suffrage Society, she pressed for women's right to vote. In 1918 women were enfranchised, but it was not until 1928, a year before Fawcett's death, that women received equal voting rights. Fawcett was made a dame for her service to Britain in two wars. She was also the author of several other books. (*Sources*: 207, 473, 681)

1870   Helen Hunt Jackson   (1830–1885) United States

Jackson's personal life was filled with tragedy: she was been orphaned at the age of seventeen, her two children died in 1854 and 1865, and her husband was killed in an accident between the deaths of her children. Jackson began studying journalism under the noted essayist Thomas Wentworth Higginson and by 1870 published her first book of poetry, *Verses*. Widespread recognition as a writer came in 1872 with the publication of *Bits of Travel*. These and many other books she published under the initials "H. H." Jackson remarried and moved to Colorado, where she became interested in Native Americans and their problems, especially after hearing SUSETTE LAFLESCHE speak. In 1881, Jackson wrote and published at her own expense an indictment of the treatment of the Indians and sent it to government officials. Receiving little response, she published *Ramona* (1884), a fictionalized account of the Indian plight. It became her best-known work, going through more than 300 printings. (*Sources*: 447, 486, 522, 562, 718, 758)

1870   Esther Morris   (1814–1902) United States

Recently widowed, Morris moved with her son to Illinois in 1845. She remarried and with her husband, son, and the two surviving sons from her second marriage went to Wyoming in the gold rush year of 1869. Morris became interested in women's rights and began to campaign vigorously for the passage of a state suffrage bill; it passed that year. In 1870 Morris was appointed the first woman justice of the peace and heard almost 100 cases during her eight-month tenure. Divorced from her husband, she continued to advocate women's rights and in 1890 was named Mother of Woman Suffrage in Wyoming. Morris kept up her work until her death in 1902. (*Sources*: 125, 325, 447, 455, 548, 627, 699)

1870   Ellen Richards   (1842–1911) United States

Richards graduated from Vassar College in 1870 and in the same year became the first woman accepted at the Massachusetts Institute of Technology to study chemistry. Three years later she earned both her bachelor's degree from MIT and her master's from Vassar. She continued her studies at MIT but was never awarded her doctorate. In 1882 she made another first, becoming the first woman elected into the American Institute of Mining and Engineering. Toward the end of the 1870s, she began to devote her career to women's education. In 1876 she established a woman's laboratory at MIT and in 1882 was one of the founders of a women's alumni society, which later became the American Association of University Women. Richards combined her knowledge of chemistry and her interest in women by investigating household products; her findings were published in the early 1880s. By 1890 she was involved in establishing home economics schools, and she devoted the remainder of her career to fostering homemaking education for women. (*Sources*: 105, 383, 522, 525, 583, 627, 718)

1870   Emily Shirreff   (1814–1897) England

Shirreff, like MARGARETHE SCHURZ, was influenced by the kindergarten system developed by Friedrich Froebel in Germany in 1841. Shirreff was also interested in the education of older girls and was one of the founders of Girton College in 1869, serving on its executive committee in 1870. Her first book was *Principles of the Kindergarten System*, written in 1870. It was revised to include the education of women and republished in 1876 and 1880. Shirreff wrote a book on kindergarten in the home in 1884 and a biography of Froebel in 1877. (*Sources*: 297, 473, 518)

1870   Caroline Yale   (1848–1933) United States

In 1870 Yale joined the faculty of the Clarke Institution for Deaf Mutes (later changed to Clarke School for the Deaf); she remained with the school for over sixty years. Under the guidance of Harriet Rogers, Yale learned to teach deaf children the newly developed lipreading and lipspeaking systems. Yale became principal of the school in 1886 and in 1889 added the first teacher training program to Clarke. In 1931 Yale wrote a book about the school entitled *Years of Building*. (*Sources*: 105, 320, 518, 748)

1871   Phoebe Couzins   (1839–1913) United States

In 1871 Couzins became the first woman to receive a law degree from Washington University in St. Louis. Although she was admitted to the bar in four states and the federal court in

Nebraska, she never practiced law. Having become avidly interested in the women's movement, Couzins devoted her time and services to women's groups and was also actively involved in prohibition. Around the turn of the century, Couzins became embroiled in bitter arguments with various women's groups and renounced her support for suffrage. She also began to lobby for a brewery to fight against prohibition. Upon Couzins's death, a friend had to provide for the funeral expenses. (*Sources*: 447, 455, 626)

1871   Marietta Holley   (1836–1926) United States

Holley's career as a humorist began in 1871, when she created the characters Samantha Allen and Betsy Bobbet for the nationally circulated *Peterson's Magazine*. Using multiple pseudonyms, she continued to write, publishing her first book about these characters in 1873. Between 1873 and 1914, Holley wrote twenty-three successful books. Although the character Samantha Allen was an outspoken advocate of women's rights, Betsy Bobbet and other figures had more traditional characterizations; Holley herself would not publicly support the women's movement. (*Sources*: 548, 617)

1871   Mary Jacobi   (1842–1906) United States

Jacobi's first career was in fiction; her work was published in the *Atlantic Monthly* when she was only seventeen. She wrote to support herself while attending medical school, first in the United States and later in Paris. She had already earned a degree in pharmacology when she decided on medicine for a career. Graduating from the École de Médecin in Paris in 1871, Jacobi was the recipient of a bronze star for her medical thesis. She returned to New York, where she set up practice, married, and had two children. She wrote medical books, including a classic study of the brain tumor that eventually killed her. In 1882 she became interested in women's medical problems and was the first to note that what was considered pathological in women was in fact normal. Jacobi wrote four books on women from a medical perspective. (*Sources*: 2, 34, 432, 447, 522, 537, 566, 567, 584, 618, 731)

1872   Susan Dimock   (1847–1875) United States

Dimock's early interest in medicine was fostered by a local physician in Washington, D.C., who allowed her to accompany him on his calls and to read his medical books. After being denied admission into U.S. medical schools, Dimock went to Zurich for training. Following an additional year of study in Vienna, Dimock returned to the United States in 1872 to become the country's first female surgeon. She was appointed to the New England Hospital, where she performed most of the surgery and established a large private practice. She took a leave of absence in 1875 to travel to Europe and drowned in a boating accident a month later. (*Sources*: 447, 518, 703, 718, 763)

1872   Charlotte Ray   (1850–1911) United States (African American)

Having graduated from Howard Law School in 1872, Ray was the first woman named to the bar in the District of Columbia. Because of sexual and racial prejudice, however, Ray was not able to support herself in private practice and so returned to teaching, which she had done to finance her studies at Howard. She taught in the New York public school system for approximately twenty years before retiring. (*Sources*: 447, 455, 627, 680, 696)

1872   Linda Richards   (1841–1930) United States

In 1872 Richards enrolled in the small class of five women at the New England Hospital for Women and Children that received the first formal training in nursing in the United States. She became a superintendent at the Bellevue Training School in New York in 1873 and at the Massachusetts General Hospital training school in Boston in 1874. Richards is credited with establishing the first classroom and hospital-ward instruction program. Following a trip to England for further training, she founded a second school of nursing in Boston and in 1896 developed the first nursing program in Japan. Richards worked to improve the nursing care in two mental hospitals in Massachusetts and one in Michigan before retiring in 1911. (*Sources*: 81, 105, 447, 455, 462, 512, 537, 583, 731, 763)

1872   Louisa Schuyler   (1837–1926) United States

Schuyler was born into a wealthy and illustrious family noted for its philanthropic work. Her great-grandmother, Elizabeth Hamilton, had been a cofounder with JOANNA BETHUNE of the first orphanage in New York City, and Schuyler's parents were active workers in New York Children's Aid Society. At the beginning of the Civil War, Schuyler was asked to chair the New York branch of the Sanitary Commission and was noted for her skills in organization, starting and supervising smaller branches and arranging for distribution of materials. After the war she traveled for several years; upon her return to New York in 1872 she organized prominent citizens into a committee that supervised the public charities of the state and became the official representative organization for New York. Schuyler was also responsible for the establishment of the first nursing school at Bellevue Hospital. Through Schuyler's efforts, in 1875 legislation was passed to remove all children under the age of three from poorhouses. In 1890, again at Schuyler's urging, New York State established separate institutions for the mentally ill. In 1907, as a trustee of the Russell Sage Foundation, she helped to establish programs for the blind that later became the National Committee for the Prevention of Blindness. Following in the family tradition of charitable work, Schuyler devoted fifty-four years to the service of others. (*Sources*: 146, 339, 548, 722)

1873   Susan Blow   (1843–1916) United States

Greatly impressed by the kindergarten theory of the German educator Friedrich Froebel, Blow, with the help of the St. Louis superintendent of schools, in 1873 established the first kindergarten in the United States. The following year she started a training program for those who would be working in classes with the preschool children. This program not only emphasized child development and care but also fostered the learning of literature, art, history, and other subjects. In 1884 Blow was forced to withdraw from the program because of a serious illness, and when she returned in 1894, she found that the kindergartens had become geared toward the care of immigrant children and preparation for grammar school. A strong believer in Froebel's theory that teaching children was the highest level to which women could aspire, she fought the expansion and utilitarian approach developed in her absence, but without success. (*Sources*: 548, 616, 783)

1873   Amanda Jones   (1835–1914) United States

A complex woman, Jones gave equal energy to writing poetry, creating inventions, running a business, and making psychic predictions. She started out teaching but gave it up to write poetry, which she in turn gave up when she became involved in inventions and business, only to return to poetry and psychic experiences at the end of her career. Her first patent was for a vacuum process for canning in 1873 and was followed by five additional patents by 1890. Jones ran a successful business until she went back to writing, at which time she wrote both poetry and articles for engineering journals. Her psychic experiences were a family tradition dating back to her grandfather, who was reputed to have been able to successfully pray for rain and, as a county sheriff, had visions of a murder and its perpetrators before the case was known. Perhaps Jones's explanation of the "dual mind" (that is, the dual existence of the intellect and the supernatural) most aptly applies to her own case. (*Sources:* 105, 452, 486, 548)

1873 Belva Lockwood (1830–1917) United States

A widow and a mother, Lockwood taught school. But throughout her career she preferred to work on a broader level and in 1860 presented her teaching ideas at a national teachers' assembly. Having moved to Washington, D.C., in 1873, she graduated from the National University Law School but had to fight to have her diploma issued. Since CHARLOTTE RAY had already become the first woman admitted to the bar in the District of Columbia the year before, Lockwood had no trouble being admitted; however, her cases were never heard in the federal claims court. Her petition to plead in the Supreme Court was denied. Lockwood took her case to Congress and in 1879 became the first woman allowed to practice before the high court. She worked through national women's organizations and the courts to get a bill guaranteeing equal pay for equal work through Congress in 1872. In 1884 and 1888 she ran on a national ticket for the presidency but was not a serious challenge. She worked for world peace by serving on an international peace committee and as a member of the nominating committee for the Nobel Peace Prize. Her most famous case before the Supreme Court was in 1906, when Lockwood won a $5-million settlement for the Cherokee tribe. (*Sources:* 447, 530, 532, 718, 728, 756)

1873 Lottie [Charlotte] Moon (1840–1912) United States

Moon's background and early years gave no indication of her willingness to devote her life to others in a foreign land: she was born into a wealthy slaveholding family that at one time owned Thomas Jefferson's home, Monticello; her mother was a devout Baptist whereas her father was indifferent to religion; and young Lottie preferred romantic novels and the irreligion of Thomas Paine. It was not until her late teens that she attended the forerunner of Hollins College, where she became interested in an education and also became devoutly Baptist. Like her older sister, who became the first southern woman physician, Moon was among the first southern women to earn the first equivalent of a master's degree. Having initially taught school, Moon went to China in 1873 to tend to her ailing missionary sister, whom she accompanied back to the United States. She then returned to China, devoting the remainder of her life to the religious education of peasants. Along with her other work, she also trained missionaries assigned to foreign service, despite the prejudice of the home office against women in the ministry that almost caused her to resign her post. When there was a need for money, Moon solicited funds on her own. This willingness to sacrifice for others cost Moon her life when, in 1912, she remained with the people of Tengchow and starved to death with them. It is reported that over time more than $400 million has been donated to the Lottie Moon Christmas Fund that honors her memory and her Baptist faith. (*Sources*: 10, 126, 434, 497, 750)

1873   Sarah Smith   (1814–1885) United States (England)

Smith, who was a minister and had tended the wounded in the Civil War, migrated to Indiana after the war and continued to help others, particularly poor women and children. She especially deplored the prison conditions for women. When Indiana finally opened the first separate prison for women in 1873 (there were seventeen inmates), Smith became its first woman superintendent. Since 1877 only women have been appointed to the board of trustees of the prison. (*Sources*: 363, 455, 696)

1874   Helen Blackburn   (1842–1903) England (Ireland)

Blackburn's family moved from Ireland to London. By the age of sixteen, she had become involved in the women's movement. She joined the National Society for Women's Suffrage in 1867 and by 1874 was secretary. Blackburn edited a women's magazine for nine years; she wrote her first book, *The Condition of Working and the Factory Acts*, in 1896. She followed this with *Women's Suffrage: A Record of the Movement in the British Isles* in 1902 and *Women Under the Factory Acts* in 1903. Blackburn devoted more than half her life to helping women. (*Sources:* 171, 473, 681)

1874   Catherine Breshkovsky   (1844–1934) Russia

Breshkovsky devoted more than sixty-five years of her ninety-year life to freeing the Russian people from autocratic rule. Born into an aristocratic family but given a liberal education, she attempted to educate the serfs on her parent's estate when she was hardly more than a child herself. In 1874, recognizing that the edict issued in 1861 to free all serfs had not changed their political or social condition, Breshkovsky joined the revolutionary party with the express intent of overthrowing the czarist government. She left her husband and joined over 2,000 young people who traveled from village to village advocating a revolution. Arrested shortly after she began her political activities, she waited in prison until 1878 before being sentenced to walk the 5,000 miles to the Siberian prison camp where she was to serve her five-year sentence. She was later forced to walk an additional 1,000 miles to the next prison camp. Caught attempting to escape, Breshkovsky was transferred to a camp near China, where she spent seven years in isolation. She was allowed to return home in 1896 and organized the People's Social Revolutionary Party. Breshkovsky traveled to the United States to raise money for the revolution and earned the name Mother of the Revolution. On her return to Russia, she was imprisoned again and after a political upheaval was sent to Czechoslovakia. She died in exile in 1934. (*Sources:* 391, 530, 584, 655)

1874   Cornelia Clapp   (1849–1934) United States

Clapp graduated from Mount Holyoke Seminary (later named Mount Holyoke College) in 1871 and within a year was teaching mathematics at her alma mater. In 1874 she attended an institute at a school of natural history in Maine, where she developed her lifelong interest in zoology. Clapp was a strong proponent of the field-observation method of studying species in their natural environment and spent much time at the newly founded marine biology center at Woods Hole, Massachusetts. Clapp went on to earn a total of three doctorates between the years 1888 and 1896 and was given an additional honorary doctorate in 1921; she also had a chair endowed in her name at Mount Holyoke. Clapp was the second in a matriarchal lineage of women zoology professors at Mount Holyoke that lasted until 1961. (*Sources*: 548, 587, 634)

1874   Lucretia Crocker   (1829–1886) United States

In 1874 Crocker and five other women were finally allowed on the Boston School Committee after having been refused the seats to which they had been elected the previous year. Two years later Crocker was elected to the board of supervisors, a position she held for ten years. Noted as a science teacher, Crocker introduced a strong science program into the school system. She wrote *Methods of Teaching Geography: Notes of Lessons* in 1883. (*Sources*: 2, 137, 447, 473, 718)

1874   Sophia Jex-Blake   (1840–1912) England

Jex-Blake is one of many women who personify the Sisyphean dilemma, having to prove something again and again. In 1869, after rejection by a medical school in London and a long fight for acceptance into the medical school at the University of Edinburgh, Jex-Blake and four other women were admitted as provisional students. One of the women was denied an academic prize because of her gender, and all were harassed by both faculty and fellow students. Their most serious problem occurred when the five women were denied permission to study at an infirmary, which was necessary to complete their medical degrees. When Jex-Blake and the others challenged this ruling, a riot resulted and professors refused to have the women in their classes. Jex-Blake filed a complaint against the medical school in 1871 and won, but the conditions at the medical school worsened, and the women filed another suit in 1873, which they lost. Unsure of earning her degree, Jex-Blake founded the London School of Medicine for Women in 1874. After being awarded her degree two years later, she founded two more women's medical schools in 1885 and 1886. She continued her efforts toward women's medical training for another thirteen years before retiring. (*Sources*: 2, 9, 473, 530, 587, 731)

1874   Bethenia Owens-Adair   (1840–1926) United States

Owens-Adair did not conform to the age-appropriate customs of her time: she was married at fourteen, a mother at sixteen, divorced at nineteen, and started her education at the age of twenty. After completing school, she opened a millinery shop in Oregon. She sold the shop in 1873 to go east to medical school. A year later she graduated from a Philadelphia medical school and returned to Oregon to practice medicine. Because the medical school she had attended had a dubious reputation, Owens-Adair returned to school, earning her medical degree from the University of Michigan medical school in 1880 at the age of forty. She resumed practice, specializing in the treatment of eye and ear diseases. In 1884 Owens-Adair remarried and became a mother for the second time, at the age of forty-seven. She continued to practice medicine until she was sixty-five. (*Sources*: 447, 455)

1874   Hannah Hadassah Smith   (1767–1810) United States
Julia Evelina Smith   (1792–1886)
Abby Hadassah Smith   (1797–1878)

A well-versed woman in mathematics, astronomy, and languages, Hannah Smith and her minister-turned-lawyer husband (he had excommunicated the congregation that in turn excommunicated him) set the precedent for the family's feistiness. Hannah had a signed petition presented to Congress in opposition to the practice of slavery and invited William Lloyd Garrison to give an antislavery speech on the front lawn of the Smith home in Glastonbury, Connecticut. Of the four unmarried daughters (Julia married at age eighty-seven), Julia and Abby, the youngest two, seem most to have inherited their parents' spirit. Julia, a polyglot, devoted much of her life to making five translations of the Bible, two in Greek, two in Hebrew, and one in Latin. Abby, a strong feminist, petitioned the local government in 1874 to lower the family's property taxes because they were unenfranchised citizens. When their petition was denied, they refused to pay the overdue taxes, and the town confiscated seven of their cows in lieu of payment. When the first three cows were auctioned, Julia and Abby were the highest bidders, but after the remaining four cows were auctioned along with some of the Smiths' property, a lively legal and public fight ensued that lasted for two years. In 1876 the courts ruled in favor of the two women, who were by then eighty-four and seventy-nine. Their case gained nationwide notoriety, and the two sisters became frequent speakers at federal, local, and women's suffrage meetings. In 1877 Julia wrote an account of their case, presenting the court and newspaper accounts of it, rebutting those that were unfavorable. (*Sources:* 105, 339, 447, 552, 674, 686, 718)

1875 Helena Blavatsky (1831–1891) United States

A charismatic woman, Blavatsky was able to recruit followers to her occult beliefs even after repeatedly being exposed as a charlatan and a plagiarist. Leaving Russia and her husband in 1850, she became the mistress of an opera singer named Metrovich and fell under the influence of the spiritualist Daniel Home. After a brief reconciliation with her husband, she rejoined Metrovich, who was killed in an explosion en route to Egypt. She soon left for the United States, where in 1875 she teamed up with Henry Olcott to establish the first Theosophical Society. Blavatsky credited "The Master" for her book on mysticism, written in 1877. By 1880 the group had defined three goals: universal fraternity, the discovery of humans' latent psychic powers, and the study of religions. It was the first goal that seemed to lure followers. On a trip to India Blavatsky enjoyed her largest audience, even raising funds to build a center there. In 1887 she established a new center in London, where she also recruited ANNIE BESANT as a convert. Besant became president of the society in 1907. (*Sources:* 447, 455, 543, 617, 731)

1875 Rosa Hazel (1852–1932) United States (African American)

Hazel was born in Rhode Island but educated in the nonsegregated schools in Worcester, Massachusetts. In 1875 she became the first African American to graduate from Rhode Island Normal School, where she had been a classmate of ANNIE PECK. She was recruited to teach by Samuel Armstrong, founder of Hampton Institute (the first black college), and later taught school in New York City. In 1882 she married William Hazel, one of the first black architects. With Elizabeth Piper, she opened one of the first circulating libraries in Boston. Hazel later taught at Tuskeegee Institute and is noted for arranging for its founder, Booker T. Washington, to speak in Boston shortly after the school's opening. Hazel was also instrumental in establishing the

Palmer Memorial Institute in Sedalia, North Carolina. (*Sources*: 92, 757)

1875 Cornelia Spencer (1825–1908) United States

As an active lifetime advocate for education, Spencer was pleased to ring the tower bell at the University of North Carolina at Chapel Hill when it reopened in 1875, an honor she had been given because of her tireless efforts to raise funds for the school. (She was also credited with raising money necessary to carry the college through another financial crisis in 1894.) In 1877 Spencer played a large role in the founding of the women's school at the college, which later became the Woman's College of the University of North Carolina. She had spent the first years of her young widowhood teaching Latin and Greek and writing articles exhorting fellow citizens to state pride following the Civil War. In 1866, because of her reputation as a citizen and a writer, she was asked to write an account of the conditions in the state at the end of the Civil War; the book was entitled *The Last Ninety Days of the War in North Carolina*. (*Sources*: 12, 105, 447, 627, 718)

1876 Louise Bethune (1856–1913) United States

In 1876 Bethune was given an apprenticeship with an architect in Buffalo, making her the first professional woman architect. Five years later, she and her husband opened their own architecture business, designing buildings until 1904. They were especially noted for their use of the Romanesque Revival style. Bethune designed eighteen schools for the New York State school system. In 1888 she became the first woman elected to the American Institute of Architects. (*Sources*: 447, 455, 518, 535, 548, 718, 720, 731)

1876 Sarah Stevenson (1841–1909) United States

First trained as a teacher, Stevenson taught high school for four years before completing medical school in 1874. A year later she both opened her private practice and wrote a high school textbook called *Boys and Girls in Biology*. In 1876 she became the first woman physician granted membership in the American Medical Association. Stevenson was also the first woman on the staff of Cook County Hospital in Chicago (1881) and the first woman appointed to the Illinois State Board of

Health (1893). From 1875 to 1894 she taught medicine at the Women's Medical College in Chicago. She was one of the founders of a nursing school in Illinois in 1880, the same year she wrote *The Physiology of Woman*. Stevenson served on numerous committees until her retirement in 1903. (Sources: 447, 455, 473, 548)

1877 Sarah Orne Jewett (1849–1909) United States
New England was the setting for all Jewett's writings, starting with her articles in the *Atlantic Monthly* and her first book, *Deephaven*, in 1877. Jewett was the first president of Vassar College. She left her sheltered New England life to travel with her lifelong friend, ANNIE FIELDS. After Jewett's death, Fields and Willa Cather collected and edited her letters and stories. (*Sources*: 426, 627, 731)

1877 Annie Besant (1847–1933) England
In 1877 Besant and the newspaper publisher for whom she worked were fined and sentenced to six months in jail for writing an article favoring birth control. The sentence was later reversed; however, the court declared her an unfit mother and took her daughter away from her. Besant bitterly noted that a man's wife had less legal right to her children than his mistress had to hers. In 1887 she founded the newspaper the *Link*, which published an article stating that girls working in a match factory contracted cancer from handling phosphorus. This shocking revelation was called the "match that fired the Thames." Besant was responsible for a strike at the factory in 1888, but none of her efforts did much to change the working conditions. In 1889 she joined the Theosophical Society started by HELENA BLAVATSKY and in 1907 took over as its leader. (*Sources*: 60, 104, 558, 621, 676, 681, 731)

1877 Helen Magill (1853–1944) United States
In 1877 Magill had the distinction of being the first woman in the United States to be granted a Ph.D. She had earned her undergraduate degree at Swarthmore in 1873 and continued her studies in the classics at Cambridge University for an additional four years. In 1883 Magill was appointed director of a women's college in Massachusetts, and she later helped to establish a women's annex at Princeton University. She married Andrew White, who was ambassador to Russia and influential in the

founding of Cornell University, serving as its first president. (*Sources*: 455, 548, 634)

1878 Caroline Anderson (1848–1919) United States (African American)

Anderson was the daughter of abolition activists William and Letitia Still, who founded the Underground Railroad. She was the only black in the class of forty-six women who graduated from Oberlin College in 1868. After teaching for a year at Howard University, she enrolled in the Women's Medical College of Pennsylvania, graduating in 1878. Anderson opened a private practice in Philadelphia, where she was also active in civic and medical organizations; she is credited with establishing the city's first YWCA. (*Sources*: 648, 697, 757)

1878 Vera Figner (1852–1942) Russia

While a medical student in Switzerland, Figner became active in the Frichi Circle, a group of students intent on leading a revolution in Russia. Leaving her studies, she returned to Russia in 1878 to participate in the revolutionary movement and within a year had become a terrorist agent. In 1881 Figner took over the leadership of the People's Will Party; she was arrested for her activities in 1883 and spent twenty-one years in jail. In 1906 she was exiled but was allowed to return to Russia nine years later. Her collected works were published in Russia in 1931. (*Sources*: 24, 209, 518, 558, 579, 599, 655, 731)

1878 Ellen Terry (1847–1928) England

Part of a theatrical family, Terry made her first stage appearance at the age of eight. She did not gain widespread recognition until 1878, when she joined the Henry Irving Company and starred in Shakespearean roles, becoming especially noted for her portrayal of Lady Macbeth. She continued with this theater group until 1902. Terry then began to appear in the plays of George Bernard Shaw, and her correspondence with the playwright came to be known as the "paper courtship." Their letters were published as *Ellen Terry and Bernard Shaw: A Correspondence* (1931) following her death. Terry had also written her autobiography in 1908; together these two works are noted for their literary style and their depiction of the history of the theater. (*Sources*: 34, 36, 74, 353)

1879 Chipeta (1842–1924) United States (Native American)

Chipeta was the wife of the chief of the Ute tribe that attacked a federal Indian agency in Colorado in 1879, killing everyone except the chief agent's wife, daughter, and one other woman. It is reported that Chipeta's intervention led to the release of the three women. Because the women stated they had been "violated" while in captivity, the Ute tribe was forced to go to an Indian reservation in Utah, where Chipeta died at the age of eighty-two. (*Sources*: 439, 718)

1879 Susette LaFlesche (1854–1903) United States
1889 Susan LaFlesche (1865–1915) (Native Americans)

Susette and Susan Laflesche were two of the four daughters of Joseph LaFlesche, chief of the Omaha tribe. Devastated by the encroachment of the white missionaries and settlers, the chief moved his tribe to a reservation. Attempting to get his people to adopt the more advanced agricultural techniques of the settlers, he established a village fashioned after theirs; his tribespeople called it the "make-believe white man's village." Susette, known as Bright Eyes because of her brilliant eyes, returned to the village to teach in 1875 after attending school in the East, but when the neighboring Ponca tribe was forced to move from its land with great loss of life, she decided to fight for Indian rights. Assisted by the reporter Thomas Tibbles, whom she later married, Susette traveled to Washington, D.C., in 1879 to petition for the right for Native Americans to keep their land, to be given full citizenship, and to retain their cultural heritage. Because her father and brother were more in favor of the right for Indians to lease their land, there was a long separation between Susette and her family. Susette traveled around the country and to Europe and wrote *Ploughed Under: The Story of an Indian Chief* in 1881 to further the Indian cause.

Susan LaFlesche graduated from what is now called Hampton University in 1886 and from the Women's Medical College of Pennsylvania in 1889. She returned to her tribe and provided medical services for both Indian and white populations for twenty-five years, often making her rounds on horseback. She was one of the organizers of the county medical society and was the founder of the Walthill Hospital, which was later renamed in her honor. The Susan Picotte Hospital (using LaFlesche's married name) was built in

1990. (*Sources*: 35, 105, 234, 417, 447, 522, 527, 529, 616, 618, 718, 731, 757)

1879   Mary Mahoney   (1845–1926) United States (African American)

Mahoney, in a class of four graduates in the 1879 New England Hospital for Women and Children, was the first black woman to become a nurse in the United States. She was a charter member of the National Association of Colored Graduate Nurses (established in 1908 and merged with the American Nurses Association in 1951). In 1921, with the black nurses' association, Mahoney went to the White House, where she presented the president and his wife with red roses and a request to place the group on the list of associations for world service. The association established the Mary Mahoney Medal in 1936; it is still awarded to nurses who make a contribution to intergroup relations. (*Sources*: 105, 135, 378, 629, 718)

1879   Tillie Paul   (1864?–1952) United States (Native American)

Paul, the child of a Scotsman and a Tlingit woman, grew up under the guidance and influence of the Presbyterian missionaries at the McFarland School in Wrangell, Alaska. She taught at the school, became a founding member of the first Presbyterian church there in 1879, and, years later, became the first woman named an elder in any Presbyterian church. Paul and her husband became missionaries in 1882; upon his death in 1887, she found herself left with three children and cheated out of the money owed to her husband for his trapping business. She returned to teaching and was assigned to Sitka, where she remained until 1904, when she took over as temporary pastor of the church. Paul is honored by Alaskans for her early insistence on retaining the native values while teaching the indigenous people the new cultural values introduced by the whites. She married Louis Tamaree in 1892. (*Sources*: 119, 344, 712, 718)

1880   Yelizaveta Kovalskaya   (1850–1933) Russia

Kovalskaya began her revolutionary activities in the 1860s, organizing a study group in her so-called Pink House in Kharkov. It was closed by the police in 1869. For the next thirteen years she was involved in various revolutionary movements. In

1880 she was a cofounder of the Union of Russian Workers of the South, which engaged in terrorist acts against landlords, factory owners, and civic officials. The following year she was arrested and sentenced to twenty years in Siberia. After her release, she went to Switzerland. She returned to Russia in 1917 and became a noted historian of the Russian Revolution. (*Sources*: 24, 558, 655, 731)

1880   Emma Nevada   (1859–1940) United States

Born in Nevada City, California, and having grown up in the state of Nevada, Emma Wixom chose the stage name Emma Nevada. A college graduate, she went to Vienna in 1877 to study voice and remained there until 1880, when she made her operatic debut in London. It is reported that when Giuseppe Verdi heard her sing in Italy, he arranged a performance for her at La Scala. After two more European concerts, she returned to the United States in 1884 for a one-year tour, then went back to Europe to give concerts, among them command performances for royalty. She again returned to the United States for additional tours but gave her final operatic performance in Berlin in 1910. She then retired to England, where she died thirty years later. (*Sources*: 325, 548, 554)

1881   Marie Bashkirtseff   (1859–1884) France (Russia)

Bashkirtseff left Russia as a young woman, and moved first to Italy and later to Paris, where she carried on a strenuous social life and enrolled in the art classes for women at the Académie Julien. Her first painting was shown anonymously. In 1881 Bashkirtseff exhibited her large-scale painting depicting sixteen of her classmates at work in an art studio. She held another exhibit in 1883 and her last exhibit, which included *The Meeting*, considered her best painting, in 1884. Although she painted almost 150 works during her short career, she is best remembered for her posthumously published journals, in which she described her frenetic social life, her years as an art student, and her ambitions as an artist—thwarted, she believed, because of discrimination against women. (*Sources*: 374, 395, 407, 598, 607)

1881   Grace Dodge   (1856–1914) United States

Dodge became interested in social and philanthropic work (she was never paid for her years of service) by helping her parents, both social advocates. Her own work began in 1881, when she took up the cause of young women working in factories. She formed a group for them that developed into the Association of Working Girls' Societies in 1896. Dodge was also involved in the founding of the New York Teachers' College, and she created the New York Travelers Aid Society in 1907. Her estate was willed to charitable organizations. (*Sources*: 339, 447, 455, 537, 731)

1881   Marie Augusta Estrela   (1861–?) Brazil
Estrela graduated from the New York Medical College and Hospital for Women in 1881. She returned to Brazil, where she practiced medicine and served on the faculty at the Medical College of Rio de Janeiro until 1938. (*Sources*: 439, 512, 529)

1881   Laura Richards   (1850–1943) United States
Richards came from an illustrious family; her mother was Julia Ward Howe, author of *The Battle Hymn of the Republic*, and her father was Samuel Gridley Howe, the founder of the Perkins Institution for the Blind. Richards's writing career developed out of the stories she created to amuse her seven children. In 1881 she published *Sketches and Scraps*, the first book of nonsense rhymes published in the United States. In one series of books she described three little girls, all named Margaret, who shared the same experiences at the same time. *Captain January*, written in 1890, is her best-known children's book. Richards also wrote books for adults, receiving the Pulitzer Prize in 1917 for a biography of her illustrious mother. Her other noteworthy biography was on LAURA BRIDGMAN, who had been a pupil at her father's school. (*Sources*: 5, 450, 522)

1882   Mary Ann Draper   (1839–1914) United States
Draper, wife of the astronomer Henry Draper, took a keen interest in astronomy when she married him; she assisted him in his studies until his death in 1882. Wishing to have his work continued, she created the Henry Draper Memorial at Harvard, giving generously of both money and her husband's papers. This memorial provided funds for the first classification of stars, completed by two women astronomers, WILLIAMINA FLEMING and ANNIE JUMP CANNON. (*Sources*: 9, 420, 718)

1883   Kageyama Hideko   (1865–1927) Japan

In 1883 Hideko and her mother opened a school. They intended to teach poor children and to provide working women with an education, running classes for them in the evening. The government closed the school after a year because of its liberal policies. Hideko traveled to Tokyo to enlist the aid of the Liberal Party, only to find it had been dissolved. Unhappy with the lack of support within her country, Hideko attempted to set up a new government in absentia in Korea but was jailed for almost a year. Her political activities made her a hero among Japanese women. She married in 1892; her three children and husband died by 1900. Hideko founded a socialist magazine that became the voice of the labor force, farmers, and women; she protested working conditions for women, concubinage, and prostitution. Hideko also wrote a book about her years as a common-law wife before her second marriage. (*Sources*: 621, 663)

1883   Sofya Kovalevsky, *aka* Kovalevskaia   (1850–1891) Russia

Although there had been women mathematicians and women in academe, Kovalevsky's family allowed her tutors provided she was not encouraged to pursue her interest in mathematics. She studied mathematics secretly under the threat of punishment (it is reported that she learned mathematical equations from old wallpaper in an unused room in the house). Denied admission to the university, she married in order to escape to Germany, where she was admitted to the University of Heidelberg. Kovalevsky soon gained a reputation as a mathematician, especially in partial differential equations; by 1883 she was given a professorship at the University of Stockholm. In 1888 she received the Prix Bordin from the French Academy of Sciences. For a short time afterwards, she collaborated on writing plays and wrote several novels. She accomplished all this in her short life of forty-one years. (*Sources*: 2, 9, 24, 60, 80, 232, 408, 467, 530, 587, 651, 731)

1883   Lucy Laney   (1854–1933) United States (African American)

Laney had the advantage of an education from an early age, which was very unusual for a poor black female of her time. Laney graduated from a black high school in Atlanta and because she was an excellent student was given the opportunity to be one of the first students to attend the newly built Atlanta University. Laney graduated in the first class in 1873 and then devoted her life to teaching other blacks. In 1883 a room in a church was set aside for Laney to start a school. Under her direction, it expanded and was chartered by the state in 1886. Laney worked unceasingly to raise funds to keep the school open and to develop high standards for teaching and learning; she herself took courses at the University of Chicago toward this end. Laney also opened the first kindergarten in Atlanta and started a nursing program that later developed into the nursing school at Atlanta University. Although her school closed in 1949, a new school has been built on the site and named in her honor. (*Sources*: 439, 447, 502, 507, 508, 627, 680, 683)

1883   Emma Lazarus   (1849–1887) United States (Jewish American)

Ralph Waldo Emerson praised the first book of poetry published by Lazarus, and she dedicated her next book to him; by and large, however, her poetry was not well received. In 1881 she began to write about the immigrant populations arriving in the United States, especially Jews and the persecution and discrimination they experienced; her books with this new theme were far more successful than her poetry had been. In 1883 her sonnet "The New Colossus" was selected for one of the inscriptions to be placed on the Statue of Liberty. Among the lines in this sonnet are "Give me your tired, your poor / Your huddled masses yearning to breathe free . . ." Lazarus died a few years after she won this honor. (*Sources*: 548, 551)

1883   Olive Schreiner   (1855–1920) South Africa

Schreiner's life was split into various dichotomies: she was an independent woman and loving wife, intellectual and dreamer, political activist and recluse, and she alternately enjoyed and suffered from happiness and depression, good health and illness. Despite her lack of formal education, she skillfully conveyed the mixture of these sentiments and agonies in her writing. Schreiner's first success and an example of her dilemma was *The Story of an African Farm*, which she published in 1883 under a man's name. In this book she used three different characters to portray her conflicting feelings. More than any of her others, this book best represents her early awareness of the struggles faced by women, her native country, and society. *The Story of an African Farm* was translated into five languages, with reprints appearing as late as 1976. A feminist, Schreiner also wrote *Women and Labour* (1911), one of her last books. (*Sources:* 45, 114, 127, 295, 336, 370, 473, 653, 731)

1883   Ella Wilcox   (1850–1919) United States

Wilcox's poetry and novels were more popular and highly regarded in her day than at present because of the social milieu of her time. By the age of eighteen she was selling her work and gaining in popularity in the Midwest. In 1883 Wilcox became nationally known with the rejection and subsequent publication of a book of poetry, *Poems of Passion*, that had been turned down because several of the poems were considered too immoral for print. In 1884 she married and moved east, continuing to publish her poetry and novels and to write for the more sensational newspapers. Her popularity spread to England in 1901 when she wrote a poem to commemorate the death of Queen Victoria and was presented at the court of Saint James. (*Sources:* 64, 447, 486, 522, 562, 616, 718, 758, 766)

1884   Lou Andreas-Salomé   (1861–1937) Germany (Russia)

Friedrich Nietzsche fell in love with Andreas-Salomé when he met her in 1880. Although she turned down his marriage proposal, she was greatly influenced by him and in 1884 wrote her first book, in which she described their relationship. Her marriage to a professor was an unhappy one, and she continued her relationship with Nietzsche, publishing her second book about him in 1897. After an affair with a poet, Andreas-Salomé's interest turned to literary works, and she wrote four books on the characters in Henrik Ibsen's books. In 1915, having met and been influenced by Sigmund Freud, she began a practice in psychoanalysis and wrote two books on analysis. In 1931 and 1933 she wrote books on Freud's influence on her, the second entitled *My Thanks to Freud.* Her autobiography was published posthumously in 1951. (*Sources:* 159, 731)

1884   Isabella Crawford   (1850–1887) Canada (Ireland)

Although Crawford only published one book of poetry, *Old Spookses' Pass, Malcolm's Katie, and Other Poems* (1884), she is considered Canada's first important woman poet. She arrived in Canada at the age of eight and used the Canadian culture and landscape as her source of inspiration. She is noted for her narrative and dialogical form. (*Sources*: 80, 195, 556)

1884   Alice Fletcher   (1838–1923) United States
   In 1878 Fletcher went to work at the Peabody Museum at Harvard, noted for its collection of Native American artifacts; as a result of working at the museum and hearing SUSETTE LAFLESCHE of the Omaha tribe speak, she became interested in Native American cultures. In 1881 Fletcher went to Nebraska to learn more about the Omaha tribe headed by Chief Joseph LaFlesche (Chief Iron Eyes.) Violating her professional training, she became subjectively involved in their problems and semiadopted Francis, one of the chief's sons, who remained with her the rest of her life. Fletcher is credited with pushing through the Dawes Act of 1887, which apportioned Indian land by individual rather than tribal ownership. This was in opposition to what Susette LaFlesche wanted, and the Dawes Act proved to be detrimental to the Indians. Fletcher also worked for the federal government on Indian issues and wrote several books, the most well known being her study on *The Omaha Tribe*, written in 1911. (*Sources*: 105, 210, 447, 527, 587, 634, 731)

1885   Ulrika, *aka* Minna Canth   (1844–1897) Finland
   Canth, widowed with seven children, ran her father's business and wrote plays and novels. There is evidence of the influence of B. M. Bjornson, Henrik Ibsen, Leo Tolstoy, and Kivi throughout her work, though these never overpowered her own unique style. A realist, she condemned the aristocracy for the conditions of the lower class. Canth's writings were made more poignant by her use of vernacular language. Her first play was *The Laborer's Wife*, written in 1885, and her first novel was *Kauppa-Lopo*, written in 1889. Her interest not only in class but also in gender is shown in her 1893 play, *Sylvi*. (*Sources*: 42, 184, 556, 718)

1885   Helen Hamilton Gardener   (1853–1925) United States
   Born Alice Chenoweth in Winchester, Virginia, Gardener later legally changed her name to the literary name she had been using, Helen Hamilton Gardener. Coming under the influence of a

well-known agnostic who urged her to write, Gardener published *Men, Women and Gods, and Other Lectures* in 1885, establishing her reputation as a free thinker. Responding to a statement made by a neurologist that the measurable difference in the sizes of male and female brains justified their unequal treatment, Gardener conducted research with a neurosurgeon and correctly retorted that if any difference in brain size existed, it had no relationship to intellectual capacity. Becoming very interested in feminist issues, Gardener wrote the well-received novel *Is This Your Son, My Lord?* (1890), a book on the victimization of women by prostitution. Her second book was on the inferior status of married women. A third book, about her father, was later produced as a play. Following her second marriage, at which time she moved to Washington, D.C., Gardener was asked to help promote women's suffrage. Using her well-placed connections in the Capitol, she promoted the enfranchisement of women, even with President Woodrow Wilson. Shortly after the passage of the Nineteenth Amendment, the president appointed Gardener the first woman civil service commissioner, a post she held until her death five years later. (*Sources*: 4, 74, 455, 470, 473, 543, 548, 750)

1885   Lilli Lehmann   (1848–1929) Germany

Taught by her mother, a noted soprano, Lehmann began her operatic career in Germany at the age of twenty-eight, sang throughout Europe to great acclaim, and made her U.S. debut at the Metropolitan Opera in 1885 in *Carmen*. Singing the parts of Isolde and Brünnhilde at the Metropolitan, she enjoyed a reputation as one of the best performers of Wagner. Lehmann became the director of the Salzburg Festival and wrote several books on opera. (*Sources*: 29, 116, 518, 731)

1885   Julia Rebecca Rogers   (1854–1944) United States

In 1885 Rogers and several other women—including M. Thomas Carey, the future president of Bryn Mawr College (a separate women's college)—founded the Bryn Mawr School for Girls. This same group of friends also established the College Club, which later became a branch of the American Association of University Women. Rogers and Mary Garrett offered to raise funds for the Johns Hopkins Medical School, with the proviso that the medical school admit women students; when Johns

Hopkins refused to allow women to enroll in its graduate schools, however, Rogers bequeathed her estate to Goucher College. (*Sources*: 409, 537, 718)

1886   Harriet Ayer   (1849–1903) United States

Ayer personally identified with beauty and femininity and carved a lucrative career out of promoting the importance to women of these two qualities. Although very assertive when she needed to be, Ayer never identified with or advocated female independence. Possessing a drive for success and only sixteen at the time of her marriage, she quickly established a reputation as a beauty and a charming hostess. She defied convention by divorcing her spendthrift and philandering husband. Hearing about a beauty formula, she bought it and established her own cosmetic company in 1886. Ayer's knowledge of the importance of clever advertisements contributed to her success: her business was boosted by the endorsements of Lillie Langtry and Ayer's claims that a Napoleonic courtesan used her product. Ten years later, emotionally depressed and possibly an addict, she was confined to a hospital and lost her business. After her release, she persuaded an editor of a New York newspaper to hire her to write a beauty column in which she extolled charm, beauty, and femininity. Ayer developed her journalistic skills and was soon covering sensational stories, particularly those involving women. This second career was short-lived, lasting only seven years before her death. (*Sources*: 518, 522, 627, 628, 731)

1886   Leonora Barry   (1849–1930) United States (Ireland)

Barry arrived in the United States with her parents in 1852. At age sixteen she secured a teaching certificate and taught in rural schools in upstate New York until her marriage in 1871. Ten years later she was left a widow with two of her three children to support, one having died shortly after her husband's death. Unskilled, she took a job in a factory and was appalled at the working conditions and low wages, especially for women. Barry joined the active Knights of Labor and soon rose within the ranks, eventually becoming investigator for the organization in 1886. An idealist and indefatigable worker who was willing to travel around the country and to investigate labor conditions upon request, Barry was soon disillusioned by the lack of response from industry, the paucity of people who attended Knights of Labor meetings, the rarity of women interested in working past marriage, and the overall apathy toward labor reform. A Catholic, Barry was also severely criticized by the church for her efforts. She was successful in starting two cooperative factories and helped to get a factory inspection law passed in Pennsylvania but otherwise made little headway. Barry's work for the Knights of Labor ended in 1890, and she devoted the rest of her life to support of temperance and women's suffrage. (*Sources*: 447, 627, 763)

1886 Sophia Hayden (1868–1953) United States (Chile)

In 1886 Hayden was the first woman admitted to the architecture school of the Massachusetts Institute of Technology, graduating with honors in 1890. In 1891 what should have been a fortuitous opportunity for a new graduate and a woman pioneer in architecture turned into a bitter disappointment and the end of Hayden's architectural career: Hayden was the finalist in the competition for the design and construction of the Woman's Building for the World's Columbian Exposition in Chicago. As part of the selection, she had to submit a scale model of her building at a cost of $150,000; she was reimbursed only one-tenth of her expenses, while most male colleagues were reimbursed in full. Harassed by construction workers and by suggestions from the exposition's committee members for alterations in her design, she nevertheless was the first architect to have her building completed; Hayden received an award and two medals for her work. Following the exposition, she was vilified in the most prestigious architectural journal for designing a building that was too feminine; it was given as an example of why architecture was a field inappropriate for women, and Hayden's ill health after the exposition was cited as proof that architecture was too demanding a career for women. Hayden lived a quiet life following this experience, especially after her husband of thirteen years died. Since the buildings at the World's Columbian Exposition were dismantled, none of Hayden's work has survived her. (*Sources*: 447, 720, 756)

1886 Matilde Serao (1856–1927) Italy

A Girl's Romance, written in 1886, is generally considered the best of Serao's novels. Although many of her other novels have been favorably reviewed, she is sometimes called a hack writer; as she produced over forty novels between 1881 and 1914, it is not surprising that not all were well received. Most of her works portray the life of poor Neapolitans. She and her husband were unsuccessful in publishing a newspaper, but after his death she founded and edited the famous newspaper *Il Giorno*, which she ran until her death in 1927. (*Sources*: 80, 296, 731)

1886 Anna Shaw (1847–1919) United States (England)
Brought to the United States as a small child, Shaw became a woman of tenacity and courage. She earned her degree in medicine at Boston University in 1886, a time in which women were not welcome in medical schools; she also received a license in ministry, another field not hospitable to women. She preached in defiance of her family, who, according to Shaw, would see it as "nothing short of personal disgrace." Those who knew her were perhaps more struck by her grit than by her sermons: at one point she held a gun on a would-be rapist who was driving her to a remote frontier town. In her account of the episode, she noted that "no touch of human fingers ever brought such comfort" as did her grip on the revolver. Shaw was also very active in the women's movement and was president of the National American Woman Suffrage Association for nine years. (*Sources*: 35, 328, 504, 556, 558, 584, 627, 676, 699, 749, 754)

1887 Maria Carreras (1872–?) Italy
At the age of six, Carreras was already noted for her brilliance on the piano, receiving a prize from Franz Liszt, the honorary president of the Academy of Santa Cecelia, which she attended. In 1887, at the age of fifteen, Carreras made her debut with the Rome Philharmonic Orchestra playing a composition by her famous teacher, Sgambati. Carreras gave concerts throughout Europe and South America and, after a tour of the United States, settled there and taught piano. (*Sources*: 431, 439)

1887 Mary Freeman (1852–1930) United States
Freeman graduated from Mount Holyoke Seminary in 1871. A novelist and short-story writer, she gave vivid accounts of New England life. Her first collection of short stories was published in 1887 and a second collection in 1891. Her description of New England mills, *The Portion of Labor*, written in 1901, is considered her most ambitious work. (*Sources*: 102, 358, 398, 583, 680)

1887 Beatrice Webb (1858–1943) England

In 1887 Webb wrote her first book on working conditions, having learned about business as her father's associate for six years following her mother's death. The book was the result of a survey on the working conditions of the poor. The next year she wrote on working conditions in the East End of London, basing her descriptions on information that she had presented to the House of Lords. She married in 1892; as ardent socialists, she and her husband published more than 100 books and articles on labor conditions. The couple founded the now famous London School of Economics in 1895. Webb was also influential in drafting social reform laws when she served on a royal commission. Although she was sympathetic to the plight of the working class, Webb is faulted for writing about it as an undifferentiated mass, with little regard for the individuals among the group. (*Sources*: 60, 104, 127, 426, 558, 584, 681, 731, 751)

1888 Gertrude Bell (1868–1926) England

Bell was educated at Queen's College and Oxford. She became interested in the Middle East when she first traveled to the region in 1888. She taught herself both Persian and Arabic and wrote two books on Persia (now Iran) in 1894 and 1897. After another visit to the Middle East, Bell wrote three books on the archaeological excavations in Syria and Asia Minor. During this time she also became interested in the politics of the region, writing a book about the Turkish rebellion then occurring. Bell became the first woman to travel unescorted through Arabia. Because of her knowledge of the Middle East and her ease in traveling within these countries, the British government asked her to collect information to help them mobilize the Arabs against the Turks. In 1920 she acted as a liaison between the British and the Arabs and is credited with helping to establish the Hashimite dynasty in Iraq—an incredible feat in view of the low status assigned to women by both custom and law in the Middle East. Bell apparently committed suicide in 1926, shortly after founding a national museum in Baghdad. (*Sources*: 169, 592, 731, 751)

1888 Elizabeth Boit (1849–1932) United States

Boit started as an office clerk in a Massachusetts factory in 1867; by 1888, in partnership with Charles Winship, she owned her own factory, the Harvard Knitting Mill. The mill employed 850 people and manufactured 2,000 garments a day. Boit enjoyed a reputation as a good employer. She was also on the board of a home for the aged that was later renamed in her honor. (*Sources*: 583, 718)

1888 Sophonisba Breckinridge   (1866–1948) United States
Breckinridge established one of the first woman's courses at the University of Chicago. Although her father was a wealthy former congressman from Kentucky, he expected her to marry or support herself. Breckinridge earned her degree from Wellesley in 1888 and became the first woman to pass the bar examination in Kentucky. She received her doctoral degree in political science at the University of Chicago in 1901. Because she had personally experienced how difficult it was for a woman to earn her doctorate, she chose teaching over legal practice; at the University of Chicago she established the pioneer School of Civics and Philanthropy, which later was renamed the Department of Social Service Administration. Breckinridge also incorporated into her courses the study of women's roles in the family as well as in business and the professions. Becoming a dean at the college, she observed that although education was considered a women's field, men generally held the administrative positions. (*Sources*: 34, 74, 339, 626, 683)

1888 Bertha Van Hoosen   (1863–1952) United States
In her autobiography, *Petticoat Surgeon*, Van Hoosen relates some fascinating facts about her life. For example, her father spent six years driving first her sister and then Van Hoosen back and forth to school on weekends. In winter her mother would bundle her into the sleigh with hot bricks and hot food, and her father would make the long round-trip in subfreezing temperatures. She also relates that when she went to medical school in 1885, women medical students were referred to as "hen medics"; that her mother was horrified that her daughter would consider such a career; and that she and another female doctor were denied office space in a home because the landlord feared no one would rent it afterward. She did much pioneer work in obstetrics and gynecology. She was also involved both personally and professionally in improving mental health, race relations, and the conditions of the poor;

in 1907, she helped to develop one of the first school sex education programs. She was founder and first president of the American Medical Women's Association. (*Sources*: 583, 703, 718, 734)

1888   Annie Peck   (1850–1935) United States

Peck graduated from the Rhode Island Normal School in 1872, a classmate of ROSA HAZEL. Like Hazel, Peck began a career in teaching. In 1888 Peck undertook a second and unusual career for a woman: she became a mountain climber. The first mountain she scaled was Mount Shasta in California; her next was the Matterhorn in 1895. By 1900 she was a world-renowned climber able to support herself and her adventures. In 1900, at age fifty, she set out to fulfill a desire to be the first to climb a particular mountain; she selected Sorata in Peru, finally reaching its peak in 1904. In 1908 Peck succeeded in climbing the northern face of Huascarán; in 1927 the Lima Geographical Society named the north peak of Huascarán "Cumbre Aña Peck." Peck continued to climb until her eighty-second year. It is reported that in 1909 she made the comment that she had climbed higher than the aviation pioneers Orville and Wilbur Wright and Charles Lindbergh had flown. (*Sources*: 446, 548, 592, 728)

1889   Maude Adams   (1872–1953) United States

Following in her mother's minor theatrical footsteps, Adams (née Kiskaddon) first appeared on the stage in 1877 at the age of five, but it was not until 1889, when she appeared in *Midnight Bell*, that she became a leading actor. She was the leading female performer in Charles Frohman's productions for most of her career, appearing with the great actor John Drew for five of those years. She was also considered an accomplished Shakespearean actor. Adams retired from the stage in 1918 but gave a farewell performance in *Twelfth Night* in 1934. In 1937 Adams launched a second career, teaching drama at Stephens College in Missouri. (*Sources*: 15, 74, 455)

1889   Johanna Gadski   (1872–1932) Germany

Gadski was one of the great Wagnerian sopranos of her day. She sang her first operatic role at the Kroll Theater in Berlin in 1889 and continued to perform in both the winter and summer concert series in Berlin until 1894. In 1895 she made her

U.S. debut with the Walter Damrosch Opera Company, with whom she was in the premiere of *The Scarlet Letter* in 1896 in Boston. Gadski first appeared at the Metropolitan Opera in 1900, performing there until 1903. During these years she also sang at Covent Garden and several international festivals. After her debut at Carnegie Hall, she went on tour from 1904 to 1906. She returned to the Metropolitan Opera in 1907 and during the next ten years added five new roles to her repertoire. At the beginning of World War I, because of the hostility she aroused with her stated allegiance to her country, Gadski went back to Germany. In 1928 she formed her own opera company and returned to the United States for a tour that lasted three years. (*Sources*: 29, 325, 326, 416, 455)

1889 Gertrude Jekyll (1843–1932) England

Jekyll had little formal education but demonstrated an artistic flair that she used as a home decorator, working for such prominent clients as the duke of Westminster. In 1889 failing eyesight caused her to change from home decorating to landscaping. Jekyll began to create the gardens for houses designed by the architect Edward Lutyens. She is best known for gardens inspired by French impressionist paintings and for simpler English country gardens. Jekyll's books remain particularly popular and have promoted her ideas about using color and texture in the garden. (*Sources*: 225, 751)

1889 Mary Richmond (1861–1928) United States

Richmond was a pioneer in the field of social work. In 1889 she began working with families as part of the Baltimore Charity Organization Society. She moved to Philadelphia in 1900 to become the general secretary of the organization and stayed until 1909, when she became charity director at the Russell Sage Foundation. Richmond was the author of four books on social welfare, her first, *Friendly Visiting Among the Poor*, written in 1899. (*Sources*: 60, 74, 79, 105, 286)

1889 Edith Somerville (1858–1949) Ireland

Somerville wrote alone and in collaboration with her cousin Violet Martin, who used the pseudonym Martin Ross. Their first book together was *An Irish Cousin* (1889); they coauthored seven more books. Somerville also illustrated the

books credited to her. From 1903 to 1919 she was the first woman to serve as master of foxhounds, and in 1935 she published a
book on fox hunting entitled *Notes of the Horn*. (*Sources*: 60, 78, 80,
301)

1889   Bertha von Suttner   (1843–1914) Austria
After the death of her family and the loss of the family
fortune, Suttner worked as a secretary for Alfred Nobel, who later
established the Nobel Peace Prize in her honor. She eloped with
Arthur von Suttner shortly after taking a job as governess for his
family. It was at this time that she began to write about peace.
Her book *Lay Down Your Arms!* (1889) brought her fame for the
controversy it caused; in 1905 Nobel awarded her the Peace Prize
for this work. Suttner founded the International Peace League in
1891 and continued to write until 1909. (*Sources*: 60, 80, 149, 305,
488, 634, 731)

1889   Margaret Washington   (1865–1925) United States (African American)
Washington graduated from Fiske University in 1889 and
began teaching at Tuskeegee Institute. In 1893 she became the
third wife of the institute's president, Booker T. Washington.
Washington was instrumental in starting rural schools, raising
money to build schools, and establishing an industrial education
program. She was the founder and first president of the Tuskeegee
Women's Club and the founder of the National Federation of
Colored Women's Clubs. Washington was the driving force
behind the merger of this federation with the National
Association of Colored Women's Clubs when it was founded in
1896. (*Sources*: 120, 541, 718)

1890   Janie Barrett   (1865–1949) United States (African American)
When the white family she worked for proposed sending
her to a northern school where she could easily pass for white,
Barrett instead chose to identify with her own racial group and
studied at Hampton Institute in Hampton, Virginia, graduating
in 1884. Barrett started a girls' weekly meeting group in her home
in Hampton; in 1890 it became the Locust Street Social
Settlement, the first black school of its kind. As president of the
Colored Women's Clubs, Barrett spearheaded the move to

establish a home for wayward girls, opening the Industrial School for Colored Girls in Peaks Turnout in 1915. The residents in the area protested against the school, but Barrett was able to obtain state and private money to build resident cottages and to start a program. She received aid from the Russell Sage Foundation to establish a program of education and rehabilitation for the young girls. By the end of the next decade, the school was judged one of the best of its kind in the country. Barrett was the recipient of the William Harmon Award and was invited to participate in a conference on child health and welfare held in Washington, D.C. Through her membership in the Richmond Urban League and the Southern Commission on Interracial Cooperation, Barrett attempted to establish organizations for troubled young girls of every race. (*Sources*: 411, 447)

1890 Carrie Catt (1859–1947) United States

When Catt's father refused to pay for her education she worked her way through Iowa State College, doing menial jobs. Widowed after a one-year marriage, she took up the cause of women's rights and in 1890 helped to organize the National American Woman Suffrage Association. Again widowed after a short marriage, Catt devoted her full energy to both the women's rights group in the United States and the international group she helped organize and that later became the International Alliance of Women. Catt assumed the leadership of the National American Woman Suffrage Association from the aging Susan B. Anthony in 1900. Using the same organizational and work skills that got her through college, Catt organized women throughout the country to campaign for women's suffrage; Catt, more than anyone else, is credited with the 1919 passage of the amendment giving women the vote. Catt was less successful in her endeavor to organize women toward an international and unified effort for world peace, to which she devoted the remainder of her life. (*Sources*: 88, 188, 447, 454, 525, 739)

1890 Kate Chopin (1851–1904) United States

Chopin wrote books with feminist themes, starting with her first novel *At Fault* in 1890. Chopin was raised in New Orleans in a genteel family of women and married a wealthy man, but because of the influence of writers like Guy de

Maupassant and Gustave Flaubert, did not conform to the traditional life for a woman of her day. She showed her strength when she had to move to Bayou country after her husband's business failure and eventual death left her with six children to support. In her novels *Bayou Folk* (1894) and *A Night in Acidie* (1897), she showed her literary skill for capturing ethnic culture and writing in dialect. She also published many of the stories she created for her own children. Chopin's writing career came to an abrupt end when her 1899 novel *The Awakening*, about sexual passion, nonrepentance, and suicide, resulted in social outrage and ostracism. (*Sources*: 14, 64, 72, 94, 370, 479, 486, 522, 680, 718, 731)

1890 Lavinia Dock (1858–1956) United States

In 1890 Dock needed financial help from her father in order to publish *Materia Medica for Nurses*; it was the first drug manual for nurses and sold over 100,000 copies. Dock had graduated from the Bellevue Hospital Nursing School in 1886, and in the same year that her book appeared, she became an assistant superintendent of nurses at the Johns Hopkins Hospital in Baltimore. It was here that Dock served as a role model for a later well-known nurse, ADELAIDE NUTTING. She and Nutting coauthored *A History of Nursing* in 1907, and Dock added two volumes to the reprint in 1912. In 1905 she was the only nurse who supported a physicians' campaign against venereal disease, writing about the crusade in the *American Journal of Nursing*. Dock also fought for the abolition rather than the regulation of prostitution, publishing her book *Hygiene and Morality* in 1910. Having the courage of her convictions, Dock was jailed for working for women's suffrage, helped to organize the first black nursing association, and resigned from nursing and social service groups that opposed her efforts toward suffrage, birth control, and the eradication of venereal disease. In 1947 Dock was honored by the International Council of Nurses, the group whose organization she had sponsored in 1899 with the royalties from her books. (*Sources*: 81, 339, 462, 470, 537, 583, 757)

1890 Williamina Fleming (1857–1911) United States (Scotland)

What is probably as remarkable about Fleming as is her work in astronomy is that she accomplished so much with less than ten years of formal education. Two years after arriving in the United States, pregnant and divorced, she gratefully accepted a job as a clerk at the Harvard Observatory. By 1886 she was in charge of compiling the *Henry Draper Catalogue*, a classification of the stars published in 1890. In addition to this work, she discovered ten novae, edited the observatory's publications, and wrote essays. Many honors were bestowed upon her for her valuable contributions to astronomy, including an honorary membership in the Royal Astronomical Society. At the time of her death at age fifty-four, she left enough material for years of additional research. (*Sources*: 9, 105, 565, 587, 583, 718)

1890   Loie Fuller   (1862–1928) United States

An innovative dancer, Fuller created the sensational serpentine dance in 1890 by using a combination of voluminous skirts, made of silk, and variegated lighting. Her equally successful fire dance featured the imaginative use of glass flooring and colored lights. Fuller danced at the Paris Universal Exposition in 1900 and was able to number Henri Toulouse-Lautrec and Auguste Rodin among her devotees. Her next dance sensation was an inferno scene for the 1923 Paris performance of Hector Berlioz's *Damnation of Faust*. It was often necessary for Fuller to develop the machinery to create the effects she needed. Fuller retired from the stage following a performance in London in 1927 in which she used lighting to create a silhouette effect. (*Sources*: 15, 211, 402, 416, 447, 478, 518, 679, 731)

1890   Rosa Luxemburg   (1870–1919) Germany

Luxemburg was a key leader in the founding of the German Communist Party in 1890 and became a controversial figure when she wrote *Reform or Revolution?* In 1905 Luxemburg organized a workers' revolt in Poland. At the end of the first World War, she was instrumental in the founding of the Spartacus League in Germany and promoted a revolution. She was associated with two other women revolutionaries, CLARA ZETKIN and ANGELICA BALABANOFF. She was arrested in 1919 and executed for her political activities. Luxemburg had written over 700 books, articles, and pamphlets in her short political career. (*Sources*: 60, 241, 558, 599)

1890   Elizabeth Seaman   (1867–1922) United States

Seaman first began her journalistic career in the 1880s writing for a Pittsburgh newspaper. During this decade she wrote two books, one on the social conditions in Mexico and the other on the treatment of the mentally ill in New York. She gathered material for her second book by having herself committed to an insane asylum for ten days. Seaman achieved fame with a publicity stunt in 1890: using the pseudonym Nelly Bly, she succeeded in going around the world in seventy-two days, beating the fictional record set by Phineas Fogg of Jules Verne's 1873 classic, *Around the World in Eighty Days. (Sources:* 34, 455, 486, 532, 626, 633, 731)

1890   Luisa Tetrazzini   (1871–1940) Italy

Tetrazzini was considered to be among the greatest coloratura sopranos in opera. She first studied with her sister, a noted opera star, and later at the Musical Institute in Florence, the city where she made her debut in 1890. Tetrazzini toured in South America and enjoyed her greatest success on a tour in Mexico in 1905. In 1907, after a sensational engagement in San Francisco, she went to England, making her first appearance at Covent Garden. Tetrazzini made her debut at the Metropolitan Opera in New York in 1911; except during the war years, she remained in the United States until 1931. She then retired to Italy to teach aspiring young singers. *(Sources:* 325, 739)

1890   Women's Industrial Exchange (United States)

Women's industrial exchanges began in the early 1880s, and by 1890 they were located in seventy-five cities throughout the country. These organizations either sold a woman's handwork on consignment or allowed her to trade her work for meals served in the restaurants set up as part of the exchange. The identity of the woman's name was protected by coding her work. This enabled many women to earn money or to supplement their family's income. The first exchange was established in a private home in Baltimore and later moved to its present location on Charles Street. It is still in operation today. *(Sources:* 636, 762)

1891   Harriet Converse   (1836–1903) United States

Converse was the first white woman to be made an honorary member of an Indian tribe. She was initially granted membership in the Seneca tribe of New York in 1884 for her efforts in their behalf. In 1891 she was given a higher honor by the Six Nations at the Tonawanda tribal reservation, who wanted to pay tribute to Converse and her family, including her grandfather (called Honest Trader) and her father (who had been named Brave Boy). In an elaborate ceremony Converse was made a sister and a clanswoman and was given the name Gayaneshaoh, meaning faith keeper. This "adoption" did not entitle her to any national Indian rights. (*Sources:* 342, 455)

1891 Selma Lagerlöf (1858–1940) Sweden

Lagerlöf was the only noted novelist in Sweden's renaissance period at the turn of the nineteenth century and in 1909 became the first woman writer to receive the Nobel Prize in literature. She was named the first director of the Swedish Academy in 1914. Lagerlöf wrote her first novel, *The Story of Gösta Berling*, in 1891. She gained international fame with her two-volume novel *Jerusalem* (1902), in which she wrote about Delecarlian peasants who emigrated to Jerusalem. A prolific as well as outstanding writer, Lagerlöf wrote thirty-three novels and four autobiographical accounts between 1891 and 1935. She is also credited with obtaining the release from a concentration camp of the Jewish writer NELLY SACHS, who was awarded the Nobel Prize in literature in 1966. (*Sources:* 80, 562, 583, 599, 717, 731)

1891 Josephine Peary (1863–1955) United States

In July 1891, Peary accompanied her husband, the explorer Robert Peary, to McCormick Bay, the halfway point between the Arctic Circle and the North Pole. It was a preliminary trip before the journey to the North Pole, completed in 1909. Peary kept a diary of her fifteen-month stay in this region, publishing it as *My Arctic Journal* in 1893. Her personal courage and faith in her husband are reflected in her positive reporting of the adventure. Peary describes how the party was nearly swept away from their temporary quarters by a severe rainstorm and how she was left with one companion while her husband made a foray north; she nearly drowned while fording an ice-cold stream. Her most harrowing experience was when she was left alone and unarmed to guard her husband, who had badly broken his leg. She had another terrifying adventure as a member of a boat party; she had to reload the guns while the men shot attacking walruses, as many as 100 of the beasts at a time attempting to overturn the boat. She reports that she was unsure whether she would be hit by the wildly fired bullets or dragged overboard by the walruses. Peary was nevertheless both kind to the Eskimos and observant of their customs; her only negative comment about the trip was about spending a night in an igloo that had an overpowering, rancid smell. In 1901 Peary wrote *Snow Baby*, describing the birth of her daughter, Marie, on Peary's second trip to the region in 1893. (*Sources*: 131, 455, 761)

1891   Clara Zetkin   (1857–1933) Germany
Educated at the teachers' college in Leipzig, Zetkin joined the Socialist Party in 1881 and was one of the few women delegates at the founding of the Second Socialist International in 1889. After a self-imposed exile, Zetkin returned to Germany in 1891 and began her political career, becoming editor of the socialist women's newspaper *Equality* and giving speeches advocating socialism and women's rights and opposing child labor. In 1918 Zetkin and ROSA LUXEMBURG founded the Spartacus League. Zetkin joined the new German Communist Party in 1919 and two years later was elected to the presidium in the Soviet Union. After the death of Lenin in 1924, she became less influential. (*Sources*: 30, 60, 323, 360, 472, 558, 599, 681)

1892   Amy Beach   (1867–1944) United States
Beach received her first piano training from her mother and later from the professional teachers Perabo, Baermann, and Hill. She made her concert debut in 1883 and performed with the Boston Symphony Orchestra in 1885. Beach also married in 1885 and chose at that time to forgo piano in favor of composing. Using J. S. Bach's well-known and difficult *Well-Tempered Clavier* and other études as her models, Beach (Mrs. H. H. A. Beach was the name she used professionally) developed her style. Her first major work was a mass for chorus, orchestra, and organ; in 1892 it became the first composition by a woman performed by the Handel and Haydn Society with the Boston Symphony Orchestra. A succès d'estime, it has not been performed since. Beach composed the *Festival Jubilate* for the World's Columbian Exposition that same year and later wrote works for the Omaha Trans-Mississippi Exposition and the San Francisco Panama-

Pacific Exposition. *Gaelic Symphony* was performed first by the Boston Symphony Orchestra and then by orchestras in New York, Kansas City, San Francisco, and Chicago. (*Sources*: 16, 167, 423, 447, 583, 731)

1892 Sendra Berenson (1868–1954) United States

The game of basketball was invented by James Naismith in Springfield, Massachusetts, in 1891, and by 1892 Berenson had introduced it into the physical education program at Smith College, where she was athletic director. Although it became a popular sport in women's colleges, the first professional women's basketball league did not form until 1978. (*Sources*: 439, 455, 548, 610, 627, 685, 718)

1892 Anna Cooper (1858–1964) United States (African American)

With a doctoral degree, Cooper was probably one of the most educated women—and was certainly the most educated black woman—of her time. An individualist dedicated to education, especially for black women, she devoted her life to teaching. She authored several books, her most noteworthy being her autobiography, *A Voice from the South* (1892); it met with an indifference in both the black and white communities that Cooper believed came about because she was black, female, and wrote on feminism, an issue unimportant to others. She criticized black women for not recognizing that they could lead the way for all blacks and criticized white women for excluding black women from the feminist movement. Ahead of her time in her awareness of the importance of feminism and adult education, Cooper ran a small college in her own home for black working adults. (*Sources*: 108, 120, 507, 508, 541, 627, 683, 696, 728)

1892 Constance Garnett (1861–1946) England

Garnett's education was sponsored by a scholarship to the women's college at Cambridge in 1879. She decided to study Russian while awaiting the birth of her first child, and in 1892 she began translating the works of the great Russian authors into English, soon establishing a reputation as a translator. Her first translation was that of a work by Ivan Goncharov entitled *A Common Story*. Altogether she translated seventy works by such noted Russian authors as Leo Tolstoy, Feodor Dostoyevsky, Anton

Chekhov, Ivan Turgenev, and Nikolay Gogol, including the complete works of the last two. (*Sources*: 214, 562, 751)

1892   Charlotte Gilman   (1860–1935) United States

Gilman first worked as a commercial artist following her graduation from the Rhode Island School of Design. Her fame did not come from her artistic work but rather from her books on mental health and feminism. She wrote her first book, *The Yellow Wallpaper*, in 1892 following her depression after the birth of her daughter and her subsequent divorce. A year later she published a book of poetry. Upon moving to California, Gilman became interested in women's issues and in 1898 wrote the highly acclaimed *Women and Economics*, translated into seven languages. She felt that it was the economic structure of society that kept women subservient and wrote five more books advocating change for women in the economic sphere. Gilman committed suicide in 1935. (*Sources*: 105, 103, 127, 358, 676, 731)

1892   Pauline Johnson   (1861–1913) Canada (Native American)

Johnson's great-grandfather took what became the family name when he was baptized into the Christian faith. Johnson had an Indian father and a white mother; except for five years during her teens when she attended school, she was largely taught by her mother and by reading the great books in her parents' library. Johnson identified more with her Native American than her white heritage, and all of her poetry was about Indian life. Her father died in 1884, and Johnson had to work to support her mother and herself. Although her first book of poems, *Gems of Poetry*, was published in 1885, Johnson had no money; in fact, her books never earned her more than $500 during her entire career. In 1892 she started to give readings that were very popular at the time; through these she launched her career. Her first poetic readings abroad were in 1894 in England, where she was a great success and took to wearing traditional Indian attire. She also published her book *The White Wampum* at this time. On a 1906 tour of England, Johnson met Chief Joe of a Canadian tribe and recorded his legends; with noted poetic license, she later wrote about the tales he had shared with her. Because she was poor at the close of her life, friends raised money for her by publishing her poems under the title she had chosen, *Flint and Feathers*. (*Sources*: 11, 226, 717, 735)

1893 Sadie American (1862–1944) United States (Jewish American)

American first devoted her energy to supporting settlement houses in her hometown of Chicago as well as promoting summer schools and playgrounds. In 1893 she established the National Council of Jewish Women, remaining with the organization until 1914. In 1912 she was the founder of an international association for Jewish women. American was equally active in New York City, where she worked with the Consumers' League and the State Federation of Women's Clubs. In all, American was involved in more than 100 Jewish and nonsectarian civic and social welfare organizations. (*Sources*: 123, 440, 455, 472, 525)

1893 Katharine Lee Bates (1859–1929) United States

Bates graduated from Wellesley College in 1880. She returned as an English instructor in 1885 and was made head of the department in 1891, remaining at Wellesley until 1925. Her primary interest was in poetry, and she founded the New England Poetry Club in 1915. Her most famous poem, written in 1893, but not published until 1895, was "America the Beautiful," which became a national hymn. At Wellesley Bates emphasized the function of poetry as an avenue to understanding human emotions and values. Bates published a total of four books of poetry. (*Sources*: 105, 165, 447, 473, 548, 556, 599, 617, 758)

1893 Florence Kelley (1859–1932) United States

Kelley earned a law degree in Switzerland, where she joined the Socialist Party and wrote the first English translation of Engels's book on working conditions in England. Returning to the United States in 1893, Kelley became chief inspector of factories in the state of Illinois. Kelly was successful in getting labor reform legislation passed and in 1899 became secretary of the National Consumers' League. She also served in the National American Woman Suffrage Association starting in 1905. Still active in reform, Kelley served as a delegate to the International Congress of Women for Permanent Peace held in Zurich in 1919. (*Sources*: 74, 627, 728, 763)

1893   Pierina Legnani   (1863–1923) Italy

Legnani became the prima ballerina of La Scala in 1892, but her highest acclaim came in 1893: dancing *Cinderella* in Russia, she astounded everyone by performing thirty-two turns in place on one leg. She established new standards for the Russian ballet and danced there every year until 1901. The Imperial Ballet of Russia gave her the honor of naming her *prima ballerina assoluta*. Legnani continued to dance throughout Europe until she was forty-seven. (*Sources*: 15, 478)

1893   Ethel Smyth   (1858–1944) England

Smyth's talent was recognized by her instructors and by Johannes Brahms when she studied composition in Germany; as a woman, however, she still had difficulty getting her work accepted in England. She finally made her debut as a composer in 1893, when her music was performed at Albert Hall, making her the first important woman composer in England. She nevertheless chose to have her three operatic compositions performed in Germany; her third, *The Wreckers* (1906), is still judged her best work. At about this time Smyth became interested in the women's movement and, when arrested for her women's rights activities, directed her fellow prisoners in the singing of her own composition, *The March of the Women*. Smyth created a prodigious number of operas, librettos, orchestral and choral works, and chamber pieces over nearly four decades. She also wrote nine books, most of them autobiographical accounts of her career. She was made a dame of the British Empire in 1923. (*Sources*: 16, 104, 455, 583, 731)

1893   Henrietta Szold   (1860–1945) United States (Jewish American)

Szold devoted her life to her fellow Jews in both the United States and Israel. In 1893 she became the editor of the Jewish Publication Society, translated Hebrew works into English, and composed the index volume to Heinrich Graetz's *History of the Jews*. As a teacher in Baltimore, she had started schools that educated over 5,000 immigrants, both Jewish and non-Jewish. In 1912 she founded Hadassah, a Jewish-American women's organization, and by 1913 had sent the first medical units to Palestine (now Israel). Szold is also credited with rescuing over 100,000 Jewish children from the Holocaust. (*Sources*: 79, 102, 525, 530)

1893   Lesya Ukrainka   (1871–1913) Ukraine

Ukrainka first wrote traditional and patriotic poems but in 1893 became noted for her narrative poems with biblical and historical settings, writing four books on these themes. In 1910 she published a book more psychological in nature. This was followed in 1911 by a book of poems on Ukrainian folklore, *The Forest Setting*, considered to be her best work. (*Sources*: 311, 715)

1893   Ida Wells-Barnett   (1862–1931) United States (African American)

Wells-Barnett fought against discrimination all her life. At an early age she won a suit against the Chesapeake and Ohio Railroad for its policy of racial segregation (the ruling was overturned by the Tennessee courts a few years later). She was a coowner of the Memphis newspaper *Free Speech*, which was destroyed by a mob after she published facts about local lynchings as well as fiery antidiscrimination articles. In 1893 Wells-Barnett moved to Chicago, where she started a campaign against racial discrimination. She made a public protest against the exclusion of blacks from the Chicago World Exposition and went to England to speak out against lynching. Upon her return to the United States, she organized the Woman's Club in Chicago, the first black women's suffrage club in the country. Wells-Barnett was a founder, cofounder, or member of no fewer than twelve civic, activist, and women's groups. She is also credited with being one of the founders of the National Association for the Advancement of Colored People. (*Sources*: 94, 510, 541, 627, 718, 728

1894   Carrie Bond   (1862–1946) United States

Bond had minimal training on the piano as a child but enjoyed playing and writing songs. She married at an early age, gave birth to her only child, and in 1887 divorced her husband. She remarried in 1889 and was widowed six years later. To support herself and her son, Bond turned to writing songs. Successful in publishing her first two songs in 1894, she gained in popularity once friends arranged for her to make public appearances. After giving concerts in New York, she was invited to perform at the White House for President Theodore Roosevelt. In 1901 she opened a small shop and published a book of songs that included her two best-known songs, "I Love You Truly" and "Just a Wearyin' for You." Her son became manager of the business. After his suicide in 1928, Bond blamed herself for never asking him if he would have preferred a different career. Bond's greatest success came in 1910 when she wrote "A Perfect Day," which sold over 5 million copies. She gradually lost public favor over the years, even though she continued to write songs until 1927. (*Sources*: 172, 442, 447, 522)

1894   Ichiyo Higuchi   (1872–1896) Japan

Higuchi grew up in a modest household in Tokyo but moved to the slums after the death of her father; she was left the sole support of her mother, her sister, and herself. Having studied poetry, she turned to writing and in 1894 published her first book of poetry, *The Last Day of the Year*. In her career, which lasted only two years, she produced her best volume of poems, *Growing Up*, and several other books. Higuchi wrote with sensitivity about women in the slums of Tokyo and about the innocence of the children who also lived there. (*Sources*: 80, 224)

1894   Mary McDowell   (1854–1936) United States

When McDowell was appointed director of the University of Chicago Settlement House in 1894, she found the neighborhood to be unsanitary and unhealthy. She worked to have a municipal bathhouse installed, founded a local library branch, and started a nursery for children, but her major projects were to have the nearby stockyards dump, full of animal waste, cleared out and to have a waste commissioner appointed in order to provide the city with a better sewage system. McDowell was instrumental in getting the women at the meat-packing company to apply for union membership in the Amalgamated Meatcutters and Butcher Workmen; when the union tried to limit the work performed by women, the women fought against it and won. This local branch of the union was also the first to admit black women as members. McDowell was rewarded for her efforts in 1923 when she was appointed the commissioner of public welfare for Chicago. (*Sources*: 718, 756, 763)

1894   Martha Thomas   (1857–1935) United States

Thomas was born into a conservative Quaker family; with the aid of her mother, she persuaded her father to allow her to go to college, completing her degree at Cornell in 1877. Five years later she earned her doctorate at the University of Zurich, both the first woman and the first foreigner to do so. When Bryn Mawr was founded in 1885, Thomas applied to be president, but the position was given to a male, and she was appointed a dean. In 1894, she became the second president of the college, a position she held until 1922. Thomas devoted her career to promoting women's higher education and was also a supporter for women's suffrage, serving in 1908 as the first president of the National College Women's Equal Suffrage League. (*Sources*: 34, 74, 79, 333, 447, 739, 755, 756)

1895   Donaldina Cameron   (1869–1968) United States (Scotland)

While the Chinese underworld in San Francisco called Cameron "Fahn Quai" (White Devil), the rest of Chinatown called her "Lo Mo" (the Mother) and the savior of young women. Cameron's family had first migrated to New Zealand when she was a small child and within a few years moved to the West Coast of the United States. In 1895 Cameron met the woman who had started a YWCA in San Francisco's Chinatown and was trying desperately to rescue Chinese girls from the thriving prostitution market. A mission had been opened for these young girls, some as young as nine, and Cameron accepted a position there; within a few years she became its director. Despite threats to her life and the lives of the girls, Cameron continued to work at the mission for the next forty years. The citizens of Chinatown, fearful of retaliation, secretly contacted the mission when they knew where girls were being held. Cameron and her staff—often aided but sometimes betrayed by the police, and frequently challenged by the henchmen of the brothels—made daring raids to rescue the girls. In order to provide the girls with legal protection, it was often necessary for Cameron to adopt them or be appointed their guardian. She once spent a night in jail with a girl who had been arrested on charges trumped up by her owner. Word of the mission and its successful work began to spread, and by 1900 it was one of the city's tourist attractions. Many of the girls lived at the mission for years, and it was not uncommon for Cameron to serve as "mother" of a bride or to become a "grandmother." In 1906 the mission was destroyed in an earthquake, and new quarters were found in San Raphael. It has since been turned into a community center. (*Sources*: 134, 539, 718)

1896 Alice Guy-Blaché (1873–1968) France

Guy-Blaché stumbled into her role as first woman movie director. As the secretary for a camera maker, she cast, directed, and supervised a short silent movie made in 1896 with one of the 60-mm cameras the company had just begun to manufacture. After the camera company was organized into a film company, she made a series of short films employing professional actors. By 1905, aided by newly hired assistants, she began to make longer films, among them the *Hunchback of Notre Dame*, and to direct short sound movies. She married in 1907, and she and her husband, a director, immigrated to the United States; in 1910 she launched her own production company named Solax. Within a few years, she had produced more than 300 films, often using natural settings rather than studio backdrops. One of her best-known movies at this time was *A Child's Sacrifice* (1910). Capitalizing on her achievement, Guy-Blaché built a new studio that soon became one of the largest and most successful independent film companies. In 1914 her husband took over as president, making Guy-Blaché vice-president; the company was sold three years later when it could no longer compete with the emerging giants in the film industry. Guy-Blaché is reported to have left her husband at this time and returned to France. In 1927 she attempted to recover her films, but they had been destroyed. She was awarded the French Legion of Honor in 1953 for her pioneering work in the cinema. (*Sources*: 341, 491, 656, 731, 745)

1896 Rose Lathrop (1851–1926) United States

Lathrop was the youngest daughter of Nathaniel Hawthorne. In 1896 she founded the religious order Servants of Relief for Incurable Cancer and devoted the remainder of her life to the care of victims of the disease. In 1897 she wrote her father's biography. (*Sources*: 81, 105, 126, 473, 532, 537, 551)

1896 Ida Minerva Tarbell (1857–1944) United States

Writing for *McClure's Magazine*, Tarbell soon established a reputation as a muckraker. Her first book for the magazine was a biography of Lincoln in 1896 entitled *The Early Life of Abraham Lincoln*; she wrote a second biography of him in 1900.

Tarbell also published books on well-known business figures. Her most sensational book was *The History of the Standard Oil Company* (1904). Tarbell wrote her autobiography, *All in the Day's Work*, in 1939. (*Sources*: 306, 339, 470, 519, 522, 548, 599, 627)

1897 Gertrude Franklin Atherton (1857–1948) United States

Atherton was a self-indulgent young woman who married into a wealthy and proper San Francisco family. She came by her inspiration to write accidentally, by reading a newspaper article about a local and somewhat colorful family named Gordon. Her new heroine, Nelly Gordon, personified the independent spirit the restless Atherton felt; Atherton chose to ignore the drunken, wasted portion of Nelly's life. The story she wrote about Nelly and the rest of the Gordons intrigued a publisher, who advised Atherton to remain anonymous as the author. The book was sensational and the Gordons easily identified; Atherton was subsequently reviled by her husband's family and the towns-people, but her writing career was launched. Her first notable novel, written in 1897, was *Patience Sparhawk and Her Times*; it again took up the theme of the independent woman doomed by fate to a lackluster life but nevertheless successful at finding a way to act on her potential. A prolific writer, Atherton wrote fifty novels, the majority of them highly successful. (*Sources*: 23, 473, 522, 627, 680)

1897 Alice Birney (1858–1907) United States

With the aid of Phoebe Hearst, Birney established the first parent-teacher association in the United States in 1897. In two years, membership grew from 2,000 to 50,000 members. Birney served as the first president of the association, for five years. In 1924 the name of the organization was changed to the National Congress of Parents and Teachers. (*Sources*: 455, 583, 718)

1897 Sarah Doyle (1830–1922) United States

In 1895 Doyle, a retired high school principal, was asked to chair a committee to raise funds to open a women's school at Brown University. By 1897 Doyle, who had been a cofounder of the Rhode Island School of Design, had raised sufficient funds to build and pay for Pembroke Hall, later renamed Pembroke College. Doyle was appointed president and remained with the college until 1919. Pembroke College has since been incorporated into Brown University. (*Sources*: 105, 718)

1897 Maud[e] Nathan (1862–1946) United States (Jewish American)

Throughout her life, Nathan worked actively for the rights of workers and consumers. A former director of Mount Sinai Hospital and a member of the New York Exchange for Women's Work, she was a cofounder of the New York City Consumers' League in 1890, assuming the presidency of the organization in 1897. Under her leadership the league conducted unofficial inspections of factories and made public lists of the employers who practiced fair conditions and paid reasonable salaries. By informing consumers of the working conditions of workers who created the products they purchased, the league was able to gain public support for the legislation it pushed to get passed. Unable to vote because she was a woman, Nathan also worked for women's suffrage, becoming the first vice-president of the New York Equal Suffrage League and making speeches throughout the country. She wrote the history of the New York City Consumers' League in 1926 and her autobiography, *Once Upon a Time and Today*, in 1933. (*Sources*: 123, 548, 584)

1898 Hertha Ayrton (1854–1923) England

In 1898 Ayrton became the first woman elected into membership in the Institution of Electrical Engineers. In 1906 the Royal Society awarded her the Hughes Medal in lieu of membership, which it denied her because of her sex and marital status. A mathematician and inventor, Ayrton first created (but did not patent) a sphygmograph to electrically monitor the human pulse. In 1884 she did patent her invention for an instrument that divided lines into any number of equal parts, which was of particular interest to engineers and architects. She did her most credited work in 1901, when she discerned the causal relationship between electrical arcs and explained the formation of sand ripples. In World War I Ayrton provided the military with better searchlights and a fan for the removal of poisonous gases. In spite of all of Ayrton's contributions, she was never elected to the Royal Society and was even denied the opportunity to present her papers until 1904. Her work was often credited to her husband, who was also a scientist. This led to Ayrton's feminist activities; she frequently housed the feminist activists who were victims of the so-called Cat and Mouse Act, by which they were force-fed in prison, released to recover, and later re-arrested. In 1920 Ayrton founded the National Union of Scientific Workers. (*Sources*: 2, 518, 587, 621, 731)

1898   Elizabeth Britton   (1858–1934) United States

Except for her teaching positions, Britton was unpaid for her invaluable work in botany and conservation from 1879 to 1930. She first joined a botanical club in 1879 after becoming interested in mosses. She married in 1885 and worked as an unpaid assistant to her husband for thirty-three years at the New York Botanical Garden, which she had helped to establish in 1891. Britton is credited with the acquisition of some of the garden's best-known moss collections. In 1902 Britton recognized the increasingly dangerous loss of wildflowers and was one of the founders of the Wild Flower Preservation Society. In 1925 she was successful in her attempt to end the use of wild holly for Christmas decorations, favoring the establishment of seed cultivation for this purpose. Britton founded the Sullivant Moss Society in 1898, which was renamed the American Bryological Society in 1949. The renaming of several plants and mosses as well as a mountain in Puerto Rico acknowledge Britton's fifty-one years of dedication to plant life and conservation. (*Sources*: 2, 447, 634)

1898   Louise Homer   (1871–1947) United States

Homer made her operatic debut in Vichy in 1898 singing the lead in *La Favorita*. She became a noted Wagnerian singer starting in 1900 at Covent Garden with her performance of the contralto role in *Lohengrin*, which she also sang for her U.S. debut the same year. Although often on tour, she gave more performances at the Metropolitan Opera in New York than at any other opera house. Homer sang the role of Maddalena for Enrico Caruso's U.S. debut in *Rigoletto* in 1903. Homer also sang in the first Metropolitan performance of *Madama Butterfly*, which the composer, Giacomo Puccini, attended. Homer retired after a highly successful twenty-one-year career. (*Sources*: 29, 326, 416, 455, 548)

1898   Käthe Kollwitz   (1867–1945) Germany

Kollwitz chose lithographs and sculptures to express her political views. In 1898 she completed a series of lithographs, entitled *The Weavers' Rebellion*, in which she portrayed the bare existence of the poor. In 1908 she completed the *Peasant War*, again depicting the grim conditions of the working class. Following the death of her son in World War I, her constant theme was the agony of mothers, especially at the loss of their children. In 1919 Kollwitz became the first woman elected to the Berlin Academy of Art. She was named its director in 1928, a position she held until dismissed by the Nazi regime in 1933. Much of her work was destroyed in the World War II bombing of Germany. (*Sources*: 231, 518, 583, 599, 739)

1898   Ellen Mussey   (1850–1936) United States
Having learned law from her husband, who taught at Howard University, Mussey was admitted to the District of Columbia bar in 1893. Recognizing that women had difficulty being accepted into law schools, she and a fellow lawyer, Emma Gillett, started the Washington College of Law in 1898. Mussey served as its first dean, remaining in this position until her retirement in 1913. The college is now affiliated with American University. (*Sources*: 105, 447, 548, 718, 728)

1898   Marion Talbot   (1858–1948) United States
Talbot earned her degrees at Boston University and the Massachusetts Institute of Technology. She soon founded the Association of Collegiate Alumnae and, by gathering statistics from this association, refuted the sensational pronouncement by Edward Clarke that women would suffer mental and physical breakdowns if they overtaxed their brains. The field having been added to college curriculums in 1884 through the efforts of ELLEN RICHARDS, Talbot accepted a teaching position in domestic science at the University of Chicago in 1895. By 1898 she was named dean of women. Throughout her professional career, Talbot continued to promote women's education, as had her father, who was the first dean of Boston University Medical School, and her mother, a teacher and reformer. (*Sources*: 74, 363, 584, 634, 683)

1899   Mary Antin   (1881–1949) United States (Russia) (Jewish American)
Antin emigrated from Russia in 1894 and was soon enrolled in Barnard College and the Columbia University. She wrote

about her arrival in the United States in a book entitled *From Polotsk to Boston* (1899). In her following book, first serialized in the *Atlantic Monthly*, she described the immigrant's experiences. "The winds rushed into outer space, roaring in my ears, 'America! America!'" she wrote, capturing an immigrant's first emotions upon arrival. In 1914, established as a lecturer, she wrote *They Who Knock at Our Gates*, her third and last book on immigration. (*Sources*: 472, 525)

1899   La Argentina   (1888?–1936) Spain (Argentina)

In 1899, at age eleven, Argentina, whose legal name was Antonia Mercé, became *première danseuse* with the Madrid Opera. She resigned her position in 1902 in order to study the native dances of Spain. Considered one of the best neoclassicist dancers, she choreographed dances based on the studies she had made. At first, not allowed to present her dances at the opera house, she performed in cafés and music halls and went on tour throughout the world. She danced at the Moulin Rouge in Paris but was not allowed to perform at the Paris Opera until the 1930s. Argentina is credited with establishing the Spanish dance as an art form. (*Sources*: 15, 162, 431, 478, 583, 731, 739)

1899   Emma Hackley   (1867–1922) United States (African American)

Hackley's first effort in behalf of blacks was in 1899, when she wrote articles against racial discrimination in her husband's newspaper in Denver and also founded a fraternal group to further the black cause. Having earned her music degree from the University of Denver in 1900 and unhappily married, she moved to Philadelphia, where she started a church choir and gave concerts. She used the money she earned to make a second trip to Paris to continue voice lessons. Upon her return, she donated her earnings to the promotion of talented blacks like Marion Anderson and Roland Hayes. In 1911 Hackley founded a vocal college in Chicago; when it suffered financial difficulties in 1916, she wrote the *Colored Girl Beautiful*, based on the series of lectures she had given to young black girls to promote racial pride. In 1916 Hackley organized folk-song festivals in black churches around the country and performed these folk songs in Japan in 1920 at her last concert. (*Sources*: 391, 508, 687, 718)

1900　Maude Abbott　(1869–1940) Canada

McGill University refused to admit women students until 1884, when it received a large grant from a private citizen for that express purpose. Shortly thereafter, Abbott won a scholarship to McGill, graduating in 1890. Abbott and others petitioned McGill to accept women into its medical school, but the petition was denied. In the first class of women who studied medicine at the University of Bishop's College Medical School, Abbott won two awards when she graduated in 1894. She then went to Europe to study for an additional three years, returning to Montreal in 1897 to open a practice. In 1900, through the influence of several noted scholars at McGill, Abbott was given the position of curator of the college's medical museum. Thrilled to be at her alma mater, she classified and catalogued all the specimens that had been collected but neglected since the medical school's inception. This work led to her publishing a textbook on gross pathology; Abbott was eventually allowed to teach a course in pathology. In 1910 McGill Medical College granted Abbott an honorary medical degree, even though the college was still unwilling to allow women into its medical school. Abbott published almost 100 papers during her career and was editor of the *Canadian Medical Association Journal*. She retired in 1936 and was writing a medical textbook at the time of her death four years later. (*Sources*: 384, 512)

1900　Yaa Asantewa　(?–1921) Ghana

Nothing is recorded of Asantewa's life prior to her becoming a hero in a war with the British in 1900 and 1901, which was fought to prevent the British from taking the Golden Stool, an important cultural and religious symbol, and ruling Ghana. A queen mother in the Ashanti tribe and living in Kumasi, Asantewa rallied other Ashanti leaders to fight the British, who had been trying to gain a foothold in the region for nearly a century. Asantewa took command of the troops and attacked the fewer than 1,000 British who had retreated to a fort previously built by them and surrounded by thousands of British refugees. Asantewa and her troops cordoned off the area and cut the lines into the fort. The food supply at and around the fort became dangerously low, and people began to die in large numbers. Because of the rapidly deteriorating conditions, the British ordered 1,400 troops from nearby African states into the region. Fierce battles raged for days, but the British had superior armament, especially cannon, and the Ashanti were defeated. Asantewa and the other leaders were sent into exile, and she died in exile in 1921. (*Sources*: 360, 547, 647, 658)

1900   Ellen Glasgow   (1873–1945) United States

Glasgow, a Virginian, purposely chose to dispel the myths of southern plantation life and the swooning belle in her writing. Her central characters, almost always women, had the strength to overcome adversity and generally came from the poor rather than the oft–written about wealthy families. Glasgow portrayed them as having a communion with the land, a theme first evident in *The Voice of the People* (1900) and apparent throughout the rest of her works. *Virginia,* written in 1913, brought her to national attention. *Barren Ground,* written in 1925, was Glasgow's personal favorite, but it was for *In This Our Life* that she received the Pulitzer Prize. (*Sources*: 64, 72, 447, 562, 599, 680, 731, 759)

1900   Ellen Key   (1849–1926) Sweden

Key was reviled and labeled a militant feminist following the publication of her first book, *The Century of the Child,* in 1900. In this book she argued against the customs and laws regarding marriage and sex roles. Key also expressed her high regard for motherhood, though not necessarily within the context of marriage. Key was equally controversial outside Sweden but was also more highly regarded on the Continent. She embarked on a speaking tour throughout Europe lasting from 1903 to 1909 and published her second book, *The Woman Movement,* in 1909. In her books and speeches, she particularly addressed the lack of representation women had in roles other than as wives and mothers only because their work went unrecognized and unrecorded. She also attributed the second-class status of women to the economic domination of men. Key's work was never as radical as it was judged to be by her opponents, who favored the status quo. In *The Renaissance of Motherhood* (1914), for example, she states, "No emancipation must make women indifferent to sexual self-control and motherly devotion." In all, Key wrote thirty books on women and family life. (*Sources*: 34, 42, 60, 67, 80, 127, 676, 681, 731)

1900 Mary Woolman (1860–1940) United States

Woolman was an educator and a conservative proponent of family life and the importance of learning a trade. Her two works on the household were *Sewing Course*, written in 1900, and *Book on Conservation of Clothing*, written in 1918. She also published four books on industrial arts and the textile industry. (*Sources*: 455, 723, 748)

1901 Lily Braun (1865–1916) Germany

Braun began writing in 1892, and is best known as a feminist writer. First married to a philosopher, she later married a socialist and, in 1896, joined the Social Democratic Party, becoming an activist in women's and workers' causes. She aroused controversy in 1901 when she wrote *The Woman Question*, in which she framed women's issues in political terms that advocated the need for socialism yet stressed the importance of independent worth. Braun was asked to resign from the party because of her stance. She continued her work in the more radical wing of a German feminist group and wrote her autobiography in 1911. (*Sources*: 24, 728, 731)

1901 Katharine Davis (1860–1935) United States

Davis brought a learned background to her position when she was appointed superintendent of the New York State Reformatory for Women in 1901: she had been a schoolteacher for ten years before entering Vassar College, from which she graduated in 1892 after two years of study; she had taken classes in nutrition at Columbia University; and she had worked in a settlement house. She had also earned a doctorate from the University of Chicago in 1900. Davis instituted many reforms at the prison and made a systematic study of the inmates, concluding that many were mentally retarded because of genetic inheritance but that many were illiterate and ignorant because of their social backgrounds. Davis hired a woman psychologist to test the women and to collect data on the inmates and convinced philanthropist John D. Rockefeller to establish a science laboratory at the prison. Davis left her post in 1914 to become the first woman commissioner of correction for New York City, a position she held for one year before becoming chairperson of the parole com-mission. Davis's last position was as general secretary of the New York

State Bureau of Social Hygiene from 1918 to 1928. (*Sources*: 351, 616)

1901 Cora Hind (1861–1942) Canada

Hind found her niche in 1898 when her newspaper assigned her to check the effect of recent storms on the wheat crop. In 1901, having already established a reputation as a prognosticator, she was hired by the *Free Press* to evaluate the annual wheat crops. Hind was able to predict within less than 1,000 bushels what the yearly wheat crop would be, making it possible to set a fairly accurate price for the crop in advance of the actual harvest. Hind's work was also used to figure the amount of wheat needed at any particular time to feed the world's poor populations. (*Sources*: 518, 583)

1901 Dita Kinney (1854–1921) United States

Kinney graduated from the Massachusetts General Hospital nursing school in 1892 and became superintendent at an almshouse in Boston and at a county hospital in Minnesota in the following years. In 1898 she joined the army and began a frustrating career as a military nurse. In 1900 Kinney was transferred to the surgeon general's office in Washington, D.C., and worked toward better care for the military patients and better nurses' training; efforts led to the passage of the Army Reorganization Act of 1901. Named the first superintendent of the Army Nurse Corps established in 1901, Kinney was hampered by bureaucratic interference as she attempted to upgrade the military nursing program, raise pay, and improve working conditions for nurses. Kinney believed more nurses would join the military if these changes were made; it is ironic, then, that Kinney was summarily dismissed in 1909 for failing to recruit more nurses. Kinney worked at a civilian hospital for three years, retiring because of poor health. (*Sources*: 81, 455, 462)

1901 Anna Noailles (1876–1933) France

Both born into and married into wealthy families, Noailles led a luxurious life, traveling throughout the world. Her first book of poetry, *The Innumerable Heart* (1901), expressed her awareness of her sensual self and her great need for love. The book was popular and launched her literary career. In subsequent writings she pursued the topic of sensuality but added references to her many travels. During her later years, Noailles became preoccupied with death, as reflected in her books of the period. Noailles was awarded the Grand Prix de Littérateur Académie Française in 1921 and was later elected into the Legion of Honor and the Belgian Academy. (*Sources*: 40, 113, 269)

1901   Renée Vivien   (1877–1909) France (England)

Vivien was born in England but spent her life in France. She was a proclaimed lesbian, and her poetry often reflected the social ostracism she experienced because of her sexual choice. A brilliant woman who, in her early twenties learned Greek in order to read Sappho in the original, Vivien is sometimes described as being one of the greatest woman poets. Vivien was influenced by Charles Baudelaire, from whom she learned to express the poetic balance between corresponding emotions. She published twelve volumes of poetry between 1901 and 1909. Vivien also wrote novels and essays that reflected her melancholy. She starved herself to death in 1909. (*Sources*: 40, 315)

1901   Akiko Yosano   (1878–1942) Japan

Yosano is considered to have revived the ancient and traditional Japanese form of poetry; however, her first book of poetry was severely criticized for its eroticism and its antipatriotism. In 1900 Yosano sent her poetry to a newspaper editor whom she married the next year; her first book, *Tangled Hair*, was published in 1901 and was followed by *Dream Flowers* in 1906. Yosano continued to write and founded a school for girls in 1921. She wrote her last book of poetry in 1942 and dedicated it to her husband, who had died a few years earlier. (*Sources*: 80, 594, 623, 681, 731)

1902   Nora Bayes   (1880–1928) United States

In 1902, at the age of twenty-two, Bayes became a vaudeville star at the Orpheum Theatre in New York. By 1904 she was performing in Europe, where she was equally successful; she returned to New York in 1907 to star in the first Ziegfeld's Follies. Bayes introduced several songs that became associated with her. "Take Me Out to the Ballgame" and "Shine On, Harvest Moon," a song she cowrote with her husband, Jack Norworth, were among her most famous. In 1919 she started a small theater in New York bearing her name on the roof. She wrote her own billing, which read "Nora Bayes, Assisted and Admired by Jack Norworth." (*Sources*: 352, 548, 679)

1902 Martha Berry (1866–1942) United States

Berry grew up in a comfortable home in Georgia but became concerned about the health and lack of education of the poor children in the nearby hills; when several children appeared at her home, she both read to them and gave them meals. Word of her generosity spread quickly, and she soon found her informal classes filled with children and adults. Asking the adults to repair an old church to use as a classroom, she began a school for children in 1902; it later developed into three schools. With her inheritance, Berry founded a boarding school that started with five children and soon burgeoned into a much larger, coeducational school. The children could pay their tuition and board by performing chores at the school. She taught home economics and crafts, the children displaying their handiwork at fairs to bring in money to help support the school. One of her greatest benefactors was Henry Ford, who donated $4 million for the erection of several new buildings and facilities. Berry was later made a regent of the university system in Georgia, was given several honorary degrees, and in 1925 was presented with the Medal for Distinguished Service by President Calvin Coolidge. (*Sources*: 337, 391)

1902 Marie Bregendahl (1867–1940) Denmark

Bregendahl published her first book, *At the Sickbed of Lars*, in 1902 at the age of thirty-five. Her stories, set on the west coast of Denmark, showed a profound understanding of the harshness of the lives of the people; this is considered to be the greatest strength of Bregendahl's writing. *A Night of Death*, which appeared in 1912, became her best-known and first-translated work, though her principal works are generally recognized as the two she wrote in 1923, *Pictures from the Life of the Sea-Valley People*, and 1935, *Holser Hauge and His Wife*, both multiple-volume books. (*Sources*: 80, 174, 673)

1902 Marguerite Carré (1881–1947) France

Although she was not favored by critics, Carré was nevertheless a popular operatic singer in Paris. After studying in the conservatories in Bordeaux and Paris, she made her debut in

1902 at the Opéra Comique and in the same year married its director. She sang several premier performances of well-known operas, playing the leading role in *Madama Butterfly* in its first production in France. Upon her retirement from the stage, she taught voice. (*Sources:* 416, 489)

1902 Margaret Murray (1863–1963) England (India)

In 1902, when Murray conducted her first archaelogical dig in Egypt, she was the first woman to lead an excavation. She continued her studies in archeaology and Egyptology in Malta and Palestine until 1938. Murray was also a professor of Egyptology at Oxford University and at University College in London between 1910 and 1932. A prolific author, she wrote and lectured on witchcraft and sorcery. (*Sources:* 262, 626)

1903 Mary Austin (1868–1934) United States

Austin began to write upon moving to California after she graduated from college in Illinois, her home state. She felt compelled to write about the Native Americans who had befriended her after her arrival. Austin's first four novels described Indian life; the first, *The Land of Little Rain*, was published in 1903. Also a feminist, she wrote *A Woman of Genius* in 1912. Austin produced more than 30 books and 200 articles in her long career. (*Sources:* 34, 163, 447, 522)

1903 Gertrude Kasebier (1852–1934) United States

Kasebier moved from the Midwest to New York City, where she married in 1874. In 1888 she began art lessons at the Pratt Institute, remaining there for several years before traveling to Paris for further study. Becoming more interested in photography than painting, she returned to the United States in 1897 to open her own portrait studio. In 1902 she was a cofounder of a photography group, many members of which went on to become well known in the field. Kasebier's career was established in 1903 when her work was featured in the prestigious photography magazine *Camera Work*. She soon became noted for her photographs of Native Americans and women and children as well as for her use of a soft focus rather than the conventional sharper one. One of Kasebier's more notable photographs, *Blessed Art Thou Among Women*, is of a woman leading her child to an open door. Kasebier had several exhibitions of her work between 1906 and 1926. (*Sources*: 538, 548)

1903   Wanda Landowska   (1879–1959) Poland

Landowska made her debut as a pianist in 1903, playing one composition on the harpsichord; this approach became her signature. She soon gained a reputation as a harpsichordist and expert on music of the seventeenth century and before. Landowska was also noted for blending old and contemporary music in her concerts. She opened her own piano and harpsichord school outside Paris, where she not only taught but also gave Sunday afternoon concerts that introduced the custom of discussing the music with her audience before each performance. Landowski's large library of music and her invaluable collection of harpsichords and other keyboard instruments were confiscated by the Nazis during World War II. She fled France at the beginning of the war and eventually settled in the United States, where she gave few concerts and devoted her time to studying Bach's *Well-Tempered Clavier*. She received numerous awards both in the United States and abroad. (*Sources*: 16, 236, 324, 326, 431, 440, 518, 583, 599, 739)

1903   Emmeline Pankhurst   (1858–1928) England

In 1903 Pankhurst founded the Woman's Social and Political Union for the express purpose of gaining legal rights for women, especially the right to vote. Although her father was reluctant to support his daughters in any other than traditional roles, her mother had played an active part in lobbying for passage of the Married Women's Property Act. Carrying on in the family feminist tradition, Pankhurst married the drafter of the first women's suffrage bill, and her daughter Christabel was also an activist in the women's movement. Pankhurst and her group became more militant when legislation failed to be enacted. She and her daughter were arrested several times, and Pankhurst was subjected to the Cat and Mouse Act (see HERTHA AYRTON). She suspended her group's activities during World War I but resumed them in 1918. Pankhurst ran as a candidate for the Conservative Party to represent Whitechapel after the passage of an act that gave the vote to women over thirty; however, Pankhurst died before she could be elected and one month before the passage of the revised Representation of the People Act enfranchising all women. (*Sources*: 277, 333, 339, 530, 699, 731)

1904   Ch'iu Chin   (1875–1907) China

Ch'iu is called the first revolutionary woman in China. She started a girls' school in Peking in 1904 and was in open opposition to the practice of binding girls' feet. She left her husband and two children to join her cousin's revolutionary group and helped to organize a secret society. Ch'iu and her cousin were captured in 1907, in an uprising in which her cousin was executed, and Ch'iu herself was first tortured, then beheaded. Ch'iu left the cryptic message, "The autumn rain and wind sadden us." (*Sources*: 60, 125, 567, 594, 621, 647, 731)

1904   Colette [Sidonie-Gabrielle Colette]   (1873–1954) France

Colette was for a time married to a novelist who forced her to write, added sensational passages, and published the result under his name. Upon embarking on her own literary career, in 1904, Colette often wrote of strong but sensuous women who dominated life. In 1906 she became a music-hall dancer, an experience she described in her novel *The Vagabond* (1911). She married a well-known editor, and during World War I turned their estate into a hospital. She divorced her second husband in 1925 and married for a third time in 1935. Colette was the recipient of many awards, including the Legion of Honor in 1920 for her war work; she was made a grand officer of the Legion of Honor in 1953. In 1945 she became the first woman to be elected to the Académie Goncourt. (*Sources*: 53, 192, 731)

1904   Marie Stopes   (1880–1958) England

Like her mother, a noted feminist, Stopes became interested in women's issues. She graduated from college in 1903 with three simultaneously earned undergraduate degrees, and a year later, writing her dissertation in German, earned her doctorate at the University of Munich. In 1904 Stopes also became the first woman professor in the science division of Manchester University and in 1910 was made a fellow of University College for her work in plant fossils. Between 1910 and 1915 she published two scientific books on fossils. Her first marriage having been annulled, she remarried in 1918 and began her crusade to educate women about birth control. Stopes viewed birth control more as a way to enhance sexual pleasure than as a means of population control for the poor. Her first book on sex, written in 1918, was widely praised and translated into several languages. In 1921 she opened a birth control clinic, which brought on long legal battles with the opponents of her educational policies. (*Sources*: 473, 558, 559, 621, 731, 739)

1905   Sarah Askew   (1877–1942) United States

Askew was born in Alabama and graduated with a degree in library science from Pratt Institute in 1904. In 1905, after having worked for a library in Cleveland, Ohio, Askew accepted a position in the New Jersey library system. At that time there were relatively few libraries in the state, and in many towns there was no access to a library. Often traveling by horse and buggy, Askew assessed the state's library needs and over the next thirty-seven years established more than 350 libraries throughout New Jersey. She also organized one of the first mobile units to carry books to isolated towns. During World War I, Askew solicited books to be sent to military hospitals and helped initiate what was called the Victory Book Campaign, a drive for books for military personnel. The new library at William Paterson College, built in 1956, was named in Askew's honor. (*Sources*: 578, 718)

1906   Anna Comstock   (1854–1930) United States

Comstock married her professor in zoology at Cornell University in 1878 and did not return to finish her degree until 1885. Following her marriage, she spent two years assisting her husband in his work at the U.S. Department of Agriculture in Washington, D.C. Upon their return to Cornell and her completion of her degree in 1906, she published her first book (though she did not use her own name until its second printing). During the depression of the 1890s, Comstock wrote and il-lustrated brochures for a program at Cornell University sponsored by the federal government. She also produced wood engravings for several of her husband's books. Comstock gained a reputation as a speaker, often traveling to colleges and schools in other states to lecture on natural history. She was named the first woman assistant professor at Cornell in 1897, an appointment that was rescinded two years later; she was reappointed to the position in 1913 and made a full professor in 1920. (*Sources*: 329, 532, 548, 556, 587)

1906　Emma Goldman　(1869–1940) United States (Russia)

Goldman arrived in the United States at the age of seventeen and began working in a clothing factory. By 1889 she had become a socialist and later became an anarchist. In 1906 Goldman became the editor of the socialist paper *Mother Earth*, in which she called for women's freedom and equality to men, an idea anarchists in general did not support. Her advocacy for free love and selective motherhood as well as her indifference to the legal changes espoused by suffragists also alienated that group. She was both admired for her courage and denounced for her policies, and on several occasions her life was threatened. Goldman's most serious problems came in 1917, when she opposed mandatory drafting for men to serve in the war. She was tried and sentenced to two years in jail for her views and upon her release was deported to Russia. Goldman became disillusioned with the new revolutionary government in Russia and wrote two books in 1923 and 1924 about her disappointment. She spent the remainder of her life traveling around the world and wrote her autobiography in 1931. (*Sources*: 102, 361, 627, 717, 728)

1906　Beatrice Grimshaw　(1871–1953) Ireland

Grimshaw started out as a journalist, writing first in Ireland and next in London. An avid cyclist, she set a new twenty-four-hour world record. She used her journalistic talents to earn travel to the Pacific South Seas. She was the first white woman to visit several of the islands. Grimshaw published her first book on her island travels in 1906 and wrote more than thirty novels and short stories in her thirty-four years in the islands. She retired to Australia at the end of her career. (*Sources*: 78, 219, 731, 751)

1906　Frieda Hempel　(1885–1955) Germany

Hempel studied piano and voice before making her operatic debut in 1906 at the Berlin Royal Opera. Following a second debut in London at Covent Garden the next year, she sang throughout Europe. Hempel returned to the Berlin Royal Opera until she was engaged to sing at the Metropolitan Opera in New York in 1912; she remained there for nearly a decade. In 1911 Hempel had been Richard Strauss's personal choice for the premier of his opera *Der Rosenkavalier* in Berlin. After 1920 Hempel preferred to give concerts and continued to be successful in the United States and Europe alike. (*Sources*: 325, 431)

1906 Zofia Nalkowska (1885–1954) Poland
A member of the literary Young Poland group that promoted new approaches in writing, Nalkowska wrote from a feminist perspective. She published her first book, *Women*, in 1906; it was translated into English in 1920. Her work was noted for its technical simplicity. Nalkowska continued to write books and essays until the year of her death. (*Sources*: 264, 394)

1906 Adelaide Nutting (1858–1948) United States (Canada)
Nutting migrated to the United States in 1874 to study art but instead embarked upon a career in nursing, graduating from the nursing school at Johns Hopkins in 1891. She was hired and advanced from teacher to superintendent of nurses at Johns Hopkins within thirteen years. During her tenure, she reduced the twelve-hour workday for nurses to eight hours and instituted a three-year nurses' training program. In 1906 Nutting was appointed a professor at Teachers College at Columbia University, becoming the first nurse to hold a teaching professorship. Nutting was also active in helping to found nursing societies as well as chair the committee that established a nursing school in France. She wrote several books on nursing, one of which she coauthored with another nursing pioneer, LAVINIA DOCK. (*Sources*: 74, 79, 81, 455, 462, 537, 583, 634)

1907 Delmira Agustini (1886–1914) Uruguay
Agustini was murdered by her husband shortly after their marriage in 1914, but before then, she had published three volumes of her poems: *The White Book* in 1907 and other collections in 1910 and 1913. Her poetry is noted for warmth, sensuality, and passion not usually found in works of the postmodern era. Agustini's fourth book of collected poems was published posthumously in 1924 and reissued in 1955. (*Sources*: 128, 155, 717)

1907 Mary Beard (1876–1958) United States
Beard graduated from DePauw University in 1897 and taught school until her marriage in 1900. Accompanying her husband to England, while he attended Oxford University, she helped found Ruskin Hall, a workingmen's college at Oxford.

Upon their return, both Beard and her husband attended Columbia University. In 1907 Beard became an organizer for the National Women's Trade Union League and organized its strike in 1909, later editing *The Woman Voter*. From 1913 to 1919 Beard was an active member of the women's suffrage group headed by ALICE PAUL but resigned because she preferred to work for protective legislation for women rather than for their equal rights. Given credit as coauthor with her husband of a series of history books, Beard until recently received little attention for her books on women's issues or for her effort to organize a World Center for Women's Archives, which was abandoned for lack of financial support. Her last and perhaps her major work was *Woman as a Force in History*, published in 1946. (*Sources*: 470, 627, 687, 728, 731, 755)

1907   Emily Bissell   (1861–1948) United States
Bissell was the organizer of the first chapter of the American Red Cross in the state of Delaware. Having heard of a project in Denmark by which funds were raised for the fight against tuberculosis (a prevalent disease at the time), Bissell in 1907 designed and printed the first stamps that became known as Christmas seals. The proceeds from these stamps were used to provide a hospital for tuberculosis sufferers. The printing and sale of the stamps was later taken over by the National Tuberculosis Association, and the hospital Bissell had established was renamed in her honor in 1953. (*Sources*: 98, 718)

1907   Frances Densmore   (1867–1957) United States
In 1907, after studying music at Oberlin College, Densmore began her study of Native American music for the Bureau of American Ethnology, later also working for the Smithsonian Institution. Through her recordings she was able to explain Indian cultures and the circumstances dictating their different types of music. In 1941 Densmore received the National Association for American Composers and Conductors Award for her expert studies. She also did work for the Library of Congress, which now houses her collection of more than 3,000 recordings of Native American music, including many recordings she transcribed at her own expense after funding was terminated. (*Sources*: 203, 634, 718)

1907   Edna Foley   (1878–1943) United States
Foley earned her degree at Smith College in 1901 and then earned a nursing degree in 1904, after which she worked at various children's hospitals. In 1907 she enrolled in the visiting nurses program at the Boston School of Social Work to increase her skills. Foley combined this interest with her interest in tuberculosis (an almost always fatal disease at the time), accepting a position as a supervisor for the visiting nurses at the Chicago Tuberculosis Institute. In 1911 she became the superintendent of the Chicago Visiting Nurses Association, where she remained until her retirement. While serving as superintendent, Foley increased the acceptance and number of black nurses in the visiting nursing field. Foley's manual for visiting nurses became the cornerstone textbook in the field and was reissued for many years. In 1916 she served as director of the National Society for the Study and Prevention of Tuberculosis, in 1919 as chief nurse for the American Red Cross Tuberculosis Commission in Italy, and in 1931 as director of the Chicago Tuberculosis Institute. She was also one of the organizers of the National Organization of Public Health Nurses in 1912 and served as its president in 1920. Foley was awarded an honorary doctorate from her alma mater, Smith College, in 1928. Among her other honors was the Florence Nightingale Medal she received in 1937. (*Sources*: 81, 462)

1907   Myra Hess   (1890–1965) England
Hess revealed her potential as a pianist by the age of seven, when she was enrolled in a major music school in London; by the age of twelve she had won a scholarship to the Royal Academy of Music. She made her professional debut with the London Philharmonic Orchestra in 1907 and received excellent reviews; however, she chose to withdraw from performing until she had studied further. She again began to perform in 1914 and established a notable reputation throughout Europe. Hess next traveled to the United States, performing concerts there for almost two decades. The outbreak of World War II curtailed her tours, and she returned to England, where she established a midday-concert series at the National Gallery; she and other great performers played even during air raids. Great morale boosters, these concerts were attended by an estimated 1 million people during the six years they were

given, endearing Hess to her compatriots. Early in her career Hess was noted for her interpretations of Robert Schumann and later for her eloquent playing of Johannes Brahms and Ludwig van Beethoven. Hess was the recipient of numerous awards: she was made a dame in the Order of the British Empire in 1936, received an honorary degree from Cambridge University in 1949, and became the only woman to receive a Gold Medal from the Royal Philharmonic Society. (*Sources*: 15, 52, 221, 326, 518)

1907   Sara Teasdale   (1884–1933) United States
Teasdale graduated from Hosmer Hall in 1903 and, with the help of her professors and friends, in 1904 began publishing a literary magazine called the *Wheel*. Her first book of poetry was published in 1907 and was followed in 1911 and 1915 by two more books of her collected poems. In 1918 Teasdale was awarded the prestigious Columbia University Poetry Society Prize for *Love Songs*. Her early writings were noted for their classical style and conventional verse, but her later work reflected a more mature and delicate style. Teasdale, in poor health, died of an overdose of barbiturates in 1933. (*Sources*: 98, 450, 548, 616)

1907   Sigrid Undset   (1882–1949) Norway (Denmark)
Undset was the daughter of an archaeologist who, although he died when she was eleven, instilled in her a knowledge and love of Norwegian history. Undset wrote her first book in 1907 after working for years in an office to support herself. This book established Undset's oft-used theme of the naive and idealistic young woman caught in her own tribulations. *Kristin Lavransdatter* (1920–1922), a three-volume historical novel set in fourteenth-century Norway, is considered her masterpiece. *Olav Audunssön* (four volumes) was published 1925–1927. She was awarded the Nobel Prize in literature in 1928. Undset wrote her autobiography, *The Longest Years*, in 1934. She lived in the United States during World War II, returning to Norway in 1945. (*Sources*: 80, 312, 731, 732)

1908   Sara Baker   (1873–1945) United States
Baker graduated from the Women's Medical College of New York in 1898 and practiced pediatrics. In 1908 she was appointed director of the new Bureau of Child Hygiene in New

York to care for children from birth to legal adulthood. Under her directorship, New York City was able to establish the lowest infant mortality rate of any major city in the United States. Baker was also the author of numerous books on child care and health. (*Sources*: 455, 556)

1908   Jane Delano   (1862–1919) United States
Delano was one of the first to recognize the need for the coordination of services in times of crisis. Through her work as superintendent of the Army Nurse Corps and as chair of the Red Cross Nursing Service, she established the first group of Red Cross nurses. As a graduate nurse holding several positions as a superintendent, Delano volunteered her services to the Red Cross during numerous crises and in 1908 devoted her full attention to developing their nursing services. She was responsible for causing the first group of Red Cross nurses to be sent to Europe in 1914 at the outbreak of the war. She also organized a nursing service during the influenza epidemic of 1918. Delano also wrote several books on nursing as well as one on home nursing care. A tireless worker, Delano died in France while reviewing the Red Cross wartime nursing program. She is buried in Arlington National Cemetery, and there is a memorial at the Red Cross Headquarters in Washington, D.C., to Delano and the almost 300 nurses who died while serving in World War I. Delano left her estate to the nursing association of her alma mater, Bellevue Hospital. (*Sources*: 81, 105, 202, 378, 447, 532, 537, 548, 556)

1908   Virginia Gildersleeve   (1877–1965) United States
In her autobiography, Gildersleeve admits that she drifted into both scholarship and education. She did not take up serious study until graduate school; under the aegis of a professor whom she greatly admired, she wrote in French her master's thesis on the feudal system in France in the Middle Ages. She happened upon the field of education when she was offered a position teaching English at Barnard College in 1900. Barnard sponsored her doctoral studies when Gildersleeve threatened to resign because of a triple teaching load; she earned her doctorate in 1908. In that same year she published her first book, *Government Regulations of the Elizabethan Drama*. She returned to Barnard to teach and also taught additional courses at Columbia University to supplement her income. In 1911

Gildersleeve, already the author of several books on education, was appointed a dean at Barnard, a position she held for thirty-six years. Gildersleeve served on many prestigious committees on education throughout her career. (*Sources:* 74, 87, 355, 364, 537, 634, 676, 759)

1908   Rose Knox   (1857–1950) United States
Upon being widowed in 1908, Knox, who had worked with her husband to build a gelatin business, became its sole proprietor at the age of fifty-one. She treated her employees well, being one of the first to establish a five-day work week and granting vacation time and sick leave. Her advertisements were aimed at women, and she wrote a food column for a local newspaper in which she gave recipes that used gelatin. Knox was civic-minded and donated generously to the city of Johnstown, New York, where her company was located. Knox did not retire as director until her ninetieth year. (*Sources:* 98, 548, 583, 628, 718)

1908   Henrietta Leavitt   (1868–1921) United States
Head of the department of photometry, Leavitt was a distinguished astronomer at the Harvard Observatory. She discovered four novae and over 2,000 variable stars. She is best known for her work on the brightness of stars and the relationship between the brightness and distance of stars. This discovery contributed greatly to the determination of the size of the Milky Way. (*Sources:* 9, 105, 238, 548, 587, 634, 739)

1909   Jelly d'Arányi   (1895–1966) Hungary
In 1909 d'Arányi gave the first of her many violin performances with her sister. She was greatly favored by composers: she gave the premier performances of two of Béla Bartók's sonatas and of pieces by Maurice Ravel and Vaughan Williams, all of whom had dedicated the music to her. Later in her career she gave recitals with pianist MYRA HESS. (*Sources:* 15, 116, 160, 468, 670, 731)

1909   Florence Blanchfield   (1882–1971) United States
Because of Blanchfield's efforts, members of the Army Nurse Corps were the first women to receive commissions in the army. She had received her nursing degree in 1906 in Pennsylvania and had worked at various hospitals until 1913,

when she went as a civil service worker to the canal zone in Panama. At the beginning of World War I, she joined the Army Nurse Corps and started her major career. Blanchfield worked as a nurse throughout the war and returned to the army in 1920 for a second tour of duty. At that time, nurses were not given relative rank or salary compared to male officers; Blanchfield began her efforts to equalize nurses' rank and promotion opportunities. Kept at the rank of lieutenant during her tenure, Blanchfield was finally promoted to captain in 1939. Within the Army Nurse Corps she worked with JULIA FLIKKE; they gained the equal standing for nurses they had sought—and both were promoted— but it was ten years before they received back pay for their military rank. Blanchfield became the seventh superintendent of the Army Nurse Corps in 1943 and continued a very active effort on behalf of army nurses. During World War II she established field hospitals in war zones, gained permission for nurses to wear battle fatigues that were more appropriate than the standard white uniforms, and increased the number of army nurses to almost 60,000. Her efforts after the war were no less ambitious or successful: in 1947 the Army Nurse Corps was incorporated into the regular army, with nurses receiving equal rank and pay with their male counterparts. Blanchfield was awarded the Distinguished Service Medal by the army and was the recipient of the Florence Nightingale Medal of the International Red Cross for her work. Blanchfield was buried in Arlington National Cemetery; an army hospital is named in her honor. (*Sources:* 81, 455, 462)

1909 Annie Burton (1859–?) United States (African American)

It is likely that nothing would ever have been recorded about the existence of Burton had she not, like HARRIET WILSON, written a book about her life. In 1909 a teacher at the Franklin Institute in Boston encouraged and assisted Burton (then forty-four) in writing her autobiography. In it, Burton described her traumatic childhood: at the age of six, she was first abandoned by and later reunited with her mother, a slave who was forced to run away without her children. Burton's sporadic schooling started when she worked as a nursemaid for a family that taught her to read and write. She did not attend school until, at the age of twenty, she spent six months in a high school. Because of illness, Burton never finished her studies at the Franklin Institute, but she did complete a composition on Abraham Lincoln she would have presented at her graduation. (*Sources*: 85, 507, 688, 696)

1909   Crystal Eastman   (1881–1928) United States
Eastman graduated from Vassar College in 1903 and earned her law degree in 1907, after which she investigated industrial accidents for the Russell Sage Foundation. In 1909 she became the first woman appointed to the New York State Employers' Liability Commission. A suffragist as well as a worker's advocate, Eastman in 1913 helped found the organization that later became the National Woman's Party. She was also a founder of the Feminist Congress, which convened in New York in 1919. When Eastman moved to England, she became involved in the women's movement there for a few years before her untimely death at the age of forty-six. (*Sources*: 34, 74, 98, 470, 584, 627, 680, 722, 728, 731, 763)

1909   Nora Stanton Blatch De Forest   (1883–1971) United States
De Forest was the granddaughter of Elizabeth Cady Stanton and the daughter of the equally famous suffragist HARRIOT STANTON BLATCH. She graduated with honors as a civil engineer from Cornell University in 1905. Her first job was in drafting, and in 1907 she was named assistant engineer for the New York Board of Water Supply. Her last position was as chief engineer for a private steel company. In 1909 De Forest was elected the first woman junior member of the American Society of Civil Engineers but was dropped from membership seven years later, when she was to become a full member. De Forest lost her suit against the society; it was 1927 before another woman was elected to the organization. In 1912 she left the engineering field to devote her full energy to women's suffrage, as had her grandmother and mother. (*Sources*: 98, 455, 501, 584, 634, 773)

1909   Alma Gluck   (1884–1938) United States (Romania)
As a young immigrant, Gluck attended secretarial school at Union College and took a job as an office clerk; it was her husband, an insurance salesman, who recognized her singing talent. In 1906 she began to study music with Arturo Buzzi-Peccia. Gluck made her operatic debut at the Metropolitan Opera in 1909

in *Werther* and sang numerous minor roles at the Met over the next three years. A short time later, Gluck began to perform as a concert singer; she was immensely popular, particularly when she performed with her second husband, the noted violinist Efrem Zimbalist. Gluck also made numerous popular recordings, and her rendition of "Carry Me Back to Ol' Virginny" is reported to have sold close to 2 million copies. Gluck was a cofounder of the American Guild of Musical Artists and the Musical Art Quartet. She retired from the stage in 1925. (*Sources:* 325, 439, 525, 616)

1909 Gabriele Münter (1877–1962) Germany
   Münter did not begin to study painting seriously until 1901, when, unable to enroll at the Royal Academy because she was female, she attended the School of the Association of Women Artists. In 1902 she took classes at the new Phalanx School founded by the famous artist Wassily Kandinsky. Münter and Kandinsky soon became lovers and remained together until 1915. Münter's work demonstrates an emphasis on color as an independent element that is much closer in style to the fauvist school than to the German expressionism popular at that time. She is also known for her innovative folk art. In 1908 Münter and Kandinsky settled in the Bavarian Alps, where they shared quarters with another famous painter, Alexej Jawlensky, and his companion, the artist Marianne von Werefkin. In 1909 these four artists founded the New Artists' Association of Munich, but a disagreement soon followed, and Kandinsky and Münter left to organize the first Blue Rider exhibit, choosing the name from an avant-garde art publication. Münter first showed her collected works at this exhibit. Münter and Kandinsky separated at about the time World War I began, Münter going to Switzerland and Kandinsky to Russia, where he later married. Münter continued to credit him for influencing her art and in 1957 donated much of his original work along with her own to a German gallery. (*Sources:* 374, 390, 395, 407, 607, 608, 717, 726)

1909 Emmuska Orczy (1865–1947) Hungary
   Orczy is best known as the author of *The Scarlet Pimpernel* (1905); none of her sequels to it were as popular. Orczy also, however, wrote a series of detective stories that enjoyed more success than the sequels to her famous book. Orczy's first detective novel, *The Old Man in the Corner,* appeared in 1909 and was followed by

two more in 1910 and 1925. She was also the author of several other books, her first *The Emperor's Candlesticks* in 1899 and her last her autobiography in 1947. Orczy was also a minor but somewhat accomplished artist. (*Sources*: 53, 78, 273, 500, 599, 751)

1909 Hazel Hotchkiss Wightman (1887–1974) United States

In 1909 Wightman won the first of forty-eight U.S. tennis titles she earned over her forty-five-year career. Noted especially for her skill in doubles matches, she won Olympic gold medals in doubles and mixed doubles in 1924 and was often referred to as the Queen of the Volley and Queen Mother of Tennis. Her love of the sport never waned. In 1923 she inaugurated the Wightman Cup tournament for women's tennis, which alternates each year between London and the College of William and Mary in Williamsburg, Virginia. (*Sources*: 20, 74, 98, 518, 685, 718)

1910 Harriot Stanton Blatch (1856–1940) United States

Blatch was the middle generation in the trigenerational suffragist family of Elizabeth Cady Stanton, Harriet Stanton Blatch, and NORA STANTON BLATCH DE FOREST. Blatch graduated from Vassar College in 1878 and, after marrying in 1882, lived in England for twenty years. During these years, Blatch was not only active in the women's suffrage movement but also earned her master's degree from Vassar, her thesis based on the women's movement in England. In 1907 Blatch organized a women's group that later merged with the National Woman's Party. In 1910 she led the first large-scale suffrage parade in New York City with Rheta Dorr, CARRIE CATT, and ALICE PAUL, all astride horses and dressed in elegant outfits. In 1917 she was one of the organizers of a 1,000-woman march on the White House to win the right to vote. Blatch wrote several books on the women's movement, weaving into them the issue of peace; she had been a pacifist during World War I. Blatch's autobiography, *Challenging Years*, was published the year of her death. (*Sources*: 34, 455, 470, 501, 504, 627, 634, 680, 699)

1910 Margaret Morris (1891–1980) England

In 1910 Morris opened her own dance school, where she taught a free style of dancing adapted to meet the needs of physical rehabilitation programs. Although her later dance schools were less successful, she continued to promote her dancing through a publication, *The Margaret Morris Movement*. Morris was also the author of three books on dance and its beneficial qualities. (*Sources*: 15, 259, 478, 518)

1910   Theodate Pope Riddle   (1868–1946) United States

One of the first woman architects in the United States, Riddle had to be privately tutored for her classes at Princeton University because the university would not admit women into its School of Architecture. She worked with the noted architect Stanford White on the design for her parents' estate, Hill-Stead, in Farmington, Connecticut. By 1910 Riddle was a registered architect in Connecticut and New York. Riddle designed eight buildings, many of them schools and private estates; she is best known for her architectural restoration and new design for the birthplace of President Theodore Roosevelt. Her other outstanding design was the Avon Old Farms School in Avon, Connecticut. The project took nine years to complete because it was built using only sixteenth-century tools, in keeping with its English Tudor design. In 1918 Riddle was elected a member of the American Institute of Architects and in 1926 was one of the first women to be made an AIA fellow. (*Sources*: 350, 432, 718, 720, 771)

1910   Huda Sharawi   (1882–1947) Egypt

Sharawi was born into an upper-class Egyptian family during a period of political instability and social repression. Egypt had been ruled by the Ottomans, the French, and, during Sharawi's lifetime, the British. The establishment of Islam as the state religion brought about radical changes in the social structure and the position of women. Mohammed gave women less than equal status with men, though he did limit the number of wives a man could have. This deemphasis of polygyny resulted in higher esteem for the monogamous family, its honor resting on the chastity and virtue of the women family members. The wearing of veils became a symbol of family honor and a way of discouraging dishonor. It was no small gesture of defiance when Sharawi cast her veil off after attending an international women's conference in 1923. A small number of women reluctantly followed her example, but the majority ignored it or were too fearful to imitate it. Sharawi had first defied custom in 1910 when she opened a school for the education of girls, later offered secondary education and eventually admission into university classes. Sharawi organized teachers' and women's unions and, in 1944, established the All-Arab Federation of Women. (*Sources*: 360, 454, 621, 728)

1910 Marina Tsvetayeva (1892–1941) Russia
A child prodigy, Tsvetayeva's first book of poetry was published to wide acclaim in 1910 when she was only eighteen. Two other successful books followed. During the Russian Revolution, she and her husband lived in exile, and she continued to write and publish her poetry. She also became a close friend of another noted poet, ANNA AKHMATOVA. With the rise of fascism, Tsvetayeva returned to the Soviet Union, where neither she nor her work were made welcome. Always a lonely and melancholy person, she committed suicide shortly after the start of World War II. Her work is only now being read in her native country. (*Sources*: 80, 309, 562, 627)

1910 Ella Young (1845–1918) United States
In 1910 Young was named the first woman president of the National Education Association. Having graduated from the Chicago Normal School in 1862, she began her teaching career in Chicago that same year. Young was named superintendent of schools in 1900 and also taught at the University of Chicago between 1899 and 1905. Young became principal of her alma mater in 1905, a position she held until 1909. (*Sources*: 548, 616)

1911 Rebecca Felton (1835–1930) United States
Felton had the quickness to capture the seemingly ordinary events going on around her, the intelligence to assess their meaning and value, and the talent needed to share her perceptions with readers. These characteristics are evident in both her books. In Felton's first book, *My Memoirs of Georgia Politics* (1911), she explains the political-legal system and how it operates within the social structure; with insight and clarity, she shows how the system fostered the conundrum of women's suffrage. Felton was able to address interpretations and rationalizations without resorting to argument or vindictiveness; she gave clear explanations of indisputable facts. In her second book, *Country Life in Georgia* (1919), Felton draws on the memories of her childhood and the events surrounding it,

presenting them from a child's perspective yet weaving in her adult reassessment of those years. Her accomplishment is all the more remarkable for having been achieved when she was eighty-four. (*Sources*: 84, 332, 750, 756)

1911   Josefina Martinez-Alvarez   (1890–) Puerto Rico

Martinez-Alvarez first entered the Peabody Conservatory of Music in Baltimore, but an interest in the health of the poorest people in her country soon led her to enroll at the Woman's Medical College of Pennsylvania. She graduated with honors in 1911, becoming one of the first women physicians from Puerto Rico. She completed additional medical studies in New York and Baltimore. Upon her return to Puerto Rico to practice, she discovered that tuberculosis was a common disease among the peasant class and caused numerous deaths; she is credited with developing a method for its detection. As well as maintaining her private practice, she taught at the medical college and at several other institutions. Martinez-Alvarez was an active proponent of women's suffrage and a leader in the women's movement (Puerto Rican women gained the right to vote in 1932). She was active in or a founder of numerous organizations and received many awards for her civic, feminist, and medical contributions, one of which was an honorary medical diploma in 1961 by the American Association of Women Doctors. At age ninety-five, Martinez-Alvarez was still a voice in the women's movement. (*Sources*: 721, 757)

1911   Harriet Quimby   (1875?–1912) United States

With an established career as a writer for a prestigious magazine, Quimby applied for a pilot's license. Sure that she would disqualify herself, the club officials allowed her to demonstrate the flight required to be licensed. Quimby not only passed the test, becoming the first woman to hold a pilot's license, but also broke the club's accuracy landing record by putting her plane down within 8 feet of where she had taken off. Like BESSIE COLEMAN and MATILDE MOISANT, Quimby did exhibition flying. Known for her flamboyant, plum-colored satin flying outfit, she was very popular with crowds because of her daring. In July 1912, a year after obtaining her license, Quimby was killed in a 20-mile speed record flight in Boston, a crowd watching her body plummet into the bay. A possible cause for the accident was that she had taken the plane to a higher altitude than it could manage, the highest altitude at which a woman had yet flown. (*Sources*: 396, 441, 465, 518, 585, 685, 779)

1911   Blanche Scott   (1886–1970) United States

In 1911 Blanche Scott and HARRIET QUIMBY became the first American women to fly an airplane. A year earlier, Scott had been the first woman to drive alone across the United States. Working with Thomas Baldwin, a pioneer in dirigibles, Scott learned to fly and in 1911 made the first solo flight by a woman. She had previously trained as a pilot in 1910 as part of an exhibition team but was dropped from the team after only one flight. The U.S. Post Office issued a stamp in Scott's honor in 1980. (*Sources*: 396, 439, 441, 672, 685)

1911   Anne Sedgwick   (1873–1935) England (United States)

Sedgwick's literary career began when she married in 1908 and moved to England. She took advantage of the opportunity to observe and contrast her old environment with her new one, which resulted in her writing her first book, *Tante*, in 1911. Sedgwick was equally successful with subsequent books, including *Adrienne Toner* and *The Little French Girl*. Her illustrious brother-in-law, Charles Marquand, and his wife were a rich source of inspiration for her. With affection and insight, she described Marquand's personality and talent and his wife's scatterbrained habits—forgetting to take the dog along when she wanted to walk her pet, having an automobile accident because she was distracted by other events—that so vexed Marquand. Sedgwick is in fact best known for her character studies. (*Sources*: 105, 363, 426, 562)

1912   Halide Adivar   (1883–1964) Turkey

Following her graduation from the American College for Girls in 1901, Adivar worked as a teacher and a writer for a liberal newspaper. Her articles on women's rights to emancipation and education were bitterly opposed by the ruling party in Turkey, and she was forced to flee for her life. Adivar returned in 1910 and by 1912 had produced her first two books, *Handan* and *Yeni Turan*, again advocating women's rights. She became one of the principal writers for the president, Kemal Atatürk; she and her husband later rejected his policies and left for England. Following the death of Atatürk in 1938, Adivar returned to

Turkey and taught at the University of Istanbul; she was also elected to the Grand National Assembly. In her memoirs she describes her efforts to establish schools for children, especially girls, and her concern with their health and well-being. (*Sources*: 8, 60, 151, 731)

1912   Anna Akhmatova   (1889–1966) Russia
Like her friend and fellow poet MARINA TSVETAYEVA, Akhmatova spent part of her life in exile because of her writing. Akhmatova joined the school of Achmeists, whose literary philosophy was to change the accepted use of symbolism to a simpler and more direct literary style. Considered the school's most distinguished poet, Akhmatova published her first book, *Vecher*, in 1912 and was a successful writer until her husband was killed for political reasons and her writings were no longer considered de rigueur. Akhmatova lived in exile for a ten-year period, publishing the successful *Air Ways* in the United States and returning to the Soviet Union in 1953. Although her work was translated into many languages, it was not until 1965, a year before her death, that she was accepted into the Soviet writers' union and recognized as one of the country's greatest poets. (*Sources*: 47, 73, 80, 156, 665, 717)

1912   Alexandra of Denmark   (1844–1925) England (Denmark)
Married to King Edward VII of England and out of favor with her mother-in-law, Queen Victoria, Alexandra was well liked by the people of her adopted country. Alexandra was noted for her interest and work in behalf of the poor, in particular her founding of the Imperial Military Nursing Service in 1902. To celebrate her fifteenth wedding anniversary, she had symbolic roses sold to commemorate the event, with the proceeds going to British hospitals. The practice continued every year on the anniversary of the first occasion and is still observed. Alexandra was the mother of a king of England and a queen of Norway. (*Sources*: 141, 158, 593, 706)

1912   Agnes Arber   (1879–1960) England
A botanist, Arber was especially known for her studies of monocotyledons (plants characterized by a single embryonic seed leaf). Her first and major book, *Herbals: Their Origin and*

Evolution, was written in 1912 and updated in 1939; she published additional books in 1920, 1925, and 1934. She was the first woman elected as fellow of the Royal Society and in 1948 she received the Linnean Society's highest award. (*Sources*: 2, 161, 518, 731)

1912   Lillian Baylis   (1874–1937) England
Baylis was a singer like her parents; accompanying them to South Africa, she became one of the first music teachers there. She returned to London in 1912 to take over the management of the Victoria Theatre, later fondly called the Old Vic, which she developed into one of the finest theaters of its day. Baylis made it the cultural center for Shakespearean plays and dramas by contemporary playwrights as well as for opera and ballet. In 1931 Baylis rebuilt and reopened the Sadler's Wells Theatre as a ballet theater, hiring NINETTE DE VALOIS as its director. The Old Vic increasingly came to present popular plays, updating its role as one of the leading and most successful theatres in Britain. (*Sources*: 166, 518, 717, 731)

1912   Sarah Conboy   (1879–1928) United States
In 1912 Conboy became one of the primary organizers for a union known as the United Textile Workers. In 1915 she became its secretary-treasurer, a position she held for the thirteen years before her death. Conboy was also a leading spokesperson for the American Federation of Labor and worked unstintingly to better working conditions, especially for women. A strong and influential union member, she advocated legislation to reduce women's working hours when the union was unable to make this provision for them. The decision to press for legislation was not always popular, even with women workers, but Conboy stressed the need because she recognized that women had limited power in the unions and were not always extended the same concern shown to male workers. (*Sources*: 105, 447, 455, 470, 763)

1912   Alberta Hunter   (1897–1984) United States (African American)
In 1912, at the age of fifteen, and with a repertoire of two songs, Hunter got her first singing job, at Dago Frank's club. When the club was closed down, she sang in other clubs, each one having a slightly better reputation, until by 1920 she was singing at Dreamland, one of the best-known clubs in Chicago. In 1921 she

recorded her own composition, "Downhearted Blues," a song made famous by another blues singer, Bessie Smith. Hunter's rise to stardom was meteoric; she continued to record popular hits and appeared at the Orpheum and at Keith's. In 1923 she replaced Bessie Smith in a Broadway show and by 1927 was the star of Oscar Hammerstein and Jerome Kern's *Show Boat*. She also had her own radio program and organized the first Black USO tour during World War II. Hunter stopped singing as abruptly as she had started; she left the theater in 1954 and became a practical nurse. Hunter resumed her musical career in 1974 after being retired from her hospital job. Still in demand but never the star she had been as a younger woman, she made an album in 1982 that received outstanding reviews; her voice was said to be still one of the finest, to have lost nothing with age. Hunter performed throughout the world, with one of her last appearances in Brazil in 1983. She gave a few concerts in 1984 and was to appear at the Republican Convention the year she died. (*Sources*: 98, 330, 331, 580, 611)

1912   Julia Lathrop   (1858–1932) United States

Lathrop graduated from Vassar College in 1880 and devoted her career to the betterment of conditions for children. She first worked at the Hull House Settlement in Chicago, noted as a shelter for troubled women and children. The first woman appointed to the Illinois State Board of Charities, she was also active in the University of Chicago's establishment of a social work program. An effective organizer, Lathrop was appointed the first director of the newly instituted Federal Children's Bureau in 1912, making her the first woman to head a federal agency. As director of the bureau, she investigated the living and working conditions of children. She also conducted national studies on maternal and infant deaths in order to improve conditions for women and children. Lathrop retired from this position in 1921 but continued her work as president of the Illinois League of Women Voters and served on the children's committee of the League of Nations until a year before her death. (*Sources*: 34, 105, 447, 455, 470, 548, 583, 584, 616, 680, 731)

1912   Matilde Moisant   (1878–1964) United States

Moisant was the second woman to obtain a pilot's license, shortly after her friend, HARRIET QUIMBY, had been licensed to fly. Her family ran the Moisant Aviation School, where her brother, later killed in an air crash, was an instructor. Moisant broke the altitude records set by Quimby and another woman pilot, Helene Dutrieu, and was the first woman to pilot a plane from Paris to London. Pressured by her family and distressed by the deaths of both her brother and Quimby, Moisant decided to fly her last exhibition flight in April 1912. As she came in for a landing following her exhibition, she shut her engine off and glided in according to standard procedure; however, the crowd had rushed onto the field to greet her, and she realized she would hit them before the plane could come to a stop. In a daring maneuver, she restarted her engine, bounced off the ground for thrust, and was able to get her plane airborne before it ran into the crowd. Because of the engine's heat, restarting the plane caused it to burst into flames. Moisant was saved from burning to death by her heavy clothing and the quick reaction of spectators who pulled her from the plane. Moisant devoted the rest of her life to working for the Red Cross. (*Sources*: 418, 439, 441, 544, 585, 631)

1912   Harriet Monroe   (1860–1936) United States

Monroe was educated in the arts by her father. Her first job was as an art critic for the *Chicago Tribune*; after a tour of Europe, she returned to the *Tribune* but also became a freelance writer. Her most successful poem was "Columbian Ode," written for the World's Columbian Exposition in 1892. In 1912 Monroe founded a monthly journal, *Poetry: A Magazine of Verse*, which started out publishing the work of notable poets and later, despite widespread protest, also included the work of lesser-known poets who used experimental forms. This daring and financially costly support for new poets was instrumental in advancing their work. Monroe edited the magazine for twenty-four years. (*Sources*: 80, 252, 522, 548, 758)

1912   Marie Rambert   (1888–1982) England (Poland)

Rambert developed a method of translating rhythm into bodily movements for ballet and began teaching this technique to the Ballet Russe in Paris in 1912. She opened her own ballet school in England and helped Vaslav Nijinsky choreograph his *Rite of Spring*. Her Ballet Rambert became one of the most important ballet companies in England, and her pupils included

Alicia Markova and Antony Tudor. Credited with developing British ballet into one of the finest in the world, Rambert was made a dame of the Order of the British Empire in 1962. (*Sources*: 283, 402, 583, 739)

1912 Mary Vorse (1874–1966) United States

Vorse grew up in a comfortable and intellectual world and in 1898 married into a similar one. She and her husband started the A Club in Greenwich Village, an avant-garde group of thinkers and writers. She is also credited with starting the Provincetown Players in Cape Cod, Massachusetts, a place that was very dear to her. Vorse wrote articles for the *Atlantic Monthly* and for *Criterion*, much of this work later becoming the basis for books such as *The Autobiography of an Elderly Woman* (1911) and *The Prestons* (1918). Vorse first became aware of the plight of ordinary working people in 1912 when she covered the strike at a factory in Lawrence, Massachusetts. Her articles on this and subsequent strikes made her the only journalist trusted by the famous strike leader Mother Jones. For thirty years, Vorse wrote articles on the working conditions both in the United States and abroad. As a correspondent during World War II, she pre-ferred to report on the effects of war on women and children rather than news of the front. Vorse also covered the women's international conventions in Amsterdam and Budapest. In both her fiction and nonfiction, she took labor and working conditions as her major theme. (*Sources*: 522, 556, 579, 680, 744, 763)

1913 Lili Boulanger (1893–1918) France

Never quite reaching the fame of her older sister Nadia, a world-renowned composer, Boulanger in 1913 became the first woman to win the Grand Prix de Rome; five years later, when it was discovered that she was a woman, the award was rescinded. Both her parents as well as her sister were musically talented, and she began to compose at an early age, her sister supervising her work. She entered the Paris Conservatoire at the age of nineteen and wrote her prize-winning cantata at the age of twenty. During her very brief career, Boulanger composed numerous choral, vocal, and instrumental works, the choral piece *Vieille Prière Bouddhique* written shortly before her death. (*Sources*: 139, 372, 515, 583, 654, 731)

1913   Elsie Parsons   (1875–1941) United States
    Parsons earned her doctorate in sociology at Columbia University in 1899 and taught at Barnard College. In 1913 she published her first book, The Old-Fashioned Woman, and, anticipating the response to its shocking theme—the repression, especially sexual repression, of women—published it under the nom de plume of John Main. Parsons met the anthropologist Franz Boas in 1915 and through his influence became interested in anthropology and the Native Americans of the southwestern part of the United States, Mexico, Peru, and the Caribbean. Her book Mitla: Town of Souls (1936), was an investigation of the Zapotecs, one of the oldest cultural groups in the Americas. Parsons wrote as a means to interest the public in diverse cultures rather than to engage her colleagues in scholarly debate, her choice of audience probably reflecting Boas's influence. Parsons was elected the first woman president of the American Anthropological Association in 1941 but died before taking office. (Sources: 103, 278, 518, 634, 676)

1913   Katherine Stinson   (1896–1977) United States
    Stinson was the oldest child in a family of four children and became as famous as a pilot as did her sister and two brothers. Stinson learned to fly in order to finance her piano studies but soon abandoned music in favor of flying. In 1912, at the age of sixteen, Stinson qualified as a pilot. She waited until 1913 before she became an exhibition pilot in shows throughout the country. In the same year, she became the first woman in the United States authorized to carry airmail, a distinction she also earned later in Canada. When her brother opened a flying school in San Antonio, Stinson and her sister moved there to give flying lessons. Stinson established several records, two of which are noteworthy: in 1917 she set a flight record of nine hours and ten minutes for a flight from San Diego to San Francisco and within six months made a record-breaking flight from Chicago to Binghamton, New York. Stinson also established records in Canada for distance and endurance. At the start of World War I, Stinson offered her services as a military pilot but was rejected; she instead flew supplies for the Red Cross. Following a serious illness, Stinson retired from flying in 1920. (Sources: 418, 441, 509, 564, 585, 672, 737, 773)

1913　Katherine Tynan　(1861–1931) Ireland

Tynan wrote about her native country and, like her compatriot William Butler Yeats, had an abiding interest in the Celtic revivalist movement. She wrote in both verse and prose. Aside from *The House in the Forest* (1928), her best-known works are her five autobiographical works, with her first, *Twenty-five Years*, written in 1913 and the final one, *Memories*, in 1924. Her last book, *Collected Poems*, was published in 1930. (*Sources*: 310, 571, 751)

1914　Elizabeth Haldane　(1862–1937) Scotland

Haldane was an intellectual who translated the works of G.W.F. Hegel and René Descartes and wrote a biography of the latter. Her later books (1923 and 1937) were about her other interests, nursing and social reform. In 1884 Haldane founded an organization to rebuild slum neighborhoods and served on various nursing boards. She also worked for the right for women to have both an education and better working opportunities. In 1914 Haldane was made a member of the board of trustees for the United Kingdom Trust, and it was through her efforts that the organization rescued the Sadler's Wells Theatre and Ballet from its impending demise. In 1920 Haldane was appointed the first woman justice of the peace in Scotland. (*Sources*: 220, 706)

1914　Elsie Inglis　(1864–1917) Scotland (India)

Inglis earned her degree in medicine in 1899 and began to work for better health for women and children, founding a free hospital for women and children in Edinburgh. By 1914 she had organized the Scottish Women's Hospitals to work for women's suffrage. Inglis's greatest work started in 1914, when she personally raised over $2 million to finance an all-women's medical team to set up hospitals in war zones. The British War Office rejected the offer, but the French government accepted, and two units were immediately sent to the combat zone, another unit going to Serbia. The unit in Serbia, in which Inglis served, had to administer to an epidemic of typhus as well as tend the wounded. When the Serbian unit was captured and the patients taken prisoners, Inglis went with them to continue to care for them. Inglis's hospital units served valiantly in the war, but while posted in Russia, Inglis recognized the danger of the impending Bolshevik Revolution and asked to have her units brought back to

Scotland. Already in poor health, she died a day after her return. (*Sources*: 384, 573, 621, 706)

1914   Lotte Lehmann   (1888–1976) Germany
Lehmann made her debut with the Vienna State Opera in 1914 and remained with the company until she emigrated to the United States. Her career with the Metropolitan Opera spanned the period from 1934 to 1945. Lehmann was noted not only for her operatic ability, particularly her expressiveness, but also for the rapport she developed with her audience. A multitalented woman, she painted, wrote novels, taught, composed an opera, and sang until she was sixty-five. She wrote her autobiography, *Midway in My Song*, when she was fifty years old, revising it as *My Many Lives* ten years later. (*Sources*: 518, 595, 620, 739)

1914   Suzanne Lenglen   (1899–1938) France
Considered to be one of the greatest women tennis players of all time, Lenglen won the first of many championships in 1914 at the age of fifteen. Starting in 1919, she won six consecutive Wimbledon championships. Moving with the grace of a dancer, Lenglen rarely allowed her opponents to win more than four games. The only match she ever lost was to Molla Bjurstedt Mallory in 1921. Her skill, grace, and personal charm are credited with making tennis a more popular sport. A champion in both lawn and hard-court tennis, Lenglen turned professional in 1926 and beat the best-known U.S. woman tennis player, Helen Wills Moody. Lenglen also earned the largest amount of money ever paid to a tennis player at that time for a tour of matches in the United States. She died of cancer at the age of thirty-nine. (*Sources*: 20, 555, 685)

1914   Gabriela Mistral   (1889–1957) Chile
Lucila Godoy Alcayaga combined the first name of Gabriele D'Annunzio and the last name of Frédéric Mistral, her two favorite poets, to become Gabriela Mistral. Using her new literary signature, she won her first prize for her first entry, "Three Sonnets," in Santiago in 1914. Her gentle and sometimes melancholy poems reflected her interest in children, the poor, and death. Having first begun a career teaching, she continued to teach throughout her life as well as acting as a cultural ambassador for her country and serving on committees in both the

League of Nations and the United Nations. She was awarded the Nobel Prize for literature in 1945. (*Sources*: 64, 80, 250, 540, 682, 731)

1914 Liubov Popova (1889–1924) Russia

Popova took art classes in Moscow and moved to Paris in 1912, where she studied with Henri Le Fauconnier and Jean Metzinger. Painting primarily portraits and still lifes, Popova used the highly representational style of cubism, later moving on to abstractionism. She held her first exhibit in 1914 and showed continuously until 1921, with an additional exhibit of her works presented posthumously in 1924. Popova also worked as a textile designer for the state and was noted for her costume and set designs. (*Sources*: 439, 607, 608)

1914 Dorothy Richardson (1873–1957) England

Richardson wrote her first book, *The Quakers Past and Present*, in 1899, but it was not published until 1914. Shortly after the book appeared, Richardson began her twelve-volume autobiography, the first volume entitled *Pointed Roofs* (1915) and the last *Dimple Hill* (1938). The work's length, intensity, and wide publication span did not make it popular reading; however, it did establish Richardson as the first of the stream-of-consciousness writers, preceding two more-famous stream-of-consciousness writers, Virginia Woolf and James Joyce. Writing from a feminist perspective, Richardson is faulted for her selective self-revelation and an unlikely reticence. (*Sources*: 80, 370, 406, 500, 681, 731, 755)

1915 Emily Balch (1867–1961) United States

Balch was in the first class to graduate from Bryn Mawr in 1889. After completing her studies in the United States and abroad, she taught economics and sociology at Wellesley College. From 1908 to 1913 Balch served on the Massachusetts Commission on Industrial Relations, moving on to the Massachusetts Commission on Immigration. She sat on the Boston City Planning Board starting in 1914. In 1915 Balch was a cofounder of the Women's International League for Peace and Freedom. As one of its directors, she sent fact-finding committees to study potential areas of political unrest and urged the government to join the World Court and to outlaw war. She also served as a delegate to the International Congress of Women and as secretary to the Women's International League. Balch shared the Nobel Peace Prize in 1946 for her efforts in behalf of world peace. (*Sources*: 74, 98, 556, 583, 584, 722, 731, 759)

1915 Edith Cavell (1865–1915) Belgium (England)

Cavell trained and worked at the privately supported London Hospital (where, under the direction of Eva Luckes, nursing training had been greatly improved). In 1901 she fought the typhoid epidemic in the slum areas of London. Hearing of her work and knowing she spoke French, Antoine Depage, a Belgian physician, hired her to direct his newly founded nursing program at the Berkendael Institute. Cavell devoted the years 1907 to 1914 to improving the nursing program and the level of patient care at the hospital. When World War I started and Belgium was invaded, Cavell and her staff treated all wounded, including enemy soldiers. She also began to hide Allied soldiers and to assist in their escape from Belgium. She was caught and arrested, and though not charged with espionage or any subversive act, she was executed along with the Belgian nurse Louise Thuliez on October 12, 1915. Several monuments have been erected to honor her bravery. (*Sources*: 87, 104, 131, 419, 518, 592, 629, 739, 751)

1915 Libbie Hyman (1888–1969) United States (Jewish American)

Hyman earned her doctorate in zoology from the University of Chicago in 1915 and remained there on the teaching staff until 1931. She wrote the first of innumerable publications, a manual on zoology, in 1919. For more than three decades, starting in 1936, Hyman did research at the American Museum of Natural History in New York. It was here that she began her major work, *The Invertebrates*, a six-volume study that was completed by colleagues shortly after her death. Hyman was the recipient of several honorary degrees and two gold medals and was the first woman to receive the Daniel Giraud Medal from the National Academy of Science. (*Sources*: 224, 525, 583, 739, 778)

1915 Freda Kirchwey (1893–1976) United States

Kirchwey started out as a cub reporter in New York in 1915 on the *Nation*, a newspaper known for its conservatism. By 1918 she had become the managing editor and began to write on the unpopular issue of women's rights. In 1926 Kirchwey began a series of articles in which she asked women about the issues of family, work, and marriage, ending the series with psychologists' evaluations of the interviews. She also began to write on labor conditions and world events. In 1937 Kirchwey bought the *Nation* as a vehicle for advocating change. She openly criticized the U.S. government for failing to recognize the threat Hitler posed and for not joining the free world in an alliance against him; she was especially critical of the 1938 Munich Pact. She also denounced the exclusion of women from jobs and praised President Franklin Roosevelt when he appointed Frances Perkins to the position of secretary of labor. Because of her outspoken criticism of Senator Joseph McCarthy, she was labeled a Communist, and her newspaper was banned in schools and elsewhere. Kirchwey remained editor in chief until 1955. (*Sources*: 13, 74, 98, 548, 583, 626, 627)

1915   Marianne Moore   (1887–1972) United States

After graduating from Bryn Mawr in 1909, Moore was uncertain about her career until she visited New York and met the poets Erza Pound and William Carlos Williams. She moved to New York to begin her long career as a poet, publishing her first work in 1915 in the *Egoist*, one of the leading literary journals of the time. She soon followed this with articles in other noted literary magazines and entire books of her own poetry. She became editor of the *Dial* in 1926 and developed it into an internationally recognized literary journal. Moore was much admired by fellow poets such as T. S. Eliot, who wrote the foreword for one of her early books. Her work *Observations* won the Dial Award in 1924. (*Sources*: 64, 72, 256, 522, 563, 731)

1916   Katherine Mansfield   (1888–1923) England (New Zealand)

Mansfield had already lived half her life when, at the age of nineteen, she left New Zealand for London to start her literary career. Her writing became dominated by the death of her brother in the war and childhood remembrances of her native country (Mansfield never returned to New Zealand, even for a visit). She was a master of the short story, the first, "Aloe," being published in 1916. She developed her poignant and delicate style with "The Garden Party" (1922), considered her best work. Mansfield died at the age of thirty-five after a five-year battle with tuberculosis. (*Sources*: 80, 245, 562, 627, 665, 717)

1916   Edith Södergran   (1892–1923) Sweden/Finland (Russia)
Writing in the symbolistic style, Södergran is considered to have been one of the greatest influences on the development of Swedish and Finnish poetry. Although her parents were Swedish and Finnish, and she was educated in Russia, she began writing poetry in German, her first language. However, influenced by several Swedish literary intellectuals, she published her first collection of poetry, entitled *Dikter* (1916), in Swedish. Despite her almost lifelong affliction with tuberculosis, which eventually took her life, and her family's being forced to leave Russia at the start of the revolution, Södergran continued writing until her death at thirty-one. (*Sources*: 80, 300, 476)

1918   Mary Donlon   (1893–1977) United States
In 1918 Donlon became the first woman editor in chief of the *Cornell Law Quarterly*, a position she held until she graduated in 1920. In 1937 she was the first woman appointed a trustee of her alma mater's alumni association. In 1944 Donlon became the first woman to chair the New York State Industrial Board and the following year was named to the chair of the Workmen's Compensation Board. Donlon's most notable first was in 1955, when she became the first woman to be made a federal judge in the U.S. Customs Court, a lifetime appointment. (*Sources*: 111, 455, 713)

1918   Zona Gale   (1874–1938) United States
Having moved to New York to establish a writing career, Gale began to publish nostalgic books about her small-town background in 1908. Unlike her contemporary, KATHERINE MANSFIELD, whose memory of her roots was never encumbered by any new reality, Gale's writing style developed after she made a return trip to her home state and reevaluated the virtues of small-town life that she had once so admired. In a style similar to that of Sinclair Lewis, she began to dramatize the conventionality and repression of middle-class life. Her first book to reflect this detached attitude was *Birth* (1918). Her next and similarly successful book, *Miss Lulu Bett*, was eventually

turned into both a play and a movie. The popularity of Gale's works continued throughout her career. (*Sources*: 53, 74, 105, 439, 548, 616)

1918   Ninette de Valois   (1898–) England (Ireland)

Valois first danced with a children's touring group, but in 1918, after more serious study, she was named principal dancer with the British National Opera. She next danced for the Ballet Russe, leaving in 1926 to open her own school and to become the choreographic director of the Old Vic Theatre, working with LILLIAN BAYLIS. She continued her innovative choreography, collaborating with such notables as Margot Fonteyn. In 1947 Valois opened several ballet schools in foreign countries, but it was not until 1956 that she was granted permission to start the Royal Ballet of England. She served as its director until 1963, at which time she was named a life governor of the Royal Ballet. (*Sources*: 15, 313, 468, 500, 518, 554, 583, 731)

1919   Sylvia Beach   (1887–1962) France (United States)

With little formal schooling, Beach moved to Paris in 1917 and in 1919 opened a bookshop to support herself. Called Shakespeare and Company, the shop became her salon, a haven for writers, a cultural center, and a publishing house. A self-educated woman, Beach devoted her life to encouraging and assisting young writers, many of whom went on to become famous. The then unknown writers Jules Romains, Valéry Larbaud, Gertrude Stein, Ernest Hemingway, Archibald MacLeish, and James Joyce gathered there to exchange ideas and often called upon Beach for literary information. When Joyce could not find a publisher for his book *Ulysses*, Beach had it published for him. She also arranged the publicity and mailing for the book, including smuggling it into the United States, where it had been banned. When her bookshop was closed during World War II, she remained in Paris and was interned in a detention camp. Beach chose not to reopen the store after the war, preferring to use her home as her salon. She helped to arrange and loan much of her literary property for a Paris exhibit, an effort for which she received many awards, including the French Legion of Honor in 1938. (*Sources*: 64, 74, 79, 369, 731)

1919 Evangeline Booth (1865–1950) United States (England)

It is not possible to write about Booth without also mentioning her mother, Catherine Booth. Although her father, William Booth, was credited with the founding of the Salvation Army in 1878, her mother was equally instrumental in its beginning and largely responsible for her daughters' introduction into and continuation in the organization. Since Catherine Booth had eight children and was often in poor health, she instilled her sense of commitment to the poor in her daughters, who often did the work she was too ill to do. Evangeline, one of the youngest children, joined her parents in their efforts and then moved to the United States. In 1904 she took over the leadership of the American Salvation Army, a position she held for thirty years, leaving only to take over as general of the International Salvation Army. Because of the early work by Catherine Booth and her daughters, women have held equal positions with men in the Salvation Army. In 1919 Booth became the first woman to receive the Distinguished Service Medal for her thirty-five years of work in the Salvation Army. (*Sources:* 59, 392, 455, 500, 518, 548, 583, 599)

1919 Alice Hamilton (1869–1970) United States

Years ahead of her time, Hamilton foresaw the danger of industrial pollutants to public health. She earned her medical degree at the University of Michigan in 1893 and joined the illustrious group of women who ran Hull House in Chicago. Here she developed her interest in working conditions and public health. In 1902 Hamilton traced the cause of a typhoid epidemic to contaminated water. By 1910 she was the head of the Occupational Disease Commission, which discovered that the lead in many common products, such as bathtubs and paint, was highly toxic. Hamilton exposed the cause of death among workers in the explosives industry: once attributed to natural causes, it was in fact due to nitrous fumes they inhaled. She was also one of the first physicians to investigate the effects of certain dangerous industries on the health of women and on maternal and fetal health. In 1919 Hamilton was named the first professor in the new Department of Industrial Medicine at Harvard Medical School. The first woman appointed to this all-male bastion, she was prevented from using the Harvard Club and from participating in the graduation procession. Hamilton remained at Harvard for sixteen years, retiring as an assistant professor, the same rank at which she had been hired. (*Sources*: 34, 74, 398, 432, 537, 603, 634, 718, 731, 739)

1919   Juana de Ibarbourou   (1895–1979) Uruguay

Ibarbourou wrote her first volume of poetry, *Diamond Tongues*, in 1919 and soon became the most celebrated poet in Uruguay. She enjoyed enormous popularity throughout her lifetime. A highly creative poet, she preferred to extol the virtues of natural life rather than use the accepted and stilted style of the time. Her poems were about nature and things natural, presenting human love and sensuality as both joyous and integral parts of nature. In 1945 she wrote radio dramas for children that were also successful. Her poetry after the year 1950 reflected the sadness she experienced in the recent and close losses of her husband and her parents. Ibarbourou's work was known throughout the world, and she received many honors from European as well as North and South American countries. Ibarbourou was given a state funeral, and a poetry competition is named in her honor. (*Sources*: 64, 124, 540, 717)

1919   Melanie Klein   (1882–1960) Austria

Klein's interest in psychotherapy developed from her own experience as a patient. The aspect of psychology that most intrigued her was the psychological development and trauma of children. She published her first paper on her pioneering work in 1919. Klein discovered that in their play behavior children revealed much about their inner feelings. In 1932 she wrote *The Psychoanalysis of Children*, in which she stated that the Oedipus complex and the aggression toward the mother emerged at an earlier date than Sigmund Freud had previously set. Klein's later studies on children and envy became highly controversial. In her book *Narrative of a Child Analysis*, published post-humously, she related how she worked with a child as an example of her psychoanalytic work with children. (*Sources*: 529, 583, 621)

1919   Sarah Millin   (1889–1968) South Africa (Lithuania)

Millin's beliefs in white supremacy and apartheid served as the foundation for the plots in her novels; the poor diggers of the diamond mines in Kimberely whom she had observed as a child became prototypes for her characters. Millin's portrayal of the meanness and smallness of their lives was in evidence from her first book, *The Dark River* (1919), to her last one, *White Africans Are Also People* (1966). Millin saw greed and money, even small amounts of money, as well as miscegenation as the dominating and demeaning forces in their existence. Her female characters are strong-willed, ruthless, highly sexual, and very cunning. Because she believed in genetic superiority, her work did not reflect any understanding, empathy, or appreciation for any redeeming characteristics the miners might possess. Her personal values were not shared by her fellow South African writers and are certainly not in favor today; this does not detract from the literary value of her work and her often forceful and compelling style. Millin wrote several notable biographies as well as her autobiography, *The Measure of My Days*. (*Sources*: 7, 80, 475, 476, 691)

1919   Emmy Noether   (1882–1935) Germany

Noether's parents, both mathematicians, provided her with an excellent education. Although she completed her doctorate in 1907, her only opportunity to teach and to continue her research on abstract algebra was to accept a less than desirable position at University of Erlangen in 1915. Noether taught as a full-time substitute in a position technically assigned to a male. It was not until 1922 that Noether was finally named to the faculty and recognized as an outstanding mathematician. In 1933, she emigrated to the United States, where she taught at Bryn Mawr and Princeton. Noether is credited with advancing theory in modern algebra. (*Sources*: 273, 408, 427, 518, 587, 634, 739)

1919   Edith Quimby   (1891–1982) United States

Part of Quimby's opportunity for acceptance and success came from being a pioneer in the field of radiation while it was still in its infancy. Quimby not only faced prejudice against women but also lacked her doctorate, an important credential in university research. She had earned her undergraduate degree in physics at Whitman College in Washington in 1912 and her master's degree with the aid of a teaching scholarship at Berkeley. In 1919 Quimby was offered the opportunity to conduct research in radiation with the collaboration of Gioacchino

Failla; their professional relationship lasted throughout their lives. Using their knowledge of physics, Quimby and Failla studied the use of radiation for medical therapy and determined correct therapeutic dosages of radiation. Their calculations involved determining dosages based on the type of tumor, its depth and size, and its relationship to other organs, as well as the safety factors for those administering the radiation, the type and safety of equipment, and its distance from the body. In 1940 Quimby became the first woman to receive the Janeway Medal and an honorary doctorate from Berkeley; she received the Gold Medal from the American Radiological Society in 1941. Quimby became a full professor at Cornell and later at Columbia Medical School, where she did pioneering work in the field of radioisotopes, the disposal of radioactive waste, and radioactive spills. (Sources: 634, 779)

1919   Lotte Reiniger   (1899–1981) Germany

Puppetry and silhouettes are ancient theatrical forms used throughout the world, particularly in the Oriental theater; Reiniger, however, was the first to develop the use of the silhouette in the cinema. She began to develop the technique in 1919, when she worked for the Max Reinhardt Theater School. In 1921, newly married, she worked with her husband to develop the sophisticated techniques necessary to transfer puppetry and silhouetting to the movie screen. She determined the type of material to be used for the silhouettes, cut them out, and, placing them on lighted glass with the camera overhead and using stop-action photography, manipulated the animation of the figures. In 1923 she produced her first full-length movie and went on to produce another twenty-five. She continued her work in England, also producing films for the United States. She and her husband made some of the first animated cartoons for television, and Reiniger remained active in the industry until the late 1970s. (*Sources*: 284, 731)

1919   Eunice Tietjens   (1884–1944) United States

Born in the United States but exposed to European cultures at an early age, Tietjens developed an insight into and knowledge of other cultures and had the talent to express her sensitivity in the form of poetry. In 1915 she became an assistant editor of the journal *Poetry: A Magazine of Verse*, established by HARRIET

MONROE. She remained at the journal for twenty-five years. In 1919 Tietjens published her first work of poetry, *Body and Raiment*. For the next few years she traveled in the Orient and, deeply admiring the cultures she visited, began to write poetry about China, Japan, and the South Pacific islands. Tietjens also wrote poetry about Tunisia and Italy. Tietjens's work reflected her empathetic view of both the beauty and cruelty she witnessed. Her eclectic and sensitive poetry appealed to adults and children from many cultures. (*Sources*: 309, 369, 522)

1919   Anzia Yezierska   (1880–1970) United States (Soviet Union) (Jewish American)
    With a poor and interrupted education, Yezierska gained fame in 1919 when she wrote her short story "The Fat of the Land." Her next story, *Hungry Hearts*, brought her a contract as a scriptwriter for films, but Yezierska chose to return to solitary writing in New York. She took as her theme the trials and tribulations of immigrant Jews, especially women, in acclimating to their new culture. Although Yezierska wrote until the late 1920s, by the time she published her autobiography, *Red Ribbon on a White Horse* (1950), she was poor and forgotten. (*Sources*: 74, 102, 321, 355, 522, 525, 763)

1920   Frieda Loehmann   (1874–1962) United States (Jewish American)
    An enterprising woman, Loehmann recognized that brand-name women's clothes that stores had been unable to sell could be sold at a discount, so in 1920 she became the pioneer in off-price retailing. She offered wholesalers cash for their unsold preseason merchandise and sold the garments in her Brooklyn store. Within ten years Loehmann had built a business worth $3 million. After her death, her son took the business over, and by the time of his death in 1977, there were close to forty Loehmann stores across the country. By the mid-1980s, the Loehmann stores, which had been sold first to Associated Dry Goods and later to the May Company, numbered eighty-two, with annual sales of better than $200 million. (*Sources*: 62, 718)

1921   Grace Abbott   (1878–1939) United States
    Interested in helping poor women and families, Abbott worked at Hull House in Chicago, one of the first and most

outstanding shelters for women. She was later the director of the Immigrants' Protective League of Chicago, helping to find housing, employment, and health care services for immigrant women who often did not speak English and had no means of support for themselves or their children. She also served in a similar position in Massachusetts. She wrote *The Immigrant and the Community* in 1916. Recognized for her organizational skills, Abbott was appointed in 1921 as the first chief of the newly established U.S. Children's Bureau, a position she held until 1934. Abbott also served as the presidential representative on the Advisory Committee for the Protection and Welfare of Children and Young People sponsored by the League of Nations in 1924. (*Sources*: 74, 105, 339, 355, 627, 763)

1921   Florence Ayscough   (1878–1942) United States (China)
Ayscough was born to American parents in China and lived there until she was sent to school in the United States when she was nine years old. She later returned to China to study its history and language, devoting her career to writing about the country she loved. Written in 1921, her first book, *Fir-Flower Tablets*, was a translation of Chinese poetry. Ayscough wrote a number of books to teach young readers both in China and abroad about China's culture and history. Since the 1920s was as much a time of social upheaval for women in China as it was for women in the West, in 1937 Ayscough wrote *Chinese Women, Yesterday and Today*, in which she contrasted the traditional roles of women in China with the changes women were seeking for themselves. Asycough's intent in her writing was to bridge the gap between the diverse Chinese and American cultures. (*Sources*: 60, 368, 522, 599)

1921   Gertrude Bonnin   (1876–1938) United States (Native American)
Bonnin—who preferred her Indian name, Zitkala-Sa (Red Bird), to her Christian name—worked tirelessly for Native American rights. This fierce devotion came about as a result of her early and traumatic experiences in U.S. schools; the schizophrenic policy of replacing the Indian children's culture with the American one yet rejecting their acceptance into the new culture left most of the children with no culture with which to identify. Bonnin nevertheless finished her schooling, studied

violin for a year, and taught in the reservation schools. Her first book on Native American life was published in 1901. In 1921, after she had moved to Washington, D.C., she conducted a survey of conditions of Native Americans for the Indian Welfare Committee and worked for years for improvements in health, education, and conservation of Indian lands. Because there was no substantive response from the Federal government, Bonnin urged Indians to vote for Democratic candidates in the next election. (*Sources*: 11, 447, 470)

1921 Rebecca Clarke (1886–1979) England

Clarke studied composition and violin at the Royal College of Music in London and was later known for her talent as a viola player. Her first composition, a piano trio, was written in 1921 following her move to the United States. Other notable works by Clarke are her *Chinese Puzzle* for violin and piano (1922) and Rhapsody for Cello and Piano (1923). Clarke is noted for her use of atonality. (*Sources*: 27, 439, 645)

1921 Maud Gonne (1866–1953) Ireland

Gonne successfully combined a literary life with her pragmatic political drive. She was a noted actor in the theater group organized by William Butler Yeats (who was in love with her and wrote poems in her honor). After her husband was executed for his political activities, she helped to organize the rebel group Sinn Fein. In 1921 the Irish Free State appointed her its first diplomat to France. She published her autobiography, *A Servant of the Queen*, in 1940. (*Sources*: 36, 42, 217)

1921 Helen Hagan (1891–1964) United States (African American)

Hagan, who first studied piano with her mother, earned her degree in music from Yale University in 1912, a diploma from the Schola Cantorum in France in 1914, and a master's degree in teaching from Columbia University Teachers' College. Hagan played her own composition, Piano Concerto in C Minor, at the All-Colored Composers' Concert in Chicago in 1915. Hagan also participated in tours to sing for black troops in France during World War I. In 1921, making her debut at Aeolian Hall, she became the first black pianist to perform in a New York concert hall. In the 1930s Hagan joined the music faculties at Tennessee

State A & M College and Bishop College in Texas; at the latter she was named a dean of the School of Music. She opened her own studio in New York in 1935 and later became interested in church music. (*Sources*: 106, 371, 684)

1921   Sophie Loeb   (1876–1929) United States (Soviet Union) (Jewish American)
Starting in 1913, Loeb used her position as a feature writer on the *Evening World* newspaper in New York to publicize the terrible conditions of poor families. Loeb herself had grown up in a fatherless home in which everyone worked in order to keep the family intact. She was successful in helping to get legislation passed that provided inexpensive school lunches for children, lower natural gas rates for poor families, and free maternity care for impoverished women. Through her efforts, the first child welfare program was enacted in 1921. Although her work was bitterly opposed, she was successful in having foster homes replace the old system of orphanages. Loeb is credited with many of the legislative acts passed to improve conditions for women and children. (*Sources*: 105, 525, 627, 718)

1921   Elinor Wylie   (1885–1928) United States
Wylie was noted as both a poet and novelist. In 1921 she won the Julia Ellsworth Ford Prize for her first book of collected poetry, *Nets to Catch the Wind*. She published additional volumes of poetry in 1923 and 1928. Wylie is also credited with four novels, her first, *Jennifer Lorn*, written in 1923. Three of her books of poems were published posthumously. (*Sources*: 562, 616)

1922   Rose Alschuler   (1887–1979) United States (Jewish American)
In 1922 Alschuler began the first private nursery school. Under her direction, the Winnetka, Illinois, public nursery school for poor children in Chicago was later established. She also organized nursery schools at the Garden Apartments Negro Housing projects. In addition, Alschuler was the author of four books on children and was a founding member of a synagogue in Chicago. From 1941 to 1943 Alschuler served as chairperson for the National Commission for Young Children and was a member of a number of other national and local committees. She received several awards, among which were the Government of Israel

Award (1958) and the Eleanor Roosevelt Humanities Award (1966). (*Sources*: 458, 525)

1922 Bessie Coleman (1892–1926) United States (African American)

Born in the segregated South, Bessie Coleman wanted to become the first black female pilot; she worked as a manicurist to save money for flying lessons. Knowing she would have to go to Europe to get training, she took French lessons and earned her pilot's license in France with the aid of Robert Abbot, editor of the *Chicago Weekly Defender*. Holding the first female international pilot's license, she started flying in exhibitions in 1922. She was killed in a plane crash in Florida four years later. Each year black pilots fly over her grave and drop flowers in her honor. A black flying club at the Gary Municipal Airport in Chicago is named the Bessie Coleman Aviators. (*Sources*: 391, 418, 601, 648, 685)

1922 Lucy Slowe (1885–1937) United States (African American)

Slowe was orphaned at an early age, but with the aid of a scholarship, she graduated from Howard University in 1908. She earned her master's degree from Columbia University in 1915 and became the principal of a junior high school in Washington, D.C. In 1922 Slowe was appointed the first dean of women at Howard University, a post she filled until her death. During Slowe's tenure, she enacted many innovative policies, such as shifting the emphasis from in loco parentis supervision to developing cultural enrichment programs for women. She was one of the founders of Alpha Kappa Alpha, the first black sorority, and initiated a cultural program that invited noted black authors and performers such as Countee Cullen and Marian Anderson to lecture to the students. Slowe was a member of the American Association of University Women and helped to found the Black National Association of College Women, which was later incorporated into the American Association of University Women. (*Sources*: 74, 120, 508, 683, 750)

1923 Louise Bogan (1897–1970) United States

Although she faced the same hurdles and frustrations, Bogan chose not to identify with the newly independent woman of the 1920s, a factor that may have played a part in her periodic emotional breakdowns. Despite her emotional frailty, Bogan had a very successful career and was greatly admired. Often doing her writing at her remote farm in New York State, she published her first book of poetry, entitled *Body of This Death,* in 1923 and continued to publish until 1955. She was the recipient of the Bollingen Prize for poetry in 1954. Along with writing poems, Bogan also worked as the poetry critic for the *New Yorker,* wrote for HARRIET MONROE's *Poetry: A Magazine of Verse,* and was named poetry consultant at the Library of Congress from 1944 to 1946. Bogan is best remembered for her highly acclaimed work *Achievement in American Poetry* (1951), in which she evaluated the best of American poetry since the turn of the century. (*Sources:* 57, 64, 425, 457, 548, 599, 758)

1923   Vera Brittain   (1893–1970) England
Brittain was a noted feminist, writer, pacifist, and controversial figure. She earned her degree at Somerville College at Oxford in 1919 and wrote her first book, *The Dark Tide,* in 1923. A prolific author, she continued writing until shortly before her death. The topics of her books were as diverse as her interests: in *Testament of Youth* (1933) she gave an account of her experiences as a volunteer in hospitals during World War I; in *Testament of Friendship* she described her long and close friendship with Winifred Holtby; and in *Testament of Experience* she wrote about her reactions to life. The controversy surrounding her writing centered on her outspoken—and often unflattering—words about contemporary figures. Brittain was a noted international speaker and an officer in the Married Women's Association, the Women's International League of Peace and Freedom, and the Society of Women Writers and Journalists. (*Sources:* 176, 406, 470, 626, 706, 731)

1923   Alexandra Kollontai   (1872–1952) Soviet Union
Despite her aristocratic background, Kollontai became a strong advocate for the overthrow of the czar and the formation of a classless society. After a visit to Europe, she wrote two books on the oppression of women. Her first book, *Love of Worker Bees,* was published in 1923 and was followed by *Revolution in Feelings and Morality.* She was later exiled to Germany. She returned to the Soviet Union after the revolution and was named the first

woman commissar for public welfare, working for collective child care and changes in the divorce laws. After she had a scandalous affair and roused the opposition of her party, Stalin appointed her trade delegate and later ambassador to several Scandinavian countries; she was essentially exiled. Kollontai was able to negotiate an end to the Soviet-Finnish war in 1944 and was allowed to return to the USSR, but she was never given another position of power in the Communist Party. (*Sources:* 24, 60, 230, 518, 599, 621, 731, 739)

1924   Annie Jump Cannon   (1863–1941) United States

Cannon was noted for her discovery of five novae and for her contribution to a stellar spectral classificatory system compiled in conjunction with WILLIAMINA FLEMING. She began her work at the Harvard Observatory in 1896, helping to develop the system that demonstrated that most stars come from a narrow range of origins. She is credited with classifying approximately half a million stars. In 1924 she published an additional eleven volumes to the *Henry Draper Catalogue* first printed in 1890 by Fleming. Cannon received many honors from several countries. The Annie Jump Cannon Prize, awarded to outstanding women in astronomy, was established shortly before her death. (*Sources:* 9, 408, 447, 583, 599, 718, 731, 739)

1924   Jessie Fauset   (1885–1961) United States (African American)

Fauset graduated from Cornell University in 1905, where she was elected to Phi Beta Kappa. She earned her master's degree from the University of Pennsylvania. First writing *There Is Confusion*, in 1924, she went on to become one of the best authors of the Harlem Renaissance. While contemporary black authors were writing largely about being black and poor, she wrote about middle-class black life from a positive and proud perspective in her books *Plum Bun*, *The Chinaberry Tree*, and *Comedy: American Style*. Her literary career began in 1919, when she resigned from her teaching position to become literary editor of the *Crisis*, a position from which she resigned after seven years in order to return to teaching. As well as a novelist, Fauset was a journalist, critic, translator, and poet. After the passage of civil rights legislation and the development of "black pride," Fauset's work was largely ignored. (*Sources*: 34, 94, 508, 583, 627, 680)

1924 Miriam Ferguson (1875–1961) United States

Ferguson's husband, the governor of Texas, was impeached in 1917. Ferguson ran for the office in 1924 and was elected, even though she was opposed by such powerful groups as the Ku Klux Klan, which battled her under the "bonnet or hood" slogan. A newspaper writer combined her initials, M. A. (for Miriam Amanda), to give her the nickname Ma Ferguson, which was soon widely used. Ferguson would have been the first woman governor of a state had not NELLIE ROSS of Wyoming taken office two weeks earlier. A respectable though not outstanding governor, Ferguson lost her bid for reelection in the following term and again lost in the subsequent election. She was, however, successful when she ran for the office in 1932. (*Sources*: 74, 98, 125, 718, 756)

1924 Ida Rosenthal (1889–1973) United States (Jewish American)

Rosenthal began her dressmaking business in her home, adding help as her business prospered. She eventually opened her own store in the fashionable shopping district of New York, where she would make the first bras for women to wear under their flapper dresses. In 1924, with the help of her husband, she standardized bra sizes and gave up dressmaking for her new enterprise, which she and her husband developed into the multimillion-dollar Maidenform company. For the next thirty years, Rosenthal traveled around the world promoting her product, turning the business over to her daughter only shortly before her death. (*Sources*: 583, 627, 628)

1924 Bricktop [Ada] Smith (1894–1984) United States (African American)

Known as Bricktop, Smith began to sing at an early age and appeared with the acclaimed Florence Mills in a group called the Panama Four. In 1924 she went to Paris and opened her own club. Chez Bricktop, as she called it, was very successful and numbered such individuals as the Prince of Wales (King Edward VIII), Evelyn Waugh, John Steinbeck, and Ernest Hemingway among its clientele. Smith returned to the United States at the start of World War II and again became known as a performer.

Cole Porter wrote the song "Miss Otis Regrets, She's Unable to Lunch Today" in Smith's honor. In 1951 Smith went to Italy, opening a club in Rome; she started another in Mexico and returned to the United States in 1964. Smith made a documentary film of her life entitled *Honeybaby, Honeybaby!* and wrote her autobiography, *Bricktop by Bricktop*, in 1983. (*Sources*: 29, 510, 612)

1924 Mary Webb (1881–1927) England

Webb wrote with a warmth and intimate knowledge about the area she loved, Shropshire, but described life there as being filled with hardship and calamity. She began writing in 1916 and published four novels that gained little recognition; however, when her fifth novel, *Precious Bane* (1924), was publicly praised by Prime Minister Stanley Baldwin, Webb became an overnight success. Because her novels lacked verve, they provided fertile ground for parody. (*Sources*: 78, 80, 316, 751)

1925 Leonie Adams (1899–) United States

Adams showed promise as a poet at an early age and was supported in her work by family and teachers. In 1925 the highly respected poet Louis Untermeyer encouraged her to publish her first book of poetry, *Those Not Elect*. Adams went to Europe on a Guggenheim Fellowship and upon her return taught at Bennington College and Columbia University. She taught in France as a Fulbright scholar from 1955 to 1956. A close friend of fellow poet LOUISE BOGAN, she followed Bogan as poetry consultant at the Library of Congress, serving from 1948 through 1949, and she and Bogan shared the Bollingen Prize for poetry in 1954. Adams wrote four books, with her poetry noted for its expression of joy and metaphysical beauty. (*Sources*: 84, 368, 413, 522)

1925 Mary Belle Harris (1868–1957) United States

In 1925 Harris was appointed superintendent of the first federal women's prison, which was located in West Virginia. Harris was selected because of her background as superintendent of the New Jersey State Home for Girls and her reputation as an innovator in prison reform. The design of the prison was similar to a college campus and had no surrounding walls, armed guards, or barred windows. Harris instituted educational programs, including a beauty school, to prepare the women for their reentry into society upon their release. Harris also established a classificatory system to determine each woman's best skills. The dining room was furnished with small tables, napkins, and linen cloths as part of the program to instill a sense of self-respect in the women, and women in each of the cottages in which they were housed were given the right to self-government. The cost of the prison proved to be only slightly more expensive than conventional prisons. Harris remained as superintendent until 1941. (*Sources*: 74, 351, 455)

1925   Helen Hokinson   (1893–1949) United States
Hokinson grew up in a small town in Illinois. In 1913 she began five years of study at the Chicago Academy of Fine Arts, continuing her studies at the New York School of Fine and Applied Art. In 1925 a cartoon Hokinson submitted to the *New Yorker* magazine launched her career as a cartoonist; she drew more than 1,700 cartoons, most of which were published in the *New Yorker*. Her characters were middle-aged matrons whom she gently chided for their garden clubs and luncheons as well as for their naivete. Her cartoons never lost favor with the public. In 1931 she began a collaboration with James Reid Parker, who wrote the captions for her cartoons. These were later published separately in six books between 1931 and 1956, the last three published following Hokinson's accidental death in 1949. (*Sources*: 439, 548)

1925   Doris Humphrey   (1895–1958) United States
The genius of Humphrey's choreography stemmed from her exploration of the relationship between the human body and the effects of gravity. Recognizing the balance between the harmony of bodily movement and gravitational forces, and the imbalance between them when the laws of gravity were defied, Humphrey artistically translated this harmony/disharmony into expressions of the harmony/disharmony in life. Humphrey also showed how the more gravity was defied, the more vigorous the attempt needed to recover, the simile being that the more we defy custom, the more vigorous our actions must be. Starting her own dance company in 1925, she developed dance movements without music and, later, dances accompanied by the natural sounds of water and wind. Humphrey eventually formed a dance company with Charles Weidman in which such celebrated dancers as Sybil Shearer and José Limón performed. Afflicted

with arthritis in 1945 and no longer able to perform, Humphrey founded the Julliard Dance Theater, where she taught until the end of her career. (*Sources*: 15, 74, 478, 538, 756)

1925 Rosalie Keliinoi (1875–1952) United States (Hawaiian American)
Both of Keliinoi's husbands were politicians in territorial Hawaii, and three of her seven sons were later to enter politics. Heavily supported when she chose to run as the Republican representative in 1925, she won, becoming the first woman in Hawaii to hold this office. Almost all of the sixteen bills she introduced involved women's rights, and she was successful in getting four of them passed during her tenure, including a maternal and infant care bill. The passage of a bill empowering women to sell property they owned prior to marriage and without the consent of their husbands is considered her most significant achievement. Keliinoi also worked for civic and social changes and was responsible for the restoration of the royal palace, which was later opened as a museum. (*Sources*: 121, 606)

1925 Ynes Mexia (1870–1938) United States
Mexia's life was singularly unimpressive until she reached her fifties. In 1921, after enrolling at Berkeley and taking courses in botany, she set out alone to Mexico on her first expedition to find new species of plants. She made many trips throughout the Americas, including Alaska. Obsessed with her project, she left the funding and presentation of her work to her friend, Nina Bracelin. Armed with minimal knowledge and equipment, Mexia faultlessly collected, dried, and preserved the rare and exotic plants she found. She stayed for three years in Brazil and Peru, collecting over 3,000 specimens. In 1925, at the age of fifty-five, Mexia joined a trek in the Andes. She followed this with a solo expedition into the head-hunting areas of the Amazon, where she was aided by one of the fiercest tribes in the region. Because her expeditions kept her from completing her degree, Mexia never considered herself a professional botanist— an opinion not shared by others in the field. (*Sources*: 2, 447, 718)

1925 Sarojini Naidu (1879–1949) India
Educated in England at Girton College, Cambridge, Naidu returned to India inspired by the English suffragists' work. She

became a disciple of Gandhi, who encouraged women to assist in his nonviolent resistance (albeit in a limited way) and believed they should have political rights. In 1925 Naidu became the first Indian woman president of the Indian National Council. Naidu was arrested several times for her political activities and promoted a strong negative response to Indian involvement in World War II. She participated in many of Gandhi's negotiations with the British and was part of the team that negotiated India's independence in 1947. She remained politically active in the Indian government until her death. (*Sources*: 60, 78, 80, 82, 263, 594, 599, 717)

1925   Edith Rogers   (1881–1960) United States

Rogers's interest in veterans started when she served overseas as a Red Cross volunteer in World War I. After the war she became the first Red Cross Gray Lady, serving in the veterans' hospital in Washington, D.C., during her husband's tenure as a U.S. congressman from Massachusetts. Upon his death in 1925, Rogers filled out her husband's term and successfully ran for reelection for sixteen terms. The first major bill she had passed was a $15 million appropriation for building additional veterans' hospitals. This was followed in 1941 by the passage of a bill for an all-woman voluntary army corps, a bill that met with resistance until the the U.S. entry into World War II a few months later. Rogers was also the major sponsor for the GI Bill of Rights passed in 1944. (*Sources*: 51, 74, 537, 548, 717, 754)

1925   Florence Sabin   (1871–1953) United States

Sabin graduated from Smith College in 1893 and remained to teach until she had saved her tuition to the Johns Hopkins Medical School. Completing her medical degree in 1900, she was invited to remain as an assistant to Franklin Mall, who influenced her decision to study anatomy. Sabin conducted research at Johns Hopkins for twenty-five years, during which time she became the first woman at that institution promoted to full professor. She pioneered research into the lymphatic system, proving it was a one-way system that developed out of preexisting veins. In 1925 Sabin was asked to head a research department on tuberculosis at the Rockefeller Institute. Rather than limiting the research to the existing department, Sabin coordinated studies being done at other universities, institutes, and pharmaceutical companies and controlled the research through the Rockefeller Institute. Sabin retired from the institute in 1938 only to become involved in public health in her home state of Colorado. By 1947 Sabin had seen most of her public health reform bills passed. She finally retired in 1951, two years before her death. (*Sources*: 103, 333, 355, 537, 554, 583, 587, 703)

1926   Marion Bauer   (1887–1955) United States

Born into a musical family (her father and sister were musicians), Bauer began her studies in Paris under the famous Nadia Boulanger and worked later in Berlin under Jean Paul Ertel. She began her teaching career in 1926 at New York University and from 1928 to 1952 was associated with the Chautauqua Institute's summer programs. Bauer later taught at the Institute of Musical Arts in New York. In Bauer's early years of composition, her work was considered radical; however, more recent critics describe her work as a cross between romanticism and impressionism. She wrote several pieces for piano with her first, *From New Hampshire Woods*, written in 1921; she is also noted for her choral and chamber music pieces. Bauer wrote four books on music between 1925 and 1955, three of these books coauthored by Ethel Peyser and several of them going into additional printings. (*Sources*: 29, 39, 74, 423, 627)

1926   Zofia Kossak-Szczucka   (1890–1968) Poland

Kossak-Szczucka wrote her first short story, "The Troubles of a Gnome," in 1926. In 1935 she wrote her first novel, *Angels in the Dust*. She was imprisoned in a German concentration camp for the duration of World War II; after her release at the end of the war, she moved to England and completed two more novels, several short stories, and many articles. Her work is known for its mastery of historical fact and its vivid imagery. (*Sources*: 80, 394)

1927   Dorothy Arzner   (1897–1979) United States

Arzner grew up in Hollywood, and her first job in the movie industry was in 1919 in the script department. Moving quickly through the ranks, Arzner had by 1923 already established a reputation as one of the best script editors, a tedious and exacting job still in its crudest stage. In 1927 she directed her first film, the successful *Fashions for Women*, which established her career; she became one of the first female directors and was later elected the first woman member of the Directors Guild of America. After directing two more comedies about women, Arzner made her first sound film in 1929; *The Wild Party* starred Clara Bow, already a leading actor. Arzner is credited with mounting the stationary microphone on a fishing pole that followed the actors as they moved, thus regaining the mobility lost when sound was first introduced. Working with fledgling stars such as Ginger Rogers, Frederick March, Claudette Colbert, and Katharine Hepburn, Arzner continued to direct until 1943. At that time, having completed the film *Craig's Wife* (which made Rosalind Russell a star) and having been seriously ill, Arzner retired from films. (*Sources*: 98, 133, 491, 597, 656, 717, 745)

1927 Ruth Elder (1904–1977) United States
Ruth Elder learned to fly at a time when women were more accepted as aviators. Women pilots who were successful, and particularly those who were physically attractive, often received lucrative commercial contracts after establishing reputations as pilots. Toward the end of the 1920s, however, though flying fascinated the country and continued to receive much press coverage, there was growing concern for the number of planes that crashed and the number of lives lost. This resulted in more cautious backing of flights to establish or break records. Despite these new restrictions, Elder had sponsors and became a nationally known pilot. In 1927, twenty-three years old at the time, Elder planned a nonstop transatlantic flight with George Haldeman, a well-known pilot. Naming their new plane *American Girl*, they took off for Paris, and because of the storms in the Atlantic at that time of year, they chose to fly directly across the ocean rather than taking the more common northerly route. The two pilots took the precaution of flying over the shipping lanes, which was fortuitous, because when their plane developed problems, they were rescued by a freighter, their plane exploding shortly after they had been rescued from the sea. Although she did not realize her ambition to become the first woman pilot to fly the Atlantic, Elder nevertheless set a record for the longest flight by a woman, having completed 2,030 miles of the trip. Capitalizing on her fame and beauty, Elder made appearances on stage and in film. (*Sources*: 98, 439, 631, 737)

1927   Fumiko Hayashi   (1904–1951) Japan
Hayashi came from a poverty-stricken family and remained poor most of her life. A novelist and poet, she wrote about the destitution of her childhood. She is especially noted for what are considered her semiautobiographical books, *Journey of a Vagabond* (1927), *Toyko*, and *The Floating Cloud*. A realist but not bitter, she tells of her love and belief in a better life in her poem "The Lord Buddha." (*Sources*: 623, 731)

1927   Helen Hogg-Priestley   (1905–) Canada (United States)
Growing up in an intellectually stimulating home, Hogg-Priestley graduated from high school at sixteen but delayed college for a year because of her age; she graduated a member of Phi Beta Kappa from Mount Holyoke College in 1926. The influence of her professors and particularly an unheard-of 100-mile trip by her class to observe the total eclipse of the sun at dawn in 1925 helped Hogg-Priestley decide on a career in astronomy. She published her first paper in 1927 while a graduate student at Radcliffe College. Her lifelong work with globular star clusters began shortly after she earned her doctorate and married an astronomer who accepted a position at the observatory in British Columbia. Given a stipend and observatory privileges, Hogg-Priestley began to photograph star clusters and found a total of 138 new variable stars. She continued her work when both she and her husband were given positions at the University of Toronto. Hogg-Priestley published a catalogue of over 1,000 globular star clusters in 1939, the most complete catalogue to date. By 1946 she had become the first woman elected to the Royal Astronomical Society of Canada. In 1950 she was named the recipient of the coveted Annie Jump Cannon Prize and by 1957 had been made full professor and became the only woman to be named president of the Royal Astronomical Society of Canada. Much of Hogg-Priestley's work led to the discovery that new stars were constantly being formed, the accepted theory having been that all stars had preexisted. (*Sources*: 439, 666, 779)

1927   Vera Menchik-Stevenson   (1906–1944) England (Soviet Union)
Menchik-Stevenson, one of the first women chess players, was also one of the most famous. Her opportunity to play professional chess came when the first women's Olympiad and

women's tournament were inaugurated in 1927. She won every women's tournament from 1927 until her death in a bombing raid in World War II. In a mixed tournament in 1934, she placed third, a record she was never able to better. Menchik-Stevenson was also a noted professional chess teacher and gave frequent lecture tours on the game. (*Sources*: 249, 421, 453, 707)

1927   Leonora Speyer   (1872–1956) United States

Speyer was a gifted violinist with great promise when she made her debut with the Boston Symphony at the age of eighteen. In a relatively few years, when she became afflicted with neuritis, her career was cut short. A multitalented woman, she turned to writing as a new career and published her first book of poems in 1926. Speyer was awarded the Pulitzer Prize in 1927 for her second book of poetry, *Fiddler's Farewell*. She incorporated her musical talent into her poems, producing melodious verse and rhythm, often to dramatic effect. Speyer's works were more successful when she wrote of natural objects rather than people. She was the president of the Poetry Society of America and taught poetry at Columbia University. (*Sources*: 48, 450, 522)

1927   Louise Thaden   (1906–1979) United States

Thaden learned to fly in her late teens, and in 1927, at the age of twenty-one, she won the first Woman's Air Derby. She also held three international flying records for endurance, altitude, and speed; by 1936 she was the recipient of the Harmon Trophy as the most outstanding woman pilot in the country. A close friend and admirer of Amelia Earhart, she tried to dissuade her from making her fatal flight in 1937. Thaden carried on Earhart's goal to get women accepted into aviation—a goal not yet fully realized. (*Sources*: 465, 509, 543, 718, 754)

1928   Katherine Esau   (1898–) United States (Soviet Union)

Esau first began studying botany in the Soviet Union and later in Berlin before immigrating to the United States, where she earned her doctorate at the University of California in 1931, a second doctorate in 1962, and her law degree in 1966. After working briefly for a commercial sugar company in California, Esau began to teach at the University of California in 1928; she was made a full professor in 1949. She also received a Guggenheim Fellowship in 1940 and was named a John Prather fellow at Harvard University in 1960. Despite her honors, numerous books, and publications, she was not made a member of the American Academy of Arts and Sciences until 1949. She was only the seventh woman so honored. (*Sources*: 2, 463, 535, 536, 634)

1928　Juanita Hall　(1901–1968) United States (African American)

Hall's Broadway debut as a singer was in 1928 in *Show Boat*. In 1930 she appeared in *Green Pastures* as part of the Hall Johnson Choir, a company with which she remained for several years. Hall organized her own singing group, which performed frequently on radio, in 1942. Six years later she began to make theater café appearances. Oscar Hammerstein and Richard Rodgers heard Hall and selected her for the role of the Tonkinese woman in their 1949 Broadway hit *South Pacific*; this was the first time an African American had been given a major role in an all-white Broadway show. Hall appeared in other shows and in 1966 gave a one-woman show in New York. (*Sources*: 455, 508, 688)

1928　Barbara Hepworth　(1903–1975) England

Hepworth won a scholarship to the Royal College of Art in London to study sculpture; she went on to Italy for two years of further training. She gave her first exhibit in conjunction with her husband, also a sculpter, in 1928. By 1933 Hepworth was experimenting with free organic forms in her work as well as using the newer pierced forms, and this type of sculpture became her trademark. Hepworth is perhaps best known for her Dag Hammarskjöld Memorial at the United Nations headquarters in New York. In addition to receiving numerous other awards and honorary doctorates, she was made a dame of the British Empire in 1965. (*Sources*: 356, 407, 538, 608, 717, 726)

1928　Ruth Bryan Owen　(1885–1954) United States

Daughter of William Jennings Bryan, the noted orator, senator, and prosecutor in the Scopes trial, Owen established a political career of her own. Her first position was as secretary of the American Woman's War Relief Fund in Britain during World War I. Following the war, she began to give public lectures. Although beaten in her first bid for Congress in Florida in 1926, she was successful in her second bid two years later, becoming the first woman from the South elected to Congress. Owen was reelected in 1930 but lost her seat in 1932. In 1933 Owen became the first woman to be appointed ambassador to Denmark. Forced to resign in 1936 because of her marriage to a Danish military officer, Owen resumed public speaking and writing. Her first book, *Elements of Public Speaking*, had been published in 1933. Her later books, written between 1935 and 1943, were primarily fairy tales and novels about Denmark. In 1954 Owen was given the Distinguished Service Medal by the king of Denmark. (*Sources*: 84, 548, 718)

1928 Mabel Willebrandt (1889–1963) United States
Willebrandt received her law degree from the University of Southern California in 1916. She became interested in the issue of criminality and women when she served as the first woman assistant public defender in Los Angeles County. Active in women's groups, she was one of the founders of the Women Lawyers Association and also helped to create an advisory board to help new lawyers become established. In 1921, at age thirty-two, Willebrandt was appointed assistant attorney general of the United States. Her vigorous work to establish separate prisons for women, especially federal prisons, met with success when the first federal women's prison was opened in 1928. (*Sources*: 74, 363, 718)

1929 Margaret Bondfield (1873–1953) England
When Bondfield took a job at the age of eighteen, she had to work a seventy-four-hour week at subsistence wages. She joined the newly formed National Union of Shop Assistants and the Independent Labour Party and was the only woman delegate to the Trades Union Congress held in 1898. In 1929, with an established record of pushing for reform in working conditions, she was elected the first woman minister of labor. In 1931 she was defeated in her bid for reelection. (*Sources*: 518, 583, 681)

1929 Aida Breckinridge (1884–1962) United States
A wealthy young student in Paris in 1903, Breckinridge took the first balloon ride by a woman, a feat her scandalized parents kept secret for almost thirty years. Her greater claim to fame occurred in 1929, when she founded the first institute for ophthalmological surgery at Johns Hopkins Medical School, named in honor of the physician who had saved partial vision in

one of Breckinridge's eyes when she was afflicted with glaucoma at the age of thirty-eight. In 1945 Breckinridge was also responsible for the establishment of the Eye Bank for Sight Restoration, which focused on publicizing the need for eye donations, a rapid system for the transport of donated eyes, and the training of physicians to perform eye surgery. Breckinridge served as the eye bank's director for the first ten years. Eye banks have since been opened throughout the country and the world, saving or restoring the sight of millions of people. (*Sources*: 568, 718)

1929　Dorothy Eustis　(1886–1946) Switzerland (United States)

In 1923, disturbed that German shepherd dogs were being bred for beauty at the cost of their intelligence and utility, Eustis moved to her husband's family's home in Switzerland to breed the dogs back to their original characteristics. An article in the *Saturday Evening Post* about the work she and her partner, Jack Humphrey, were doing in training dogs to assist the blind led to a flood of requests for the dogs from the United States. Eustis agreed to teach Frank Morris, who was sightless, how to train his dog, Buddy, to serve as his guide. As a result, a Seeing Eye school with two students was started in Tennessee in 1929, and Eustis was named its first president. The school later moved to New Jersey, where its headquarters are now located. In the system Eustis developed, the pups are placed in families with young children for a year and are then returned to the school for their Seeing Eye training. The sightless are also given one month of training in the procedure at the school. Eustis's ambition to return the dogs to their natural traits and her willingness to develop their abilities to assist the sightless became an immeasurable humanitarian service. (*Sources*: 346, 455)

1929　Kathleen Kenyon　(1906–1978) England

Kenyon's interest in archeaology was fostered by her father, who was the chief librarian at the British Museum. Having completed her studies at Oxford, she went on her first dig to Rhodesia (now Zimbabwe) in 1929 to investigate the site of King Solomon's mines. She also helped to unearth a Roman amphitheater in London. She conducted her own digs in Jericho and Jerusalem and established that the cities were permanent rather than nomadic settlements, that nonnomadic life was not possible until the agricultural age, and that the walls of Jericho had collapsed as a result of an earthquake, not a battle. Kenyon was a supporter of the slow but, she believed, reliable Mortimer grid method rather than the Wheeler method of digging directly along an exposed wall—both methods are still highly controversial. Kenyon's other major contribution was in helping to found the London Institute of Archaeology. (*Sources*: 228, 583, 621, 752)

1929   Phoebe Omlie   (1902–1975) United States
Omlie was seventeen years old when she started to make spectacular parachute jumps in order to finance her flying lessons. She soon gained a national reputation as a pilot and, with her new husband, Vernon Omlie, began the Phoebe Omlie Flying School. In 1927 she was issued pilot's license number 199 by the U.S. Department of Commerce. Omlie won the first and second women's Powder Puff Derby in 1929 and 1930. For winning the National Air Races (opened to women for the first time in 1931 but closed to them in 1934), she received a new car and what was then considered the astronomical amount of $12,000. Little is known of Omlie after she discontinued flying. (*Sources*: 98, 418, 441, 509, 631)

1929   Mary Lou Williams   (1910–1981) United States
(African American)
With very little formal training, Williams carved out an illustrious career as a pianist, arranger, and composer in the field of jazz. She began her career in 1929 as a pianist with the Andy Kirk Orchestra and was soon arranging music for the group. She later became an arranger for some of the famous bands of the era, including those of Benny Goodman and Duke Ellington. She played her own composition, *Zodiac Suite,* at a Town Hall concert in 1945. Williams gave theater performances, made records, and appeared on radio and television. She was awarded four honorary degrees in music and a Guggenheim Fellowship and was named artist in residence at Duke University in 1971. Following her conversion to Catholicism, she wrote primarily religious music. (*Sources*: 330, 583, 611, 717, 718)

1930   Ellen Church   (1905?–) United States
Church, a licensed pilot and a registered nurse, suggested to Boeing Air Transport that they hire her as a nurse aboard their

aircraft to attend to any passenger emergencies that might arise. Initially reluctant, the airline hired Church as the first airline stewardess. Her initial route was from Cheyenne to San Francisco, a flight that took fourteen hours because of the numerous stops made along the way. Since passengers responded favorably to the security of having a nurse aboard, Church was told to recruit seven more nurses. Along with their nursing services, these first stewardesses loaded baggage, cleaned the interior of the planes, and found shelter for passengers when there were unexpected landings due to bad weather. Within a few years, other airlines were hiring women as attendants, and training schools were soon established. (*Sources*: 98, 439, 441, 631, 636, 672)

1930   Ruth Crawford [Seeger]   (1901–1953) United States

Crawford never developed her talent as a poet and because of tendinitis was thwarted in her efforts to become a pianist. She instead turned to composing and earned her bachelor's degree from the American Conservatory of Music in Chicago in 1923 and her master's degree in 1927. In 1930 Crawford was the first female recipient of a Guggenheim Fellowship and went to Europe for further study in classical composition. She wrote several classical pieces, especially for chamber ensembles; a string quartet composed in 1931 is considered her best. Influenced by Carl Sand-burg, whose poetry she had set to music, and by Charles Seeger, a folksinger whom she later married, Crawford began to write popular rather than classical pieces, publishing them under her married name and often collaborating with her husband and others. She also transcribed more than 200 folk recordings housed in the archives at the Library of Congress. It was 1952 before Crawford resumed composing classical music, but she died a year later. Because her folksongs became better known, Crawford is not usually associated with classical music. (*Sources*: 423, 439, 571, 627, 717, 754)

1930   Nancy Cunard   (1896–1965) England

An avant-garde poet and journalist, Cunard in 1930 wrote an exposé on the racist attitudes of the English gentry. Calling it *Black Man and White Ladyship,* she used her mother, a well-known, wealthy, and very much envied woman, as an example of this racism. Objecting to her daughter's association with blacks, particularly her romantic liaisons, Cunard's mother threatened to leave her nothing in her will. Cunard nevertheless wrote scathingly of her, even posting her mother's annual clothing expenditure. Cunard's article was a sensation but was severely criticized for its viciousness even by those sympathetic to her views. (*Sources*: 47, 717)

1930 Edith Hamilton (1867–1963) United States

Edith and her sister, ALICE HAMILTON, were both intellectual. Alice chose medicine as her field, and Edith became a classical scholar. Interested in classics from an early age, she studied at both Bryn Mawr and Munich University. Hamilton wrote her first book, *The Greek Way*, in 1930 and her second, *The Roman Way*, in 1932. Hamilton was elected to the American Academy of Arts and Letters and was made an honorary citizen of Athens for her contribution to classical knowledge. (*Sources*: 718, 731)

1930 Amy Johnson (1903–1941) England

A newly licensed pilot and ground engineer with only fifty hours of flying experience, Johnson attempted to better the time record from England to Australia in 1930. Her plane developed engine problems while en route, but she managed to communicate with people who had never seen a white woman before nor understood English and to obtain barely usable spare parts. Although she completed the flight, she failed to break the existing record. She next made flights from London to India and then Tokyo and from London to the United States across the North Atlantic Ocean. In 1931 she married; with her husband, she set several new flying records. She was divorced in 1938 and at the beginning of World War II helped to establish the Women's Auxiliary Air Force. When Johnson's plane went down while she was ferrying it across the Thames River, she swam to within 20 yards of the rescue ship before disappearing under the water. (*Sources*: 377, 424, 441, 455, 500, 509, 518, 614, 731, 739)

1930 Rachel Queiroz (1910–) Brazil

Queiroz's first book, *The Year '15* (1930), established what would become one of her most frequently used themes, that of a woman who is victimized by her role in life but fights back and survives. She also wrote of a woman's need to experience not only passionate love and maternal love but a feeling of love for humankind in general. Queiroz subtly weaves the greater social injustice and differences in social class into the lives of her characters. Highly respected by her fellow Brazilians, Queiroz was offered the post of minister of education and culture in 1961 but declined the honor. (*Sources*: 64, 124, 280, 697)

1930 Rose Schneiderman (1882–1972) United States (Jewish American)

Schneiderman, a Polish immigrant, joined the Women's Trade Union League in 1903, after she had been fired from her clerical position for making her first error and after she had been forced to purchase her own sewing machine in order to work as a seamstress in a factory. Interested in improving working conditions and wages for women, Schneiderman became the president of the league in 1930 and was active in organizing strikes and rallies, frequently speaking at local union meetings. Concerned that the depression focused attention only on the plight of male workers, Schneiderman raised awareness of the treatment of women workers, who were either unemployed or paid lower wages than men for the same amount of work and number of hours. She was fearful that jobless and desperate women would turn to prostitution. A feminist, Schneiderman emphasized that women who worked in foundries and laundries in unbearable heat would not, as men had charged, lose their femininity if they were given the vote. Schneiderman is considered one of the best speakers of the time on working women's issues. (*Sources*: 339, 439, 584, 699, 754, 763)

1931 Florence Bailey (1863–1948) United States

While a student at Smith College, Bailey became interested in ornithology, and her articles on birds were published in the *Audubon Magazine*. She contracted tuberculosis shortly after leaving college; while recuperating in New Mexico, she wrote about the birds of that region. For her book *Birds of New Mexico* she won the Brewster Medal in 1931. In 1899 she had married naturalist Vernon Bailey and, accompanying him on his field trips, added natural history to her books. Bailey is credited with writing popular books on nature for a wide audience. (*Sources*: 2, 548, 587)

1931 Irmgard Flügge-Lotz (1903–1974) Germany

Flügge-Lotz earned her doctorate in engineering from the Technical University of Hannover in 1929. She was made chair of the Department of Aerodynamics at Göttingen University, where in 1931 she developed the method for calculating the distribution of the lifting force of an airplane's wings. Because of their technical knowledge, both she and her husband, also an aerodynamics professor, were allowed to remain in Germany during World War II in spite of their anti-Nazi sentiments. It was during this period that Flügge-Lotz began to develop the principles of automatic flight control to replace the existing manual controls found in aircraft. She and her husband emigrated to the United States shortly after the war and were appointed professors at Stanford University, with Flügge-Lotz the first woman appointed a full professor in the engineering school. She was named a fellow of the American Institute of Aeronautics and Astronautics in 1970 and also received the Achievement Award of the Society of Women Engineers. (*Sources*: 583, 627)

1931 Nancy Mitford (1904–1973) England

Mitford wrote charming novels in which she wittily parodied the British upper class. Her first novel, written in 1931, was entitled *Highland Fling*; once established as a successful author, she wrote two more novels in the 1930s, another three in the 1940s, and in her most prolific decade, the 1950s, wrote four novels and translated and adapted a comedy for the London stage. Mitford published *Don't Tell Alfred* and *The Water Beetle* in the early 1960s. Intrigued by the French court, she also wrote biographies of Madame de Pompadour, Louis XIV, and Voltaire. (*Sources*: 251, 626)

1931 Marguerite Yourcenar (1903–1987) France (Belgium)

Yourcenar was the daughter of a wealthy scholar who encouraged her to write at an early age and helped her to change the family name of Crayencour into the anagrammatic Yourcenar. She was noted as a classic novelist as early as 1931, when she wrote *La nouvelle Eurydice* (The new Eurydice). In her writing Yourcenar skillfully blended past and contemporary events to emphasize the continuity of history and its impact on the present. In 1939 her inheritance was lost, and she emigrated to the United States. Although she became a U.S. citizen and wrote about themes such as black American poetry and Negro spirituals, she continued to write in French. Yourcenar's *Les mémoires d'Hadrien* (Memories of Hadrien; 1951) is considered her greatest work. The French Academy, limited to forty people—all of them men up to that point—elected her a member in 1980; she was also granted French citizenship. (*Sources*: 98, 731, 739)

1932 Hattie Caraway (1878–1950) United States

Not unlike President Calvin Coolidge, who had left office with the nickname "Silent Cal" shortly before Caraway arrived in the capital, she soon acquired the moniker "Silent Hattie." She had been sent to Washington at the end of 1931 to complete her husband's term of office as the senator from Arkansas. Her quiet manner and plain dress led everyone to assume she would leave as soon as a new senator from Arkansas was elected; instead, she successfully ran for office and in 1932 became the first woman elected senator. Caraway was reelected in 1938 and served as a senator from 1931 to 1944. (*Sources*: 98, 125, 455, 583, 718, 724)

1932 Dorothea Lange (1895–1965) United States

Struggling to make her name as a photographer, Lange was touched by the homeless men wandering the streets as victims of the Great Depression and in 1932 began to take pictures of them. The first photograph that brought her attention was entitled *White Angel Breadline*. Lange was then hired by the state of California to document the lives of migrant workers. Because of her ability to convey both the economic despair and the personal dignity of her subjects, her photographs became classics. Lange was among the first photographers hired by a newly established federal agency, the Farm Security Administration, to document the living conditions of the poor. During World War II, with the same skill and compassion she exhibited in her photography of the Depression, Lange captured on film the devastation of the Japanese Americans as they were being sent to detention camps. (*Sources*: 34, 237, 532, 548, 627, 754, 756)

1932 I[rene] Rice Pereira (1907–1971) United States

Pereira began a modest and conventional career in art as a poor young woman attending art classes at night. It was not until she had the opportunity to study in Paris and Italy and—most important in her case—to visit the Sahara Desert that she was able to develop her unique style. Influenced by the vastness of the ocean and the luminescence of the desert, Pereira began to develop ways to capture these dimensions on canvas. Her first exhibit, a one-woman show in 1932, included many of her paintings of the ocean. Experimenting with cubism and surrealism, Pereira did a series of paintings depicting humans as smaller than the machinery over which they were supposed to be masters. Still searching for additional ways to convey space and translucence, Pereira in 1939 began to combine paint and glass. Using lighter and darker shades in oil in different densities on several different layers of corrugated glass, she was able to create the sense of motion, infinite space, and texture. *Undulating Arrangement* (1947) and *Shooting Stars* (1952) are considered excellent examples of this cosmic space effect. Pereira also wrote poetry and metaphysical pieces; she was given an honorary doctorate from the Free University of Asia and was named poet laureate of the Philippines in 1968 for her work in these fields. (*Sources*: 407, 496, 608, 639, 727, 754)

1932 Florence Price (1888–1953) United States (African American)
Price graduated from the New England Conservatory of Music in 1906 at the age of eighteen. Talented as both a pianist and a composer, she won her first prize for piano composition in 1928. Her initial major success came in 1932, when her Symphony in E Minor, which won the Wannamaker Prize, was played by the Chicago Symphony Orchestra at the Century of Progress Exhibition. That same year, she performed another of her compositions with the Chicago Women's Symphony. Price composed such diverse pieces as the chorus and orchestral *Wind and the Sea*, Rhapsody for Piano, and *Negro Folksongs in Counterpoint* for string quartet. (*Sources*: 29, 99, 516, 372, 698, 718, 754)

1932 Josephine Tey (1897–1952) Scotland
Elizabeth Mackintosh wrote under the pen names of Josephine Tey and Gordon Daviot. She used the name Daviot for most of her plays and some of her novels and biographies and Tey for her murder-mystery novels. She had had to give up her position as a physical education instructor when both of her

parents became ill in the late 1920s. While caring for them, she had begun to write plays and novels. Her first play, *Richard of Bordeaux*, written in 1932, was not only a success but also provided the showcase for one of John Gielgud's earliest performances. Tey also wrote four additional plays between 1934 and 1949. She wrote eight murder-mysteries, with her last, *The Singing Sands*, published posthumously in 1952. (*Sources*: 36, 307, 571, 739)

1933 Caterina Jarboro (1903–1986) United States (African American)

Born Catherine Yarborough, Jarboro was once refused membership in the New York Opera Association because she was black. In 1931, however, she became the first black opera singer to perform in New York City, singing the lead role in *Aida*. Jarboro had previously performed in a number of Broadway shows, starting with *Shuffle Along* in 1921. She sang in both Europe and the United States, giving a concert at Carnegie Hall in 1944. The Caterina Jarboro Company, a theater group, was renamed in her honor in 1971. (*Sources*: 98, 120, 439, 524, 678, 684)

1933 Alicia Markova (1910–) England

Markova began to dance professionally at the age of ten, and by sixteen she had danced the lead in a ballet by the choreographer George Balanchine. In 1933 Markova was named prima ballerina with Vic-Wells Ballet Company. In the years that followed, she danced with the Rambert Ballet Club, formed her own ballet group, and danced with the Ballet Russe. She danced for the American Ballet Theater in New York from 1941 to 1944, creating a lead for the ballet *Aleko* and the role of Juliet in *Romeo and Juliet*. Markova retired from performing in 1963 and became the director for the Metropolitan Opera Ballet in New York. Named a dame of the British Empire in 1973, she was also appointed governor of the Royal Ballet. (*Sources*: 15, 246, 402, 478, 583, 731)

1933 Maria Cadilla de Martinez (1884–1951) Puerto Rico

Martinez began a modest career as a teacher in Puerto Rico following her teachers' training at Washington Institute in the United States in 1902. She became certified to teach English in 1910 and by 1916 was teaching history and literature at the University of Puerto Rico. Martinez completed her bachelor's degree in 1928 and earned a master's degree in education in 1930. She studied for her doctorate in Spanish literature in Spain, completing her degree in 1933. Her doctoral thesis, *Popular Poetry in Puerto Rico*, published in 1933, is still a major textbook on the subject. Over a twenty-year period, Martinez wrote nine books on her work in Puerto Rican culture, folklore, and children's fairy tales. She also published numerous books on the cultural history of Puerto Rico and several other countries. Martinez was honored by several countries for her poetry and art as well as for her writing. Noted as an educator, historian, poet, and artist, Martinez was active in the women's movement in Puerto Rico and served as president of the Association for Mental Health in her native country. (*Sources*: 721, 757)

1933   Barbara McClintock   (1902–) United States
McClintock earned her bachelor's degree in botany at Cornell University in 1923 and her doctorate in science, graduating with honors from the University of Rochester in 1947. Although noted for her research in genetics for the Guggenheim Foundation (1933–1934) and the Carnegie Institute (1941–1947), McClintock was never given a research post at a major university; instead, she taught at Cornell University and at the University of Missouri. She was the recipient of numerous awards for her work in genetics and was honored by the American Association of University Women in 1947. (Sources: 2, 98, 393, 408, 536)

1933   Nellie Ross   (1876–1977) United States
Ross, like MIRIAM FERGUSON, was asked to complete the two years left in her husband's term in the gubernatorial office upon his death. Sworn in a few days before Ferguson, Ross became the first woman governor. She was not reelected but in 1933 became the first woman named to the post of director of the U.S. Mint, a position she held for twenty years. During Ross's tenure, three new mints were added: Fort Knox, the West Point Depository, and one in San Francisco. (*Sources*: 125, 548, 583, 718, 754)

1933   Dorothy L. Sayers   (1893–1957) England
In 1915, with a degree in medieval literature, Sayers became one of the first women to graduate from Oxford University. She began her literary career by editing three murder-

mysteries in the late 1920s. Although she herself began writing detective novels in 1930, she received little acclaim until 1933, when she wrote *Murder Must Advertise*. By 1937, tired of detective novels, she began to write religious books. Several of her stories were performed on the radio during religious holidays. Sayers also began an English translation of Dante's *Inferno* but only completed the *Purgatorio* before her death. (*Sources*: 80, 294, 518, 731, 751)

1933   Phyllis Tate   (1911–1987) England
Tate studied composition at the Royal Academy of Music in London. Not satisfied with some of her early efforts, she published pieces under fictitious names and later destroyed some of this work. The first public performance of one of her compositions was in 1933, when her cello concerto was played. Tate reached the apex of her career for instrumental composition in 1944 with her Concert for Alto Saxophone and Strings. By 1960 Tate had elected to write more vocal music; *The Lodger*, based on the story of Jack the Ripper, was her most successful opera. She also wrote several operettas between 1970 and 1980. Tate's distinctive style is marked by its rhythmic dissonance and asymmetry. (*Sources*: 29, 116, 731)

1934   Florence Allen   (1884–1966) United States
Allen came from a family noted for its accomplishments: a progenitor, Samuel Fuller, arrived in the New World on the *Mayflower*; her maternal grandfather, Jacob Tuckerman, with an interrupted education, became president of Farmer's College in Cincinnati; her paternal grandfather, Cyrus Allen, founded the dental school at the University of Buffalo; her father, Emir, was a legislator who helped to draft the Ohio constitution; and her mother, Corinne, helped to establish the first free public library in Salt Lake City. Allen graduated from Case Western Reserve University in 1904 and earned her law degree from New York University in 1913. Having become interested in women's suffrage, Allen returned to Ohio to practice law and to help secure the passage of the suffrage bill. Not hired by any law firm because she was a woman, Allen became interested in worker compensation laws through her work in legal aid. She also became involved in politics and in 1921 was elected a judge in the court of common pleas. While serving on this bench, she became the first

woman judge to sentence a man to death. In 1922, without the support of either party but with the backing of women's groups, Allen was elected to the Ohio State Supreme Court. Allen reached the apogee of her career in 1934, when President Franklin D. Roosevelt appointed her to the Federal Circuit Court of Appeals, making her the first female judge to sit on a federal court only one step below the Supreme Court. (*Sources*: 34, 74, 125, 455, 713, 729)

1934   Maria Dabrowska   (1889–1965) Poland
Dabrowska used the peasant life in Poland to show the strength of her native country. In 1934, depicting a poor couple as her central characters, she wrote her masterpiece, *Nights and Days*, in which she portrayed the endurance, particularly the endurance of the woman, to bravely cope with life's adversities and to show the importance of the roots provided by family life and native culture. Always writing in a positive vein, in 1955 Dabrowska chose the description and meaning of a village wedding to illustrate the calamities experienced by the Poles during and after World War II. Dabrowska first began writing in 1909 and died before she finished her last novel, started in 1961. (*Sources*: 476, 739)

1934   Marie Drake   (1887–1965) United States
In 1907 Drake moved to Alaska with her new husband, who went to work for the Bureau of Public Roads. In 1917 she was hired as a secretary in the Department of Education and found there was no office and few records. In order to establish an accurate record system, she often traveled to remote school districts by dogsled or plane to get the needed information. In 1934 she became the first woman appointed assistant commissioner of education; one of her duties was to edit and write the district school newspaper. In 1935 she published a poem about Alaska that was later set to music by Elinor Dusenbury and became the state song. Drake remained with the department until 1945 and was awarded an honorary doctorate from the University of Alaska in 1958 for her contributions to the Alaska school system. (*Sources*: 712, 718)

1934   Katharine [Kit] Hepburn   (1878–1951) United States
Perhaps best known as the mother of the famous actress Katharine Hepburn, Kit Hepburn was active in her own right.

She worked toward both women's suffrage and improved working conditions, taking along her four-year-old daughter when she picketed the White House for better working conditions for women. Hepburn, who had six children, came from a wealthy background and was married to a prosperous physician; aware that a large family such as hers would be a hardship for a poorer woman, she supported the legalization of birth control. In 1934, she appeared before the House Judiciary Committee to tell the members that their fears about legalizing birth control were as unfounded as had been their earlier fears about the passage of the suffrage bill. (*Sources*: 415, 603, 680)

1934   Tillie Lewis   (1901–1977) United States
Lewis went to work at the age of twelve and within twenty years she was earning top commission selling securities. In 1934, noting that all Italian tomato products were imported, she borrowed money, arranged for the purchase of tomato seeds from an Italian exporter, and experimented with growing Italian tomatoes in the San Joaquin Valley. A skilled entrepreneur, she turned her original loan into a multimillion-dollar business, bought out the canning firm, and, when the firm was in turn purchased by Ogden Foods, served as president of the company. (*Sources*: 518, 525, 583, 718)

1934   Alice Paul   (1885–1977) United States
Paul earned her bachelor's degree from Swarthmore College in 1905, her master's and doctoral degrees in 1907 and 1912, a law degree from the Washington College of Law in 1922, and master's and doctoral degrees in law in 1927 and 1928 from the American University of Law. The pursuit of these latter three degrees was stimulated by an interest in the women's movement; in 1906, when she had gone to England for further studies, she had become involved in women's rights groups. Arrested and jailed several times and a victim of the Cat and Mouse Act (under which British authorities force-fed hunger-striking women prior to their release from prison), Paul returned to the United States determined to aid in the fight for equal rights. She organized groups, led marches on the White House, and was credited with writing the original draft of the Equal Rights Amendment in 1934 (it was later reworded by a Senate committee when it was presented to Congress). Paul is also credited with the

incorporation of an equal rights statement into the United Nations Charter of 1945 and into the Civil Rights Act of 1964, which specifically forbids discrimination on the basis of sex. By the time of Paul's death in 1977, she had lived to see women given the right to vote and the Equal Rights Amendment only seven votes short of being enacted into law. (*Sources*: 400, 401, 470, 548, 584, 603, 627, 631, 687, 699)

1934   Hanna Reitsch   (1912–1979) Germany

Reitsch had to cajole her father into allowing her to take flying lessons. A petite woman, she was not taken seriously by flight instructors and students until within a short time she became not only a pilot but an expert in flying a new invention, the glider plane. Needing money to accompany an expeditionary force to test gliders in South America in 1934, Reitsch did stunt flying for a movie. She participated in research on gliders and performed aerial shows, for which the government of Argentina gave her the Silver Soaring Medal. The only woman in the program, Reitsch continued working with the Institute for Glider Research for eleven years, during which time she helped to design and test a new braking system to prevent the loss of control of a glider, which often led to crashes. Flying at 19,000 feet, she dove toward earth at 125 miles an hour; at 600 feet she retracted the dive brakes, landing safely. In 1937 Reitsch was invited to become a test pilot for the only recently revealed German air force, becoming the first female pilot to fly yet another new invention, the helicopter. She was also one of the five German pilots to be the first to fly a glider over the Swiss Alps. With the outbreak of World War II, Reitsch began testing military planes. She was awarded an Iron Cross, second class, for her pioneer work in testing planes with scissor-edged wings to cut through the British balloons equipped with cables that would slice the wings of planes as they approached for an attack. Although she had to terminate these tests when she contracted scarlet fever, by 1942 Reitsch was testing rocket-powered Messerschmitts. On her fifth test flight she crashed and was seriously injured, requiring months of reconstructive facial surgery; she was subsequently awarded an Iron Cross, first class. In the last year of the war, she became the only woman to test the V-l, a small rocket carrying a gyroscope-guided bomb; two male test pilots had been killed and four seriously wounded testing the V-1s. The war ended before

manned rockets were successfully developed. Following the end of
World War II, Reitsch was questioned by the liberating forces:
because she had flown through Soviet lines to Hitler's last
bunker, the Allies suspected her of having flown the Führer out of
Germany. These charges were dismissed; however, Reitsch was
imprisoned until 1946 for her war activities. She lived in
seclusion until 1952, when she competed as part of the German
team in the World Gliding Championships in Spain and went on
to establish several new records. Honored by a number of
countries, including the United States, Reitsch was elected Pilot
of the Year by the state of Arizona in 1972. She continued to fly
until shortly before her death a few years later. (*Sources*: 441,
509, 564, 622, 631)

1934   Florence Seibert   (1897–) United States

Robert Koch, a bacteriologist, identified the tubercle
bacillus in 1892 and developed the skin test that determined
the presence of tuberculosis; the test was not reliable, however,
because of the impurities found in the live tuberculin used.
Having worked on developing the technique for ten years, Seibert
in 1934 was able to extract the pure tuberculin that makes the test
accurate, establishing a special batch of the tuberculin that is
used today as the standard of measurement. A victim of polio,
Seibert was lame all her life. Coming from a poor family, she
relied on scholarships to finance her education, graduating from
Goucher College and obtaining her medical degree from Yale
University in 1923. Financing part of her education by working
in a laboratory, she soon took more of an interest in research
than in the practice of medicine and devoted her career to
medical research. Seibert is also credited with developing
the means to isolate bacteria from the distilled water used in
medical procedures. She later worked on methods to determine
the size, weight, and structure of molecules. (*Sources*: 463, 535,
634, 778)

1934   Tess Slesinger   (1905–1945) United States

Slesinger, a graduate of Swarthmore College and
Columbia University, published short stories at the age of
twenty-three and wrote her first novel, *The Unpossessed*, at the
age of twenty-nine. In 1935 she moved to Hollywood and became a
successful scriptwriter. Her best-known screenplay was for *The*

Good Earth in 1937. She died of cancer at thirty-nine. (*Sources*: 522, 680)

1934   Christina Stead   (1902–1983) Australia

In her first book, *Seven Poor Men of Sidney* (1934), Stead described the harsh waterfront life. Her skill at succinctly portraying the uglier side of life was very much in evidence in *The Man Who Loved Children* (1940), but the work's brilliance went unrecognized for twenty-five years. Compared to the writings of Leo Tolstoy and other literary giants, Stead's book portrayed the harsh life of a married couple, the wife a bitter woman barely able to survive her brutish husband. The author of fourteen novels and several short stories, Stead was nominated several times for the Nobel Prize in literature but never received the award. (*Sources*: 80, 303, 599)

1934   Simone Weil   (1909–1943) France

A brilliant child, Weil was the first female accepted at the École Normale Supérieure. Obsessed by humanitarian causes, she became a social activist. In 1934 she went to work in an auto factory to experience and identify with industrial working conditions. She also went to Spain during the civil war, but returned to France after being badly burned in an accident. Already as a child she had often endangered her health by self-starvation; in 1943, unable to return to France to share the war with her compatriots, she refused to eat more than the French were receiving in rations and died of malnutrition. In spite of her poor health, Weil wrote extensively on politics, social philosophy, and spirituality. (*Sources*: 558, 583, 599, 731, 751)

1935   Patricia [Patty] Berg   (1918–) United States

Berg started golf lessons at the age of thirteen and by the age of seventeen had won her first tournament, the Minnesota State Women's Championship. Winning several more championships, Berg was awarded the National Women's Amateur Title in 1938. In 1940 she turned professional and went on to earn thirteen more titles, which included one in which she beat the famous woman golfer Babe Didrikson Zaharias. Berg was inducted into the World Golf Hall of Fame in 1974 and in 1976 won the Ben Hogan Award. (*Sources*: 98, 439, 548, 685)

1935   Juliette Fraser   (1887–1983) United States (Hawaiian American)

Fraser studied art at Wellesley College, graduating in 1915, and at the Art Students' League in New York City. Through the early 1900s she taught art at Hawaiian high schools and worked for an art shop. In 1934 Fraser was one of only four artists granted a commission under the federal Works Project Administration; the painting she completed for the WPA is now housed at the Hawaiian State Library. In 1935 Fraser received her first private commission, a mural for the home of a Mrs. Charles Adams, and she later painted the murals for the Hawaiian Pavilion at the 1938 World's Fair in San Francisco. At the outbreak of World War II, Fraser began to work in the camouflage department of the military; working with 100-gallon drums of paint, she stained camouflage netting and credited this experience with teaching her to do large murals and to work comfortably on scaffolding. This led to her first fresco work in 1949 depicting the Konane Players and titled in their honor. For her mural for the Board of Water Supply in 1954, she began to do more symbolic representations of Hawaiian legends, the most common theme in her murals. In 1967 Fraser was selected to paint the mural for the Ipapandi Chapel, a gift from Hawaii to Greece, for which the Greeks renamed a street in her honor. Fraser also worked in other mediums: in 1972 she supervised the making of the 1,900 handcrafted tiles used in her *Ka Haku Beniamina* mural for a school in Hawaii. A noted illustrator as well, Fraser won an award for her writing and illustrations for a book entitled *Ke Anvenue* in 1952. (*Sources*: 19, 61, 121, 382, 606)

1935   Marja Kuncewiczowa   (1897–) England (Poland)

A novelist, Kuncewiczowa wrote her books, *The Stranger* (1935) and *Polish Milestones* (1942), in her native country before moving to England in 1946. Noted for her original and sensitive writing style, she is considered an experimentalist. (*Sources*: 80, 394)

1935   Audrey Richards   (1899–1984) Uganda (England)

Richards earned her doctorate at the University of London School of Economics and Political Science in 1929 and was hired as a lecturer in social anthropology. In 1935 Richards moved to South Africa, where she taught at the University of Witwatersrand. After a brief return to England, she next taught at Makerere University in Uganda, leaving to become the director of the East African Institute of Social Research. During her years in Africa, Richards conducted field research in Rhodesia (now Zimbabwe), the Transvaal, and Uganda. From 1944 to 1962 Richards was associated with the Colonial Research Council. (*Sources*: 285, 398, 634)

1935 Kate Roberts (1891–1985) Wales

Already a noted writer, Roberts became the director of a publishing house in Denbigh, Wales, in 1935. She was the major force in developing the short story in Welsh writing. Taking as her subject the struggles of miners and their families, she wrote of their hopes and endurance rather than focusing on their hardships. Using a mix of conventional language and dialect, she was able to convey the essence of mining village life. (*Sources*: 80, 118, 287)

1935 Muriel Rukeyser (1913–) United States

An eclectic poet whose works are often described as romantic and lyrical, Rukeyser was alert to her environment and infused her poetry with real-life drama. A contributor to sophisticated literary magazines and theatrical publications, she wrote her first book, *Theory of Flight*, in 1935. For this work, Rukeyser drew on such experiences as the 1933 Scottsboro Boys trial (in which nine young black males were convicted of raping a white woman, all but two of the hasty convictions later being overturned) and learning how to fly. Her later books—*Mediterranean* and *U.S. 1* (1938) and *A Turning Wind* (1939)—reflect her impressions of her travels. Rukeyser made a social statement in her symbol-laden book on abolitionist John Brown (1940) but was equally comfortable writing a biography of a physicist in 1942. After receiving two monetary awards and a Guggenheim Fellowship in 1943, Rukeyser was able to concentrate exclusively on writing poetry, and between 1944 and 1978 she published fifteen books of her collected poems. Rukeyser is also noted for her children's books and for the several works she translated. (*Sources*: 3, 548, 728, 754, 758)

1936 Dolores Ibarruri (1895–1989) Spain

Ibarruri, called La Pasionaria for her strong political views, was elected to the Cortes (the Spanish parliament) in

1936. The founder of the Spanish Communist Party and editor of several Communist newspapers, she used every means available, including walking the streets, to urge people to oppose the Fascist Party. She was forced to leave Spain during Francisco Franco's regime, spending the better part of forty years in the Soviet Union as an officer in the Spanish Communist Party there. When Ibarruri returned to Spain in 1977 at the age of eighty-two, she was again elected to the Cortes. The title of the English translation of her autobiography, *They Shall Not Pass* (1966), was taken from her well-known slogan. (*Sources*: 361, 558, 583, 621, 731, 739)

1936 Beryl Markham (1902–1986) Kenya (England)
Markham's independence and sense of adventure derived in part from having been raised as one of the few white children in East Africa (now Kenya) by her divorced father, who left her alone at the age of seventeen when it became necessary for him to leave the country. Using the knowledge of horse breeding and racing her father had taught her and hunting skills she had learned from her African contemporaries, Markham was able to support herself. In 1930, having met the pilot Tom Black, she learned to fly; by age twenty-eight she was a bush pilot carrying mail and passengers and leading aerial hunting expeditions throughout Africa. Although Markham had often flown from Africa to London, in 1936 she decided to make what would be the first flight from London to New York, considered an almost impossible and dangerous trip because of headwinds and foul weather. Markham had to fly by instruments and instinct; she had planned to stop in Nova Scotia only for refueling, but when her plane developed engine problems, she safely crash-landed there. The flight had taken twenty-one hours and twenty-five minutes, and though she did not complete the planned trip, she was the first to have completed any east-west solo flight. Markham had led an often scandalous life, but in her 1984 autobiography, she wrote only about Africa, her love for the place that had always been her home, her African friends and contemporaries, and her life as a pilot. She called her book *West with the Night* in remembrance of her famous flight. (*Sources*: 418, 441, 500, 509, 513, 528, 631)

1937   Josephine Bell   (1897–1987) England

Bell was a physician who came from a family of physicians and married a physician. She practiced medicine with her husband until his death in 1936 and then incorporated her medical background into the murder-mysteries she began to write. Her first book, *Murder in Hospital*, appeared in 1937. Her protagonists—a young physician is usually her central character—use physical evidence to solve murders. A prodigious writer, she added drug addiction and modern crimes to her list of themes by the 1960s. (*Sources*: 626, 694)

1937   Julia Flikke   (1879–1965) United States

In 1937 Flikke became the sixth superintendent of the Army Nurse Corps, often said to be her most significant contribution to the nursing field. But this appointment was in fact preceded by many valuable services. Flikke grew up in Viroqua, Wisconsin. Widowed at thirty-three, she enrolled in the nursing program at the Augustana Hospital Training School in Chicago and graduated in 1915. Working at her alma mater, Flikke took additional courses in nursing education and administration at Columbia University over a ten-year period. In World War I Flikke began her military nursing career, serving first in the United States and later in France, where she was appointed chief nurse; at the end of the war, she directed the evacuation of thousands of wounded troops back to the United States. Flikke then served both in the United States and in the Philippines and China, returning in 1922 when she was named chief nurse at Walter Reed General Hospital. By 1927 she became a captain in the Army Nurse Corps, assuming the position of superintendent of the corps ten years later. Holding what was called a "relative rank" (i.e., rank without the concomitant pay and benefits accorded male officers), Flikke challenged this discrepancy; although she attained the rank of colonel, nurses were not officially recognized and given equal status with their male counterparts until 1947. During Flikke's tenure as superintendent, World War II began, and she again served wartime duty, recruiting, mobilizing, and assigning thousands of nurses to stateside and field hospitals. Field hospital assignments were possible because Flikke had instituted changes in the Army Nurse Corps training to include the necessary skills should the need arise. Flikke was buried in Arlington

National Cemetery with full military honors. (*Sources*: 98, 378, 462, 759)

1937 Eleanor Macdonald (1909–) United States
Having earned a bachelor's degree in statistics at Radcliffe College in 1928, Macdonald began a career in her home state of Massachusetts. She gathered statistical data on cancer deaths and cancer autopsy results that had never been systematically collected before, publishing her results in 1937. With her reputation in the field of epidemiology established, Macdonald, who never earned advance degrees, began a campaign for public awareness of cancer (she had a radio show for several years) and a long and illustrious teaching career. Over the years, she had public service appointments in Connecticut, where she established a cancer record registry, and in New York, Massachusetts, and Texas. Macdonald also held teaching positions at Yale University, Tufts Dental School, Regis College, Emmanuel College, Baylor University College of Medicine, and Anderson Hospital and Tumor Institute; she held the position of full professor at the School of Medicine at the University of Texas. Macdonald served on numerous national cancer advisory boards and committees and established the causal relationship between intensity of exposure to sun rays and skin cancer. (*Sources*: 536, 583)

1937 Anne McCormick (1880–1954) United States
(England)
In 1937 McCormick became the first woman to win the Pulitzer Prize for international journalism. A year earlier she had become the first woman to write editorials for the *New York Times*. Drawing on her mother's experience as a reporter and on her own experience traveling through Europe with her husband, she began to write for the *New York Times* shortly after World War I and as early as 1922 was writing about the then unknown Benito Mussolini. In the early 1930s she wrote about farm women in the United States, citing their fortitude and ingenuity as the hope for economic recovery from the depression. In these articles she also urged women to use their newly won right to vote to elect the most responsible public officials at both the local and national levels. In the 1950s, McCormick, a Catholic, wrote extensively about the position of the Catholic church during the war, the prejudice against Catholicism in the United States, and

the Vatican's theological position against the rise of communism. McCormick also wrote in-depth articles on such political figures as Adolf Hitler, Josef Stalin, and Dwight Eisenhower. (*Sources*: 65, 522, 583, 627, 680)

1937 Vijaya Pandit (1900–) India
Pandit was the sister of Jawaharlal Nehru and aunt of Indira Gandhi, both of whom were prime ministers of India. Although she never reached the political heights of her brother and niece, Pandit was politically successful in her own right. Between 1930 and 1940 she was imprisoned four times for her political involvement in India's fight for independence. In 1937 Pandit became the first woman to be appointed to the cabinet post of a local minister by the United Provinces government. After India gained its independence in 1946, Pandit was appointed the head of the Indian delegation to the United Nations and in 1953 became the president of the United Nations General Assembly. She served at various times as ambassador to the Soviet Union, the United States, Mexico, and Ireland. Returning to India in the early 1960s, she held various government posts and joined the Congress Party in opposition to her niece, Indira Gandhi. In her memoirs, published in 1979, Pandit detailed her political life and views, her personal observations of the world, and her position as a woman in government. (*Sources*: 82, 276, 594, 599, 731)

1937 Jean Rosenthal (1912–1969) United States
Recognizing her talent, Orson Wells hired Rosenthal as lighting director for the Mercury Theatre in New York in 1937; she immediately gained notice for her lighting effects for Wells's production of *Julius Caesar*. In addition to working on Broadway, Rosenthal designed lighting for New York ballet and opera companies as well as for the Los Angeles Music Center. She is credited with developing the first notational system, which coordinated lighting for every production, doing away with the need for separate schemes. Rosenthal also originated two-dimensional lighting by using lights on the side of the stage as well as the conventional overhead lights and footlights. Rosenthal created the lighting for such Broadway hits as *West Side Story* and *Hello, Dolly!* Her last show, shortly before her death, was Neil Simon's *Plaza Suite*. (*Sources*: 15, 478, 583, 627)

1937 Evelyn Sharp (1919–1944) United States

Sharp was licensed as a pilot in 1937 when she was eighteen years old. She later became the first woman airmail pilot and the first woman to fly from the West to the East Coast. When World War II began, Sharp joined the Women's Auxiliary Ferry Squadron, ferrying U.S.-built planes to England. In April 1944 Sharp was killed after taking off in a plane in Pennsylvania. Since women pilots received no military recognition, friends had to contribute to Sharp's burial expenses. It was 1977 before the women pilots from World War II were finally given full military benefits. (*Sources*: 418, 465, 564, 718)

1937 Angela Thirkell (1890–1961) England

The granddaughter of the artist Edward Burne-Jones and a cousin to Rudyard Kipling, Thirkell made her own literary mark in 1937 with the publication of her first novel, *Coronation Summer*. Most of her novels were published in the 1940s with her last, *The Duke's Daughter*, appearing in 1951. Her characters are sometimes considered the descendants of Anthony Trollope's fictional characters. Using understatement to create absurdity, she is known for her gentle parody of upper-class British life. (*Sources*: 12, 571)

1938 Beatrice Auerbach (1887–1968) United States (Jewish American)

At the time of her father's death in 1938, Auerbach took over G. Fox & Company in Hartford, Connecticut, and turned it into the largest department store in New England. Noted for her excellent management of personnel, Auerbach was one of the first employers to give workers medical and retirement benefits. An active feminist, she sponsored a women's managerial course at Connecticut State College. The service division of the Beatrice Fox Auerbach Foundation served as a center for women's civic issues. (*Sources*: 525, 603, 718)

1938 Angelica Balabanoff (1878–1965) Soviet Union (Italy)

As a young woman, Balabanoff returned with her Ukrainian parents to Russia, but her education was completed in Belgium, Germany, and Italy. Aware of enormous disparities between socioeconomic classes and influenced by Socialists CLARA

ZEKTIN, Lenin, Mussolini, and Marx's daughter, Eleanor Marx, Balabanoff joined the Socialist Party, and later the Communist Party. In Italy she joined the socialist group Avanti and wrote for the socialist newspaper *Difesa*, eventually becoming an opponent of Mussolini because of his fascist political stand. She returned to the Soviet Union following the revolution, but, after a disagreement with party officials, left again in 1926. She spent many years in the United States, where in 1938 she wrote her autobiography, *My Life as a Rebel*. In her memoirs she revealed her romantically high ideals for social reform throughout the world and her disillusionment with the Socialist and Communist parties. Balabanoff returned to Italy at the end of World War II but was no longer active in politics. (*Sources*: 30, 60, 556, 681, 731)

1938 Katharine Blodgett (1898–1979) United States

Blodgett graduated from Bryn Mawr College in 1918 and went on the earn her master's degree from the University of Chicago before taking a job at the General Electric research laboratory in Schenectady, New York. She started as an assistant to the future Nobel Prize winner Irving Langmuir, an association that lasted until his death in 1957. In 1926 Blodgett became the first woman awarded a doctorate by Cambridge University. She returned to the General Electric laboratory in 1933 and was assigned to continue Langmuir's earlier work on molecules. Langmuir had discovered that, spreading a thin layer of oil on a surface of the water, he could show how molecules were attracted to the water by floating a waxed thread that moved in front of the molecules as they were activated. Using stearic acid, he established that the molecules "stood on end," with their active end on the water's surface, thus creating a minuscule layer of molecules over a surface. Although the discovery was recognized for its academic value, it was not seen as having any practical application, so the research had been discontinued until Blodgett took it over. Blodgett's contribution to this study came in 1933, when she lowered a metal ruler into the solution and discovered that the molecules were then attracted to the metal; by reinserting and withdrawing the ruler, she found thin layers of molecules developed on the ruler. She also discovered that after multiple layers had been built up, colors began to appear on the surface, and a color gauge could be used to determine the thickness of the layers. Again, her experiments were seen as impractical because of the fragility of the components. Then, in 1938, Blodgett found that when she created a film exactly four-millionths of an inch thick, the light rays at the bottom and top cancelled each other so that no light was reflected; she thus invented nonreflecting glass. Its use has so far been limited to cameras and telescopes, in which a thin glass lens can be sealed against breakage or contamination. (*Sources*: 439, 778)

1938   Crystal Bird Fauset   (1893–1965) United States (African American)
Fauset was elected to the state legislature of Pennsylvania in 1938, becoming the first African American woman in the United States elected to such a position. Fauset also served as an adviser to both the mayor of New York and President Franklin D. Roosevelt. During World War II, she served as a racial relations adviser in the Office of Civil Defense. (*Sources*: 447, 583, 756)

1938   Frida Kahlo   (1910–1954) Mexico
Kahlo's resolution, made when she was thirteen, to bear the child of the well-known painter Diego Rivera is almost as famous as her paintings. She did in fact wed Diego six years later; their stormy marriage was fraught with deception and despair and led to their divorce and eventual remarriage. Shortly after declaring her intentions toward Diego, however, Kahlo was involved in an accident in which her spine, pelvis, and foot were crushed, her foot later having to be amputated. Thirty-five operations and a long hospitalization were required to repair the damage to her body; during this time she taught herself to paint. She presented her first paintings to Diego. Never free of pain and never able to fulfill her promise to bear Diego's child, Kahlo developed a distinctive style in which she depicted Mexican peasant art, color, and culture and her own physical pain; her paintings were almost all self-portraits. Kahlo's first exhibition in 1938 was followed shortly by a second one in New York City. It was not until 1953 that there was a major exhibit of her work in Mexico, for which she had to be propped up in a bed because of her pain. She died the following year. Described first as a primitive artist and later as a surrealist,

Kahlo disputed such labels, saying she painted only reality. (*Sources*: 376, 395, 407, 639, 717)

1938 Nathalie Sarraute (1902–) France (Russia)
When she was a small child, Sarraute and her family moved to France; she was educated there and earned degrees in law and literature from the Sorbonne. She practiced law in France from 1922 until 1939. In 1938 she published her first novel, *Tropisms*. Labeled an antinovel because it violated conventional writing styles, Sarraute's work was built upon theses and their antitheses, the attraction/repulsion inherent in them portraying the similar complexities in human feelings. After 1940, she devoted her career to writing, publishing books, reviews, critical essays, and plays for radio. In her most recent book, *You Don't Love Yourself* (1990), she explores self-hatred, a characteristic she describes as universal. (*Sources*: 80, 293, 716, 731, 739)

1939 Jane Drew (1911–) England
Drew graduated from the Architectural Association School in London in 1933 and in 1939 was elected the society's first woman member. She later became the first woman president of the Architectural Association. Drew was an international architect, designing buildings in Ceylon, Ghana, India, Kenya, Kuwait, and Nigeria. She first became interested in architectural designs for hot climates in 1942 and by 1945 had coauthored a book on tropical architecture that became a classic. Also in 1945 Drew founded the *Architect's Yearbook*. She was especially interested in creating functional structures that met complex needs, as evidenced in her design for the School for the Deaf in London. Drew lectured at the Massachusetts Institute of Technology in 1966 and did not retire until 1974. (*Sources*: 350, 438, 511, 602, 731)

1939 Pearl Kendrick (1890–1980) United States
After earning her medical degree from Johns Hopkins, Kendrick elected to use her knowledge of medicine and microbiology in the public health field, first working for the New York State Department of Health. In 1920 she accepted a position with the Michigan State Health Department, becoming an associate director in 1932. It was during this tenure that she and Grace Eldening developed a vaccine for whooping cough, a

common and sometimes fatal disease in children. It was primarily through Kendrick's effort that the standardized immunization program for diphtheria, whooping cough, and tetanus was established for young children. She continued her work in public health until her death at the age of ninety. (*Sources*: 634, 718, 731)

1939   Cecília Meireles   (1901–1964) Brazil
    Meireles was orphaned at the age of three and raised by her maternal grandmother. At the age of twenty she began to write poetry, much of it a nostalgic recollection of her grandmother's gardens. In 1939 she was awarded the Brazilian Academy of Letters Poetry Prize, becoming one of her country's most revered poets. Using traditional literary forms, she composed melodious descriptions of nature to portray the transience of life and the mystery and finality of death. Meireles's themes of life and death are not surprising in view of the tragedies she experienced in her younger years: her grandmother died in 1933, and her husband committed suicide a short time later, leaving Meireles with three young daughters. (*Sources*: 64, 80, 124, 247, 682)

1939   Lise Meitner   (1878–1968) Austria
    Meitner experienced prejudice both as a Jew and as a woman. After earning her doctorate in physics at the University of Vienna, she went to Berlin to continue her studies of radioactivity, a new field. Barred from other facilities because she was a woman, she set up her own laboratory with Otto Hahn; their professional association lasted throughout their lives. Although they were unaware of their accomplishment at the time, in 1934 they succeeded in splitting the atom. Shortly afterward Meitner had to flee Germany because she was a Jew. After settling in Sweden and resuming her work, she realized what she and Hahn had done and published their findings in 1939. She refused to work on the development of the first atomic bomb and was deeply affected by the knowledge that her work had led to this destructive use. It was Hahn alone who received the Nobel Prize for their discovery. She continued her work until her death in 1968, having outlived her lifelong collaborator by only a few months. (*Sources*: 248, 383, 408, 627, 651, 731)

1939   Marguerite Perey   (1909–1975) France
Perey was a brilliant scientist who was invited to join the Marie Curie research group in 1929. In 1939 Perey isolated the eighty-seventh element, francium, a natural and rare radioactive isotope not found as a free metal but rather as combined with simple or complex compounds. Perey's experiments with the radioactive element eventually caused her death in 1975. (*Sources*: 2, 408, 627, 731)

1940   Frances Bolton   (1885–1977) United States
Bolton was elected in 1940 to finish her late husband's congressional term; Bolton did not leave at the end of the term, however, but was reelected many times, serving until 1968. During her tenure Bolton became the ranking minority leader on the powerful House Foreign Affairs Committee. She made trips to the Soviet Union and Africa and wrote what became a famous report on Communist tactics in 1948 following several of her trips abroad. Bolton helped shape Republican foreign policy platforms and was the country's delegate to the United Nations in 1953. Bolton also promoted nursing and was closely associated with the development of the Army Nurse Corps. Concerned with the entry of the United States into World War II, Bolton was the force behind a drive to finance nursing training, and in 1941 $1 million was appropriated to begin a federally sponsored nursing program; the amount was tripled in 1942. The program enabled young women to become nurses with the proviso they serve in the military upon completion of their training; it provided the military with over 100,000 nurses. (*Sources*: 81, 87, 125, 439, 759)

1940   Katherine Dunham   (1910–) United States (African American)
A lifelong victim of arthritis, Dunham nevertheless became a dancer and choreographer. Using federal grants in the 1930s, Dunham organized African American and Caribbean dance companies for which she choreographed music that combined cultural themes into modern dance. First performing in 1940 in New York, her Katherine Dunham Dance Group was one of the longest continuous black dance groups, performing for more than twenty years. Dunham teaches dance and choreography at several universities. (*Sources*: 1, 345, 611, 705)

1940 **Living Computers** (United States)
Vivian Adair, Laura Bateman, Roena Becker, Marie Burcher, Katherine Johnson, Helen Willey, Emma Landrum, Kathleen Wicker, Virginia Biggins, Lona Howser
These are some of the women who were "living computers" working for the National Advisory Committee for Aeronautics, at Langley, starting in 1940. They graduated from college in the 1930s with degrees in mathematics or physics. Using only a T-square and a pencil, these women performed all of the computations for the early space program. They worked six days a week in an un–air-conditioned office and because of the high level of security often had no way to check their own work. Each woman had to recompute the work of the others; it is reported that very few errors were ever found. When calculators were first introduced into the program, the women were said to perform the calculations faster than the computers. Their accomplishments were "rediscovered" in 1990, and the women were honored at a symposium at the NASA Langley facility in Virginia. (*Source*: NASA videotape, December 1990)

1941 **Margaret Leech** (1893–1974) **United States**
Leech graduated from Vassar College in 1915 and published her first book in 1924. She continued to publish throughout the 1920s and in the 1930s began writing an account of the capital during the Civil War. She won the Pulitzer Prize for the work, *Reveille in Washington*, in 1941. In 1959 she again won the Pulitzer Prize for her book *In the Days of McKinley*, making her the first woman to receive two Pulitzer Prizes for literature. Among her other noteworthy books is *Roundsman of the Lord* (1927), which she coauthored with Heywood Broun. (*Sources*: 455, 571)

1941 **Marina Raskova** (1912–1943) **Soviet Union**
By 1941 the German invasion of the Soviet Union had cost the lives of most of the Soviet pilots, and Raskova, an experienced pilot, organized 200 women pilots into three regiments. On their first mission, the women flew without fighter escorts in three groups of ten planes in subzero temperatures, each carrying 2,000 pounds of explosives; they completed the mission successfully without the loss of a single plane. Using new airstrips throughout the Soviet Union, these pilots, led by Raskova,

completed hundreds of missions, first at strategic defense positions within the country and later all the way into Berlin. Because of the limitations of planes at the time, bad weather, and the necessity of flying low due to the weight of bombs, the death toll among the women pilots ran high. Raskova, who both directed operations and flew missions herself, was killed on a return flight from a bombing raid when her plane crashed into a mountain in a snowstorm. Despite the war, Raskova was buried with full military honors in an elaborate ceremony at the Kremlin. (*Sources*: 54, 441, 564, 572)

1942   Natalia Ginzberg   (1916–) Italy
Ginzberg is a short-story writer, essayist, dramatist, translator, and a member of the Italian Parliament. Her first published novel was *Road to the City*, written in 1942. Portraying frailty, ennui, and fatalism, Ginzberg eloquently uses colloquial language to discuss inner hopes and disappointments and failed relationships. She won the Strega Prize in 1963 for her novel about family life in which she employed the words and phrases the family repeatedly used to capture their shared sense of entrapment and fatalism. Ginzberg also wrote three plays, *The Advertisement* (1968) being presented simultaneously by the National Theatre of Brighton and the British Broadcasting Company. (*Sources*: 80, 103, 476, 635, 704, 717)

1942   Susanne Langer   (1895–1985) United States
Possessing an unusual insight into why writers and artists use artistic forms to express their intuitive knowledge and meaning, Langer wrote about the linguistic analysis and aesthetics of art forms, using the distinctions between nondiscursive and discursive symbols as her premise. For example, Langer stated that the adjective "virtual" expresses the aesthetics of meaning while the adjective "actual" conveys factual meaning. In her discourse *Philosophy in a New Key: A Study in the Symbolism of Reason, Rite and Art* (1942), she claimed that the languages of art, music, and writing are as accurate and, therefore, as appropriate, as scientific language in their meaning. Most of Langer's academic career was as a professor at Connecticut College for Women. (*Sources*: 64, 380, 439, 522, 538, 731)

1942   Alice Mason   (1904–1971) United States
Mason was a direct descendant on her paternal side of the famous early American artist John Trumbull. Starting in 1921,

Mason began studying art in Rome and later in New York, where, in 1927, she came under the influence of Arshile Gorky, one of the earliest abstract artists. Reflecting her knowledge of Byzantine architecture, Mason's works are noted for moving from pure abstraction to more architecturally motivated compositions. Although she was also greatly impressed by the work of Piet Mondrian, her style remains distinctive from his. Mason first exhibited her work in New York in 1942 and held several later exhibits; however, Mason's art received little attention until fairly recent times. Depressed by personal tragedy and the lack of recognition, she became alcoholic and died in 1971. (*Sources*: 395, 607, 639)

1942   Agnes Meyer   (1887–1970) United States
Meyer told how rereading Leo Tolstoy and Henry Thoreau helped her recapture the feelings she had as a child; she also described how close to death she came when her brother accidentally fired a bullet that lodged in the right side of her brain and was never fully removed. This combination of the ethereal and the pragmatic was present in much of what Meyer wrote and believed throughout her life. With her husband Meyer was co-owner of the *Washington Post*, and she wrote many investigative reports for their newspaper. She wrote extensively about the value of the public school system and appeared before Congress to lend support to the Taft bill for federal funding for public schools. She was a vocal opponent of communism and a strong supporter of U.S. involvement in World War II. Her first article for the *Post*, written in 1942, was an account of the struggles and courage of British women that she witnessed firsthand. She admonished American women, especially students, to seek careers so that they could make a contribution to society rather than going to college to find a husband to support them; yet she charged married women with the duty of preserving the family. Meyer unabashedly stated that her life was a pursuit of the promised land and that this promised land had to be governed by democratic principles. (*Sources*: 4, 34, 557, 718)

1942   Dorothy Stratton   (1899–) United States
Stratton earned a bachelor's degree at Ottawa University (1920), a master's degree at the University of Chicago (1924), and a doctorate at Columbia University (1932). She began teaching at

Purdue University in 1933 and remained with the university until she enlisted in the Women Accepted for Volunteer Emergency Service (WAVES) in 1942. Within a short time, she planned and developed a women's reserve corps later called the SPARS, an acronym of the Coast Guard motto. Stratton was appointed director of the SPARS, a position she held until 1946; during that time, enrollment was increased to more than 10,000. Working as director of the Girl Scouts of America and the International Monetary Fund between 1947 and 1960, Stratton was later appointed to the President's Commission on the Handicapped. (*Sources*: 98, 548, 759)

1943 Emily Barringer (1876–1961) United States

Barringer was influenced by a family friend, the physician MARY JACOBI, who urged her to study medicine. Barringer earned her undergraduate degree in three years and entered the Women's Medical College in New York, completing her medical training at Cornell Medical College after it accepted women into its program in 1898. She completed her medical degree in 1901, but it took a two-year battle to be allowed to take the internship required to qualify for a medical license. Barringer devoted much of her career to caring for the poor, first as an ambulance doctor and later as chief of staff at the Gouverneur Hospital in New York. Continuing her mentor's struggle for the acceptance of women physicians, Barringer fought for years to have women physicians commissioned in the military. She won this battle in 1943 when the U.S. Senate voted favorably on the passage of the bill. (*Sources*: 142, 383, 512, 529)

1943 Cornelia Fort (1919–1943) United States

Fort grew up in Nashville, Tennessee, and earned her pilot's license when she was nineteen; by the age of twenty she was an instructor. On December 7, 1941, Fort was instructing a student pilot in Hawaii when she nearly collided with a Japanese plane that was attacking Pearl Harbor. Since women pilots were not accepted into the military, she joined the Air Transport Command, which allowed some of the qualified women pilots to ferry planes. While ferrying a bomber in 1943, Fort was killed, becoming the first woman pilot to die in the war. (*Sources*: 564, 718, 759)

1943   Leona Libby   (1919–1986) United States

Libby was a brilliant scientist and the only woman officially assigned to the Manhattan Project (the building of the first atomic bomb) in 1943—although neither she nor the other women who worked on the project were included in any of the official pictures of this group of scientists. Libby also helped to build seven other plutonium-producing reactors, assisted in building the first thermal column, and invented the rotating neutron spectrometer. Her last major discovery was the method for measuring historical climates from the isotopes in tree rings. (*Sources*: 443, 583, 627)

1943   Lydia Litvak   (1921–1943) Soviet Union

One of the women pilots recruited by MARINA RASKOVA for the Soviet air force in World War II, Litvak was assigned to the Seventy-Third Fighter Regiment, a mostly male unit known as the "free hunters" who sought out the enemy. The regimental leader was deeply opposed to having women assigned to the group, but given the opportunity to prove herself, Litvak became one of the unit's ace pilots. She was soon called the White Rose of Stalingrad because she had white roses painted on the fuselage of her plane and a rose for each of her "kills" on the nose. In love with the second in command, she was present when his plane crashed. Already flying frequent sorties, Litvak increased the number she flew; on her eleventh "kill," she shot down one of the German aces. As reported in detail in *Night Witches* (Miles, 1981), the downed pilot apparently refused to believe a woman had shot him down until she reviewed their dogfight with him maneuver by maneuver. Her twelfth victory was her last; Litvak was killed in action in 1943. (*Sources*: 54, 441, 564, 647)

1943   Myra Logan   (1908–1977) United States (African American)

Logan accomplished three firsts: she was the first African American to win a scholarship to the New York Medical College, the first woman to perform heart surgery, and the first African American elected a fellow in the American College of Surgeons. Logan graduated from Atlanta University in 1927 and earned her master's degree; she graduated from New York Medical College in 1933. Logan developed a specialty in heart surgery, concentrating on pediatric heart surgery, and also did research on the effects of the then new antibiotics on children. Married to the noted artist Charles Alston, Logan retired from practice in 1970 and accepted a position with the Physical Disability Program of the New York State Workmen's Compensation Board, a position she held until shortly before her death. (*Sources*: 383, 618)

1943   Nancy Newhall   (1908–1974) United States

In 1943 Newhall became acting curator of the New York Museum of Modern Art to replace her husband, who had been called to military service. Newhall is credited with making photography accepted as an art form. In all, Newhall published and edited twenty-two photography books, among which, in 1960, was the work of the photographer Ansel Adams. She also published a biography of Adams in 1963. (*Sources*: 267, 626)

1944   Sue Dauser   (1888–1972) United States

Dauser graduated from nursing school in 1914 and joined the navy in 1918. While serving as a navy nurse in 1923, she attended President Warren Harding at his death. By 1939 Dauser was appointed superintendent of the Navy Nurse Corps, and even though women did not receive comparable rank to men, was able to recruit enough women to enlarge the nursing corps tenfold. Dauser was made a captain in 1942, but it was not until 1944 that equal military rank for women also implied equal privilege and pay in the navy. In 1945 Dauser was also the first military woman to be awarded the Distinguished Service Medal. (*Sources*: 83, 98, 378, 455, 549, 629)

1944   Violette Szabo   (1921–1945) England

Recruited as a spy because she spoke French, Szabo was parachuted into occupied France in the early months of 1944. Following her return after a successful mission, she was again sent to France as part of a team of four agents. Two days after their arrival the team was detected by a unit from the famous Panzer Division; in their attempt to escape, Szabo injured her ankle and was unable to keep up with the others. Noted for her marksmanship, Szabo remained behind to cover their escape. She was captured and imprisoned; seven months later, along with two other women agents, she was executed by firing squad. (*Sources*: 439, 500, 727)

1945   Mary Hallaren   (1907–) United States

Following a brief teaching career in Massachusetts, Hallaren entered the Officer Candidate School of the newly formed Women's Army Auxiliary Corps in 1942. A year later she commanded the first Women's Army Corps (WAC) unit sent overseas and in 1945 was appointed the director of all the women's overseas units. By 1947, having first served as an assistant director, Hallaren was named WAC director. In 1948, when the WAC had been officially integrated into the army, Hallaren, by then a colonel, became the first woman to receive a commission in the U.S. Army. She remained as director until 1953, retiring from the military in 1960. (*Sources*: 548, 583, 614)

1945   Kathleen Lonsdale   (1903–1971) England

One of the few women crystallographers (ROSALIND FRANKLIN was doing similar work in France at about the same time), Lonsdale was elected to the Royal Society in 1945 for her molecular work on diamonds and health problems. Working with William Bragg, who was doing research on diamonds, Lonsdale was able to demonstrate how the carbon atoms in the benzene nucleus are arranged in a diamond. By using x-ray techniques, she was also able to demonstrate the intramolecular phenomena found in certain medical problems. A pacifist, Lonsdale devoted much energy to the peace movement and was once jailed for her war protestations. (*Sources*: 240, 621, 739)

1945   Helen Taussig   (1898–1986) United States

Taussig had tuberculosis as a child, was dyslexic, and in her early adulthood became deaf. Despite these physical limitations, she graduated Phi Beta Kappa and was a member of the honor society at Johns Hopkins Medical School, overcoming her deafness by learning lipreading. In 1928 she became a pediatrician and began to work with children in the children's wing of Johns Hopkins Hospital. Early in her career, Taussig made extensive studies of the heart; she invented the fluoroscope to enable her to see and study heart anomalies in children. The most common childhood heart malformation was the failure to develop one of the ventricles. Taussig noted that the ductus, which closed off shortly after birth, could be enlarged or rebuilt to compensate for the missing ventricle. In 1945 she and heart specialist Alfred Blalock developed the surgery that saved thousands of "blue babies," the term applied to children with this defect. In 1962 Taussig discovered that phocomelia, a condition in which children are born with malformed or absent limbs, was caused by their mothers' taking the sedative thalidomide. Her findings led to the drug's being banned in the United States and several other countries. Taussig was elected president of the American Heart Association in 1963, becoming the first woman to hold this position. She was the recipient of many honors and awards. (*Sources*: 383, 432, 529, 535, 618)

1946   Hannah Arendt   (1906–1975) United States (Germany)

Arendt earned her degrees in Germany studying under the philosophers Martin Heidegger, Edmund Husserl, and Karl Jaspers. Although she had published in Germany and was not a practicing Jew, she was forced to flee the country with the rise of the Nazi regime. She spent the next six years helping European Jews emigrate to Palestine; after being arrested, she fled to the United States in 1941. In 1946 Arendt was hired as editor in chief at Schocken Books, a publishing house in New York City where she edited books about Jaspers, her former professor. She also translated and edited the works of Franz Kafka. From 1949 to 1952 Arendt helped to relocate and retrieve Jewish property taken by the Nazis. Having taught at Princeton and other universities, in 1959 she was given the post of visiting professor at Princeton. Arendt published several works of importance. Her book on the Nazi leader Adolf Eichmann (1963) was highly controversial because of her philosophical stance that Eichmann was only one of a collective of parties guilty for the Jewish extermination. Arendt spent much of her later years expressing her fears about the evils of both totalitarianism and bureaucracy. (*Sources*: 64, 149, 525, 530, 583, 739)

1946   Elizabeth Bishop   (1911–1979) United States

Because Bishop's mother suffered a mental breakdown after the death of Bishop's father, from the age of three Bishop was shuttled from one household to another. At first a shy and often sickly child, Bishop eventually became more self-assured. She began to write when she was a student at Vassar, where she met one of her lifelong friends, the writer Mary McCarthy; Bishop also shared a lifetime friendship with the poet

MARIANNE MOORE. Following her graduation in 1934, Bishop traveled throughout Europe until she settled in the United States, spending the winter in the Florida Keys and the summer in New York. Published in 1946, her first book of poetry was entitled *North and South* and won her the Houghton Mifflin Poetry Award. Her second most notable work was based on her visits to the poet Ezra Pound, who was confined to a mental hospital in Washington, D.C., while Bishop was a consultant to the Library of Congress. Writing in a meter often used in nursery rhymes, she described Pound and his fellow patients in *Visits to St. Elizabeth's*. Bishop received the Pulitzer Prize for poetry in 1956. Bishop's later years were divided between teaching at Harvard and traveling. She continued to receive numerous other awards for her poetry. (*Sources*: 368, 369, 522)

1946   Ellabelle Davis   (1907–1960) United States (African American)

Having sung on tour throughout South America and performed with the Philadelphia and Indianapolis symphony orchestras (singing under the direction of the renowned Eugene Ormandy when she appeared with the Philadelphia Orchestra), Davis was named Outstanding American Singer of the Year by the League of Composers in 1946. The following year she sang the cantata "The Song of Songs," a work commissioned especially for her by the League of Composers and written by Lukas Foss. She gave the first performance in Boston with the Boston Symphony under the direction of Serge Koussevitzky. It is reported that Koussevitzky was so enthralled by the work that he conducted the piece eight times in nine days, an unprecedented event for a symphony orchestra. Davis toured Europe in the 1950s and gave additional concerts in the United States. She died shortly after completing her second tour of South America. (*Sources*: 324, 510, 524)

1946   Connie Guion   (1882–1971) United States

In the course of her medical career, Guion became the first woman to be appointed a professor of clinical medicine at New York Hospital, the first woman to win the Alumni Award of Distinction at New York University, the first woman physician to serve on the medical board of New York Hospital, and the first woman named an honorary member of the New York Hospital's board of governors. Guion was born in North Carolina, earned her bachelor's degree from Wellesley College in 1906, and graduated first in her class from Cornell Medical College in 1917. She was named professor in 1946. A building at the Cornell Medical College (New York Hospital) was named in her honor in 1963. (*Sources*: 512, 535, 536, 567, 583)

1946   Nadia Nerina   (1927–) England (South Africa)
Nerina studied ballet in Durban under Eileen Keogan and Dorothea MacNair and performed in South Africa until 1945, when she moved to London. She became a dancer with the Sadler's Wells Ballet in 1946, was a soloist by 1947, and was named prima ballerina of the company in 1952. Her greatest performance with Sadler's Wells was in *Elektra*, performed in 1963. Nerina toured in Europe, the United States, and South Africa; while in the Soviet Union she appeared at the Bolshoi and Leningrad Kirov ballets, dancing with two legendary performers, Rudolf Nureyev and Nicolai Fadeyechev. (*Sources*: 7, 265, 478, 498)

1946   Galina Nikolayeva   (1911–1963) Soviet Union
Nikolayeva graduated from the Gorky Medical Institute in 1935 and worked as a physician during World War II. Following the war she began to write, publishing *Through Fire* in 1946. A multitalented and prolific writer, she produced ten books of verse, coauthored the play *The First Spring*, and wrote the scripts for three movies. She was awarded the Stalin Prize in 1951. Much of her work has been translated into other languages. (*Sources*: 268, 655)

1946   Olga Orozco   (1920–) Argentina
Orozco's poetic style reflects the mixture of fantasy and reality to which she was exposed from childhood. Her grandfather was both an idealist and a pragmatist who was the mayor of their small town, presiding over all functions, working to have the town provided with electricity, and worrying about the poor. He and Orozco's grandmother cared for those who escaped from jails and mental institutions. Her father, also a town official, read the classics to her at an early age. In her first book, published in 1946, Orozco elusively and delicately treads between the harshness of life and the dreams of idealism. The

theme of transfiguration is found in all her poetry and especially in her autobiographical work, *Darkness Is Another Sun* (1967). Orozco's style is considered unique among Argentinian poets. (*Sources*: 540, 717)

1946   Ann Petry   (1911–) United States (African American)

Carrying on a family tradition, Petry earned a degree in pharmacy in 1934 and practiced her profession until 1938, when she moved to New York City following her marriage. There she began to write for the *Harlem Amsterdam News*. In 1946, as the winner of the Houghton Mifflin Fellowship for 1945, Petry wrote her first novel, *The Street*. This was followed by additional novels, more short stories, and newspaper articles. She later wrote four children's books. In 1978 Petry received an award for her writing from the National Endowment for the Arts. (*Sources*: 106, 603, 627)

1946   Nelly Sachs   (1891–1970) Sweden (Germany)

Sachs grew up in a prosperous Jewish family in Germany and was rescued from a concentration camp early in World War II through the intercession of poet and friend SELMA LAGERLÖF. Emigrating to Sweden, Sachs learned Swedish and wrote in her new language. Her first book of verse was published in 1946 and, like her later work, was written about the suffering of the Jews and their fate. In *O the Chimneys* (1967) she wrote

O you chimneys,
O you fingers,
And Israel's body as smoke through the air!

In *The Seekers* (1970), fifty-eight of her poems are about death, seventy-six are about despair and flight from despair, and only two are about love and hope. In 1965 Sachs was awarded the Peace Prize given by German publishers. She shared the 1966 Nobel Prize for literature with the Israeli poet Shmuel Agnon. (*Sources*: 80, 291, 599, 627, 644)

1946   Florence Van Straten   (1913–) United States

Straten joined the Women Accepted for Volunteer Emergency Service (WAVES) in 1942 and by 1946 was a technical adviser in the Office of Chief of Naval Operations. She had graduated with honors from New York University in 1933 at the age of nineteen, earning her doctorate there. The navy had sent

Straten to the Massachusetts Institute of Technology for certification in meteorology and then to the Pacific war theater, where there was an urgent need for this work. Launching planes from a ship was still relatively new and required precise coordination of the speed of the ship, the plane, and the wind; therefore, optimum weather conditions as close to a planned target as possible needed to be calculated. It was also discovered that weather conditions a distance away could later affect operations at a critical juncture. For example, troop landings on shore might be set at several days after a ship began an operation, and it was critical to know the predicted weather for the time of the landing. Following the war, Straten began research critical to the new space program. Her studies of higher atmospheric and stratospheric weather conditions helped to determine the types of materials needed in spacecraft passing through these conditions. Her later and equally important work was in radioactive fallout, work that was not recognized for its value until Japanese fishermen became victims of such fallout a few years later. Straten's research helped to determine the path of the fallout following the explosion. She was the recipient of the Meritorious Civilian Service Award for this work in 1956 and in 1958 was honored as Woman of the Year by the Women's Wing of the Aero Medical Association. (*Sources*: 98, 548, 759)

1946   Judith Wright   (1915–) Australia

Although Wright's poems are warm and affectionate accounts of motherhood, family, and her native country, they are not without critically sharp observations. Her first volume of verse, *The Moving Image*, was written in 1946 and was followed by a number of later publications. Wright has also published numerous children's books and is noted for her critical biographies on the Australian writers Charles Harpur, Charles Lawson, and John Shaw Neilson. (*Sources*: 6, 80, 319)

1947   Ethel Andrus   (1884–1967) United States

Andrus's first teaching position was as a principal at a high school in Los Angeles, making her the first woman principal in the California school system. She went on to earn her doctorate in 1930, retiring from teaching in 1944. Aware that the low salary and low esteem given to teachers led to their social and financial difficulties upon retirement, Andrus lobbied for better benefits for retired teachers and in 1947 founded the National Retired Teachers Association. In 1955 Andrus founded the American Association of Retired Persons, later winning medical, travel, and pharmaceutical benefits for its members. She was also responsible for starting the International Retired Persons Association. Andrus was honored as National Teacher of the Year in 1954 and was awarded the University of Chicago's Citation for Public Service in 1955. She received Freedom Foundation and Golden Rule Foundation awards in 1964, and the first school of gerontology at the University of Southern California was named in her honor in 1973. (*Sources*: 583, 718)

1947   Betty Carter   (1929–) United States (African American)
Carter got her big break as a singer in 1947, when Lionel Hampton hired her to sing with his orchestra. Lillie Mae Jones had started by performing in small clubs at the age of seventeen; she later combined her first stage name, Lorraine Carter, with the Betty Bebop that Hampton called her to create the stage name Betty Carter. Initially known as a jazz singer, she later gained a reputation for her unique style of scat singing: she would scat for longer periods than most performers, changing tempo, speed, and key numerous times or holding a note for several minutes while changing its tempo and speed in a mercurial pattern. Carter cut her first record in 1964 and by 1969 was singing under her own label, Bet-Car. Along with her numerous appearances on television and in theaters, Carter performed at Carnegie Hall in 1979. (*Sources*: 32, 352, 524, 611)

1947   Gerty Cori   (1896–1957) United States (Czechoslovakia)
Cori and her husband were born in Czechoslovakia, graduated from medical school together in 1920, emigrated to the United States in 1922, and were professors at Washington University Medical School in St. Louis. Teaming up to do research, they made two renowned discoveries: that carbohydrates are stored in the liver and muscles and are changed into glucose that can be used by the body, and that certain hormones affect the metabolism of carbohydrates. The Coris shared the Nobel Prize for physiology and medicine in 1947 with Bernardo Houssay, making Cori the first woman physician to win a Nobel Prize. (*Sources*: 194, 455, 583, 739)

1947 Flemmie Kittrell (1904–1980) United States (African American)

Kittrell, an international educator, also took part in many outstanding programs in the United States, including numerous federal programs. Much of her work in home economics was done while a professor at Howard University and as a visiting professor in several foreign countries. A graduate of Hampton Institute in 1928, Kittrell earned her master's and doctoral degrees at Cornell University in 1930 and 1935, respectively. In 1947 she conducted a nutrition survey of West Africa for the U.S. Department of State, work for which she was honored by the Liberian government. In 1950 Kittrell helped found the Baroda College of Home Economics in India and later aided the college in setting up a nutrition research program. She continued to assist in the establishment of several other programs in India over the years. Between 1957 and 1961 Kittrell made trips to Hawaii, Japan, Thailand, and several countries in West and Central Africa to promote better nutrition, especially for children, and create departments of home economics and nutrition centers. She received numerous national and international awards, among them one personally presented by President Harry Truman in 1946. An international scholarship is also named in her honor. (*Sources*: 338, 474, 700)

1947 Alma Morani (1907–) United States

Morani was the oldest child of Italian immigrant parents. She states that her desire for an education was fostered by her mother, who had received a good education in Italy, and her ambition to become a plastic surgeon was inspired by her father, who was a sculptor of some repute. Her father, however, preferred that she study sculpting because, as he noted, his work was forever while hers would die with her patients. Because of the depression, it was difficult for Morani to afford to stay in medical school, but she graduated from the Women's Medical College of Pennsylvania in 1931. Although it was rare for surgeons to tutor female physicians, Morani was fortunate enough to befriend a surgeon who admired her skill and determination and taught her surgery. Morani practiced surgery at her alma mater for fifteen years while attempting to be accepted into a plastic surgery program. Not until 1947, after experiencing much discrimination and discouragement, did she finally become the first woman plastic surgeon. In 1972, as president of the Medical Women's International Association, she inaugurated a family planning program in several Far Eastern countries. She later performed surgery gratis at a hospital in Taiwan, where she earned the name Orchid Lady. Morani has received many awards, including some for sculptures she created with the training her father gave her. (*Sources*: 566, 583)

1948 Esther Brown (1898–1990) United States
While expressing a great deal of respect for the women who had served in a nursing capacity for many years and through several wars, Brown devoted her career to improving and expanding nursing care and to upgrading professional nursing. Although a nursing training program had been established as early as 1798, it was 1872 before a standardized nursing school program was set up and not until nursing associations were founded that the quality of training began to make greater and more rigorous improvements in the profession. Brown was one of the early proponents of postgraduate and degree nursing training. Public health nursing had fared no better at its inception; in 1836 a woman had only to be of good character and observe six deliveries before being awarded a certificate to deliver babies in private homes, and it was 1897 before a one-year training program was inaugurated. Starting in 1949, Brown conducted extensive studies into nursing school programs, nursing degree programs, and public health nursing in order to accomplish her dual goals of better nursing care and upgraded professional nursing. Among the awards Brown received for her years of work was the highest nursing award, the Mary Adelaide Nutting Award, in 1973. (*Sources*: 75, 76, 178)

1948 Elsa Morante (1918–1985) Italy
Originally from Rome, Morante had to take refuge in the small southern Italian town of Cassino during World War II. The town later became the site for her most noted books, *House of Liars* (1948) and *Arturo's Island* (1957). Morante's first book won the Viareggio Prize in the year that it was written, and *Arturo's Island* won her the coveted Strega Prize. Her other best-known book, written in 1974, is *History: A Novel*, which portrays the naive hopes of youth that fade with the reality of maturity. Morante is noted for her controlled handling of the gothic and

romantic aspects of her work interwoven with the realities of life. (*Sources*: 257, 476, 715, 739)

1948 Eleanor Raymond (1887–) United States

In 1915, when Harvard would not admit women (the policy would not change until 1942), an instructor named Henry Frost, who later became the director of the Harvard School of Architecture, and his partner, Bremer Pond, agreed to tutor five young women in architectural design in their office; this modest venture was derogatorily referred to as the "Frost and Pond Day Nursery." Raymond was one of the first women students; she later became a partner in Frost's office. By 1933 she was credited with building the first contemporary house in Massachusetts. Raymond served as the director of the program that developed radar at Massachusetts Institute of Technology in the early years of World War II. Raymond's most renowned design is the solar home she created with Maria Telkes in 1948. The sun's energy was trapped in sheet-metal containers behind glass panels and was stored in a sodium compound until fans blew the heat into the interior vents in the house. Although the principles used were still rudimentary, Raymond's was the first solar-powered house in the United States. (*Sources*: 101, 455, 583, 720)

1949 Louise Bourgeois (1911–) United States (France)

Working with marble, wood, wax, latex, and metal, Bourgeois gives an organic quality with an emotional subtext to her sculptures. Many of her works are of women and convey the emotions of helplessness, confinement, and frustration; others are of groups representing family units or people with a common cause. Bourgeois received her inspiration for these sculptures when flying over the Sahara Desert, where she observed the clustering of huts and their isolation from other groups; she refers to this work as her Cumul series, named for the type of clouds that follow the same pattern. Bourgeois came from a family of tapestry weavers in France, where she learned both to draw the outlines for repairs and to do the repairs. At first majoring in mathematics at the Sorbonne, she soon switched to art, studying at some of the finest art schools in France. Following her marriage in 1938, she moved to the United States, where she continued her work. Bourgeois had her first one-woman exhibit in New York in 1949 and was recognized as a new major sculptor. One of her most unusual series, started in 1964, is of what she called lairs, sculptures in the shape of caves and hiding places concealing bodies. Bourgeois's skill appears to lie in her power to elicit strong emotional responses to her abstract works. (*Sources*: 407, 639, 717)

1949 Angella Ferguson (1925–) United States (African American)

Ferguson earned her undergraduate degree in 1945 and her medical degree in 1949, both from Howard University. Shortly after starting her private practice, she became particularly interested in the health and development of black children. Forming a research team with Roland Scott, Ferguson began to tour the United States investigating the health of black children. The results of this study led Ferguson to narrow her research to sickle-cell anemia, a genetic disease more commonly found among blacks than among whites. Aware that the disease was not curable, Ferguson focused on its symptoms and treatment. By carefully monitoring afflicted children, she was able to plot the pattern of the disease by age groupings, observing that some symptoms were prevalent at certain ages. She also identified the conditions under which a child might go into a sickle-cell crisis, with infection the most likely contributor to a crisis. She discovered that, because of the unusual blood-cell configuration associated with the disease, postoperative sickle-cell anemia patients need larger supplies of oxygen to ward off a disease crisis. She also studied the effects of drugs on the disease and found that they were not only of limited help but could even be dangerous. She discovered that consuming large amounts of water containing minute doses of the common alkaline bicarbonate was as effective as other drugs and less dangerous. She also advised suspending many hygiene procedures such as dental treatment when a child had an infection or showed signs of an impending disease crisis. One of her most important discoveries was that sickle-cell anemia often caused changes in physical appearance that had once been interpreted as evidence of lower intelligence; she was able to disprove this fallacy. (*Sources*: 404, 648)

1949 Alison Smithson (1928–) England

Smithson was an honors graduate in architecture at the University of Durham in 1949. She married an architect, and she and her husband began a professional partnership. In 1954 they created their most notable structure, the Hunstanton Secondary School, in which the steelwork, brick walls, and heating and electrical conduits are exposed. They are also known for the building they designed for St. Hilda College at Oxford in 1970. The Smithsons coauthored six books on architecture published between 1960 and 1969. (*Sources*: 299, 602, 625, 643)

1950 Margaret Bonds (1913–1972) United States (African American)

Bonds earned degrees in piano and composition from the Julliard School of Music and Northwestern University. Her musical compositions are unique combinations of classical music and Negro idiom; she has also written intricate compositions combining Native American, Negro, and classical forms. In 1933 Bonds gave a solo performance at the Chicago World's Fair. In 1950 she became the first African American pianist to perform with the Scranton Symphony Orchestra in Pennsylvania. In addition to her cultural-classical works, Bonds composed music to accompany librettos written by poet Langston Hughes. From 1968 until her death in 1972, she devoted her career to the Inner City Cultural Center of Los Angeles. (*Sources*: 372, 510, 524, 439, 688)

1950 Rachel Brown (1898–) United States

It was only with the help of private and scholarship funds that Brown was able to graduate from Mount Holyoke College in 1920. After earning her master's degree in organic chemistry from the University of Chicago, she began to teach in order to support her aging grandmother and mother and to begin her doctoral studies. A financial crisis during her studies led Brown to accept a research position with the New York State Department of Health, but later returned to the University of Chicago to complete her doctorate. Brown's primary work with the health department was in categorizing and standardizing the various serums used to combat pneumonia. With the discovery of penicillin and streptomycin in the early 1940s, interest in further research into earlier serum studies abated; however, the new antibiotics had serious side effects as well as levels of toxicity. This led Brown and fellow researcher Elizabeth Hazen to search for a nontoxic and antifungal serum. In 1950 they succeeded in isolating antibiotics from the actinomycetes found in soil and developed the serum nystatin, which has both of the desired characteristics. Brown and her colleague did not accept the royalties from this commercially valuable discovery, choosing instead to direct the money to the advancement of scientific research. Brown has earned numerous awards for her work, among which was becoming the first woman awarded the Pioneer Chemist Award by the American Institute of Chemists in 1975. (*Sources*: 383, 439, 779)

1950   Rosario Castellanos   (1925–1974) Mexico

At an early age, Castellanos experienced the devaluation of females in Hispanic culture: her parents were disappointed that their firstborn was a girl and more displeased when their only other child, a son, died in childhood. Her frequent reference to exile in her work reflects her personal sensitivity as well as her awareness of the societal rejection of the native Indians, a group she worked among and wrote about. Castellanos's commitment to writing, especially to writing about the effects of culture on women and their roles, was evident in her master's thesis on feminine culture (1950). Fellowships in 1953 and 1954 to conduct research on the contributions of women to the Mexican culture led to the 1957 publication of her first book, which won two prestigious awards. Castellanos later taught literature at the University of Mexico and at several colleges in the United States. In 1971 she was appointed ambassador to Israel; she is said to have done her best writing there. She died in an accident in Israel and was given a state funeral in Mexico City, where she is buried in the Tomb of National Heroes. (*Sources*: 80, 124, 540, 641, 637)

1950   Marguerite Duras   (1914–) France (Indochina)

Duras used a narrow point in time in order to dramatize the events in her narratives. This style may be due to her early childhood in Indochina, where she became aware of the effects of political events on human lives and formed her pacifist political viewpoint. Her book *A Sea of Troubles*, written in 1950, established Duras's reputation as a writer; it is typical of Duras's work in its use of a woman protagonist to depict people as alienated or at best living on the fringes of society, letting alcohol numb their despair. Duras won the Prix Goncourt in 1984 for her semiautobiographical novel *L'Amante Anglaise*. Duras is also noted for her screenplays and her work as a director; *Hiroshima Mon Amour* (1959) is her best-known screenplay. Duras has continued her career as a novelist, playwright, scriptwriter, and director. (*Sources*: 626, 731)

1950 Ingrid Jonker (1933–1965) South Africa

Following in the steps of other Afrikaaners who wrote to protest, Jonker expressed her belief in the wrongness of the white supremacy that has dominated South African culture and the evils of the exploitation exercised through the system of apartheid. Only writing one book, *Selected Poems* (1950), Jonker chose suicide at the age of thirty-two to show her deep and troubled feelings about her country. (*Sources*: 227, 659, 691)

1950 Ludmila Rudenko (1904–1986) Soviet Union

In 1950, Rudenko was the first Soviet woman to win the Women's World Chess Championship, with two of her countrywomen claiming second and third places in a field of sixteen women. She continued to win the title for the next three years, also becoming the Soviet women's champion in 1952. She lost her international championship to ELIZAVETA BYKOVA in 1953 but won the Women's International Grandmaster Tournament in 1976. (*Sources*: 132, 290, 366)

1951 Janet Collins (1917–) United States (African American)

At the age of fifteen, Collins auditioned for the Ballet Russe de Monte Carlo; she was recognized for her talent but not hired because of her race. Appearing in black roles in the United States, she danced in the movie *Thrill of Brazil* in 1946 and made a solo appearance in 1947, which led to a scholarship to study with the great dancer DORIS HUMPHREY. Her Broadway appearance in the 1951 Cole Porter production of *Out of This World* earned her the Donaldson Award for of the Year; she then made her Metropolitan debut as the first black prima ballerina. Collins continued to dance with the Met for the next four years, appearing in both traditionally black and traditionally white roles. Having left the Met in the late 1950s, she devoted the rest of her life to teaching dance, though she gave performances well into her fifties. (*Sources*: 1, 403, 705)

1951   Maria Dermout   (1888–1962) Netherlands (Indonesia)
Dermout wrote her first book in 1951 at the age of sixty-three and had written seven books by the time of her death, with the last two published posthumously. She began her career out of a desire to write about her love of her life in Indonesia before its independence in 1949. Her stories are lyrical accounts of the pleasures of island culture and life. (*Sources*: 80, 204)

1951   Martha Eliot   (1891–1978) United States
Eliot's professional career focused on better health care for children. A first cousin to the poet T. S. Eliot and a member of Phi Beta Kappa, she graduated from Radcliffe College in 1913 and earned her medical degree from Johns Hopkins University Medical School in 1918. Eliot's medical appointments from 1918 to 1924 were all in pediatrics, and in 1924 she was named director of the Division of Child and Maternal Health for the U.S. government under GRACE ABBOTT. In 1951 Eliot was appointed chief of the U.S. Children's Bureau, a post she held until 1956, when she accepted a position at Harvard University. During her long career, Eliot was responsible for the passage of several child health care bills, such as the child health care provision in the Social Security Act of 1935 and the Emergency Maternal and Infant Care program of 1943. This latter program provided maternal and child care for lower-ranking military personnel during wartime conditions. It helped to improve the health of more than 1 million children during the war years. Eliot also served on a number of international child welfare committees and was responsible for a study that isolated the causes of rickets in children. (*Sources*: 432, 439, 676, 722)

1951   Janet Frame   (1924–) England (New Zealand)
Frame wrote her first collection of short stories, *The Lagoon*, in 1951; she emigrated to England in 1956. Her most poignant books are about her periodic confinements in mental institutions, with her three autobiographical books (1982, 1984, and 1985) the best examples of the prose style in which she questions where the sanity in life lies. She has also written several novels on the difficulty of communications. *An Angel at My Table* (1990), directed by Jane Campion, is a biographical film about Frame. (*Sources*: 626, 646, 665, 731)

1951   Doris Lessing   (1919–) England (Zimbabwe, Iran)
Because her father was a British officer assigned to foreign duty, Lessing was born in Iran and moved to Rhodesia at the age of five. Lessing remained in Southern Rhodesia (now Zimbabwe) until the age of thirty, and used it as the setting for many of her early novels. Lessing's first novel, *The Grass Is Singing* (1951), reflects her abhorrence of racism and her interest in social reform. The major focus of her later work was women's independence and women's relationship to men. Beginning in 1950, Lessing spent almost twenty years writing the novel-series, "The Children of Violence," in which she expresses her disillusionment with communism and her feelings about racism, sexism, and war. Lessing won the Somerset Maugham Award in 1954; her most recent book, *The Fifth Child*, was written in 1987. (*Sources*: 456, 503, 583, 704, 731)

1951   Margaret O'Neill   (1900–1975) United States
O'Neill graduated from the Women's College at the University of Delaware in 1922 and began a long teaching career in the school system in Smyrna, Delaware. In 1951 she became the first woman principal of the high school and later served as president of the state board association. O'Neill served as the Delaware delegate to the White House Conference on Children and Youth and on the National Commission on Human Rights. In 1964 she was named Mother of the Year in Delaware for her years of dedication to the education and well-being of children. (*Sources*: 526, 718)

1952   Virginia Apgar   (1909–1974) United States
Apgar probably made the greatest contribution of any physician to neonatal survival rate. In 1952, while serving as an anesthesiologist, she became concerned about the need to note the vital signs in newborns and developed the Apgar Score System on which infants are checked within moments of birth for heart rate, respiratory effort, muscle tone, reflex, and color, with each of these signs measured on a scale of zero to two, ten being the highest cumulative score for good health. Apgar had graduated with honors from the Columbia College of Physicians and Surgeons in 1933. In 1937 she had become board certified in anesthesiology and began her long association as a professor of anesthesiology at Columbia Medical College. In 1959, at the age

of fifty, Apgar returned to school to earn a master's degree in public health and was named by the National Foundation as director of research on birth defects and anomalies. She was the author of more than fifty papers on birth defects and anomalies, writing several articles on precautionary measures for expectant mothers. (*Sources*: 14, 18, 122, 443, 480, 568, 583, 649, 782)

1952   Helen Delich Bentley   (1923–) United States

Bentley, who started as a cub reporter on the *Baltimore Sun* in 1945 following her graduation from the University of Missouri a year earlier, soon became an expert on maritime traffic. She was named maritime editor of the newspaper in 1952, the same year she also began to write a nationally syndicated maritime column. In 1969 she became the first woman given a presidential appointment as a chairperson of a U.S. regulatory agency when she was named chair of the Federal Maritime Commission. In 1984 Bentley was successful in her bid for a congressional seat in Maryland, a seat she still holds in 1992. (*Sources*: 33, 43, 455, 463, 607)

1952   Hanya Holm   (1898–) United States (Germany)

In 1952 Holm had the distinction of being the first choreographer to obtain a copyright, for her work in *Kiss Me Kate*. Holm had immigrated to the United States in 1919 and opened a dance studio in New York City in 1936. She taught summer courses in dance at a school she founded in Colorado and in 1961 was appointed head of the New York Musical Theater Academy. Holm's best-known choreography was in the musicals *My Fair Lady* in 1956 and *Camelot* in 1960. (*Sources*: 423, 478, 583)

1952   Fusaye Ichikawa   (1893–1981) Japan

A feminist and politician, Ichikawa began as a teacher in a rural village. She launched her political career by founding the New Women's Association, dedicated to gaining the right for women to make political speeches and for suffrage, and by directing women's labor organizations in their campaign for better working conditions. Ichikawa was also the president of the New Japan Women's League. Running as an independent, she was elected to the Upper House of Councilors in 1952, a position she held, except for a brief interim, for eighteen years. She was noted for her fight against prostitution, pay raises for members of the

Diet, and corruption in elections. While a member of the Diet, she donated her salary to women's organizations. (*Sources*: 583, 621, 681, 728, 731, 739)

1952   Patricia McCormick   (1930–) United States

McCormick studied with some of the most notable matadors of Mexico, making her debut as a *torera* (woman bullfighter) in 1952. McCormick appeared in the ring a dozen times in her first year, killing fifteen bulls. She was noted as the only *torera* able to plant the barbed hooks into the bull before making her kill. McCormick was one of the few *toreras* invited to perform in Mexico, where she became a popular figure. She was especially praised for her courage, often continuing a *corrida* (performance) after being wounded; her popularity soared after she returned to the ring following several serious injuries. McCormick appeared in some of the most famous rings in the world, later teaching bullfighting and coaching movie actors for their roles as bullfighters. (*Sources*: 455, 545, 647, 685)

1952   Shushila Nayar   (1914–) India

Nayar earned her medical degrees at the Lady Hardinge Medical College in Delhi and Johns Hopkins Medical School in Baltimore. After she returned to India, she became a supporter of Gandhi and was jailed for three years for her political activism. After India won its independence, she was appointed minister of health, rehabilitation, and transport in 1952 and later became a member of the lower parliamentary house, a seat she held until 1971. She was minister of health from 1962 to 1967 and director of the Mahatma Gandhi Institute of Medical Sciences in 1969. (*Sources*: 60, 731)

1953   Fae Margaret Adams   (1918–) United States

A native Californian, Adams was the first woman to earn her medical degree under the GI Bill of Rights. A reserve officer in the Women's Army Corps (WAC), Adams in 1953 became the first woman physician commissioned after the corps was made a part of the regular army. (*Sources*: 98, 439, 455, 583)

1953   Clare Benedict   (1871–1961) United States

The granddaughter of James Fenimore Cooper, Benedict was also a writer. Interested in chess throughout her life, she sponsored her first chess tournament in 1953, which was named in her honor. This tournament became an annual event between the years 1955 and 1974, with two additional ones played in 1977 and 1979. Most of the competitions were held in Switzerland, which had become her adopted country in her later years. (*Sources*: 132, 421)

1953   M. Hildred Blewett   (1911–) United States (Canada)

Blewett earned her bachelor's degree in physics at the University of Toronto and her doctorate at Cornell University. She is noted for her work in designing nuclear reactors and particle accelerators (mechanisms to release more energy from the nucleus of an atom). Blewett has served as consultant in many countries including working for CERN, the first European nuclear physics research center, developed in 1953 and located in Switzerland. (*Sources*: 583, 627)

1953   Elizaveta Bykova   (1911–1989) Soviet Union

Taught to play chess by her brother, Bykova won her high school chess championship in 1927. Continuing to play chess, she captured the Soviet women's championship in 1947, 1948, and again in 1950. In 1953 Bykova beat the famous chess player LUDMILA RUDENKO for the Women's World Chess Championship, a title she held until 1956 and recaptured in 1958; she was undefeated until 1963. Bykova also won the Grand Master Championship in 1976. She later wrote a book on Soviet women chess players and a column for an international chess magazine. (*Sources*: 132, 366, 707)

1953   Rosalind Franklin   (1920–1958) England

Franklin worked as a crystallographer in Paris, where she helped to pioneer work in carbon-fiber technology by photographing the crystals in coal and granite. She went to King's College in London in 1951. In 1953 she was able to isolate and photograph the DNA molecule. Because Franklin was a recluse by nature and the victim of discrimination by her male colleagues, her work went unnoticed. After her death, it was discovered that her studies corroborated and verified the research done by James Watson, Francis Crick, and M.H.F. Wilkins, who were awarded the Nobel Prize in 1962 for the discovery of DNA. (*Sources*: 367, 393, 408, 583, 739)

1953   Sara Lidman   (1923–) Sweden

In Lidman's first novel, *The Tar Still* (1953), she described a small Swedish village and won immediate acclaim. Her second book about village life was equally successful. Following trips to South Africa, Rhodesia, and Vietnam, she created two documentaries about the conditions of the populations in those countries. She wrote three plays between 1954 and 1970, and in the 1970s wrote a trilogy about oppression of people. (*Sources*: 80, 239, 438, 476, 715, 717)

1953   Ruth Sager   (1918–) United States

Sager earned her doctorate in genetics at Columbia University in 1948. Five years thereafter she joined the Rockefeller Institute and began her pioneer work in genetic studies by challenging the existing theories of the exclusivity of the chromosomal reproductive system and by postulating that there was a separate genetic transmitting system outside the chromosomes. Sager discovered in 1953 that reproduction of the alga Chlamydomonas, a small plant found in muddy ponds, could be accomplished by nitrogen deprivation. This established her theory of a second set of genes existing outside the nucleus chromosomes of a living cell. Sager was elected to the National Academy of Science in 1977 for her outstanding work in genetics. (*Sources*: 292, 583, 739)

1954   Brigid Brophy   (1929–) England

Brophy's literary career got off to an auspicious start when she won the Cheltenham Literary Festival's award in 1954 for her first novel, *Hackenfeller's Ape*. Brophy published ten books between 1954 and 1967, winning the London Magazine's award for prose in 1962. During this time she also collaborated with her husband, Michael Levey, and Charles Osborne on two additional books. In 1967 and 1968, she wrote two plays that, although produced, were less successful than her novels. Brophy was at her best when she wrote about contemporary marriage and the relationship between women and men; her venture into psychoanalytic behavioral characterization, *Of Black Ships to Hell* (1962), was derisively reviewed, as was *Fifty Works of English and American Literature We Could Do Without*, one of the two books she coauthored. (*Sources*: 80, 177, 398)

1954   Miriam Makeba   (1932–) South Africa
Makeba began singing as a child and later gave amateur performances at local events in South Africa. Her first professional performance was in 1954 when she became a member of the Black Manhattan Brothers and toured throughout Africa. In 1958 Makeba starred in the U.S.-made anti-apartheid movie *Come Back Africa* and began appearing in U.S. clubs. Makeba was later banned from her native country and lived in exile until the late 1980s, when she was allowed to return. (*Sources*: 403, 731)

1954   Penelope Mortimer   (1918–) England (Wales)
Mortimer is a novelist and journalist. She graduated from London University and began her literary career in 1954 with *A Villa in Summer*. Mortimer's central characters are usually unhappy or neurotic women; her plots reach a crescendo of intensity. Her best-known work was the *Pumpkin Eater* (1962), which was made into an equally successful film. Mortimer coauthored a book with her husband, the playwright John Mortimer. She has also been a contributor to the London *Times* and the *New Yorker* magazine. (*Sources*: 260, 626)

1955   Consuelo Northrop Bailey   (1899–) United States
By her mid-fifties, Bailey had earned a total of five law degrees. She was admitted to the Vermont bar in 1926 and by 1933 was presenting cases before the U.S. Supreme Court. Politically active throughout her career, Bailey served in several capacities for the state and national branches of the Republican Party. She served as a state senator in Vermont in 1930 and in 1955 became the first woman ever elected lieutenant governor of a state, winning a landslide victory. Bailey has served on numerous state, federal, and civic boards throughout her career and is the author of a book on Vermont politics. (*Sources*: 98, 439, 455, 536)

1955   Louise Boyd   (1887–1972) United States
Boyd was a wealthy woman who developed an insatiable interest in the Arctic after she made her first trip to the region in 1924 on a passenger cruise. Because she was able to finance her own trips, her explorations were considered to be nothing more than an extravagant and eccentric self-indulgence; newspaper accounts made much of the number of polar bears killed on her first expedition in 1926. Boyd was not thought of as a serious

explorer until 1928, when she organized an unsuccessful expedition to find the lost explorer, Roald Admunsen, for which she was honored by the governments of both Norway and France. Her third trip, in 1931, was funded by the American Geographical Society, which also sponsored her expeditions in 1933, 1937, and her final one in 1938. Boyd's photographs and records were among the earliest documents of the Arctic region; the data from her 1937 and 1938 expeditions were classified because of World War II but in 1948 were published as a book entitled *The Coast of Northeast Greenland*. In 1955, at the age of sixty-eight, Boyd became the first woman to fly over the North Pole. At her death her ashes were dropped over the Arctic Ocean. (*Sources*: 583, 592, 631, 634, 718)

1956   Bette Graham   (1924–1980) United States

A divorced single parent who lacked an education (she later earned her GED), Graham took a job as a typist without knowing how to type. In order to keep her job, she used white paint to cover over her typing errors. Since this had unsatisfactory results, she developed a correction liquid that she called Mistake Out and sold from her home. In 1956, after trying unsuccessfully to sell her invention, she opened her own business. She changed the product name to Liquid Paper and by 1968 had developed it into a multimillion-dollar business. (*Sources*: 583, 627)

1956   Rose Heilbron   (1914–) England

Heilbron graduated with honors from Liverpool University in 1935 and earned her law degree from Gray's Inn in 1937. In 1956 she was the first woman ever appointed recorder on the Queen's Council, a position she held until 1974. In 1974 Heilbron was made a dame of the British Empire and also appointed high court judge on the Northern Circuit, becoming only the second woman to be appointed to this post. Heilbron was named chair of the Home Secretary's Advisory Group on Rape in 1975. (*Sources*: 463, 731)

1956   Wen-Ying Hsu   (1909–) Taiwan (China)

Hsu gave her first piano concert of her own composition in Taiwan in 1956 after studying musical composition in both China and the United States. After continuing her studies in the United

States and doing research into ancient Chinese music, she returned to Taiwan, where she pursued her research into the ancient seven-string instrument called the *ku-ch'in* that served to develop the Western seven-note musical scale. Her findings were published in 1972 as *Origin of Music in China*. Hsu was also the author of a book entitled *The Ku-ch'in* (1976). In addition to composing music, Hsu translated Chinese poems into English and wrote original poems in her adopted language. She is listed in both the international *Who's Who in Music* and the *World Who's Who of Women*. (*Sources*: 99, 698, 781)

1956   Olga Rubtsova   (1909–) Soviet Union
In 1956 Rubtsova became only the fourth competitor to win the Women's World Chess Championship. She retained her title the following year but lost the championship to ELIZAVETA BYKOVA in 1958. Rubtsova had won the Soviet women's cham-pionship first in 1931 and again in 1937 and 1949. In 1950 she was given the title of international woman master. She was given the Order of the Red Banner of Labor in 1956 and received the title of international woman grandmaster in 1976. (*Sources*: 132, 289, 366)

1956   Chien-Shiung Wu   (1912–) United States (China)
Wu was born and educated in China and earned her doctorate in physics at the University of California after immigrating to the United States. Her first work was for the Manhattan Project at Columbia, where she developed the process for producing the fissionable uranium used in making the first atomic bomb. As chief experimenter, Wu and Tsung-Dao Lee and Chen-Ning Yang in 1956 disproved the conservation of parity theory, which stated that nature is totally symmetrical because all atomic particles move in an identical direction. They demonstrated that all atomic particles do not act similarly but rather are in different systems—which they called left- and right-handedness—the direction of their movement determined by the handedness of the particles' spin. Lee and Yang received the Nobel Prize in physics in 1957 for this work; Wu did not. She later hinted at her frustration, remarking that atoms and molecules do not show a preference for mas-culine or feminine treatment. Wu did, however, receive many other awards for her work, and was the first woman to

receive the prestigious Comstock Award. (*Sources*: 583, 621, 627, 647, 779)

1957   Daisy Bates   (1911–) United States (African American)
When Bates was a young woman, she was told that her father had disappeared after attempting to avenge her mother's rape by four white men. Having experienced prejudice in the segregated South all her young life, she joined the civil rights movement in Arkansas in the early 1950s. Because of her political activities, her home was vandalized and burned following numerous telephone threats on her life and the lives of her family, but Bates continued to fight. On September 23, 1957, Bates was able to announce that President Dwight Eisenhower had sent troops to Arkansas to ensure that the African American children could return to Central High School safely. (*Sources*: 98, 705)

1957   Ekaterina Furtseva   (1910–1974) Soviet Union
Furtseva holds the distinction of being the only woman ever named to the All-Union Politburo, a post she held from 1957 to 1961. She was later named minister of culture, a position she filled until her death. Women educators were often appointed as indoctrination specialists, giving them membership and a minor status in the Communist Party; however, Furtseva, a graduate of the Moscow Lomonosov Institute, had a degree in chemistry. She had risen through the ranks by serving as second and later first party secretary in Moscow, holding the latter office for eight years. (*Sources*: 24, 439)

1958   Mary Roebling   (1905–) United States
Roebling was made one of the thirty-two governors of the New York Stock Exchange in 1958, becoming the first woman ever appointed to this board. Named one of the three public members of the board, she was entitled to walk on the floor of the exchange, even though she was not directly connected with the Wall Street community. Roebling was also one of the first women bank presidents; when her institution, the Trenton Trust, merged with the National State Bank of New Jersey, she became chair of the newly combined banks. Roebling is a member of a state advisory group, the New Jersey Investment Council. Among her many awards is the Department of Defense Medal for Distinguished Public Service in 1984. (*Sources*: 455, 533, 583, 615)

1958   Efua Sutherland   (1924–) Ghana
Sutherland founded the Ghana Drama Studio and the Ghana Society of Writers in 1958 and subsequently established schools in upper and middle Ghana as well as one at the University of Ghana. Although she writes and produces many plays and stories, especially for children, an equal part of her career has been devoted to helping young Ghanian writers and popularizing drama for children. Much of Sutherland's work has been heard on "The Singing Net," a nationally known radio program. In each of her works, including her poetry, she captures the essence of African culture while placing it in more contemporary settings. (*Sources*: 411, 429, 640, 717)

1959   Maria Bueno   (1939–) Brazil
Bueno won her first championship at Wimbledon in 1959 and successfully defended her title in 1960, reclaiming the title in 1964 following a serious illness. She is best known for her series of matches against Margaret Smith (Court) of Australia between 1960 and 1968. Considered one of the most graceful women tennis players, Bueno retired in 1968, having won thirteen titles during her career. Bueno is in the International Tennis Hall of Fame. (*Sources*: 20, 179, 610)

1959   Karen De Crow   (1937–) United States
Author, editor, lawyer, and feminist, De Crow earned her bachelor's degree from Northwestern University in 1959 and her law degree from Syracuse University in 1972. Her first position was as editor of *Golf Digest* from 1959 to 1960. This was followed by several other editorial positions for a variety of magazines on topics ranging from education to sports. A prolific writer as well, De Crow published her first book in 1967. Most of her books are about feminism; she served as president of the National Organization of Women from 1974 to 1976. De Crow has also been a contributor to several national newspapers and has written a column for the *Syracuse New Times*. (*Sources*: 98, 533, 728)

1959   Muriel Spark   (1918–) Scotland
Spark's literary career started in 1947 when she was an editor and took a different course in 1951 when she became biog-

rapher of the literati Mary Shelley, John Masefield, and Charlotte and Emily Brontë. In 1959 Spark began to write witty, engaging novels, her first, *Momento Mori*, followed by three additional novels in the same genre. The best known of these is *The Prime of Miss Jean Brodie*, which was made into both a successful Broadway play and a film. Spark again changed her literary style in 1965, writing more serious and sinister novels such as *The Mandelbaum Gate* and *Not to Disturb*. (*Sources*: 80, 302, 438, 717)

1959   Rosalyn Yalow   (1921–) United States (Jewish American)

Yalow earned her undergraduate degree from Hunter College in 1941 and her doctorate from the University of Illinois in 1945. She began working with Solomon Berson at the Veterans Administration hospital in New York in 1950 investigating the medical uses for radioactive isotopes. One of their earliest discoveries was in the use of radioisotopes in the diagnosis and treatment of thyroid disorders. They developed radioimmunoassay, more commonly known as RIA, as a diagnostic tool to measure concentrations of hormones, proteins, and other substances in the body. The most dramatic result of the use of RIA occurred in 1959 when Yalow and Berson were able to demonstrate that adult diabetics do not always have an insufficiency of insulin in their blood. RIA is also used to diagnose the presence of the hepatitis virus in blood. Yalow was named director of the nuclear medicine service at the Veterans Administration hospital in 1970 and also serves as consultant at several other research facilities. (*Sources*: 98, 383, 412, 548)

1960   Sirimavo Bandaranaike   (1916–) Sri Lanka

Bandaranaike was not taken seriously when she completed her husband's term as prime minister of Ceylon (now Sri Lanka) after his assassination in 1959. She successfully ran for the post in 1960, becoming the first woman prime minister in history. Her political career followed a mercurial path from her election in 1960 to her defeat in 1965 and her reelection in 1970 to her ouster in 1977. Initially praised for her strong policies and for her efforts to rid the government of corruption, Bandaranaike was later criticized for the country's economic weaknesses and for nepotism. She was also expelled from Parliament in 1980 following her conviction for misuse of power. (*Sources*: 347, 463, 558, 583, 716, 731)

1960   Dorothy Brown   (1919–) United States (African American)

Raised in an orphanage, Brown earned her college degree in 1941 from Bennett College and her medical degree from Meharry Medical College in Tennessee in 1948. Working at Riverside Hospital in Nashville, Brown had been appointed chief of surgery by 1960, becoming the first woman to hold this post. She remained at Riverside until 1983. Brown also has the distinction of being the first African American woman elected to the American College of Surgeons. (*Sources*: 648, 688)

1960   Jeraldyn [Jerri] Cobb   (1931–) United States

In 1960, Cobb became the first woman to pass the physical test for the astronaut program. Although never selected for the space program, Cobb served as a consultant for the women's astronaut program for NASA. Cobb's father had taught her to fly at the age of twelve, and within six years she was earning her living as a bush pilot. In 1959 she was named both Woman of the Year in Aviation and Pilot of the Year by the National Pilots Association. Cobb also set several light-plane flying records. (*Sources*: 98, 441, 418, 455, 535)

1961   Tenley Albright [Gardiner]   (1935–) United States

Tenley Albright (now Tenley Gardiner) is known as a world champion figure skater, having won five straight U.S. figure skating championships starting in 1951, the world championship in 1953, and the gold medal in the 1956 Olympics. Albright had learned to ice skate as a child to strengthen her muscles after contracting a mild form of poliomyelitis. What is less well known about her is that she went on to a second career in medicine. Having earned her undergraduate degree from Radcliffe College, Albright graduated from Harvard Medical School in 1961 and has since practiced surgery in Boston. (*Sources*: 98, 439, 684)

1961   Virginia Carter   (1936–) United States (Canada)

Carter's career path has diverged widely from her educational background. After earning her degrees in physics, she first planned to become a nuclear physicist, but finding the scientific field unreceptive to women, she became interested in the women's movement and served as the president of the Los Angeles branch of the National Organization of Women. It was while she was in Los Angeles that she met the television producer Norman Lear, who offered her a consulting position in the television industry. Her first job was as a creative adviser on public issues, especially women's issues. By 1960, within three years of starting her new career, she had been promoted to a vice-presidency in the Lear company in charge of developing new programs. Her stated career goal is to become a chief executive officer (CEO) in the television industry within the next few years. (*Sources*: 3, 439)

1961   Carol Sloane   (1937–) United States

Sloane's first singing job was with a small New England band that often played at a ballroom near her hometown in Rhode Island. Marrying in 1957, she accompanied her husband, who was in the army, to Germany, where she organized a production of *Kiss Me, Kate* that toured throughout Germany. Returning to the United States and soon divorced, she began to sing for the then unknown Larry Elgart Band. Her big break came in 1961, when she appeared at the Village Vanguard in New York on the same program as Oscar Peterson and was given her first recording contract. Between 1961 and 1968 Sloane appeared on several national radio programs with some of the most important stars of the time. After this initial success, and with the rapid growth in popularity of rock music, she alternately experienced success and failure. She moved to Raleigh, North Carolina, where she worked in a law office days and sang in a small club at night. She lived with pianist Jimmy Rowles for four years, only to end up penniless and on the verge of alcoholism, and she returned to New England. In 1981 Sloane went back to North Carolina to sing and by 1982 had her own music show on a local radio station. This success lasted only three years; again penniless, she returned to New England and resumed singing in small clubs throughout New England and hosting a jazz radio program in Massachusetts. (*Sources*: 32, 352, 611)

1961   Janet Travell   (1901–) United States

Travell earned her bachelor's degree from Wellesley College in 1922 and her medical degree from Cornell University

Medical College in 1926. She was an instructor at Cornell until her most prestigious appointment, as physician to President John F. Kennedy in 1961, making her the first woman physician to a president. Following his assassination in 1963, she was physician to President Lyndon B. Johnson until 1965. She has since served on several national boards, including the Office of the Surgeon General and the Joseph P. Kennedy Foundation. Besides contributing to medical journals, Travell wrote her autobiography, *Office Hours: Day and Night* (1969). (*Sources*: 438, 455, 583)

1962   Jessie de la Cruz   (1919–) United States (Hispanic American)
Although strongly family-oriented, Cruz at an early age rejected the traditional role of Hispanic women. She insisted on more independence and a greater voice in her marriage. Having worked in the migrant labor force for many years, she was aware of the deplorable working conditions and became one of the first volunteer recruits for César Chávez in 1962. She risked her life and her job when she challenged the farm owners regarding conditions and pay. In 1967 Cruz became an official union organizer and was also appointed to the Fresno County Economic Opportunity Commission. In 1974 she helped to found the National Land for People, a farm cooperative. Cruz has been honored by the Mexican American Women's Association for her outstanding work in the labor movement. (*Sources*: 88, 358, 627, 755)

1962   Nona Gaprindashvili   (1941–) Soviet Union
Gaprindashvili won her first Women's World Chess Championship in 1962 at the age of twenty-one. She successfully defended her championship in the four world matches between 1965 and 1975. It was not until the fifth defense of her title in 1978 that she lost to a fellow Soviet, Maya Chiburdanidze. She was also the Soviet women's champion five times. Competing under the Swiss system of nine rounds and forty-eight players, Gaprindashvili finished first in the Lone Pine Tournament in 1977 and second in the Dortmund Tournament in 1978; these two tournaments were the best in her career. Gaprindashvili is among the few women chess players compared to the greatest woman chess champion, VERA MENCHIK-STEVENSON. (*Sources*: 132, 213, 421)

1962 Ruth Ginsburg (1933–) United States (Jewish American)

Ginsburg earned her undergraduate degree from Cornell University in 1954 and her law degree from Columbia University in 1959 and soon after entered private practice. In 1962 Ginsburg was appointed an assistant professor at Columbia Law School and served as a delegate to the International Congress on Comparative Law. She has authored and coauthored several books on foreign law and has been coeditor for *Trade Regulation in the Common Market*. (*Sources*: 103, 536, 550)

1963 Marie Goeppert-Mayer (1906–1972) United States (Germany)

Goeppert-Mayer was born into a highly educated family and earned her doctorate in physics from Göttingen University in 1930. In 1931 she married Joseph Mayer and fled from Nazi Germany. Much of her work was in collaboration with her husband, but it was she who in 1948 discovered that some neutrons and protons were peculiar in their structure and stability. This discovery is now often referred to as "magic numbers" or "shell theory." Mayer won the 1963 Nobel Prize for this work but had to share it with two other physicists, Hans Jensen and Eugene Wigner, who had made a similar discovery. She was author and coauthor of a number of books, including one she wrote with Jensen in 1955. She also worked on the separation of uranium isotopes and was a member of the Manhattan Project team that developed the atomic bomb. Even after a stroke, she spent the remaining years of her career teaching. (*Sources*: 22, 216, 583, 627, 731, 739)

1963 Shulamit Ran (1949–) Israel

Ran has devoted almost as much of her life to studying as she has to performing. Starting in 1960, at the age of eleven, she studied composition and piano in Israel and in 1963 studied with Aaron Copland and Lucas Foss at the prestigious Berkshire Music Center in Tanglewood, Massachusetts. In 1967 she graduated from the Mannes College of Music in New York, where she had studied on a scholarship; she received additional private tutoring until 1976. Ran played her own composition, *Capricco*, with the New York Philharmonic Orchestra under the direction of Leonard Bernstein in 1963; although she had performed several times in both Israel and the United States, the year 1967 is given as the official date for her U.S. debut. In 1971 Ran gave the premiere of her *Concert Piece* with the Israel Philharmonic Orchestra under the direction of Zubin Mehta. Ran has been the recipient of several grants, including a Guggenheim Fellowship; she was awarded the Pulitzer Prize in music in 1991, and has been teaching at the University of Chicago since 1973. (*Sources*: 12, 29, 357, 515)

1963   Bridget Riley   (1931–) England

Riley studied art for six years before giving her first exhibit in 1963. Playing up the sharp contrast between black and white in unique compositions, she creates op art; the psychological sight effect gives the illusion of motion and fluidity where none exist. Her style is considered basically mechanical because she employs illusory lines and images in order to obtain the optical effect she desires. (*Sources*: 356, 407, 586, 608, 717)

1963   Valentina Tereshkova   (1937–) Soviet Union

Tereshkova, making forty-eight orbits of the earth over a three-day period aboard *Vostok 6* in 1963, became the first woman to go into space. The Soviet government rewarded her for her pioneer flight by presenting her with the Order of Lenin and the Gold Star Medal and naming her Hero of the Soviet Union. Tereshkova was also honored by a number of foreign countries. Now holding the rank of lieutenant colonel, she is connected with the Soviet Air Force Engineering Academy. (*Sources*: 441, 471, 560, 565)

1963   Judith Zaimont   (1945–) United States

Zaimont made her debut as a pianist at Carnegie Hall in 1963. Most of her career since then has been devoted to composing pieces for orchestra and piano as well as vocal, chamber, and sacred music; she composed *The Thirteen Clocks*, a chamber opera, in 1983. After studying at the Julliard School of Music, she earned her bachelor's degree with honors from Queens College in 1966 and her master's in music from Columbia University in 1968; she continued her studies in Paris until 1972. Having taught at other colleges earlier, she was named a professor in music theory at the Peabody Conservatory of Music in Baltimore in 1980. Zaimont has been the recipient of numerous awards, fellowships, grants, and honors, including the Gold Medal from the Louis

Moreau Gottschalk centenary competition, and has frequently been commissioned to create works. (*Sources*: 99, 117, 698, 781)

1964 Margaret Bailey (1915–) United States (African American)
Bailey graduated from the Fraternal Hospital School of Nursing in Montgomery, Alabama, and earned a certificate in psychiatric nursing and her bachelor's degree from San Francisco State College in 1959. Entering the Army Nurse Corps in 1944, she remained in the army for twenty-seven years. In 1964 Bailey became the first African American promoted to the rank of lieutenant colonel, and in 1965 she was the first African American appointed chief nurse at an integrated army hospital. In 1970 she was promoted to full colonel. After her retirement from the army, Bailey worked with the Office of Economic Opportunity and the Manpower Administration. (*Sources*: 451, 648)

1964 Marga Richter (1926–) United States
Richter became an internationally known composer in 1964 when she wrote the score for the ballet *Abyss*. This was also the year her piano sonata was performed for the first time. Having first started composing teaching pieces in 1947, Richter then expanded her repertoire to include compositions for the ballet, piano and orchestral works, chamber and sacred music, as well as vocal pieces and band music. In 1972 she cofounded the Long Island Composers' Alliance. Richter won numerous awards and several grants from the National Endowment for the Arts. (*Sources*: 16, 29, 99, 416, 698, 781)

1965 Ama Ata Aidoo (1942–) Ghana
Aidoo was a graduate of the writing school at the University of Ghana in 1964 and also studied in the United States. She produced her first play, *The Dilemma of a Ghost*, in 1965. Like EFUA SUTHERLAND, Aidoo combines African tradition with modern themes, but she has been criticized as weakly presenting both worlds and for finding solutions for her characters' nettling problems within tradition yet failing to make its meaning clear. For example, in *Anowa* (1970) both husband and wife commit suicide, Aidoo giving no explanation for this end to the woman's (contemporary) need for independence and her husband's (traditional) fear of it. In Aidoo's *Dilemma of*

a Ghost, a Ghanian man is married to an African American woman, the man's family distressed because she is the descendant of slaves and the woman horrified at her in-laws' primitive lifestyle. A later novel (1977) is about women's rights, including their right to self-expression. (*Sources:* 107, 411, 717, 731, 739)

1965 Shulamit Aloni (1931–) Israel

Aloni was elected to the Knesset in 1965 and is also the head of the Civil Rights Party. She earned her degree in law from the Hebrew University of Jerusalem. In 1966 Aloni was named chair of the Israeli Consumer Council. She has a radio program and writes columns for Israeli newspapers. An ardent feminist, Aloni is pushing for better working conditions for women and better child care centers for working mothers. (*Sources:* 439, 458, 525, 731, 739)

1965 Jeanne Holm (1921–) United States

Holm was the first woman to attend the Air Command and Staff School and as a major general held the highest military rank of any woman in 1965. Holm enlisted in the army in 1942, serving until 1946. She was recalled to duty in 1946 and in 1948 was transferred to the air force. In 1965 Holm was made the first director of women in the air force. She was promoted to her present rank of brigadier general in 1971. Holm served at NATO headquarters in Europe for four years, and in 1975, after her retirement from the air force, she served as special assistant for women under President Gerald Ford. (*Sources:* 125, 451, 455, 463, 583, 664)

1965 Sheila Scott (1927–1988) England

Scott had difficulty staying in school or finding anything of interest to her until 1959, when she discovered flying. By 1965 she had completed the longest consecutive flight around the world. In 1969 she won the very competitive and much-publicized Top of the Tower race from London to New York in just over twenty-six hours. Her greatest feat, accomplished in 1971, was becoming the first pilot to fly over the North Pole in light aircraft. Tracked by NASA throughout most of her trip, she provided them with valuable information for the space program. By the time of her death she had broken more than 100 world records. (*Sources:* 441, 509, 583)

1966   Lynn Margulis   (1938–) United States

Margulis, a microbiologist, was among the first supporters of the still widely debated theory of symbiotic evolution of microorganisms first proposed by chemist James Lovelock. This theory states that living matter cannot survive alone and that, in fact, it is critically dependent on other matter for its existence and evolution. Margulis entered the University of Chicago in 1952 at the age of fourteen and married noted astronomer Carl Sagan when she was nineteen. Seven years later, she earned her doctorate from the University of California at Berkeley. Shortly after graduating, she divorced and began what has been a highly controversial career. She assumed her first major research position in 1966 at Boston University, where she remained for twenty-two years, often working with Lovelock. Their prediction that Mars would show no evidence of living organisms was vigorously disputed until the NASA *Viking* space probe proved them right. Margulis contends that the first cells on earth were forced to accept a symbiotic relationship with existing bacteria, the end result being the merger of the two into nucleated cells, the cells without nuclei evolving later. Her development of this theory led her to postulate that the recently discovered DNA molecule was once codependent with free-living spirochetes but had evolved to become an independent organism, retaining only the critically needed motility system of the spirochetes. Despite her earlier successes, her recent proposal is meeting with much controversy. The author of numerous articles and books, Margulis was elected to the National Academy of Sciences in 1983 and is presently a professor at the University of Massachusetts. (*Sources*: 546, 730)

1966   Grace Ogot   (1930–) Kenya

Ogot has divided her time between careers in nursing and writing. Trained as a nurse and midwife in Uganda and Britain, she has worked as a midwife and served as a community relations officer in Kenya and public relations officer for Air India in Nairobi; she was also a writer and announcer for the BBC in London. In 1966 Ogot published her first novel, *The Promised Land*, in which she wove witchcraft and folklore into her plot; similar themes occur in her short stories and children's stories. Her recent books address more contemporary issues, and she is a frequent contributor to the "Voice of Kenya" radio program. (*Sources*: 107, 385, 594, 731)

1967 Delores Brown   (1945–) United States (African American)

In 1967 Brown became the first woman to graduate from the Tuskeegee Institute's School of Engineering. Her first position was as an associate engineer for the General Electric Company, working on their contract with the U.S. Atomic Energy Commission project. Brown has since worked for the Sperry Univac Corporation and Honeywell Aerospace, as well as for several other companies. In 1981 Brown became a licensed minister in St. Petersburg, Florida. (*Sources*: 145, 648)

1967 Jo Freeman   (1945–) United States

Freeman has a history of political and social activism; she campaigned for Alan Cranston in his unsuccessful bid for the presidency in 1964 and for the similarly unsuccessful presidential candidate Eugene McCarthy in 1968. A civil rights worker from 1965 to 1966, she came to recognize the discriminatory practices toward women—even among those who advocated civil rights legislation. It was then that she became committed to changing the institutions that fostered this discrimination. In 1967 Freeman and several coactivists created an independent women's caucus to fight for women's rights, and that same year she organized the first consciousness-raising women's group in Chicago. In 1968 she founded the *Voices of Women's Liberation* newsletter, and she wrote two books on feminism in 1975. Freeman has also been an editor and coeditor for several publications as well as a freelance photographer. She began teaching at the University of Chicago, where she earned her doctorate, and has since taught political science at several State University of New York campuses. (*Sources*: 102, 358, 398, 583, 680)

1967 Muriel [Mickey] Siebert   (1928?–) United States

It is reported that in 1967 Siebert paid almost $.5 million to become the first woman to own a seat on the New York Stock Exchange. Her first job in investments was as a security analyst with Bache & Company in 1954, and by 1961 she was a partner in Stearns & Company. In 1968 Siebert opened her own financial investing corporation, which after a few years restricted its services to large corporations and institutions. Along with the many boards she has served on in various capacities, she was appointed New York State banking commissioner in 1974. (*Sources*: 349, 397, 533, 535, 583, 628, 756)

1967 Jane Wright (1919–) United States (African American)
Wright, the daughter and granddaughter of physicians, earned her medical degree from New York Medical College in 1945. She joined the Harlem Hospital medical staff and, after the death of her father, took over the research division that he had established. Wright's research focused on the effects on humans of animal-tested anticancer drugs. Her work in chemotherapy involved studying the effects of drugs on different types of cancer. The results led her to develop a research method by which cancer cells are removed and treated with the same drug at the same time the patient receives the medication in order to better understand the drug's effects. Through her specimen-control research, Wright was able to demonstrate that the drug interfered with the division of the invasive cells. This simultaneous patient-cell treatment aids in the determination of the correct drug to use on a particular patient with a particular form of cancer. In 1963 Wright was appointed to the President's Commission on Heart Disease, Cancer, and Stroke. In 1967 Wright was made dean and professor of surgery at Harlem Hospital, becoming the first woman appointed to this post. (*Sources*: 348, 383, 404, 618, 648)

1968 Marian Edelman (1939–) United States (African American)
Edelman learned compassion and concern for others from her parents, who, when there was no facility available for the African American elderly in Bennettsville, South Carolina, opened a home for them; her mother died there still caring for people younger than herself. In 1968, concerned about the needs of young children and the care provided for them, Edelman founded the Children's Defense Fund and moved to Washington, D.C., where she could lobby in behalf of poor children. Edelman states that it is the grace of ordinary women and their continuing struggle that serves as her inspiration. (*Sources*: 391, 705)

1968 Audre Lorde (1934–) United States (African American)

A declared lesbian and a strong advocate of feminism, Lorde chose poetry as her means of expression. She uses nature for her analogy for goodness and beauty, stating that the Hebraic-Christian focus on the "I" judges differences as right and wrong. Lorde contends that seeking sameness or merely tolerating differences robs us of the opportunity to use polarity as a source of creativity. Having published *The First Cities* in 1968, Lorde is the author of more than ten books of poetry. (*Sources*: 77, 496, 717, 728)

1969 Marguerite Chang (1923–) United States (China)

Chang was born and educated in China, earning her doctorate at Tulane University after immigrating to the United States. Much of Chang's work is still classified by the Department of the Navy. She is credited with many inventions, some of which deal with nuclear propellants, one of her areas of expertise. In 1969 she invented the triggering device used in testing underground nuclear explosives. She received several awards from the navy as well as the Federal Woman's Award in 1973. (*Sources*: 583, 627)

1969 Barbara Kolb (1939–) United States

Kolb's father, an instrumentalist and music director of a radio station, financed her college education but refused to pay for her graduate studies in an attempt to dissuade her from a musical career. She financed her own graduate work and was soon the recipient of numerous fellowships and grants for further study, including a Fulbright scholarship in 1966 and two Guggenheim awards in the early 1970s. One of the few contemporary artists able to support herself on commissioned work, Kolb is also the first U.S. woman composer to win the Prix de Rome in 1969. She received much acclaim for her music, in which the rondeau is performed by the repetition of groups of instruments rather than the melody. She is also known for the addition of electronics into her piece *Soundings*, played by both the New York Philharmonic and Boston Symphony orchestras. (*Sources*: 16, 99, 627)

1970 Martina Arroyo (1936–) United States (African American)

Arroyo was born in Harlem and was educated at Hunter College in New York. She made her operatic debut on opening night at the Metropolitan Opera in 1970 and has since sung nineteen major operatic roles at the Metropolitan. On her European tours she has sung at the Vienna Opera, La Scala, and Covent Garden; she has sung in many of the opera houses of South America. Arroyo often has MARGARET BONDS write special music for her recitals and still performs lieder and oratorio, the music in which she received her first training while studying under Marinka Gurevich. She has appeared with the major symphony orchestras of the United States and Europe, often as guest soloist, and records with four large record companies. (*Sources*: 1, 372, 463, 510, 756)

1970 Christine Beshar (1929–) United States (Germany)

Beshar left Germany at the end of World War II and studied in Sweden before earning a Fulbright scholarship to attend Smith College, where she graduated in 1953. After marrying a Yale Law School graduate, Beshar went to work in his office as a clerk. Learning that she qualified to take the bar examination because she had clerked for more than the required four years, Beshar took the examination in 1960, becoming the first woman in the state of New York to pass without first attending law school. In 1964 both she and her husband left the law firm where they had worked together for more than ten years; Beshar was hired by Cravath, Swaine & Moore, one of the most prestigious firms on Wall Street. In 1970 Beshar was named the first woman full partner in the firm. The mother of four children, Beshar had moved from law clerk to full partner in sixteen years. (*Sources*: 531, 534, 535, 671)

1970 Elizabeth Hoisington (1918–) United States

Hoisington came from a military family: her father and three of her brothers were West Point Academy graduates, and one of her brothers was made a brigadier general in the army in 1958. She graduated from the College of Notre Dame in Baltimore in 1940 and enlisted in the army in 1943 as a lieutenant; she was commissioned in the regular army in 1948 when the Women's Army Corps (WACs) was incorporated into the regular army. From 1944 to 1950 Hoisington served in both Europe and Japan, returning to the United States to work for MARY HALLAREN, director of the WACs. After a second assignment in Europe,

Hoisington returned to the United States, where in 1964 she was appointed commandant of the U.S. Women's Army Corps School. In 1970 Hoisington was promoted to brigadier general, becoming the first woman to hold this rank. Hoisington holds an impressive record of citations and decorations, including the Bronze Star and the French Croix de Guerre. (*Sources*: 98, 439, 455, 583, 733)

1971   Chantal Akerman   (1950–) Belgium

Akerman made her first film, *Blow Up My City*, with very little training and no financial backing; it did not receive attention until 1971, when it was critically acclaimed as one of the outstanding avant-garde films of the day. Working in black and white, Akerman uses repeated settings, minimal dialogue, and the depiction of an ordinary life that is altered with a spectacular ending to highlight personal emotions. In *Blow Up My City*, a thirteen-minute film, a housewife is shown scrubbing the floor in her apartment only to turn on the gas and blow up the entire building. Noted for her use of a fixed camera, Akerman herself often appears in her films. Akerman's 1974 film *I . . . You . . . He . . . She* was her first work to be screened at both the Brussels and Nice festivals and one of the films in which she plays the lead role. She is much admired by feminists for her dramatic portrayals of the drudgery of women's work and lives as well as their sexuality. Akerman has directed more than fifteen short and full-length films and was named Director of the Year in 1978 at both the Chicago and Paris film festivals. (*Sources*: 669, 728, 746)

1971   Alison Bauld   (1944–) Australia

Having first studied acting before turning to composing in 1969, Bauld writes music for unique blends of actors, singers, and instruments. She studied composition in London on a scholarship, receiving her doctorate from York University in 1974. Bauld composed her first piece, called *On the Afternoon of the Pigsty*, in 1971; other works have such unusual titles as *Dead Brown Land* (1972), *Pumpkin 2* (1973), and *Mad Moll* (1976). One of her compositions is written for two mimes, a soprano, a tenor, and various instruments; another combines a speaker, a piano, and percussion instruments. In 1975 Bauld was appointed musical director for the Laban Centre for Dance at Goldsmiths' College,

University of London. Bauld has written several compositions for the British Broadcasting Company, most notably her music for *Richard III*, as well as for numerous festivals. (*Sources*: 117, 731)

1971   Judith Jamison   (1944–) United States (African American)
Jamison first trained in ballet at the Philadelphia Dance Academy and later studied modern dance at Joan Kerr's Dance School. She made her debut in Agnes DeMille's *The Four Marys* and joined the Alvin Ailey Dance Company in 1965. Jamison reached stardom in 1971 when she performed one of the longest and most demanding solos in a production called *Cry*. In 1976 she danced with Mikhail Baryshnikov in a program presented by the Ailey Company in honor of Duke Ellington. She has also appeared with the American Ballet and the San Francisco Ballet companies as well as with several ballet and dance companies in Europe. In 1972 Jamison was named to the board of directors of the National Endowment for the Arts. She now teaches at the Maurice Hines Dance School in New York City. (*Sources*: 98, 345, 533)

1972   Maria Barreno   (1939–) Portugal
In 1972, under a new law that held authors responsible for the morality of their work, Barreno and her coauthors, Maria Horta and Maria da Costa, were arrested for publishing *The New Portuguese Letters*. The book was a compilation of their notes and letters to each other over a period of several months. These three friends and writers discovered they held the common belief that women were oppressed, but they also discovered that each held a different view as to why: Barreno felt it was the social institutions, particularly motherhood, that enslaved women; Horta felt is was because of men and their aggression, including that of fathers, husbands, and even sons; and da Costa argued that both men and women share equally in suffering. Out of this disagreement came the idea of writing missives and sharing them with each other, meeting once a week to discuss what each had written. They chose MARIANNA ALCOFORADO as their unifying theme because she had been confined to a convent by her family and had been betrayed by her lover. The case became an international cause célèbre among women's and writers' groups. Shortly after their trial began, the judge dismissed the charges

against them and proclaimed the book a work of literary merit. (*Sources*: 37, 479, 583)

1972 [Eleanor] Margaret Burbridge (1922?–) England

Burbridge is noted for her work in discovering the origin of stars, quasars (bodies that are not stars but resemble them), galaxies (aggregates of stars such as the Milky Way), and star formation. Her research led to the discovery of pulsars (short-period radio sources) and the source of supernovas (the explosion of material in a star). Burbridge first began her studies in astronomy at the Observatory of the University of London in 1948. In 1955 she and her husband, also an astronomer, moved to California, where he had a fellowship at the Mount Wilson Observatory while she had to accept a minor teaching position at the California Institute of Technology. By 1965 Burbridge was a professor at the University of California, a position she held until accepting an appointment in 1972 as the first woman director of the Royal Greenwich Observatory. She coauthored a book with her husband in 1967. (*Sources*: 180, 561, 739)

1972 Sally Priesand (1946–) United States (Jewish American)

Priesand earned her bachelor's degree from the University of Cincinnati in 1968. Next earning a degree in Hebrew letters in 1972, Priesand became the first ordained woman rabbi in the Reform sect of Judaism, the only sect willing to accept women rabbis at that time. Her first post was as an assistant rabbi at the Stephen Wise Free Synagogue in New York City; beginning in 1979 she was rabbi at Temple Beth El in Elizabeth, New Jersey. She has served on no fewer than fifteen major commissions, both religious and secular. The National Conference of Christians and Jews named Priesand one of its ten Outstanding Young Women of America in 1972 and one of its fifty Extraordinary Women of Achievement in 1978. She is also the author of a book (1975) that examines the changing role of women in Judaism. (*Sources*: 98, 439, 455, 533, 617, 652, 692)

1972 Nawal el Saadawi (1930–) Egypt

As one of the few women physicians in Egypt, el Saadawi was appointed director of education in the Ministry of Health and editor of the magazine *Health*. The more she saw the physical, social, and psychological effects of the Arab culture on women, the more she felt a need to speak out in their behalf. In 1972 she published her first book on the conditions of Arab women, *Women and Sex*, and was immediately dismissed from both of her official posts. Continuing her campaign to change the political and social status of women, she wrote the novel *Woman at Point Zero* in 1978 and a nonfiction book, *The Hidden Face of Eve: Women in the Arab World*, in 1979. In her novel, el Saadawi tells the story of a woman imprisoned in the notorious Qanatir prison—where el Saadawi herself was placed in 1981 for having written the book, which the government had banned shortly after its publication. One of the cultural practices el Saadawi is fighting to have outlawed is the performance of clitoridectomy (female circumcision) on young girls. Having experienced this ceremony herself, she was particularly sensitive to the pain, infection, and deaths resulting from this tradition that she witnessed as a physician. In 1977 el Saadawi organized the African Training and Research Center for Women in Ethiopia and in 1982 founded a pan-Arab women's rights organization. (*Sources*: 147, 717, 728)

1973 Nguyen Thi Binh (1927–) Vietnam

As the official representative of the National Liberation Front, Binh signed the 1973 peace accord that ended the Vietnam War. The daughter and granddaughter of two of the most highly regarded Vietnamese patriots, she had devoted most of her early life to carrying on this heritage. At the age of twenty-four she was imprisoned for her political activities and was not released until the end of French rule in 1954. She resumed her political activities, first fighting the Vietnamese dictator Diem and later the U.S. forces. In 1969 Binh was appointed a foreign minister in the provisional government; in 1976, when Vietnam was again unified, she was appointed minister of education. Known as the "flower and fire" of the revolution, she expressed her gratitude for peace. (*Sources*: 583, 621)

1973 Charlotte Murphy (1925–) United States

Murphy earned her law degree at Catholic University in 1948 and was appointed that same year to the U.S. Court of Appeals in Washington, D.C. She was editor of the *Young*

Lawyers, an American Bar Association publication, from 1951 to 1957. In 1956 Murphy became the youngest lawyer and first woman elected director of the District of Columbia Bar Association. Beginning in 1960, she worked for the Internal Revenue Service and in 1973 became the first woman to be appointed trial judge in the U.S. Court of Claims. (*Sources*: 455, 583, 713)

1973   Twyla Tharp   (1941–) United States
Tharp began studying music as a child, first playing the piano, violin, and viola. She later studied dance and ballet at Barnard College, where she graduated in 1963. She joined the Paul Taylor Dance Company but left to form her own company in 1965. Her first choreography was presented at Hunter College in 1965. Continuing to choreograph and dance, she built a modest following of fans. Tharp's big success came in 1973, when she wrote her first major ballet, *Deuce Coup*, a combination of Beach Boys music, modern dance, and ballet presented in nineteen sections for the Joffrey Ballet. It premiered at the New York City Center Theater and established Tharp as a major figure in U.S. choreography. Other major successes have been *Push Comes to Shove*, written for the American Ballet Theater and starring Mikhail Baryshnikov, and her role as dancer in the movie version of *Hair*. *Push Comes to Shove* was performed twice each year for the first ten years after it was written. Still using combinations of modern dance and ballet, rock and roll, jazz, and classical music, Tharp chose a more serious theme in her 1980 and 1981 productions, focusing on the breakdown of family life in the United States. (*Sources*: 345, 548, 709)

1974   Muriel Fox   (1928–) United States (Jewish American)
Impatient to start her career in communications, Fox worked as an art critic and bridal editor for a Miami newspaper and as a UPI reporter before she graduated with honors from Barnard College in 1948. Her first position out of college was as a speech writer and publicist with Carl Byoir and Associates in New York City; she later became the director of the company's television and radio department and was promoted to vice-president of the firm in 1956. After working for several other companies, Fox was appointed to the federal task force on women in 1968. In 1974, Fox was one of the founding members of the

Women's Forum; she later became its president The first organization of its kind, the forum is a roster of names that connects people with women experts in a large number of fields and has become a major referral service—a sophisticated answer to the old-boy network. Fox has served on numerous business and civic boards and was one of the founding members of the National Organization of Women. She was named one of the 100 Top Corporate Women by *Business Week* magazine (1976) and received a business leader of the year award in 1979. (*Sources*: 3, 533, 535)

1974 Faith Popcorn (1948–) United States

Popcorn is seen as having an uncanny ability to predict trends in U.S. taste; however, she is methodical in arriving at her predictions. A graduate of New York University, Popcorn began a career in advertising, opening her own company, Brain Reserve, in 1974. Noting that fads are unimportant because of their short duration, she focuses instead on trends that have a longer life expectancy and are usually incorporated into the culture. Popcorn uses the brainstorming technique with her staff to elicit the best predictions in the marketplace. Her approach saves industries the costly, lengthy, and not always accurate procedure of marketing research. Popcorn defines new markets, develops strategies for new products, and invents effective ways to reposition older brand names. Among the major companies that have used her services as a marketing consultant are AT&T, Borden, Eastman Kodak, and Campbell's Soup. There are often feature articles on Popcorn in the *New York Times* and the *Wall Street Journal*. (*Sources*: 130, 143, 349, 448, 460, 613)

1974 Armi Ratia (1912–1979) Sweden (Finland)

Ratia studied textile design in both Finland and Germany and in 1935 opened her own weaving business. In 1944 she was forced to flee to Sweden because of the war and took a job in a U.S. advertising company's Swedish office. She left her job in 1949 to help her husband rebuild the oilcloth company he had purchased; here she began to design dresses for women as well as fabrics. In 1974 Ratia established a dressmaking company named Marimekko (Mary's dress), and within four years it was an internationally known company with sales in the millions of dollars. (*Sources*: 583, 621, 731)

1974 Simone Veil (1927–) France

The same year that Veil received her bachelor's degree, she and her family were deported to the concentration camp at Auschwitz, which only she and her sister survived. She studied law and entered politics in 1946. By 1969 Veil had drafted her first law on adoption; she was appointed minister of health in 1974. Knowing of the resistance to liberalized abortion laws that had been going on for many years, she fought valiantly and successfully to get an abortion law passed—the first such law in any country with Catholicism as its national religion. In 1979 Veil became president of the European Parliament, a post she held until her resignation in 1982. Starting in 1982, she chaired both the Legal Affairs Committee and the Liberal and Democratic Group. (*Sources*: 464, 558, 583, 621, 731)

1975 Ellen Zwilich (1939–) United States

Zwilich earned her bachelor's and master's degrees in music from Florida State University in 1960 and 1962 and in 1975 became the first woman awarded a doctorate in musical composition at the Julliard School. From 1965 to 1972, she was a violinist with the American Symphony Orchestra under the direction of Leopold Stokowski. She began composing in 1971 and became a freelance composer in 1973. In 1983 Zwilich became the first woman awarded a Pulitzer Prize for music. Her pieces have been played and recorded in several countries, winning her numerous awards and honors. (*Sources*: 29, 99, 117, 386, 781)

1976 Paula Hyman (1946–) United States (Jewish American)

Hyman earned her B.A. from Radcliffe College in 1968 and her M.A. and Ph.D. in Judaic history from Columbia University in 1970 and 1975. Her first teaching position was at the Seminary College of Judaic Studies (1973–1974); in 1974 she was appointed assistant professor at Columbia, where she still teaches. Hyman was a coauthor of *The Jewish Woman in America* in 1976 and wrote *Dreyfus to Vichy* in 1979. Hyman has devoted much of her study to the role of the Jewish American woman, stereotypically referred to as the Jewish American princess, or JAP. Pampered and indulged, the young Jewish woman is also charged with the preservation of the Jewish family, the root of Jewish community life and survival. She notes that in the 1970s, Jewish women's personal identity and change in roles were the focus of much discussion; by the 1980s, however, the focus had shifted back to her obligations to family, community, and Jewish survival, with little to no emphasis on her importance as an individual. Hyman states that it is not family life but rather community life that preserves the minority group and that the myth of the Jewish woman as the keeper of Jewish life is an attempt to perpetuate her servile role within the family. (*Sources:* 224, 583)

1976 Ntozake Shange (1948–) United States (African American)
Shange, primarily a poet, chose the infrequently used art forms of choreopoem and poemplay as the major vehicles for her work. She called on her own painful experiences as a woman and as an African American for her material. Shange was raised in a middle-class home and graduated from Barnard College in 1970, earning her master's degree from the University of California at Los Angeles in 1973. Having experienced racism at an early age and aware of the injustices to women, Shange wrote about these topics in a lengthy poem that she later developed into a poemplay and finally presented as a choreopoem entitled *for colored girls who have considered suicide when the rainbow is enuf*. Produced on Broadway in 1976, it was an immediate success, winning several awards, including the Obie and the Golden Apple, and being nominated for Grammy and Tony awards; later made into a movie for PBS, it was also nominated for an Emmy award. Her work was praised for its appeal to women and African Americans. Each of the twenty verses presents an aspect of women's lives, some of them happy, others sad, several depicting the injustices women suffer; the final one is a dramatic portrayal of a woman witnessing the death of her children at the hands of her lover. Shange followed this initial success with *A Photograph: A Still Life with Shadows* in 1977 and two more works in 1979, all staged in both U.S. and European theaters. Along with her choreopoems and choreoplays, Shange has written fiction and nonfiction and is the author of three volumes of poetry. (*Sources:* 77, 439, 717)

1977 Debbi Fields (1956–) United States
Deciding to capitalize on the popularity of her chocolate chip cookies among her friends and her husband's business

associates, Fields borrowed $50,000 from her husband to open her own cookie shop in southern California. The prediction that her business would fail appeared to be accurate until she developed the marketing strategy of giving out free cookies to passersby. Her cookies became so popular that Fields used profits to expand her business, turning it into a $60-million entrepreneurship within ten years. She has begun to expand into markets throughout Europe and Asia. (*Sources*: 349, 448)

1977 Kay Koplovitz (1945–) United States
Koplovitz faced her first real challenge as a child when she fought to recover from a serious illness by learning to speed skate. She then took up baseball and tennis. After graduating with honors from the University of Wisconsin in 1967 and earning her master's degree two years later from Michigan State University, Koplovitz drew on her knowledge of sports to host a radio sports talk show. Having written her master's thesis on the emergence of satellite television, Koplovitz broke into the burgeoning field of cable television, going to work for UA/Columbia. Noting the success of a satellite broadcast of a major boxing event in 1975, UA/Columbia (later renamed USA Network) in 1977 decided to establish a cable television network with Koplovitz as chief executive officer. Although the network was at first limited to sports events, Koplovitz expanded the programming to twenty-four hours, diversified into other events, and added talk shows to compete with other new cable channels. In 1986 she was among the first to purchase successful television programs before they went into syndication. Under her direction, USA Network developed into a business that generates $200 million a year. (*Sources*: 49, 86, 349, 439, 448, 517, 533, 613)

1977 Leslie Silko (1948–) United States (Native American)
Born into a family of Pueblo, Mexican, and white ancestry that was socially and financially privileged relative to those around it, Silko developed both sensitivity and strength at an early age. She also chose to identify with her Native American heritage, particularly her Laguna ancestry. In 1969 she graduated from the University of New Mexico, where she later taught creative writing. Although Silko has written many short stories and poems, all of them about her culture, both past and present, she is best known for her novel *Ceremony* (1977). In it, the central

character, Tayo, who had traumatic experiences both as a child and as a soldier in World War II, develops serious mental problems that are not solved by the white doctors. Only with the help of two fellow tribespeople, a man and a woman, is he able to recover. Interwoven into the story of Tayo is the plight of his tribe, which is suffering from a severe drought that ends at the time Tayo regains his health. She writes within the Native American context of the inevitability of things past, repeated, and to be experienced again—a continuity of the events in life. (*Sources*: 11, 446, 605, 738)

1978 Anne Fisher (1950–) United States

Along with five other women, including Sally Ride (the first U.S. woman to go into space) and Judith Resnick (killed in the *Challenger* flight), Fisher was accepted into the first NASA women astronaut training group in 1978. Fisher had earned her bachelor's and medical degrees from the University of California at Los Angeles in 1971 and 1976. She and her husband, also a physician, applied to the space program together; it was not until he was accepted in 1980 that they became the first wife-husband astronaut team. Not yet selected for a mission flight, Fisher has helped to develop and test the remote manipulator arm used in space shuttles and also developed emergency medical treatment programs for use in space travel. (*Sources*: 90, 418, 455, 583)

1978 Kay Gardner (1941–) United States

One of few women orchestral conductors, Gardner became the musical director and conductor for the New England Women's Symphony in Boston in 1978. A proponent of the idea that women may develop musical forms different from those men have created (which are still the only accepted forms), Gardner has been composing since 1977. Her first composition was *When We Made the Music;* she has since written more than ten additional pieces, including an opera based on a text by Gertrude Stein and a composition for eleven flutes. Gardner won the American Society of Composers, Authors, and Publishers' Standard Award in 1980 and 1983 and the Palestrina–Schönberg Award in 1982. (*Sources*: 445, 728)

1980 Vigdis Finnbogadottir (1930–) Iceland

Finnbogadottir received her education in Iceland, Denmark, France, and Sweden, studying French, theater, and literature. Returning to Iceland, she began a diversified career first as a French teacher, later as a drama instructor, and then as a popular television host presenting French and art lessons. In 1972 Finnbogadottir was appointed director of the Reykjavik Theater Company and in 1978 was named chair of the Advisory Committee on Cultural Affairs in the Nordic Countries. In 1972, divorced and childless, she became the first single woman in Iceland to adopt a child. Finnbogadottir made a successful bid for president in 1980, defeating three male opponents and becoming the first woman elected president in Iceland. She was reelected, unopposed, in 1984; in 1988 she beat out the one candidate opposing her, another woman, and was reelected to her third term. Finnbogadottir's presidency has been noted for its emphasis on the preservation of the integrity and culture of Iceland as well as on the ecological reclamation and preservation of the country's natural resources. (*Sources*: 335, 438, 558, 615)

1980   Betty Welch   (1913–1985) United States

Welch was one of the few women with a degree in mechanical engineering when she graduated from Cornell University in 1936. She worked as an aeronautical engineer for thirty years, first at United Aircraft Corporation and later at Kaman Aircraft, both in Connecticut. In 1964 Welch earned her master's degree in physics at Trinity College in Hartford and began a new career teaching physics at the Torrington branch of the University of Connecticut, retiring in 1978. In 1980 Welch was presented with the Centennial Medallion, the highest award given by the American Society of Mechanical Engineers. (*Source*: 68)

1981   Alexa Canady   (1950–) United States (African American)

Born in Lansing, Michigan, Canady earned her bachelor's degree from the University of Michigan and graduated from the university's medical school with honors in 1975. She is the first female African American neurosurgeon. In 1981 Canady was appointed chief of pediatric neurosurgery of the Detroit Children's Hospital, and she remains the only African American neurosurgeon in that city. She is also a clinical instructor in neurosurgery at Wayne State University. (*Sources*: 391, 648, 705)

1981   Anne St. Clair   (1947–) United States
St. Clair was born in Bluefield, West Virginia. She earned her bachelor's degree in chemistry from Queens College, North Carolina, in 1969 and her master's degree in bioinorganic chemistry in 1971 from Virginia Polytechnical Institute and State University. She is a senior research scientist and manager of the Advanced Aircraft Program at the NASA-Langley Research Center in Virginia, where she conducts research on polymer films and coatings for aerospace vehicles. Married to a fellow NASA scientist, St. Clair is the author of 100 scientific journal articles and has been the presenter of seventy technical papers at symposiums. She holds sixteen patents, with an additional seventeen patents pending in the United States, Europe, and Asia. St. Clair has been named NASA Inventor of the Year four times since 1981 and has received a total of sixty-five awards to date, including a NASA medal for exceptional scientific achievement in 1985. St. Clair serves on the editorial review board of the *Society for Materials and Processing Engineers (SAMPE) Quarterly*. (*Source*: 690)

1981   Ellen Terry   (1934–) United States
Terry was compelled to carve out a career when she abruptly found herself a single parent responsible for two children. Although she held a physical education degree from Southern Methodist University, she had never worked and needed to find a new field that would enable her to support her family and pay the $100,000 debt with which she was left. Starting on a commission basis for a real estate firm in 1976, she left in 1978 to open a company with two other women, again leaving in 1981 to open her own residential real estate company, Ellen Terry Realtors, in Dallas, Texas. Within the first four years of operation, the company showed a profit of $400 million. Terry has also developed a second career as a paid management motivational speaker. (*Sources*: 397, 448)

1983   Jean Yokum   (1931–) United States
Among the few woman banking executives in the country, Yokum was named Credit Union Professional of the Year in 1983 by the National Association of Federal Credit Unions. Appointed president of the Langley Federal Credit Union in Hampton, Virginia, in 1979, she began her career in banking as a teller at

this local institution in 1953 after completing a three-year course at the Credit Union Business School in Wisconsin. Under Yokum's aegis, Langley Federal Credit Union assets have quadrupled. Among her many other honors is to have been elected the first woman chair of the board for the Peninsula Retail Merchants Association in Hampton; she also became the first woman chair for Peninsula Family Services. Yokum currently serves on both national- and state-level credit union boards as well as several community services boards. (*Source*: 777)

1985 Sherian Cadoria   (1940–) United States (African American)

When Cadoria was promoted to the rank of brigadier general in 1985, she became the highest-ranking African American woman in the U.S. Army. She had earned a bachelor's degree in business education from Southern University in 1961 and a master's degree in human relations from the University of Oklahoma in 1974 as well as several military college diplomas. Having served as a protocol officer in Vietnam for almost three years, Cadoria had considered leaving the military upon her return in 1969. When she was selected to attend the Commanding General Staff College, however, she felt a responsibility toward all African Americans in the military; she attended and graduated from the military staff college and continued her career in the army. (*Sources*: 391, 648, 705)

1986 Ruth Pater   (1939–) United States (Taiwan)

Born in Taiwan, Pater earned her bachelor's degree in chemistry before emigrating to the United States, where she earned her master's degree at Southeastern Massachusetts University in 1972 and her doctorate at Brown University in 1977. Hired in 1986 as a senior polymer scientist at NASA-Langley Research Center in Hampton, Virginia, her work has involved research and development of new, improved high-temperature polymeric composite materials for aircraft engine applications. She is author or coauthor of sixty scientific papers. Pater has received numerous awards, including seven NASA awards in 1989 (one of these being the Special Invention Award), three NASA awards for the year 1988, and the NASA-Lewis Invention Award for the year 1985. In addition, she holds patents on thirteen inventions. (*Source*: 600)

1988   Ekanem Esu Williams   (1950–) Nigeria

Williams graduated from the University of Nigeria in 1975 and earned her doctorate in immunology at the University of London in 1984. She is presently a senior lecturer at the University of Calabar. Williams credits Hilliard Festenstein of the London Hospital Medical College for promoting her education in immunology and encouraging her to accept challenges. In 1988 Williams and seven women doctors from Sudan, Ethiopia, Zambia, Zaire, Tanzania, Uganda, and Angola founded the Society for Women and Aids in Africa (SWAA), an expanding pan-African organization dedicated to challenging the existing legal and cultural oppression of women and children, especially the laws and cultural restrictions that fail to protect women and children from contracting AIDS. As an immunologist, Williams is doing research on AIDS in Nigeria. She is also a member of Women in Nigeria (WIN), a feminist group that has disclosed the abuse of women and children, child marriages, and the subjugation of women in her native country. Williams is also a technical adviser for the International Center for Research on Women. (*Sources*: 580 and personal interview)

1991   Merrill Waserman Sherman   (1948–) United States (Jewish American)

Sherman earned her bachelor's degree from Mount Holyoke College in 1970, having attended the University of Manchester in England during her junior year. She received her degree in law from the University of Denver in 1974. Sherman began her practice with the Providence, Rhode Island, law firm of Hinckley, Allen, Snyder & Comen and was named a partner in 1980. Specializing in real estate, administration of mortgages, and lending closings, she was involved in real estate transactions throughout the country. Developing a second area of expertise in commercial and savings banks, Sherman left the firm in 1991 to join Eastland Bank of Woonsocket, Rhode Island, as executive vice-president and chief general counsel. In June 1991 she was named president, becoming one of the few woman bank presidents in the United States. She is charged with improving the performance of the troubled financial institution, worth $750 million. (*Sources*: 414, 604, 661)

Indexes

The following indexes are provided to help you locate information on specific individuals or groups of women. Each index entry lists both the year and page number of a woman's biographical sketch. The **Index by Name** lists women alphabetically. The **Index by Country** will help you locate women from specific countries, and also, in the case of the United States—where racial and ethnic identity are highly prized—women who belong to specific ethnic groups. The **Index by Profession** lists individuals according to profession or nature of accomplishment.

Index by Name

Index by Country

GERMANY

UNITED STATES BY ETHNIC CATEGORY. These subcategories list women who identified themselves not only by their citizenship but by their ethnic background as well.

African Americans

Index by Profession
and Accomplishment

327

EXPLORERS

FEMINISTS

FILM DIRECTORS

GOVERNMENT OFFICIALS

SCIENTISTS

Sources

1. Abdul, Raoul. *Famous Black Entertainers of Today*. New York: Dodd, Mead, 1974.
2. Abir-am, Pina G., and Dorinda Outram, eds. *Uneasy Careers and Intimate Lives*. With a foreword by Margarete W. Rossiter. New Brunswick: Rutgers University Press, 1987.
3. Adams, Jane. *Women on Top*. New York: Hawthorn Books, 1979.
4. Adams, Mildred. *The Right to Be People*. Philadelphia: J. B. Lippincott, 1967.
5. Adams, Oscar Fay. *A Dictionary of American Authors*. 5th ed. Boston: Houghton Mifflin, 1904.
6. Adcock, Fleur, ed. *The Faber Book of Twentieth Century Women's Poetry*. London: Faber and Faber, 1987.
7. Adey, D., ed. *Companion to South African English Literature*. Johannesburg: Donker, 1986.
8. Adivar, Halide Edib. *Memoirs of Halide Edib*. New York: Century, 1926.
9. Alic, Margaret. *Hypatia's Heritage*. Boston: Beacon Press, 1986.
10. Allen, Catherine B. *The New Lottie Moon Story*. Nashville, Tennessee: Broadman Press, 1980.
11. Allen, Paula Gunn, ed. *Spider Woman's Granddaughters*. Boston: Beacon Press, 1989.
12. Allibone, S. Austin. *A Critical Dictionary of English Literature and British and American Authors*. Philadelphia: J. B. Lippincott, 1902.
13. Alpern, Sara. *Freda Kirchwey*. Cambridge: Harvard University Press, 1987.

14. American Medical Association. *Encyclopedia of Medicine.* New York: Random House, 1989.

15. American Society of Composers, Authors and Publishers. *American Society of Composers, Authors and Publishers Biographical Dictionary.* New York: R. R. Bowker, 1980.

16. Ammer, Christine. *Unsung.* Westport, Connecticut: Greenwood Press, 1980.

17. Anderson, Bonnie S., and Judith P. Zinsser. *A History of Their Own.* 2 vols. New York: Harper & Row, 1988.

18. Apgar, Virginia, and Joan Beck. *Is My Baby All Right?* New York: Trident Press, 1972.

19. Arlen, Lorna. "Juliette May Fraser, Honolulu Artist." *Paradise of the Pacific* 57, 2 (February 1945).

20. Arlott, John, ed. *The Oxford Companion to World Sports and Games.* London: Oxford University Press, 1975.

21. Arthur, Mildred H. *Williamsburg, Virginia: Colonial Williamsburg.* Williamsburg: Colonial Williamsburg, 1990.

22. Asimov, Isaac. *Asimov's Biographical Encyclopedia of Science and Technology.* New York: Doubleday, 1964.

23. Atherton, Gertrude Franklin Horn. *Adventures of a Novelist.* N.p.: Atherton Company, 1932; reprint, New York: Arno Press, 1980.

24. Atkinson, Dorothy, Alexander Dallin, and Gail Warshofsky Lapidus. *Women in Russia.* Stanford: Stanford University Press, 1977.

25. Axtell, James. "The Vengeful Women of Marblehead." *William and Mary Quarterly,* 3rd ser., 31 (1974): 650-652.

26. Baker, H. Barton. *History of the London Stage.* New York: Benjamin Blom, 1969.

27. Baker, Samuel W. *Exploration of the Nile Tributaries of Abyssinia.* Hartford: O. D. Case, 1868.

28. Baker, Samuel W. *Ismailia: A Narrative of the Expedition to Central Africa for the Suppression of the Slave Trade.* New York: Harper & Brothers, 1875.

29. Baker, Theodore. *Baker's Biographical Dictionary of Musicians.* New York: Macmillian, 1984.

30. Balabanoff, Angelica. *My Life as a Rebel.* N.p.: Harper & Brothers, 1938; reprint, Bloomington: Indiana University Press with Harper & Row, 1973.

31. Balbontin, José Antonio. *Three Spanish Poets*. With an introduction by José Picazo. London: Alvin Redman, 1961.
32. Balliett, Whitney. *American Singers*. New York: Oxford University Press, 1988.
33. "Baltimore County Women, 1930–1975." *American Association of University Women*. Towson, Maryland.
34. Banner, Lois W. *Women in Modern America: A Brief History*. San Diego: Harcourt Brace Jovanovich, 1984.
35. Barnes, R. H. *Two Crows Denies It*. Lincoln: University of Nebraska Press, 1984.
36. Barnhart, Clarence L., ed. *The New Century Handbook of English Literature*. New York: Meredith, 1967; reprint, New York: Appleton-Century-Crofts, 1956.
37. Barreno, Maria Isabel, Maria Teresa Horta, and Maria Velho da Costa. *The Three Marias: New Portuguese Letters*. Translated by Helen R. Lano. Garden City: Doubleday, 1975.
38. Barrington, Lewis. *Historic Restorations of the Daughters of the American Revolution*. Foreword by Sarah Corbin Robert. New York: Richard R. Smith, 1941.
39. Bauer, Marion, and Ethel R. Peyser. *Music Through the Ages*. New York: G. P. Putnam's Sons, 1932; rev. ed. Elizabeth E. Rogers and Claire Lingg, 1967.
40. Bede, Jean-Albert, and William B. Edgarton, eds. *Columbia Dictionary of Modern European Literature*. 2d ed., rev. and enl. New York: Columbia University Press, 1980.
41. Bell, Susan Groaf, ed. *Women from the Greeks to the French Revolution*. Stanford: Stanford University Press, 1973.
42. Benét, William Rose. *The Reader's Encyclopedia*. 2d ed. New York: Thomas Y. Crowell, 1965.
43. Bentley, Helen Delich, to Beverly Golemba, July 1991.
44. Berkin, Carol Ruth and Mary Beth Norton. *Women of America*. Boston: Houghton Mifflin, 1979.
45. Berkman, Joyce Avrech. *Olive Schreiner: Feminism on the Frontier*. Montreal: Eden Press Women's Publications, 1979.
46. Bernard, Bayle, Mrs. *Retrospection of America*. Edited by John Bernard. With an introduction by Laurence Hutton and Brander Matthews. New York: Benjamin Blom, 1969.
47. Bernikow, Louise. *Among Women*. N.p.: Crown, 1980; reprint, New York: Harper & Row, 1981.

48. Bernikow, Louise. *The World Split Open*. New York: Random House, 1974.
49. Billard, Mary. "Women on the Verge of being CEO." *Business Month*, April 1990.
50. Billington, Ray Allen. *American History Before 1877*. Totowa, New Jersey: Littlefield, Adams, 1965.
51. Binkin, Martin, and Shirley J. Bach. *Women and the Military*. Washington, D.C.: Brookings Institution, 1977.
52. Birdwell, Russell. *Women in Battle Dress*. New York: Fine Editions Press, 1942.
53. Blain, Virginia, Patricia Clements, and Isobel Grundy. *The Feminist Companion to Literature in English*. New Haven, Connecticut: Yale University Press, 1990.
54. Blitzstein, Madelin. "How Women Flyers Fight Russia's Air War." *Aviation*, July 1944.
55. Bodie, Idella. *South Carolina Women*. Lexington, South Carolina: Sandlapper Store, 1978.
56. Boehm, Eric, ed. *America, History and Life*. Santa Barbara: American Bibliographical Center of ABC-CLIO, 1976.
57. Bogan, Louise, and William J. Smith, comps. *The Golden Journey*. Chicago: Contemporary Books, 1990.
58. Bogin, Meg. *The Women Troubadours*. New York: W. W. Norton, 1976.
59. Booth-Tucker, F. de L. *The Life of Catherine Booth*. 2 vols. New York: Fleming H. Revell, 1892.
60. Boulding, Elise. *The Underside of History*. Boulder, Colorado: Westview Press, 1976.
61. Bowker staff, eds. *Who Was Who in American Art*. Madison, Connecticut: Sound View Press, 1989.
62. Boyd, Belle. *Belle Boyd in Camp and Prison, Written by Herself*. With an introduction by George Agusta Sala. New York: Blelock, 1865.
63. Boyko, Hugo, ed. *Science and the Future of Mankind*. The Hague: Dr. W. Junk, 1961; reprint, Bloomington: Indiana University Press, 1964.
64. Bradbury, Malcolm, Eric Mottram, and Jean Franco, eds. *The Penguin Companion to American Literature*. New York: McGraw-Hill, 1971.
65. Brady, Haldeen. "Lady Bullfighters," *Password* (El Paso Historical Society) 8, (Winter 1963).

66. Brewerton, George D. *Ida Lewis, the Heroine of Lime Rock.* Newport, Rhode Island: A. J. Ward, 1869.
67. Bridenthal, Renate, Claudia Koonz, and Susan Stuard, eds. *Becoming Visible.* 2d ed. Boston: Houghton Mifflin, 1987.
68. Briggs, Sherry, and Christopher Welch to Beverly Golemba, August 1991.
69. Brill, Paul, to Beverly Golemba, January 1990.
70. Brink, J. R. *Female Scholars.* Montreal: Eden Press Women's Publications, 1980.
71. Broadbent, R. J. *Annals of the Liverpool Stage.* New York: Benjamin Blom, 1969.
72. Brooks, Cleanth, R. W. B. Lewis, and Robert Penn Warren, eds. *American Literature.* New York: St. Martin's Press, 1974.
73. Brown, Archie, John Fennell, Michael Kaser, and H. T. Willets, eds. *The Cambridge Encyclopedia of Russia and the Soviet Union.* Cambridge: Cambridge University Press, 1982.
74. Brown, Dorothy M. *Setting a Course.* Boston: G. K. Hall, 1987.
75. Brown, Esther Lucille. *Nursing as a Profession.* New York: Russell Sage Foundation, 1936.
76. Brown, Esther Lucille. *Nursing for the Future.* New York: Russell Sage Foundation, 1948.
77. Brown-Guillory, Elizabeth. *Their Place on the Stage.* New York: Greenwood Press, 1966.
78. Browning, D. C., comp. *Everyman's Dictionary of Literary Biography English and American.* New York: E. P. Dutton, 1960.
79. Brugger, Robert J. *Maryland.* Baltimore: Johns Hopkins University Press for the Maryland Historical Society, 1989.
80. Buchanan-Brown, J., ed. *Cassell's Encyclopaedia of World Literature.* 3 vols, rev. and enl. New York: William Morrow, 1973.
81. Bullough, Vern L., Olga Maranjian Church, and Alice P. Stein. *American Nursing.* vol. 4. New York: Garland Publishing, 1988.
82. Bumiller, Elisabeth. *May You Be the Mother of a Hundred Sons.* New York: Random House, 1990.

83. Bureau of Medicine and Surgery, Department of the Navy: Washington, D.C., 1991. N. Puksta, executive assistant, Navy Nurse Corps, to Beverly Golemba, May 1991.

84. Burke, W. J., and Will D. Howe. *American Authors and Books*. Rev. ed. N.p. Gramercy, 1943; reprint, New York: Crown, 1962.

85. Burton, Annie L. "Memories of Childhood Slavery Days." In *Six Women's Slave Narratives*, ed. Henry Louis Gates, Jr., 3–58. New York: Oxford University Press, 1988.

86. "Cable TV: Koplovitz Sets Sights on Banner Year." *Advertising Age*, April 1988.

87. Campbell, D'Ann. *Women at War with America*. Cambridge: Harvard University Press, 1984.

88. Cantarow, Ellen. *Moving the Mountain*. Westbury, New York: Feminist Press with McGraw-Hill, 1980.

89. Carter, Samuel, III. *Cherokee Sunset: A Nation Betrayed*. Garden City, New York: Doubleday, 1976.

90. Cassutt, Michael. *Who's Who in Space: The First Twenty-Five Years*. Boston: G. K. Hall, 1987.

91. Catalog and Circular of the Satate Normal School, at Providence, R.I. (June 25, 1875). Providence: Providence Press, 1875.

92. Catalog and Circular of the State Normal School, at Providence, R.I. (June 28, 1872). Providence: Providence Press, 1872.

93. Chapin, Howard Millar. *Ann Franklin of Newport, Printer*. n.p.: Rhode Island Historical Society, n.d.

94. Christian, Barbara. *Black Women Novelists: The Development of a Tradition, 1892–1976*. Contributions in Afro-American Studies, 52. Westport, Connecticut: Greenwood Press, 1980.

95. Citron, Marcia J., ed. *The Letters of Fanny Hensel to Felix Mendelssohn*. N.p.: Pendragon Press, 1987.

96. Clapp, Jane. *Sculpture Index*. Metuchen, New Jersey: Scarecrow Press, 1970.

97. Clark, George L. *A History of Connecticut*. New York: G. P. Putnam's Sons, 1914; London: Knickerbocker Press, 1914.

98. Clark, Judith Freeman. *Almanac of American Women in the Twentieth Century*. New York: Prentice-Hall, 1987.

99. Cohen, Aaron I. *International Encyclopedia of Women Composers*. vol. 1. 2d ed., rev. and enl. New York: Books & Music, 1987.

100. Cohen-Stratyner, Barbara Naomi. *Biographical Dictionary of Dance*. New York: Macmillan, 1982.

101. Cole, Doris. *From Tipi to Skyscraper*. Boston: i press, 1973.

102. Cole, Johnnetta B., ed. *All American Women*. New York: Free Press, 1986.

103. Cole, Jonathan R. *Fair Science*. New York: Free Press, 1979; reprint, New York: Columbia University Press, 1987.

104. Cole, Margaret. *Women of To-Day*. Freeport, New York: Books for Libraries Press, 1938; reprint, 1968.

105. *Concise Dictionary of American Biography*. New York: Charles Scribner & Sons, 1964.

106. Connecticut Historical Society. *Black Women of Connecticut: Achievements Against the Odds*. Connecticut Historical Society, 1984.

107. *Contribution of the Federal Republic of Germany to the International Book Year*. Tübingen, Germany: Horst Erdmann, 1972.

108. Cooper, Anna Julia. *A Voice from the South*. Xenia, Ohio: Aldine Printing House, 1892; reprint, New York: Oxford University Press, 1988.

109. Cooper, James Fenimore. *The Last of the Mohicans*. With an introduction by Susan Fenimore Cooper. Edited by Alan K. Blackmer. Boston: Houghton Mifflin, 1930.

110. Cooper, Susan Fenimore. *Rural Hours*. With an introduction by David Jones. Syracuse, New York: Syracuse University Press, 1968.

111. *Cornell University News*, October 8, 1966.

112. Craft, William, and Ellen Craft. *Running a Thousand Miles for Freedom*. New York: Arno Press and the New York Times, 1969.

113. Croft, Nancy L. "Smart Selling: Training Your Eye to See the Future." *Nation's Business* 76, 3 (March 1988).

114. Cronwright-Schreiner, S. C. *The Life of Olive Schreiner*. Brooklyn, New York: Haskell, 1972.

115. Cummings, David, *The New Everyman Dictionary of Music*. 12th ed. Cambridge: Melrose Press, 1990.

116. Cummings, David, ed. *The New Everyman Dictionary of Music*. 6th ed. New York: Weidenfeld and Nicolson, 1988.
117. Cummings, David, and Dennis K. McIntire, eds. *International Who's Who in Music and Musicians' Directory*. 12th ed. Cambridge: Melrose Press, 1990.
118. Daiches, David. *The Penguin Companion to English Literature*. New York: McGraw-Hill, 1971.
119. Davis, Mary Lee Cadwell. *We Are Alaskans*. Boston: W. A. Wilde, 1931.
120. Davis, Nancy, and Andrea Stevens, eds. *Black Women: Achievement Against the Odds*. New York: GMG Publishing, 1978.
121. Day, A. Grove. *History Makers of Hawaii: A Biographical Dictionary*. Honolulu: Mutual Publishing of Honolulu, 1984.
122. Dazé, Anne Marie, and John W. Scanion. *Code Pink: A Practical System for Neonatal/Perinatal Resuscitation*. Baltimore: University Park Press, 1981.
123. De Haas, Jacob, ed. *The Encyclopedia of Jewish Knowledge*. New York: Behrman's Jewish Book House, 1949.
124. De Zapata, Celia Correas, ed. *Short Stories by Latin American Women: The Magic and the Real*. Houston: Arte Publico Press, 1990.
125. Deckard, Barbara Sinclair. *The Women's Movement: Political, Socioeconomic, and Psychological Issues*. New York: Free Press, 1986.
126. Deen, Edith. *Great Women of the Christian Faith*. New York: Harper & Row, 1959.
127. Dell, Floyd. *Women as World Builders*. Westport, Connecticut: Hyperion Press, 1913.
128. Delpar, Helen. *Encyclopedia of Latin America*. New York: McGraw-Hill, 1974.
129. Department of Veterans Affairs, New Bern National Cemetery, Karen J. Duhart, director, to Beverly Golemba, 1991.
130. Deutschman, Alan. "A Popcorn Packet." *Fortune*, April 1990.
131. Diebitsch-Peary, Josephine. *My Arctic Journal*. New York: Contemporary Publishing Company, 1893; reprint, New York: AMS Press, 1975.

132. Divinsky, Nathan. *The Chess Encyclopedia*. New York: Facts on File, 1990.
133. Dixon, Wheeler W. *The "B" Directors: A Biographical Directory*. Metuchen, New Jersey: Scarecrow Press, 1985.
134. Dobie, Charles Caldwell. *San Francisco's Chinatown*. New York: D. Appleton-Century, 1936.
135. Dolan, Josephine A. *History of Nursing*. 12th ed. Philadelphia: W. B. Saunders, 1968.
136. Dowie, Menie Muriel. *Women Adventurers*. London: T. Fisher Unwin, 1893.
137. Drachman, Virginia G. *Hospital with a Heart*. Ithaca: Cornell University Press, 1984.
138. Drake, William. *The First Wave: Women Poets in America, 1915–1945*. New York: Macmillan, 1988.
139. Drinker, Sophie. *Music and Women*. New York: Coward-McCann, 1948; reprint, Washington, D.C.: Zenger, 1977.
140. Driver, Harold E. *Indians of North America*. 2d ed. Chicago: University of Chicago Press, 1975.
141. Dunkling, Leslie. *A Dictionary of Days*. New York: Facts on File, 1988.
142. Dunnahoo, Terry. *Emily Dunning: A Portrait*. Chicago: Reilly & Lee Books, 1970.
143. Dun's Marketing Services. *Dun's Consultants Directory*. Parsippany, New Jersey: Dun's Marketing Services, Dun and Bradstreet Corporation, 1991.
144. Dun's Marketing Services. *Reference Book of Corporate Managements*. Parsippany, New Jersey: Dun's Marketing Services, Dun and Bradstreet Corporation, 1991.
145. Educational Communications. *Who's Who Among Black Americans*. Lake Forest, Illinois: Educational Communications, 1988.
146. Ehrenreich, Barbara, and Deirdre English. *Witches, Midwives and Nurses: A History of Women Healers*. Feminist Press with McGraw-Hill, 1973.
147. El Saadawi, Nawal. "The Question No One Would Answer." *Ms.*, March 1980.
148. "Elizabeth Taylor Greenfield." *The Colored American Magazine* 4, 1 (November 1901).
149. Elon, Amos. *The Israelis: Founders and Sons*. New York: Holt, Rinehart and Winston, 1971.

150. *Encyclopaedia Britannica*, 15th ed. (hereafter *E.B.*), s.v. "Abington, Fanny."
151. *E.B.*, s.v. "Adivar, Halide."
152. *E.B.*, s.v. "Agnesi, Maria."
153. *E.B.*, s.v. "Agoult, Marie d'."
154. *E.B.*, s.v. "Aguilar, Grace."
155. *E.B.*, s.v. "Agustini, Delmira."
156. *E.B.*, s.v. "Akhmatova, Anna."
157. *E.B.*, s.v. "Aleksyeevna, Sofya."
158. *E.B.*, s.v. "Alexandra of Denmark."
159. *E.B.*, s.v. "Andreas-Salomé, Lou."
160. *E.B.*, s.v. "Arányi, Jelly d'."
161. *E.B.*, s.v. "Arber, Agnes."
162. *E.B.*, s.v. "Argentina (La), Antonia Mercé."
163. *E.B.*, s.v. "Austin, Mary."
164. *E.B.*, s.v. "Bateman, Hester."
165. *E.B.*, s.v. "Bates, Katharine."
166. *E.B.*, s.v. "Baylis, Lilian."
167. *E.B.*, s.v. "Beach, Amy."
168. *E.B.*, s.v. "Beale, Dorothea."
169. *E.B.*, s.v. "Bell, Gertrude."
170. *E.B.*, s.v. "Bickerdyke, Mary Ann."
171. *E.B.*, s.v. "Blackburn, Helen."
172. *E.B.*, s.v. "Bond, Carrie."
173. *E.B.*, s.v. "Braddon, Mary."
174. *E.B.*, s.v. "Bregendahl, Marie."
175. *E.B.*, s.v. "Bremer, Fredrika."
176. *E.B.*, s.v. "Brittain, Vera."
177. *E.B.*, s.v. "Brophy, Brigid."
178. *E.B.*, s.v. "Brown, Esther."
179. *E.B.*, s.v. "Bueno, Maria."
180. *E.B.*, s.v. "Burbridge, Eleanor."
181. *E.B.*, s.v. "Burney, Fanny."
182. *E.B.*, s.v. "Camargo, Marie-Anne."
183. *E.B.*, s.v. "Cameron, Julia."
184. *E.B.*, s.v. "Canth, Minna."
185. *E.B.*, s.v. "Carpenter, Mary."
186. *E.B.*, s.v. "Carter, Elizabeth."
187. *E.B.*, s.v. "Castro, Rosalía de."
188. *E.B.*, s.v. "Catt, Carrie."
189. *E.B.*, s.v. "Chatelet, Gabrielle-Emilie du."

190. *E.B.*, s.v. "Child, Lydia."
191. *E.B.*, s.v. "Clough, Anne."
192. *E.B.*, s.v. "Colette, Sidonie-Gabriele."
193. *E.B.*, s.v. "Collett, Camilla."
194. *E.B.*, s.v. "Cori, Gerty."
195. *E.B.*, s.v. "Crawford, Isabella."
196. *E.B.*, s.v. "Cruz, Sor Juana de la."
197. *E.B.*, s.v. "Cushman, Charlotte."
198. *E.B.*, s.v. "Dacier, Ann."
199. *E.B.*, s.v. "Darling, Grace."
200. *E.B.*, s.v. "Dashkova, Ekatrina."
201. *E.B.*, s.v. "Deken, Agatha."
202. *E.B.*, s.v. "Delano, Jane."
203. *E.B.*, s.v. "Densmore, Frances."
204. *E.B.*, s.v. "Dermout, Maria."
205. *E.B.*, s.v. "Drew, Louisa."
206. *E.B.*, s.v. "Droste-Hülshoff, Annette von."
207. *E.B.*, s.v. "Fawcett, Millicent."
208. *E.B.*, s.v. "Fiennes, Celia."
209. *E.B.*, s.v. "Figner, Vera."
210. *E.B.*, s.v. "Fletcher, Alice."
211. *E.B.*, s.v. "Fuller, Loie."
212. *E.B.*, s.v. "Fuller, Sarah."
213. *E.B.*, s.v. "Gaprindashuili, Nona."
214. *E.B.*, s.v. "Garnett, Constance."
215. *E.B.*, s.v. "Germain, Sophie."
216. *E.B.*, s.v. "Goeppert-Mayer, Maria."
217. *E.B.*, s.v. "Gonne, Maud."
218. *E.B.*, s.v. "Green, Hetty."
219. *E.B.*, s.v. "Grimshaw, Beatrice."
220. *E.B.*, s.v. "Haldane, Elizabeth."
221. *E.B.*, s.v. "Hess, Myra."
222. *E.B.*, s.v. "Higuchi, Ichiyo."
223. *E.B.*, s.v. "Huntington, Selina."
224. *E.B.*, s.v. "Hyman, Libbie."
225. *E.B.*, s.v. "Jekyll, Gertrude."
226. *E.B.*, s.v. "Johnson, Pauline."
227. *E.B.*, s.v. "Jonker, Ingrid."
228. *E.B.*, s.v. "Kenyon, Kathleen."
229. *E.B.*, s.v. "Knight, Sarah."
230. *E.B.*, s.v. "Kollontai, Alexandra."

231. *E.B.*, s.v. "Kollwitz, Käthe."
232. *E.B.*, s.v. "Kovalevsky, Sofya."
233. *E.B.*, s.v. "LaFayette, Marie-Madeleine."
234. *E.B.*, s.v. "LaFlesche, Susette."
235. *E.B.*, s.v. "Lamb, Mary Ann."
236. *E.B.*, s.v. "Landowska, Wanda."
237. *E.B.*, s.v. "Lange, Dorothea."
238. *E.B.*, s.v. "Leavitt, Henrietta."
239. *E.B.*, s.v. "Lidman, Sara."
240. *E.B.*, s.v. "Lonsdale, Kathleen."
241. *E.B.*, s.v. "Luxemburg, Rosa."
242. *E.B.*, s.v. "Lyon, Mary."
243. *E.B.*, s.v. "Maintenon, Madame de."
244. *E.B.*, s.v. "Mance, Jeanne."
245. *E.B.*, s.v. "Mansfield, Katherine."
246. *E.B.*, s.v. "Markova, Alicia."
247. *E.B.*, s.v. "Meireles, Cecelia."
248. *E.B.*, s.v. "Meitner, Lise."
249. *E.B.*, s.v. "Menchik-Stevenson, Vera."
250. *E.B.*, s.v. "Mistral, Gabriela."
251. *E.B.*, s.v. "Mitford, Nancy."
252. *E.B.*, s.v. "Monroe, Harriet."
253. *E.B.*, s.v. "Montagu, Elizabeth."
254. *E.B.*, s.v. "Montagu, Mary."
255. *E.B.*, s.v. "Moodie, Susanna."
256. *E.B.*, s.v. "Moore, Marianne."
257. *E.B.*, s.v. "Morante, Elsa."
258. *E.B.*, s.v. "More, Hannah."
259. *E.B.*, s.v. "Morris, Margaret."
260. *E.B.*, s.v. "Mortimer, Penelope."
261. *E.B.*, s.v. "Mott, Lucretia."
262. *E.B.*, s.v. "Murray, Margaret."
263. *E.B.*, s.v. "Naidu, Sarojini."
264. *E.B.*, s.v. "Nalkowska, Zofia."
265. *E.B.*, s.v. "Nerina, Nadia."
266. *E.B.*, s.v. "Neuber, Caroline."
267. *E.B.*, s.v. "Newhall, Nancy."
268. *E.B.*, s.v. "Nikolayeva, Galina."
269. *E.B.*, s.v. "Noailles, Anna."
270. *E.B.*, s.v. "Noether, Emmy."
271. *E.B.*, s.v. "Norton, Caroline."

272. *E.B.*, s.v. "Opie, Amelia."
273. *E.B.*, s.v. "Orcy, Emmuska."
274. *E.B.*, s.v. "Orzeskowa, Eliza."
275. *E.B.*, s.v. "Osborne, Dorothy."
276. *E.B.*, s.v. "Pandit, Vijaya."
277. *E.B.*, s.v. "Pankhurst, Emmeline."
278. *E.B.*, s.v. "Parsons, Elsie."
279. *E.B.*, s.v. "Patti, Adeline."
280. *E.B.*, s.v. "Queiroz, Rachel."
281. *E.B.*, s.v. "Rachel, Elizabeth."
282. *E.B.*, s.v. "Radcliffe, Ann."
283. *E.B.*, s.v. "Rambert, Marie."
284. *E.B.*, s.v. "Reiniger, Lotte."
285. *E.B.*, s.v. "Richards, Audrey."
286. *E.B.*, s.v. "Richmond, Mary."
287. *E.B.*, s.v. "Roberts, Kate."
288. *E.B.*, s.v. "Roche, Sophie von la."
289. *E.B.*, s.v. "Rubtsova, Olga."
290. *E.B.*, s.v. "Rudenko, Ludmila."
291. *E.B.*, s.v. "Sachs, Nelly."
292. *E.B.*, s.v. "Sager, Ruth."
293. *E.B.*, s.v. "Sarraute, Nathalie."
294. *E.B.*, s.v. "Sayers, Dorothy."
295. *E.B.*, s.v. "Schreiner, Olive."
296. *E.B.*, s.v. "Serao, Matilde."
297. *E.B.*, s.v. "Shirreff, Emily."
298. *E.B.*, s.v. "Smith, Charlotte."
299. *E.B.*, s.v. "Smithson, Alison."
300. *E.B.*, s.v. "Södergran, Edith."
301. *E.B.*, s.v. "Somerville, Edith."
302. *E.B.*, s.v. "Spark, Muriel."
303. *E.B.*, s.v. "Stead, Christina."
304. *E.B.*, s.v. "Strickland, Agnes."
305. *E.B.*, s.v. "Suttner, Bertha."
306. *E.B.*, s.v. "Tarbell, Ida."
307. *E.B.*, s.v. "Tey, Josephine."
308. *E.B.*, s.v. "Tietjens, Eunice."
309. *E.B.*, s.v. "Tsvetayeva, Marina."
310. *E.B.*, s.v. "Tynan, Katherine."
311. *E.B.*, s.v. "Ukrainka, Lesya."
312. *E.B.*, s.v. "Undset, Sigrid."

313. *E.B.*, s.v. "Valois, Ninette de."
314. *E.B.*, s.v. "Visscher, Anna."
315. *E.B.*, s.v. "Vivien, Renée."
316. *E.B.*, s.v. "Webb, Mary."
317. *E.B.*, s.v. "Willard, Emma."
318. *E.B.*, s.v. "Wolff-Bekker, Elizabeth."
319. *E.B.*, s.v. "Wright, Judith."
320. *E.B.*, s.v. "Yale, Caroline."
321. *E.B.*, s.v. "Yezierska, Anzia."
322. *E.B.*, s.v. "Yonge, Charlotte."
323. *E.B.*, s.v. "Zetkin, Clara."
324. Ewen, David. *The Complete Book of Twentieth Century Music.* Rev. ed. Englewood Cliffs, New Jersey: Prentice-Hall, 1963.
325. Ewen, David. *Encyclopedia of the Opera.* New York: A. A. Wyn, 1955.
326. Ewen, David. *Musicians Since 1900.* New York: H. W. Wilson, 1966.
327. Ewen, David. ed. *Great Composers.* New York: H. W. Wilson, 1966.
328. Faber, Doris. *Petticoat Politics.* New York: Lothrop, Lee & Shepard, 1967
329. Falk, Peter Hastings, ed. *Who Was Who in American Art.* New York: Sound View Press, 1985.
330. Feather, Leonard. *The Encyclopedia of Jazz.* New ed., rev. and enl. New York: Crown, 1960.
331. Feather, Leonard. *The Encyclopedia of Jazz.* New York: Horizon Press, 1955.
332. Felton, Rebecca Latimer. *Country Life in Georgia.* Atlanta: Index Printing Company, 1919; reprint, New York: Arno Press and the New York Times, 1980.
333. Finch, Edith. *Carey Thomas of Bryn Mawr.* New York: Harper & Brothers, 1947.
334. Finn, Donald F. X. "Eliza Greenfield." n.p., 1983.
335. Finnbogadottir, Vigdis, to Beverly Golemba, June 1991.
336. First, Ruth, and Ann Scott. *Olive Schreiner.* New York: Schocken Books, 1980.
337. Fleming, Alice. *Great Women Teachers.* Philadelphia: J. B. Lippincott, 1965.
338. "Flemmie Kittrell." Moreland Spingarn Research Center, Howard University, Vertical Files, Washington, D.C.

339. Flexner, Eleanor. *Century of Struggle*. New York: Atheneum, 1968.
340. Foner, Philip S., and Josephine F. Pacheco. *Three Who Dared*. Westport, Connecticut: Greenwood Press, 1984.
341. Foreman, Alexa L. *Women in Motion*. Bowling Green, Ohio: Bowling Green University Popular Press, 1983.
342. Foreman, Carolyn Thomas. *Indian Women Chiefs*. Washington, D.C.: Zenger Publishing, 1976.
343. Forrest, Mary. *Women of the South*. New York: Garrett Press, 1969.
344. Foster, Scott, ed. *Alaska Blue Book*. 7th ed. Juneau, Alaska: Department of Education, Division of State Libraries, 1985.
345. Fowler, Carol. *Contributions of Women: Dance*. Minneapolis: Dillon Press, 1979.
346. Frank, Morris. *First Lady of the Seeing Eye*. Morristown, New Jersey: Seeing Eye, 1957.
347. Fraser, Antonia. *The Warrior Queens*. New York: Alfred A. Knopf, 1989.
348. Fraser, Antonia. *The Weaker Vessel*. New York: Alfred A. Knopf, 1984.
349. Fraser, Edie, ed. *Risk to Riches*. Institute for Enterprise Advancement, 1986.
350. Free Press. *Encyclopedia of Architects*. New York: Free Press, 1982.
351. Freedman, Estelle B. *Their Sister's Keepers*. Ann Arbor: University of Michigan Press, 1981.
352. Friedwald, Will. *Jazz Singing*. New York: Scribner's, 1990.
353. Furniss, Harry. *Some Victorian Women: Good, Bad, and Indifferent*. New York: Dodd, Mead, 1923.
354. Gade, John Allyne. *The Life and Times of Tycho Brahe*. London: Princeton University Press, 1947; reprint, New York: Greenwood Press, 1969.
355. Gale Research Company. *Who Was Who Among North American Authors, 1921–1939*. Vol. 1. Gale Composite Biographical Dictionary Series, no. 13. Detroit: Gale Research, 1976.
356. Gardner, Louise. *Gardner's Art Through the Ages*. 6th ed. New York: Harcourt Brace Jovanovich, 1975.

357. Gaster, Adrian, ed. *International Who's Who in Music and Musicians' Dictionary*. 8th ed. Cambridge: Melrose Press, 1977.

358. Gatlin, Rochelle. *American Women Since 1945*. Jackson: University Press of Mississippi, 1987.

359. Gerson, H., and E. H. Ter Kuile. *Art and Architecture in Belgium*. Baltimore: Penguin Books, 1960.

360. Giele, Janet Zollinger, and Audrey Chapman Smock. *Women: Roles and Status in Eight Countries*. New York: John Wiley & Sons, 1977.

361. Giffin, Frederick C. *Woman as Revolutionary*. New York: New American Library, 1973.

362. Gifford, Carolyn De Swarte. *Women in American Protestant Religion, 1800–1930*. New York: Garland Publishing, 1987.

363. Gilder, Rosamond. *Enter the Actress*. New York: Theater Arts Books, 1931; reprint, Freeport, New York: Books for Libraries Press, 1971.

364. Gildersleeve, Virginia. *Many a Good Crusade*. New York: Macmillan, 1954; reprint, New York: Arno Press and the New York Times, 1980.

365. Glanville, Philippa, and Jennifer Faulds Goldsborough. *Women Silversmiths, 1685–1845*. Washington, D.C.: National Museum of Women in the Arts, 1990.

366. Golombek, Harry, ed. *Golombek's Encyclopedia of Chess*. New York: Crown, 1977.

367. Gornick, Vivian. *Women in Science*. New York: Simon & Schuster, 1983.

368. Gould, Jean. *American Women Poets*. New York: Dodd, Mead, 1980.

369. Gould, Jean. *Modern American Poets*. New York: Dodd, Mead, 1984.

370. Goulianos, Joan, ed. *By a Woman Writt*. Indianapolis: Bobbs-Merrill, 1973; reprint, Baltimore: Penguin Books, 1974.

371. Gray, John. *Blacks in Classical Music*. New York: Greenwood Press, 1988.

372. Green, Mildred Denby. *Black Women Composers: A Genesis*. Boston: G. K. Hall, 1983.

373. Green, Norma Kid. "Four Sisters: Daughters of Joseph LaFlesche." *Nebraska History*, July 1964.

374. Greer, Germaine. *The Obstacle Race.* New York: Farrar, Straus, and Giroux, 1979.
375. Greer, Germaine, Susan Hastings, Jeslyn Medoff, and Milinda Sansone, eds. *Kissing the Rod.* New York: Farrar, Straus, and Giroux, 1988.
376. Gresham, Charles. "An Essay on Menstruation." M.D. diss., University of Pennsylvania, 1850.
377. Grey, Elizabeth. *Winged Victory.* Boston: Houghton Mifflin, 1966.
378. Griffin, Gerald Joseph, and Joanne King Griffin. *History and Trends of Professional Nursing.* Vol. 1. 7th ed. St. Louis: C. V. Mosby Company, 1973.
379. Grigson, Geoffrey, ed. *The Concise Encyclopedia of Modern World Literature.* 2d ed. New York: Hawthorn Books, 1971.
380. Grumet, Madeleine R. *Bitter Milk.* Amherst: University of Massachusetts Press, 1988.
381. Gunnis, Rupert. *Dictionary of British Sculptors, 1660–1851.* London: Adhams Press, n.d.
382. Haar, Francis, and Prithwish Neogy. *Artists of Hawaii: Nineteen Painters and Sculptors.* Vol. 1, p. 57. Honolulu: University of Hawaii, 1974.
383. Haber, Louis. *Women Pioneers of Science.* New York: Harcourt Brace Jovanovich, 1979.
384. Hacker, Carlotta. *The Indomitable Lady Doctors.* Toronto: Clarke, Irwin & Company, 1974.
385. Hafkin, Nancy J., and Edna G. Bay, eds. *Women in Africa.* Stanford: Stanford University Press, 1976.
386. Hall, Charles J., comp. *A Twentieth-Century Musical Chronicle: Events, 1900–1988.* Westport, Connecticut: Greenwood Press, 1989.
387. Hall, Ruth. *Passionate Crusader.* New York: Harcourt Brace Jovanovich, 1977.
388. Hall, Sarah Ewing. *Selections from the Writings of Mrs. Sarah Hall.* Philadelphia: Harrison Hall, 1833.
389. Hamilton, Alice. *Exploring the Dangerous Trades.* Boston: Little, Brown, 1943.
390. Hamilton, George Heard. *Painting and Sculpture in Europe, 1880 to 1940.* New York: Penguin Books, 1970.
391. Hampton University Archives. Clip no. 231.U5. Philadelphia Tribune, October 4, 1910.

392. Hardesty, Nancy Ward. *Great Women of Faith.* Grand Rapids, Michigan: Baker Book House, 1980.
393. Harding, Sandra. *Whose Science? Whose Knowledge?* Ithaca: Cornell University Press, 1991.
394. Hargreaves-Mawdsley, W. N. *Everyman's Dictionary of European Writers.* New York: E. P. Dutton, 1968.
395. Harris, Ann Sutherland, and Linda Nochlin. *Women Artists: 1500–1950.* New York: Alfred A. Knopf, 1977.
396. Harris, Sherwood. *The First to Fly.* New York: Simon and Schuster, 1970.
397. Harrison, Patricia, ed. *America's New Women Entrepreneurs.* Washington, D.C.: Acropolis Books, 1986.
398. Harte, Barbara, and Carolyn Riley, eds. *Contemporary Authors.* Vols. 5–8. Detroit: Gale Research, 1969.
399. Harter, Hugh A. *Gertrudis Gomez De Avellaneda.* Boston: G. K. Hall, 1981.
400. *Hartford Courant.* "Alice Paul Dies at 92, Drew ERA," July 10, 1977.
401. *Hartford Courant.* "Author, 91, Still Awaits Passage of Equal Rights Amendment," March 7, 1976.
402. Haskell, Arnold. *Balletomania Then and Now.* New York: Alfred A. Knopf, 1977.
403. Haskins, James. *Black Dance in America.* New York: Thomas Y. Crowell, 1990.
404. Hayden, Robert C., and Jacqueline Harris. *Nine Black American Doctors.* Reading, Massachusetts: Addison-Wesley, 1976.
405. Hayward, John, comp. *The Oxford Book of Nineteenth-Century English Verse.* London: Oxford University Press, 1964.
406. Heilbrun, Carolyn G. *Hamlet's Mother and Other Women.* New York: Ballantine Books, 1990.
407. Heller, Nancy G. *Women Artists: An Illustrated History.* New York: Abbeville Press, 1987.
408. Hellmans, Alexander, and Bryan Bunch. *The Timetables of Science.* New York: Simon and Schuster, 1988.
409. Helms, Winifred G., ed. *Notable Maryland Women.* Centreville, Maryland: Tidewater Publishers, 1977.
410. Henry, Sondra, and Emily Taitz. *Written out of History: Our Jewish Foremothers.* 3d ed. Sunnyside, New York: Biblio Press, 1988.

411. Herdeck, Donald E. *African Authors*. Vol. 1. 2d ed. Washington, D.C.: INSCAPE Corporation and Black Orpheus Press, 1974.
412. Hersenberg, Caroline. *Women Scientists from Antiquity to the Present: An Index*. West Cornwall, Connecticut: Locust Hill Press, 1986.
413. Herzberg, Max J. *The Reader's Encyclopedia of American Literature*. New York: Thomas Y. Crowell, 1962.
414. Hiday, Jeffrey. "Easland Appoints Lawyer as President." *The Providence Journal*, June 1991.
415. Higham, Charles. *Kate*. New York: W. W. Norton, 1975.
416. Hixon, Don L., and Don Hennessee. *Women in Music: A Bibliography*. Metuchen, New Jersey: Scarecrow Press, 1975.
417. Hodge, Frederick Webb, ed. *Handbook of American Indians North of Mexico*. Smithsonian Institution Bureau of American Ethnology Bulletin 30. Washington, D.C.: Government Printing Office, 1907–1910; reprint, Totowa, New Jersey: Rowman and Littlefield, 1979.
418. Hodgman, Ann, and Rudy Djabbaroff. *Sky Stars*. Harrisonburg, Virginia: R. R. Donnelley and Sons, 1981.
419. Hoehling, A. *Women Who Spied*. New York: Dodd, Mead, 1967.
420. Hoffman, Ronald, and Peter J. Albert, eds. *Women in the Age of the American Revolution*. Charlottesville: University Press of Virginia for United States Capitol Historical Society, 1989.
421. Hooper, David, and Kenneth Whyld. *The Oxford Companion to Chess*. New York: Oxford University Press, 1984; reprint, 1987.
422. Horno-Degado, Asuncion, Eliana Ortega, Nina M. Scott, and Nancy Saporta Sternbach. *Breaking Boundaries: Latina Writing and Critical Readings*. Amherst: University of Massachusetts Press, 1989.
423. Howard, John Tasker. *Our Contemporary Composers*. New York: Thomas Y. Crowell, 1941; reprint, 1942.
424. Howat, Gerald, ed. *Who Did What*. New York: Crown, 1974
425. Howe, Florence, and Ellen Bass, eds. *No More Masks!* Garden City, New Jersey: Anchor Press, 1973.
426. Howe, Helen. *The Gentle Americans*. New York: Harper & Row, 1965.

427. Hoyrup, Else. *Women and Mathematics, Science and Engineering.* Roskilde, Denmark: Roskilde University Library, 1978.
428. Hoyt, Mary Finch. *American Women of the Space Age.* New York: Atheneum, 1966.
429. Hughes, Langston, comp. *An African Treasury.* New York: Crown, 1960
430. Hughes, Langston, comp. *Famous Negro Music Makers.* New York: Dodd, Mead, 1955.
431. Hughes, Rupert. *The Biographical Dictionary of Musicians.* McClure Phillips, 1913; rev. ed., Deems Taylor and Russell Kerr. New York: Blue Ribbon Books, 1940.
432. Hume, Ruth Fox. *Great Women of Medicine.* New York: Random House, 1964.
433. Hunt, Margaret, Margaret Jacob, Phyllis Mack, and Ruth Perry. *Women and the Enlightenment.* New York: Institute for Research in History and Haworth Press, 1984.
434. Hyatt, Irwin T., Jr. *Our Ordered Lives Confess.* Cambridge: Harvard University Press, 1976.
435. Icolari, Dan. *Reference Encyclopedia of the American Indian.* 2d ed. Rye, New York: Todd Publications, 1974.
436. Insko, W. Robert. "Early New England Clergyman." *Rhode Island History* 18, 3 (July 1959): 84.
437. *L'Institut des Religieuses Hospitalières de Saint-Joseph: L'Hôtel-Dieu.* Preface by Olivier Maurault. Montreal: Joseph Charbonneau, 1942.
438. *The International Who's Who, 1990–91.* London: Europa Publications, 1990.
439. Ireland, Norma Olin. *Index to Women of the World.* Westwood, Massachusetts: F. W. Faxon, Inc., 1970.
440. Ireland, Norma Olin. *Index to Women of the World: A Supplement.* Metuchen, New Jersey: Scarecrow Press, 1988.
441. Jablonski, Edward. *Ladybirds: Women in Aviation.* New York: Hawthorn Books, 1968.
442. Jacobs-Bond, Carrie. *The Roads of Melody.* New York: D. Appleton, 1927.
443. Jacques Cattell Press, eds. *American Men and Women of Science.* Vol. 1. 12th ed. New York: R. R. Bowker Company, 1971.

444. Jacques Cattell Press, eds. *ASCAP Biographical Dictionary*. Compiled for the American Society of Composers, Authors and Publishers. New York: R. R. Bowker Company, 1980.

445. Jacques Cattell Press, eds. *Who's Who in American Music: Classical*. New York: R. R. Bowker Company, 1983.

446. Jahner, Elaine. "The Novel and Oral Tradition: An Interview with Leslie Marmon Silko." *Book Forum* 3 (1981): 383–99.

447. James, T., Janet W. James, and Paul S. Boyer, eds. *Notable American Women*. Cambridge: Harvard University Press, 1971.

448. Jennings, Diane. *Self-Made Women*. Dallas: Taylor, 1987.

449. Johnson, Allen, ed. *Dictionary of American Biography*. New York: Charles Scribner's Sons, 1929.

450. Johnson, Edna, Evelyn R. Sickles, and Frances R. Sayers. *Anthology of Children's Literature*. 3d rev. ed. Cambridge: Riverside Press, 1959.

451. Johnson, Jesse J., ed. *Black Women in the Armed Forces*. Hampton, Virginia: Hampton Institute, 1974.

452. Jones, Amanda T. *A Psychic Autobiography*. New York: Greaves, 1910.

453. Jones, Katharine M. *Heroines of Dixie*. Indianapolis: Bobbs-Merrill, 1955.

454. Kader, Soha Abdel. *Egyptian Women in a Changing Society, 1899–1987*. Boulder, Colorado: Lynne Rienner Publishers, 1987.

455. Kane, Joseph Nathan. *Famous First Facts*. New York: H. W. Wilson, 1981.

456. Kaplan, Carey, and Ellen Cronan Rose, eds. *Doris Lessing: The Alchemy of Survival*. Athens: Ohio University Press, 1988.

457. Kaplan, Cora. *Salt and Bitter and Good*. New York: Paddington Press, 1975.

458. Karpman, I. J. Carmin, ed. *Who's Who in World Jewry*. New York: Pitman Publishing Corporation, 1972.

459. Katzenstein, Mary Fainsod, and Carol McClurg Mueller, eds. *The Women's Movement of the United States and Western Europe*. Philadelphia: Temple University Press, 1987.

460. Kauffman, Joanne. "The World According to Faith Popcorn." *Newsday*, March 1988.
461. Kaufman, Debra R., and Barbara L. Richardson. *Achievement and Women: Challenging the Assumptions.* New York: Macmillan, 1982.
462. Kaufman, Martin, ed. *Dictionary of American Nursing Biography.* Vol. 5. New York: Greenwood Press, 1988.
463. Kay, Ernest. *The World Who's Who of Women.* Cambridge: Melrose Press, 1973.
464. Keckley, Elizabeth. *Behind the Scenes.* New York: G. W. Carleton, 1868; reprint, New York: Oxford University Press, 1988.
465. Keil, Sally Van Wagenen. *Those Wonderful Women and Their Flying Machines.* New York: Rawson, Wade Publishers, 1979.
466. Kelly, Linda. *Women of the French Revolution.* London: Hamish Hamilton, 1989.
467. Kennedy, Don H. *Little Sparrow: A Portrait of Sophia Kovalevsky.* Athens: Ohio University Press, 1983.
468. Kennedy, Michael. *The Oxford Dictionary of Music.* Rev. and enl. ed. London: Oxford University Press, 1985.
469. Kerber, Linda K. *Women of the Republic.* Chapel Hill: University of North Carolina Press for the Institute of Early American History and Culture, Williamsburg, Virginia, 1980.
470. Kerber, Linda K., and Jane DeHart-Mathews, eds. *Women's America: Refocusing the Past.* 2d ed. New York: Oxford University Press, 1982.
471. Kerrod, Robin. *NASA Visions of Space.* Philadelphia: Courage Books, 1990,
472. Keter Publishing House. *Encyclopedia Judaica.* Jerusalem: Keter Publishing House, 1972.
473. Kirk, John Foster. *A Supplement to Allibone's Critical Dictionary of English Literature and British and American Authors.* Vol. 1. Philadelphia: J. B. Lippincott, 1902.
474. Kittrell, Flemmie P. "University of Baroda Establishes Home Economics in Higher Education." *Journal of Home Economics* 44, 1 (January 1952).
475. Klein, Leonard S. *African Literature in the Twentieth Century.* Rev. ed. New York: Frederick Ungar, 1986.

476. Klein, Leonard S., ed. *Encyclopedia of World Literature in the Twentieth Century*. Rev. ed. New York: Frederick Ungar, 1981.

477. Knight, Charlotte. "Now Women Are Ferrying AAF Combat Planes." *Air Force Journal*, September 1943.

478. Koegler, Horst, ed. *Concise Oxford Dictionary of Ballet*. 2d ed. Oxford: Oxford University Press, 1982.

479. Kolbenschlag, Madonna. *Kiss Sleeping Beauty Good-bye*. New York: Doubleday, 1979.

480. Korones, Sheldon B. *High-Risk Newborn Infants*. 4th ed. St. Louis: C. V. Mosby, 1986.

481. Krantz, Les, ed. *American Architects*. New York: Facts on File, 1989.

482. Kronenberger, Louis, ed. *Atlantic Brief Lives*. Boston: Little, Brown, 1971.

483. Kulik, Gary. "The Beginnings of the Industrial Revolution in America: Pawtucket, Rhode Island, 1672–1829." Ph.D. diss., Brown University, 1980; Michigan: University Microfilms International, 1981. Microfiche.

484. Kulp-Hill, Kathleen. *Rosalia De Castro*. Boston: G. K. Hall, 1977.

485. Kunitz, Stanley, J., ed. *British Authors of the Nineteenth Century*. New York: H. W. Wilson, 1936.

486. Kunitz, Stanley J., and Howard Haycraft, eds. *American Authors, 1600–1900*. New York: H. W. Wilson, 1938.

487. Kunitz, Stanley J., and Howard Haycraft, eds. *British Authors Before 1800*. New York: H. W. Wilson, 1952.

488. Kunitz, Stanley J., and Vineta Colby. *European Authors, 1000–1900*. New York: H. W. Wilson, 1967.

489. Kutsch, K. J., and Leo Riemens. *A Concise Biographical Dictionary of Singers*. Philadelphia: Chilton, 1969.

490. Labalme, Patricia H., ed. *Beyond Their Sex*. New York: New York University Press, 1984.

491. Ladoul, Georges. *Dictionary of Film Makers*. Translated, edited, updated by Peter Morris. Berkeley: University of California Press, 1972.

492. Lahaise, Robert. *L'Hôtel-Dieu de Montréal*. Montreal: Huttubise, 1973.

493. Lamphere, Louise. *From Working Daughters to Working Mothers*. Ithaca: Cornell University Press, 1987.

494. Land, Barbara. *The New Explorers*. New York: Dodd, Mead, 1981.
495. Larison, C. W. *Sylvia Dubois, A Biografy of the slav who whipt her mistress and gand her fredom.* Edited, translated, and introduced by Jared C. Lobdell. New York: Oxford University Press, 1988.
496. Lauter, Estella. *Women as Mythmakers*. Bloomington: Indiana University Press, 1984.
497. Lawrence, Una Roberts. *Lottie Moon*. Nashville, Tennessee: Sunday School Board of Southern Baptist Convention, 1927.
498. Lawson, Joan. *A History of Ballet and Its Makers*. London: Pitman & Sons, 1964.
499. Lee, Elinor. "She's Off to the Congo to Organize a College." *Washington Post*, July 30, 1962.
500. Leggett, Jane. *Local Heroines: A Women's History Gazetteer of England, Scotland and Wales*. London: Pandora, 1988.
501. Leonard, John William, ed. *Woman's Who's Who of America: 1914–1915*. New York: American Commonwealth Company, 1914.
502. Lerner, Gerda. *Black Women in White America*. New York: Random House, n.d.
503. Lessing, Doris. *A Small Personal Voice: Doris Lessing*. New York: Random House, 1975.
504. Levinson, Nancy Smiler. *The First Women Who Spoke Out*. Minneapolis: Dillon Press, 1983.
505. Lewis, Arthur H. *The Day They Shook the Plum Tree*. New York: Harcourt, Brace & World, 1963.
506. Livermore, Mary A. *My Story of the War: A Woman's Narrative of Four Years' Personal Experience*. Hartford, Connecticut: A. D. Worthington, 1888.
507. Loewenberg, Bert James, and Ruth Bogin, eds. *Black Women in Nineteenth-Century American Life*. University Park: Pennsylvania State University Press, 1976.
508. Logan, Rayford W., and Michael R. Winston, eds. *Dictionary of American Negro Biography*. New York: W. W. Norton, 1982.
509. Lomax, Judy. *Women of the Air*. New York: Dodd, Mead, 1987.

510. Long, Richard A. *Black Americana*. Secaucus, New Jersey: Chartwell Books, 1985.
511. Lorenz, Clare. *Women in Architecture*. New York: Rizzoli, 1990.
512. Lovejoy, Esther Pohl. *Women Doctors of the World*. New York: Macmillan, 1957.
513. Lovell, Mary S., comp. *The Splendid Outcast*. San Francisco: North Point Press, 1987.
514. Lowens, Irving. *Music and Musicians in Early America*. New York: W. W. Norton, 1964
515. Lyle, Wilson. *A Dictionary of Pianists*. New York: Macmillan, 1985.
516. Lynn Farnol Group, ed. *The ASCAP Biographical Dictionary of Composers, Authors and Publishers*. New York: American Society of Composers, Authors and Publishers, 1966.
517. Machan, Dyan. "Never Look Down." *Forbes*, July 1989.
518. Macksey, Joan, and Kenneth Macksey. *The Book of Women's Achievements*. New York: Stein and Day Publishers, 1976.
519. Madison, Charles A. *Leaders and Liberals*. New York: Frederick Ungar, 1961.
520. Magill, Frank N., ed. *Cyclopedia of World Authors*. New York: Harper & Brothers, 1958.
521. Magnus, Laurie. *A Dictionary of European Literature*. Rev. with addenda. New York: E. P. Dutton, 1927.
522. Mainiero, Una, ed. *American Women Writers*. 4 vols. New York: Frederick Ungar, 1981.
523. Mann, Herman. *The Female Review*. New York: Arno Press and the New York Times, 1972.
524. Mapp, Edward. *Directory of Blacks in the Performing Arts*. Metuchen, New Jersey: Scarecrow Press, 1978.
525. Marcus, Jacob R. *The American Jewish Woman: A Documentary History*. New York: KTAV Publishing House, 1981.
526. "Margaret Moffett O'Neill." Randy L. Goss, archivist for the Delaware Bureau of Archives and Record Management, to Beverly Golemba, 1990.
527. Mark, Joan. *A Stranger in Her Native Land*. Lincoln: University of Nebraska Press, 1988.
528. Markham, Beryl. *West with the Night*. San Francisco: North Point Press, 1983.

529. Marks, Geoffrey, and William K. Beatty. *Women in White*. New York: Charles Scribner's Sons, 1972.

530. Marlow, Joan. *The Great Women*. New York: A & W Publishers, 1979.

531. Marquis Who's Who, ed. *Who Was Who in America: Historical Volume*. Chicago: A. N. Marquis Company, 1963.

532. Marquis Who's Who, ed. *Who Was Who in America: Historical Volume*. Rev. ed. Chicago: A. N. Marquis Company, 1967.

533. Marquis Who's Who, ed. *Who's Who in America*. 46th ed. Wilmette, Illinois: Macmillan Directory Division, 1990.

534. Marquis Who's Who, ed. *Who's Who in American Law*. 6th ed. Chicago: A. N. Marquis Company, 1989.

535. Marquis Who's Who, ed. *Who's Who of American Women*. 15th ed. New York: Macmillan, 1986.

536. Marquis Who's Who, ed. *Who's Who of American Women with World Notables*. 6th ed. Chicago: A. N. Marquis Company, 1971.

537. Marshall, Helen E. *Mary Adelaide Nutting*. Baltimore: Johns Hopkins University Press, 1972.

538. Martin, F. David, and Lee A. Jacobus. 3d ed. *The Humanities Through the Arts.* New York: McGraw-Hill, 1983.

539. Martin, Mildred Crowl. *Chinatown's Angry Angel*. Palo Alto, California: Pacific Books, 1977.

540. Marting, Diane E., ed. *Spanish American Women Writers*. Westport, Connecticut: Greenwood Press, 1990.

541. Mather, Frank Lincoln, ed. *Who's Who of the Colored Race*. 1915; reprint, Detroit: Gale Research, 1976.

542. Maxwell, William, ed. *The Virginia Historical Register and Literary Note Book*. Vol. 3. Richmond: McFarlane & Ferguson, 1850.

543. May, Antoinette. *Different Drummers*. Mallabrai, California: Les Femmes, 1976.

544. May, Charles Paul. *Women in Aeronautics*. New York: Thomas Nelson & Sons, 1962.

545. McCormick, Patricia. *Lady Bullfighter*. New York: Henry Holt, 1954.

546. McDermott, Jeanne. "A Biologist Whose Heresy Redraws Earth's Tree of Life." *Smithsonian* 20, 5 (August 1989).

547. McFarland, Daniel Miles. *Historical Dictionary of Ghana.* Metuchen, New York: Scarecrow Press, 1985.

548. McHenry, Robert. *Famous American Women.* New York: Dover, 1980.

549. McHenry, Robert, ed. *Liberty's Woman.* Springfield Massachusetts: G. N. C. Merriam, 1980.

550. McHugh, Mary. *Law and the New Woman.* New York: Franklin Watts, 1975.

551. McKown, Robin. *Heroic Nurses.* New York: G. P. Putnam's Sons, 1966.

552. McNulty, Marjorie Grant. *Glastonbury: From Settlement to Suburb.* Glastonbury, Connecticut: Woman's Club of Glastonbury, 1970.

553. Mehren, Elizabeth. "Lifestyle in the '90s, According to Popcorn." *Los Angeles Times,* January 16, 1987.

554. Mellow, James R. *Charmed Circle: Gertrude Stein and Company.* New York: Avon Books, 1975.

555. Menke, Frank G. *The Encyclopedia of Sports.* 5th rev. ed. South Brunswick, Maine: A. S. Barnes and Company, 1975.

556. Merriam Company, eds. *Webster's Biographical Dictionary.* Springfield, Massachusetts: G. N. C. Merriam, 1980.

557. Meyer, Agnes E. *Out of These Roots.* Boston: Little, Brown, 1953.

558. Miles, Rosalind. *The Women's History of the World.* Topsfield, Massachusetts: Salem House, 1989.

559. Miller, Bertha Mahony, et al. *Illustrators of Children's Books.* Vol. 2. Boston: Horn Book, 1958.

560. Mitroshenkov, V. "They Were First." *Soviet Military Review,* 1969.

561. Mitton, Simon. *The Cambridge Encyclopaedia of Astronomy.* Foreword by Martin Ryle. New York: Crown, 1977.

562. Moers, Ellen. *Literary Women.* Garden City: Doubleday, 1976.

563. Molesworth, Charles. *Marianne Moore.* New York: Atheneum, 1990.

564. Moolman, Valerie. *Women Aloft.* Alexandria, Virginia: Time-Life Books, 1981.

565. Moore, Patrick, ed. *The International Encyclopedia of Astronomy.* New York: Orion Books, 1987.

566. Morantz, Regina Markell, Cynthia Stodola Pomerleau, and Carol Hansen Fenichel, eds. *In Her Own Words.* New Haven, Connecticut: Yale University Press, 1982.

567. Morantz-Sanchez, Regina Markell. *Sympathy and Science.* New York: Oxford University Press, 1985.

568. Moritz, Charles, ed. *Current Biography Yearbook.* New York: H. W. Wilson, 1968.

569. Moshansky, Mozelle. *Mendelssohn.* New York: Midas Books, 1982.

570. Mowatt, Anna Cora. *Autobiography of an Actress.* Boston: Ticknor, Reed, and Fields, 1854: reprint, New York: Arno Press, 1980.

571. Myers, Robin, ed. and comp. *A Dictionary of Literature in the English Language.* Vol. 1. London: Pergamon Press, 1970.

572. Myles, Bruce. *Night Witches.* Novato, California: Presidio Press, 1981.

573. Neilson, Winthrop, and Frances Neilson. *Seven Women: Great Painters.* Philadelphia: Chilton Book Company, 1968.

574. Neithammer, Carolyn. *Daughters of the Earth.* New York: Macmillan, 1977.

575. "Never Look Down." *Forbes,* July 1989.

576. Newman, John Gentry Cardinal. *Essays.* 2 vols. London: Longmans, Green, 1919.

577. Nicholas, Janet. *American Music Makers.* New York: Walker, 1990.

578. Niemeyer, Mable J. "Memories of Sarah Byrd Askew." *New Jersey Library Association Newsletter,* 1991.

579. Nies, Judith. *Seven Women.* New York: Viking, 1977.

580. Noble, Kenneth B. "Nigeria Is Spared the Worst of AIDS, but Experts Wonder for How Long." *New York Times,* March 18, 1990, 10L.

581. O'Connor, Ellen M. *Myrtilla Miner: A Memoir.* New York: Arno Press and the New York Times, 1969.

582. O'Faolain, Julia, and Lauro Martines, eds. *Not in God's Image.* New York: Harper & Row, 1973.

583. O'Neil, Lois Decker, ed. *The Women's Book of World Records and Achievements.* Garden City: Doubleday, 1979.

584. O'Neill, William L. *Everyone Was Brave*. Chicago: Quadrangle Books, 1971.

585. Oaks, Claudia M. *United States Women in Aviation Through World War I*. Washington, D.C.: Smithsonian Institution Press, 1978.

586. Ocvirk, Otto G., Robert O. Bone, Robert E. Stinson, and Philip R. Wigg. *Art Fundamentals: Theory and Practice*. Dubuque, Iowa: Wm. C. Brown, 1975.

587. Ogilvie, Marilyn Bailey. *Women in Science*. Cambridge: MIT Press, 1986.

588. Ohles, John F., ed. *Biographical Dictionary of American Educators*. Westport, Connecticut: Greenwood Press, 1978.

589. Old Colony Historical Society. "Collections of the Old Colony Historical Society." Taunton, Massachusetts: C.A. Hach and Son, 1880.

590. Old Colony Historical Society. "Commemorative of the Fiftieth Anniversary." Taunton, Massachusetts: Old Colony Historical Society, 1903.

591. Old Stone Bank. "Awashonks and Church." Providence: Old Stone Bank, June 1933.

592. Olds, Elizabeth Fagg. *Women of the Four Winds*. Boston: Houghton Mifflin, 1985.

593. Opfell, Olga S. *Queens, Empresses, Grand Duchesses and Regents*. Jefferson, North Carolina: McFarland, 1989.

594. Organization of American Historians. "Restoring Women to History." Bloomington, Indiana: Organization of American Historians, 1988.

595. Orrey, Leslie, ed. *The Encyclopedia of Opera*. New York: Charles Scribner's Sons, 1976.

596. Palmer, William P., ed. and arranger. *Calendar of Virginia State Papers*. Richmond, 1875; reprint, New York: Kraus Reprint Corporation, 1968.

597. Parish, James Robert, and Michael R. Pitts. *Film Directors: A Guide to Their American Films*. Metuchen, New York: Scarecrow Press, 1974.

598. Parker, Rozsika, and Griselda Pollock. *Old Mistresses*. New York: Pantheon Books, 1981.

599. Partnow, Elaine, ed. and comp. *The Quotable Woman*. Garden City: Doubleday, 1978.

600. Pater, Ruth, to Beverly Golemba, July 1991.

601. Patterson, Elois Coleman. *Memoirs of the late Bessie Coleman, Aviatrix: Pioneer of the Negro People in Aviation.* n.p., 1969.
602. Pehnt, Wolfgang. *Encyclopedia of Modern Architecture.* New York: Harry N. Abrams, 1981.
603. Permanent Commission on the Status of Women. *Great Women in Connecticut History.* Hartford: Permanent Commission on the Status of Women, 1986.
604. Perreault, Denise. "Eastland President Stresses Bank's Local Roots." *Woonsocket Call* (Rhode Island), July 11, 1991.
605. Perrone, Bobette, H. Henrietta Stockel, and Victoria Krueger. *Medicine Women, Curanderas, and Women Doctors.* Norman: University of Oklahoma Press, 1989.
606. Peterson, Barbara Bennett, ed. *Notable Women of Hawaii.* Honolulu: University of Hawaii Press, 1984.
607. Petteys, Chris, Hazel Gustow, Ferris Olin, and Verna Ritchie. *Dictionary of Women Artists.* Boston: G. K. Hall, 1982.
608. Phaidon Press. *Dictionary of Twentieth-Century Art.* London: Phaidon Press, 1973.
609. Phillips, J. S. *Pocasset and the Pocassets.* n.p.: Rhode Island Historical Society, 1931.
610. Phillips, Louis, and Karen Markoe. *Women in Sports.* New York: Harcourt Brace Jovanovich, 1979.
611. Placksin, Sally. *American Women in Jazz.* New York: Seaview Books, 1982.
612. Ploski, Harry, and Warren Marr, II, eds. *The Afro-American.* New York: Bellwether, 1976.
613. "Popcorn: Trends Last, but Fads Fade Fast." *Marketing News* 22, 5 (March 1988).
614. Power, James R. *Brave Women and Their Wartime Decorations.* New York: Vantage Press, 1959.
615. Pragnell, Marvyn O., and Helga Castle. *The International Yearbook and Statesmen's Who's Who.* West Sussex, England: Reed Information Services, 1990.
616. Preston, Wheeler. *American Biographies.* New York: Harper & Brothers, 1940.
617. Priesand, Sally. *Judaism and the New Woman.* New York: Behrman House, 1975.

618. Ranahan, Demerris C. *Contributions of Women: Medicine*. Minneapolis: Dillion Press, 1981.
619. Randall, Margaret, ed. and trans. *Breaking the Silences*. Vancouver: Pulp Press, 1982.
620. Rasponi, Lanfranco. *The Last Prima Donnas*. New York: Alfred A. Knopf, 1982.
621. Raven, Susan, and Alison Weir. *Women of Achievement*. With a foreword by Elizabeth Longford. New York: Harmony Books, 1981.
622. Reitsch, Hanna. *Flying Is My Life*. Translated by Lawrence Wilson. New York: G. P. Putnam's Sons, 1954.
623. Rexroth, Kenneth, and Ikuko Atsumi, eds. and trans. *The Burning Heart*. New York: Seabury Press, 1977.
624. Rhode Island Historical Society. "The Franklin Press." Rhode Island Historical Society, 18, 3 (1959).
625. Richards, J. M., ed. *Who's Who in Architecture from 1400 to the Present*. London: Weidenfeld and Nicolson, 1977.
626. Riley, Carolyn, ed. *Contemporary Literary Criticism*. Detroit: Gale Research, 1975.
627. Riley, Glenda. *Inventing the American Woman*. Arlington Heights, Illinois: Harlan Davidson, 1987.
628. Robinson, Richard. *United States Business History, 1602–1988*. New York: Greenwood Press, 1990.
629. Robinson, Victor. *White Caps*. Vol. 3. Philadelphia: J. B. Lippincott, 1946.
630. Romero, Patricia W., ed. *Life Histories of African Women*. London: Ashfield Press, 1988.
631. Roseberry, C. R. *The Challenging Skies*. Garden City: Doubleday, 1966.
632. Roses, Lorraine Elena, and Ruth Elizabeth Randolph. *Harlem Renaissance and Beyond*. Boston: G. K. Hall, 1990.
633. Ross, Ishbel. *Charmers and Cranks*. New York: Harper & Row, 1965.
634. Rossiter, Margaret W. *Women Scientists in America*. Baltimore: Johns Hopkins University Press, 1982.
635. Roth, Cecil, and Geoffrey Wigoder, eds. *The New Standard Jewish Encyclopedia*. Rex. ed. Garden City: Doubleday, 1970.
636. Rothman, Sheila M. *Woman's Proper Place*. New York: Basic Books, 1978.

637. Rowbotham, Sheila. *Women, Resistance and Revolution.* New York: Pantheon Books, 1972.
638. Rowlandson, Mary. *A Narrative of the Captivity and Removes of Mrs. Mary Rowlandson.* Fairfield, Washington: Ye Galleon Press, 1974.
639. Rubenstein, Charlotte Streifer. *American Women Artists.* New York: Avon Books, 1982.
640. Rush, Theressa Gunnels, Carol Fairbanks Myers, and Ester Spring Arata. *Black American Writers Past and Present: A Biographical and Bibliographical Dictionary.* Vol. 1. Metuchen, New Jersey: Scarecrow Press, 1975.
641. Ryan, Bryan, ed. *Hispanic Writers.* Detroit: Gale Research, 1991.
642. Rywell, Martin, ed. *Afro-American Encyclopedia.* North Miami, Florida: Educational Book Publishers, 1974.
643. Sachar, Brian. *Atlas of European Architecture.* New York: Van Nostrand Reinhold, 1984.
644. Sachs, Nelly. *The Seeker.* New York: Farrar, Straus, and Giroux, 1970.
645. Sadie, Stanley, ed. *The New Grove Dictionary of Music and Musicians.* 20 vols. London: Macmillan, 1986.
646. Salamon, Julie. "Bizarre Life of New Zealand's 'Mad Writer.'" *Wall Street Journal,* May 16, 1991, A14.
647. Salmonson, Jessica Amanada. *The Encyclopedia of Amazons.* New York: Paragon House, 1991.
648. Sammons, Vivian Ovelton. *Blacks in Science and Medicine.* New York: Hemisphere, 1990.
649. Scanlon, John W., Thomas Nelson, Lawrence J. Grylack, and Yolande F. Smith. *A System of Newborn Physical Examination.* Baltimore: University Park Press, 1979.
650. Scarborough, Ruth. *Belle Boyd.* Macon, Georgia: Mercer University Press, 1983.
651. Schiebinger, Londa. *The Mind Has No Sex?* Cambridge: Harvard University Press, 1989.
652. Schneider, Susan Weidman. *Jewish and Female.* New York: Simon and Schuster, 1984.
653. Schoeman, Karl. *Olive Schreiner.* Cape Town, South Africa: Herman Y. Rousseau, 1989.
654. Scholes, Percy A. *The Oxford Companion to Music.* London: Oxford University Press, 1963.

655. Schulz, Heinrich E., ed. *Who Was Who in the USSR.* Metuchen, New Jersey: Scarecrow Press, 1972.
656. Schuster, Mel. *Motion Picture Directors: A Bibliography of Magazine and Periodical Articles, 1900–1972.* Metuchen, New Jersey: Scarecrow Press, 1973.
657. Scott, Sheila. *Barefoot in the Sky.* New York: Macmillan, 1974.
658. Sertima, Ivan Van. *Black Women in Antiquity.* N.p.: Journal of African Civilizations, 1984; reprint, New Brunswick: Transaction Books, 1988.
659. Seymore-Smith, Martin. *Who's Who in Twentieth Century Literature.* New York: Holt, Rinehart and Winston, 1976.
660. Sheldon Jackson College. "The Verstovian." *SJC Today* 51, 2 (December 1971).
661. Sherman, Merrill, to Beverly Golemba, July 1991.
662. Sherr, Lynn, and Jurate Kazickas. *The American Woman's Gazetteer.* New York: Bantam Books, 1976.
663. Sievers, Sharon L. *Flowers in Salt.* Stanford: Stanford University Press, 1983.
664. Simon and Schuster. *Celebrity Register.* New York: Simon and Schuster, 1973.
665. Simpson, Helen M. *The Women of New Zealand.* Auckland and Hamilton, New Zealand; London: George Allen and Unwin, 1962.
666. Simpson, Kieran, ed. *Canadian Who's Who.* Toronto: University of Toronto Press, 1990.
667. Simpson-Poffenbarger, Livia. *Ann Bailey: The Thrilling Adventures of the Heroine of the Kanawha Valley.* Point Pleasant, West Virginia: Point Pleasant Publishers, 1907.
668. Skenazy, Lenore. "Welcome Home: Trend Experts Point to 'Neo-Traditional.'" *Advertising Age* 59 (May 1988).
669. Slide, Anthony. *The International Film Industry.* New York: Greenwood Press, 1989.
670. Slonimsky, Nicolas. *The Concise Baker's Biographical Dictionary of Musicians.* New York: Macmillan, 1988.
671. Smith, Betsy Covington. *Breakthrough: Women in Law.* New York: Walker, 1984.
672. Smith, Elizabeth Simpson. *Breakthrough: Women in Aviation.* New York: Walker, 1981.

673. Smith, Horatio, ed. *Columbia Dictionary of Modern European Literature.* New York: Columbia University Press, 1947.

674. Smith, Julia E. *Abby Smith and Her Cows.* New York: Arno Press, 1972.

675. Smith, Mary. *At the Office.* Hanover, New Hampshire: Harper & Row, 1982.

676. Smith, Page. *Daughters of the Promised Land.* Boston: Little, Brown, 1970.

677. Smyers, Virginia L., and Michael Winship, eds. *Bibliography of American Literature.* New Haven, Connecticut: Yale University Press, 1983.

678. Smythe, Mabel M., ed. *The Black American Reference Book.* Englewood Cliffs, New Jersey: Prentice-Hall, 1976.

679. Sobel, Bernard. *A Pictorial History of Vaudeville.* New York: Citadel Press, 1961.

680. Sochen, June. *Herstory.* New York: Alfred, 1974.

681. Soldon, Norbert C., ed. *The World of Women's Trade Unionism.* Contributions in Women's Studies, no. 52. Westport, Connecticut: Greenwood Press, 1985.

682. Solé, Carlos A., ed. *Latin American Writers.* 3 vols. New York: Macmillan, 1989.

683. Solomon, Barbara. *In the Company of Educated Women.* New Haven, Connecticut: Yale University Press, 1985.

684. Southern, Eileen. *Biographical Dictionary of Afro-American and African Musicians.* Westport, Connecticut: Greenwood Press, 1982.

685. Sparhawk, Ruth M., Mary E. Leslie, Phyllis Y. Turbow, and Zina R. Rose. *Women in Sport, 1887–1987: A 100-year Chronology.* Metuchen, New Jersey: Scarecrow Press, 1989.

686. Speare, Elizabeth. "Abby, Julia and the Cows." *American Heritage Magazine,* June 1957.

687. Spender, Dale, ed. *Feminist Theories.* New York: Pantheon Books, 1983.

688. Spradling, Mary Mace, ed. *In Black and White.* 3d ed. Detroit: Gale Research, 1980.

689. Spuler, Bertold. *Rulers and Governments of the World.* Vol. 2. London: Bowker Press, 1977.

690. St. Clair, Anne, to Beverly Golemba, June 1991.

691. *Standard Encyclopedia of South Africa*. Capetown: Mason, 1972.
692. Standard Who's Who. *Who's Who in American Jewry*. Los Angeles: Standard Who's Who, 1980.
693. Starnes, Lucy G. "Girl Spy of the Valley." *Virginia Cavalcade* 10, 4 (Spring 1961): 35–40.
694. Steinbrunner, Chris, and Otto Penzler, eds. *Encyclopedia of Mystery and Detection*. New York: McGraw-Hill, 1976.
695. Stenton, Doris Mary. *The English Woman in History*. With an introduction by Louise A. Tilly. London: Allen & Unwin, 1957; reprint, New York: Schocken Books, 1977.
696. Sterling, Dorothy, ed. *We Are Your Sisters*. New York: W. W. Norton, 1984.
697. Stern, Irwin. *Dictionary of Brazilian Literature*. Westport, Connecticut: Greenwood Press, 1988.
698. Stern, Susan. *Women Composers*. Metuchen, New Jersey: Scarecrow Press, 1978.
699. Stevenson, Janet. *Women's Rights*. New York: Franklin Watts, 1972.
700. Stewart, Alice. "The Flemmie P. Kittrell Fellowship for Minorities." *Journal of Home Economics* 65, 5 (May 1973).
701. Stewart, John. *For the Ancestors*. Urbana: University of Illinois Press, 1983.
702. Strane, Susan. *A Whole-Souled Woman*. New York: W. W. Norton, 1990.
703. Stratton, Eugene Aubrey. *Plymouth Colony*. Salt Lake City, Utah: Ancestry Publishing, 1986.
704. Sullivan, Victoria, and James Hatch, eds. *Plays by and About Women*. New York: Random House, 1974.
705. Summers, Anne. *Angels and Citizens*. London: Routledge & Kegan Paul, 1988.
706. Summers, Barbara, ed. *I Dream A World*. New York: Stewart, Tabori & Chang, 1989.
707. Sunnucks, Anne. 2d ed. *The Encyclopaedia of Chess*. New York: St. Martin's Press, 1976.
708. Sweetman, David. *Queen Nzinga*. London: Longman, 1971.
709. Switzer, Ellen. *Dancers! Horizons in American Dance*. New York: Atheneum, 1982.
710. Taylor, Frank C. *Alberta Hunter: A Celebration in Blues*. Santa Barbara, California: Landmark Books, 1987.

711. Taylor, John M. *The Witchcraft Delusion in Colonial Connecticut.* New York: Grafton Press, 1908.
712. Tewkesbury, David, and Tewkesbury, William. *Tewkesbury's Who's Who in Alaska and Alaskan Business.* Vol. 1. Juneau: Tewkesbury Publishers, 1947.
713. Thomas, Dorothy, ed. and comp. *Woman Lawyers in the United States.* New York: Scarecrow Press, 1957.
714. Thompson, Oscar, ed. *The International Cyclopedia of Music and Musicians.* 11th ed. New York: Dodd, Mead, 1985.
715. Thorlby, Anthony, ed. *The Penguin Companion to European Literature.* New York: McGraw-Hill, 1969.
716. Thorne, J. O., and T. C. Collocott, eds. *Chambers Biographical Dictionary.* Rev. ed. Edinburgh: W & R Chambers, 1974.
717. Tierney, Helen. *Women's Studies Encyclopedia.* New York: Greenwood Press, 1990.
718. Tinling, Marion. *Women Remembered.* New York: Greenwood Press, 1986.
719. Tomlinson, R. G. *Witchcraft Trials of Connecticut,* n.p.
720. Torre, Susana, ed. *Women in American Architecture: A Historic and Contemporary Perspective.* New York: Watson-Guptill Publications, 1977.
721. Torres, Lola Kruger. *Enciclopedia Grandes Mujeres de Puerto Rico.* Hato Rey, Puerto Rico: Ramollo Brothers, 1975.
722. Trattner, Walter I., ed. *Biographical Dictionary of Social Welfare in America.* New York: Greenwood Press, 1986.
723. Traub, Hamilton, ed. *The American Literary Yearbook.* Vol. 1. Henning, Minnesota: Paul Traub, 1919; reprint, Detroit: Gale Research, 1968.
724. Truman, Margaret. *Women of Courage.* New York: William Morrow, 1976.
725. Tucker, Barbara M. *Samuel Slater and the Origins of the American Textile Industry, 1790–1860.* Ithaca, New York: Cornell University Press, 1984.
726. Tufts, Eleanor. *Our Hidden Heritage.* New York: Paddington Press, 1974.
727. Tunney, Christopher. *A Biographical Dictionary of World War II.* New York: St. Martin's Press, 1972.
728. Tuttle, Lisa. *Encyclopedia of Feminism.* New York: Facts on File, 1986.

729. Tuve, Jeanette E. *First Lady of the Law*. New York: University Press of America, 1984.

730. Twin, Stephanie L. *Out of the Bleachers*. Old Westbury, New York: Feminist Press, 1979.

731. Uglow, Jennifer S., ed. and comp. *The Continuum Dictionary of Women's Biography*. New ed. New York: Continuum, 1989.

732. Undset, Sigrid. *Four Stories*. Translated by Naomi Walford. New York: Alfred A. Knopf, 1959.

733. United States Army Military History Institute. Carlisle Barracks, Pennsylvania, to Beverly Golemba, n.d.

734. Van Hoosen, Bertha. *Petticoat Surgeon*. New York: Arno Press and the New York Times, 1980.

735. Van Steen, Marcus. *Pauline Johnson*. Toronto: Musson Book Company, 1965.

736. Vare, Ethlie Ann, and Greg Ptacek. *Mothers of Invention*. With a foreword by Julie Newmar. New York: William Morrow, 1988.

737. Vecsey, George, and George C. Dade. *Getting Off the Ground*. New York: E. P. Dutton, 1979.

738. Velie, Alan R. *Four American Indian Literary Masters*. Norman: University of Oklahoma Press, 1982.

739. Vernoff, Edward, and Rima Shore. *The International Dictionary of Twentieth Century Biography*. New York: New American Library, 1987.

740. Vinson, James, ed. *Contemporary Dramatists*. 2d ed. With a preface by Ruby Cohn. New York: St. Martin's Press, 1977.

741. Virginia Historical Society. *The Virginia Magazine of History and Biography*. Vol. 11 (June 1904); reprint, New York: Kraus Reprint Corporation, 1968.

742. Virginia Historical Society. *The Virginia Magazine of History and Biography*. Vol. 14 (June 1907).

743. Virginia Historical Society. *The Virginia Magazine of History and Biography*. Vol. 23 (December 1915).

744. Vorse, Mary Heaton. *A Footnote to Folly*. New York: Arno Press, 1980.

745. Wakeman, John. *World Film Directors, 1890–1945*. New York: H. W. Wilson, 1987.

746. Wakeman, John. *World Film Directors, 1945–1985*. New York: H. W. Wilson, 1988.

747. Waldman, Carl. *Who Was Who in Native American History: Indians and Non-Indians from Early Contacts Through 1900.* New York: Facts on File, 1990.

748. Wallace, W. Stewart, comp. *A Dictionary of North American Authors Deceased Before 1950.* Toronto: Ryerson Press, 1951; reprint, Detroit: Gale Research, 1968.

749. Walsh, Mary Roth. *Doctors Wanted, No Women Need Apply.* London: Yale University Press, 1977.

750. Wamsley, James S., and Anne M. Cooper. *Idols, Victims, Pioneers.* Richmond, Virginia: Virginia State Chamber of Commerce, 1976.

751. Ward, A. C. *Longman Companion to Twentieth Century Literature.* 3d ed. Revised by Maurice Hussey. London: Longman, 1970.

752. Ward, Annie, trans. *Larousse Encyclopedia of Archaeology.* Paris: Larousse, 1969; reprint, n.p.; Hamlin Group, 1972.

753. Ward, W. E. F. *A History of Ghana.* London: George Allen and Unwin, 1958.

754. Ware, Susan. *Holding Their Own: American Women in the 1930s.* Boston: Twayne, 1982.

755. Ware, Susan. *Modern American Women.* Chicago: Dorsey Press, 1989.

756. Warren, Ruth. *A Pictorial History of Women in America.* New York: Crown, 1975.

757. Waters, Bertha, comp. *Women's History Month in Pennsylvania.* Philadelphia: Pennsylvania Department of Education, 1988.

758. Watts, Emily Stipes. *The Poetry of American Women from 1632 to 1945.* Austin: University of Texas Press, 1977.

759. Weatherford, Doris. *American Women and World War II.* New York: Facts on File, 1990.

760. Weddell, Alexander Wilborne, ed. *Virginia Historical Portraiture, 1585–1830.* Richmond: William Byrd Press, 1930.

761. Weems, John Edward. *Peary.* Boston: Houghton Mifflin, 1967.

762. Welsh, Lillian. *Reminiscences of Thirty Years in Baltimore.* Baltimore: Norman, Remington, 1925.

763. Wertheimer, Barbara Mayer. *We Were There.* New York: Pantheon Books, 1977.

764. Wier, Albert E. *The Macmillan Encyclopedia of Music and Musicians.* New York: Macmillan, 1938.
765. Wilbour, Benjamin F. *Some Little Compton History.* Providence: Rhode Island Historical Society, n.d.
766. Wilcox, Ella Wheeler. *The Worlds and I.* New York: Arno Press, 1980.
767. Williams, Henry. "Was Elizabeth Pool the First Purchaser of the Territory, and Foundress, of Taunton?" Address read before the Old Colony Historical Society, January 12, 1880.
768. Willoughby, Charles C. "The Virginia Indians in the 17th Century." *American Anthropologist* 9, 1 (1905): 57–86.
769. Wilson, Harriet E. *Our Nig: or Sketches from the Life of a the Black, in a Two-story White House, North.* New York: Random House, 1983.
770. Wilson, James Grant, and John Fiske. *Appleton's Cyclopaedia of American Biography.* New York: Appleton, 1891.
771. Withey, Henry F., and Elsie Rathburn Withey. *Biographical Dictionary of American Architects (Deceased).* Los Angeles: New Age Publishing, 1956.
772. Woloch, Nancy. *Women in the American Experience.* New York: Alfred A. Knopf, 1984.
773. *Women in Engineering.* New York: Society of Women Engineers, 1958.
774. Wood, Peter H., Gregory A. Waselkov, and M. Thomas Hatley, eds. *Powhatan's Mantle.* Lincoln: University of Nebraska Press, 1989.
775. Worthington, C. J., ed. *The Woman in Battle: A Narrative of the Exploits, Adventures and Travels of Madame Loreta Janeta Velazquez.* Richmond, Virginia: T. Belknap, 1876; reprint, New York: Arno Press, 1972.
776. Wroth, Lawrence C. *A History of Printing in Colonial Maryland.* Baltimore: Typothetae of Baltimore, 1922.
777. Yokum, Jean, to Beverly Golemba, September 1991.
778. Yost, Edna. *American Women of Science.* Philadelphia: Frederick A. Stokes, 1943.
779. Yost, Edna. *Women of Modern Science.* New York: Dodd, Mead, 1959.
780. Young, Agatha. *The Women and the Crisis.* New York: McDowell, Obolensky, 1959.

781. Zaimont, Judith Lang, and Karen Famera. *Contemporary Concert Music by Women*. Westport, Connecticut: Greenwood Press, Inc., 1981.
782. Zimmerman, David R. *Rh: The Intimate History of Disease and Its Conquest*. New York: Macmillan, 1973.
783. Zophy, Angela Howard, ed. *Handbook of American Women's History*. New York: Garland Reference Library of the Humanities, 1990.